M Robinson

1988

3144

FAIR PLAY

FAIR PLAY

CBS,
General Westmoreland,
and How
a Television Documentary
Went Wrong

BURTON BENJAMIN

An Edward Burlingame Book

HARPER & ROW, PUBLISHERS, New York
Cambridge, Philadelphia, San Francisco, Washington
1817   London, Mexico City, São Paulo, Singapore, Sydney

FIRST EDITION

Designer: Sidney Feinberg

Copyeditor: Ann Adelman

Indexer: Judith Hancock

Library of Congress Cataloging-in-Publication Data

Benjamin, Burton.
  Fair play.

  "An Edward Burlingame book."
  Includes index.
  1. Television broadcasting of news. 2. Westmoreland, William C. (William Childs), 1914–   . 3. CBS Inc. 4. Uncounted enemy. 5. Vietnamese Conflict, 1961–1975 — Military intelligence—United States. 6. Journalistic ethics—United States. I. Title.
  PN4784.T4B45 1988   070.1'9   87–46115
  ISBN 0–06–015928–6

88 89 90 91 92 HC 10 9 8 7 6 5 4 3 2 1

For my wife, Aline

CONTENTS

ILLUSTRATIONS

ACKNOWLEDGMENTS

This book began as an assignment to write an internal memorandum about a CBS News documentary that was under attack. I had no idea when I began my examination of *CBS Reports:* "The Uncounted Enemy: A Vietnam Deception" in May of 1982 that it would grow into a fifty-nine-page document that became known as "The Benjamin Report." Nor did I ever imagine that it would be further expanded into this book.

It was Everette E. Dennis, executive director of the Gannett Center for Media Studies at Columbia University, who offered me a fifteen-month senior fellowship, giving me the time and space to write it. I am in his debt.

Three researchers, all professional journalists, were tireless in their assistance. Toby Wertheim of CBS News was my principal assistant during my investigation and helped with the research for this book. At Columbia, Randall Prior worked with me until he left to go to work for the Cable News Network in Washington. Sally Sloan succeeded him and was with me until the end of my fellowship when she joined ABC News.

Three good friends read the manuscript and offered valuable insights: Herbert Mitgang, Richard Witkin, and Elaine Greene.

During my years at CBS, I worked most closely with Walter Cronkite, and I am grateful to him for contributing an introduction.

At Harper & Row, it was Edward L. Burlingame who saw promise in a sprawling outline and encouraged me to go ahead. His taste and professional judgment have guided me throughout. Kathy Walton Banks came up with the title and was unfailingly helpful.

My long-time agent and dear friend, Dorothy Olding, read the manuscript with her usual unerring eye.

I must acknowledge the critical assistance of Jan S. Rifkinson, a friend and former colleague, who has not read a word of this book. Halfway through, when my computer broke down, I turned to him for his technical expertise. He set me aright, thus preserving my sanity.

My wife, Aline W. Benjamin, an editor in publishing when we were married during World War II, read every word of the manuscript with a loving but coldly professional eye, and while endlessly supportive was uncompromising in her standards.

As we say in television, these people deserve to have their names on the credits. Any faults are mine alone.

—BURTON BENJAMIN

Scarborough, N.Y.

"The judgments must be professional news judgments—nothing more, nothing less."

—CBS News Standards, 1976

INTRODUCTION

by Walter Cronkite

Reporting, writing, editing, publishing, or broadcasting the news is a unique calling, and of its many peculiarities one stands out particularly. Its participants, who are quick to label others for what they do or what they believe, can't agree on what to call what *they* do.

The practice of journalism is certainly an occupation, but how can one define it beyond that? Is it a trade, a business, a craft, or, perhaps, even a profession?

At times and in certain respects it certainly is a trade, business, and/or craft. The question and the debate really centers on whether it can be called a profession. By one dictionary definition (i.e., a profession is "any vocation or business") there can be no doubt. The argument, however, centers on another definition, in most dictionaries the first listing: "a vocation requiring knowledge of some department of learning or science."

Practitioners of the two most visible professions, medicine and the law, after suffering years of specialized training, are properly possessive of the title, and along with certain academicians, are likely to be the most critical when journalists claim admission to the sacred halls.

They do have a point if the definition is to be limited to detailed knowledge of a particular learning or science. Suppose, however, that we apply another definition that, it seems to me, is perfectly valid, perhaps even more descriptive than the dictionary offers.

"A profession," this definition would read, "is a vocation that is governed by a particular code of ethics, written or unwritten, beyond that which is generally applied to normal business practices."

By my definition journalism is clearly worthy of being called a profession. If further argument is needed it might be noted that the ethics of journalism are honored in the breach with about the same frequency as the ethics that govern the law and, perhaps a little less often, medicine.

The major difference among the professions is that the ethics of journalism are unwritten and, in any punitive sense, unenforceable, whereas medicine has its Hippocratic Oath and standards and the law has its canons of conduct that are guarded by professional societies with powers of investigation and punishment.

Occasionally, at times when the press is for one reason or another under heavy assault by one offended interest or another, the suggestion comes again that journalism *should* have a written set of rules to which all practitioners should be required to adhere or else face punishment.

It then becomes necessary for us to explain why we do not. The argument is embodied in the First Amendment to our Constitution. It is a question of freedom of speech and press. The Amendment states that Congress shall make no law abridging these freedoms. By extension, this conviction that all of our vaunted American freedoms are based on the fundamentals of free speech and press precludes any one person or any group of persons from saying what any other person or group may print or broadcast.

This principle is not endorsed universally by all members of the press by any means. Some if its most distinguished and thoughtful leaders have from time to time proposed various ways to police our publications and broadcasts. Their solutions with rare exceptions recognize two maxims: The monitoring body should be composed of, or at least dominated by, journalistic peers and colleagues and not outsiders, and there should be no prior rules (which could be interpreted as restricting the freedom of speech and press) but only a process of review to assure that the privilege of freedom was not abused and was exercised with fairness to all parties.

The most recent and most ambitious of these attempts was the National News Council founded in 1972. It provided a forum to hear the complaints by aggrieved citizens of unfair press treatment and to hear the defense of the alleged offender. Subscribing news organizations agreed to print any council findings against them.

The council seemed to work fairly well. However, too many newspapers and broadcasters, including some of the largest, refused to participate and, its scope thus considerably limited, the council died.

The council's principal value, and one not missed by its founders, may have been to demonstrate to the public that, far from being the irresponsible bomb-throwing anarchists depicted by many press critics, journalists are concerned with the fairness of their performance and do apply an unwritten code of ethics to themselves.

Further, these matters are under constant review by standing or special committees of the numerous journalistic organizations—the American Society of Newspaper Editors, the American Newspaper Publishers Association, the AP Managing Editors Association, Sigma Delta Chi-Professional Society of Journalists, the National Association of Broadcasters, the Radio-Television News Directors Association—and the increasingly influential network of critical journalism reviews, journalism foundations such as the excellent Gannett Center at Columbia University, and university journalism schools generally.

It is noteworthy that, regarding the National News Council, few, perhaps none, of the nonparticipating organizations argued that there was no need for restraint in the exercise of journalistic freedom. What nearly all of them objected to was the concept of *outside* restraint. Indeed, several of the nonparticipants are honored for their own high standards and are among the most vociferous in arguing ethical questions before various journalistic bodies.

One of the prime movers in founding the National News Council was the then president of CBS News, Richard Salant. Besides a deep commitment to the concept of independent, impartial, unintimidated, and fair news gathering and presentation, Salant brought to the job the keen and incisive mind of a lawyer.

He was offended by the chaos of unwritten law and memos and directives scattered over the years and the confusion of presiding over an organization that lived under such regulatory disarray. So, over the objections of not a few of the CBS News executives and journalists, he codified the rules into the CBS News Standard of Practices.

The Standard of Practices addressed the knotty problems of lights and cameras inciting street violence, of terrorists demanding air time, of electronic eavesdropping and hidden cameras, of "hand-out" film provided by propagandists and publicists, of news figures demanding payment for interviews, and on and on. Of course it spoke at length of fairness, of the concepts of free press-fair trial, of the FCC's Fairness Doctrine and Equal Time rules.

While every newspaper in modern times has adhered to its own or someone else's style book to assure some uniformity in its writing and editing, the CBS News Standard of Practices was a pioneering effort in setting rules of conduct in the gathering of news.

In effect it put into a law of its own the high standards to which CBS News had always aspired, usually with widely recognized success. For the first time there was in print testimony to the ethics to which all responsible news organizations seek to comply.

It was against this background that the then president of CBS News, Van Gordon Sauter, read the harsh criticism of the CBS Reports broadcast on General Westmoreland and chose one of the company's most respected and senior journalists to conduct an in-house inquiry.

How ironic that this very attempt by CBS News to enforce its own strict rules of conduct was used against the company by Plaintiff Westmoreland's lawyers! But the publicity this legal move engendered at least helped in its own way to underline the existence, shared by all responsible media, of a journalistic ethic.

FAIR PLAY

1

SETTING
THE STAGE

The lunch with Howard Stringer on September 17, 1986, was at one of his favorite restaurants, the Maurice in the Parker Meridien Hotel on West 57th Street in New York. It is a large, pricey, mock-elegant room and, at lunch, it is heavily funded by corporate expense accounts. The head waiter was ritualistically obeisant, and we were seated at a fine table in an alcove near the front.

If you had graphed our careers at CBS, there would be four points of convergence—Lyndon Johnson, the Rockefellers, a documentary on Vietnam, and the presidency of CBS News. At our lunch on this warm, end-of-the-summer day, we reminisced about the first two, dealt fleetingly with the third and heavily with the fourth: Who would be the next president of CBS News?

Stringer, forty-four, a tall, Oxford-educated Welshman, who had become an American citizen in 1985, told me if I got the presidency, which he freely conceded he wanted very badly, he would stay at CBS News. If any of the several outsiders who were being mentioned got it, he would resign.

In 1985, I had taken early retirement from CBS after twenty-eight years and had been appointed a Senior Fellow at the Gannett Center for Media Studies at Columbia University. Early retirement was a misnomer; I was sixty-eight years old at the time. The assignment at Columbia was to research a book on fairness in the media, a subject that had been thrust upon me in my last years at the network. I was well into it, and the focus would be on Stringer's last documentary, the highly controversial 1982 *CBS Reports:* "The Uncounted Enemy: A Vietnam Deception."

I had conducted the internal investigation of that program, and had written a fifty-nine-page internal report sharply critical of it. When General William Westmoreland sued CBS for $120 million over the documentary's assertion that there had been a conspiracy on the part of his command in undercounting enemy strength in Vietnam (a suit he finally abandoned), the court ruled that the internal report had to be made public. It became known as "The Benjamin Report," and Stringer did not fare well in it. It was one of the few blemishes on his otherwise notable career.

From the first time I met Howard Stringer, in August of 1969, there was no doubt in my mind that his ascendancy at CBS News would be swift. I liked to remind him about that first meeting: I was executive producer of the Walter Cronkite conversations with former President Lyndon Johnson, and Stringer was writhing in pain in a ditch in Fredericksburg, Texas. Producer John Sharnik had assigned him to be our researcher for the interviews at the LBJ Ranch. I had arrived a few hours later than the others in the production unit and found them on a public tennis court in Fredericksburg, standing over Stringer, who had twisted his ankle badly and was lying on the ground next to the courts. We got him to a local hospital where his British accent charmed the staff and the orthopedist, who came from his home to treat him.

A six-foot-three-inch, blond, blue-eyed, humorous man, whose father was a career RAF officer, Stringer spent much of his childhood living on military bases. He would say that he understood Westmoreland better than most people. When he was growing up, many of his father's friends were generals.

As a teenager, Stringer was in ROTC and became regimental sergeant major of his corps. He won scholarships to Oundle, a prestigious all-boys boarding school in Northamptonshire where he spent seven years, and to Oxford's Merton College, where he spent three more. At Oxford, where he read history, he was influenced by Americans who were Rhodes and Fulbright scholars, and he decided that the United States was where he wanted to be. In February 1965, with $200 in his pocket, he boarded the S.S. *United States* and came to this country. Through a friend he was able to get a clerk's job at WCBS-TV in New York.

Three months after arriving in the United States, Stringer received a draft notice from the U.S. Army. A British subject, it would have been easy for him to take a cab to Kennedy Airport and a plane to London and without any serious penalty or stigma avoid what was likely to be a tour of duty in Vietnam. He was twenty-three years old. But Stringer was challenged by the idea, and after training in South Carolina and Texas, he was indeed sent to Vietnam—as a military policeman.

He was the only college graduate in his unit and no one could quite figure out what he was doing there. There were some who suspected he must be a plant by British intelligence which might have resulted in his odd assignment as an M.P. He was stationed at Long Binh and during his ten-month tour of duty was soon moved out of the police to become personnel sergeant of a battalion. He was under fire during his tour—twice by accident from American troops, once in a plane that was machine-gunned as it left Bien Hoa, and another time when an ammunition dump was blown up setting off a chain of explosions that lasted for six hours.

Stringer's captain was struggling to get a college degree through an Army correspondence course and when he discovered his young, Oxford-educated sergeant, his academic career prospered. With Stringer as his secret weapon, the captain was on his way to graduation with honors.

When he returned to CBS, Stringer moved into network news, first with the election unit and then as a researcher, where Sharnik found him and got him assigned to the LBJ unit. He was so obviously overqualified that he was soon made a producer on his own.

In 1973, our career paths crossed again—the second convergence. After a long campaign, I had persuaded the Rockefellers to cooperate in a profile of the family. I would be the executive producer, and I gave Stringer the assignment as producer. It was the first documentary he would produce alone. He did a brilliant job and the program, which was given an unusual two hours on the air, won an Emmy. From then on, he was on his own, and his work was distinguished. Two of his *CBS Reports*, "The Palestinians" and "A Tale of Two Irelands," were especially well received.

In 1976, Stringer became executive producer of *CBS Reports* and his credits were substantial: "The People Versus Gary Gilmore," "The Fire Next Door," "The CIA's Secret Army," "Any Place but Here" (all with Bill Moyers), "The Boat People," "The Boston Goes to China,"

"Teddy," and "The Defense of the United States," a highly successful series that ran for five successive nights in prime time on the network.

From *CBS Reports*, Stringer went to the *CBS Evening News* and then into management. He soon became executive vice president of the news division. In 1985, twenty years after his arrival in the United States, when he became an American citizen, a group of us helped celebrate in his office with champagne and a red, white, and blue cake.

His last documentary would be the Vietnam program. For us, it would be the third time our career graph lines had converged. But this was not like the Johnson or Rockefeller programs where we had been co-workers. On the Vietnam program, he had been the executive producer and I had come in after the fact to investigate his work. It was a part of the history that brought us to the lunch table at the Parker Meridien on that September day in 1986.

Two corporate shakeups in the news division also were part of that history. By 1981, it was clear that William Leonard, who had been extended beyond the normal retirement age of sixty-five, was soon to retire as CBS News president and that his successor would be Van Gordon Sauter, a bearded, flamboyant executive then president of the sports division. Sauter's number two would be Edward M. Joyce, another executive on a fast track, who had been managing CBS owned-and-operated stations in Chicago, Los Angeles, and New York. Joyce and Sauter had been the leading candidates for the CBS News presidency, and Sauter had won it. The changing of the guard—Leonard outgoing, Sauter incoming—took too long and for the staff the overlap was often uneasy and confusing.

In February of that year, there were the first reassignments, and they would not only shake the organization but profoundly affect a program in progress, "The Uncounted Enemy: A Vietnam Deception." For Robert Chandler, an experienced fifty-two-year-old executive, who gave the program a first, tentative go-ahead, it was a move in the wrong direction. He was replaced as vice president, public-affairs broadcasts, by Roger Colloff, just turned thirty-five. It took Chandler out of the program mix; he otherwise would have supervised the Vietnam broadcast.

Chandler was a forceful manager and editor, with a strong screening-room eye. His forte was looking at a broadcast before it aired and findings its flaws, its inconsistencies, and its imbalances. He had done this for *60 Minutes* during its most successful years and even that program's producers, notably resistant to any management input, freely conceded that they were in Chandler's debt. Chandler was moved to an administrative vice presidency and was never invited to screen the Vietnam program during any stage of its production.

Colloff, who was bright and energetic, had no experience in producing or supervising documentaries. He had been Bill Leonard's assistant and during the production of "The Defense of the United States"—the five-part series under Howard Stringer's aegis—Colloff was sent to Germany for a crash course to observe first hand how the producers, correspondents, and crews worked in the field.

Andrew Lack, a producer in his early thirties, was also affected by the changes at the top. He had solid credits, especially his *CBS Reports* program "Teddy," in which Roger Mudd left Senator Edward M. Kennedy confused and inarticulate, substantially damaging his bid for the Democratic presidential nomination in 1980. In November of 1981, two months before air, Lack was named senior producer for *CBS Reports*, but he was involved in other projects. It was far too late for him to have any real influence on the Vietnam program.

But no move that the new managers made would have as profound an effect as the reassignment of Howard Stringer in December of 1981. Then thirty-nine, at the very top of his game, he was taken off the Vietnam program a critical month before it was scheduled to be broadcast, and reassigned by Sauter to be executive producer of the *CBS Evening News with Dan Rather*. It was a full-time, consuming job for Stringer, who had never worked in hard news for CBS and was taking on a Rather program that was floundering in the ratings.

Left behind was an intensely controversial Vietnam program, its executive producer gone; its senior producer too new on the scene to help; its vice president inexperienced; and most important its producer, George Crile, embarking on his first solo effort. Crile, who in the past had always collaborated with other producers, was a controversial figure at CBS News. His last effort had been censured by the National News Council.

The Vietnam program was to become one of the most explosive and bitter episodes in the history of CBS News. In my opinion, it had been made vulnerable by the series of high-level changes and staff reassignments that had taken place during the most crucial phase of its production. It was a documentary that slipped through the cracks.

Following the documentary came other changes that had an even more telling impact on the destinies of CBS. Sauter after two years had been promoted to the CBS Broadcast Group and Ed Joyce had replaced him as president. Then Joyce was dismissed and Sauter was back as president. And finally, Thomas H. Wyman, chairman and chief executive officer of CBS, was fired and so was one of his key supporters, Van Gordon Sauter, leaving open the presidency of CBS News.

As Howard Stringer and I faced each other over lunch, all of this history was squarely on the table. In the career-path analogy, this was the fourth convergence—one hardly anticipated by either of us. We were now candidates for the same job: president of CBS News. Stringer was openly and aggressively campaigning for it, and I was trying as hard as I could to resist it.

I was under considerable pressure from four former associates to take the job. Frank Stanton, former president of CBS, a man I regarded as the driving force of the organization during its best years, had phoned and urged me to accept. So had Richard Salant and Bill Leonard, two former news presidents. Some of the stronger entreaties came from Walter Cronkite, who more than anyone else had been my closest associate and co-worker during nearly three decades at CBS. It was Cronkite who began with me *The Twentieth Century* series, my first assignment, which ran for nine years. It was with Cronkite that I produced conversations with two former presidents, Eisenhower and Johnson, many *CBS Reports* documentaries, and the *CBS Evening News*. We were close personally and professionally.

I told Stringer I was dead serious: I had no intention at this stage of my life of becoming president of CBS News, interim or otherwise—and he could bank on that.

I knew that whoever was selected would face an array of problems, and we talked a bit about that. Good as CBS News was, it and the other networks were embroiled in a fierce struggle in a vastly new environment. There were the problems created by a new technology which had deprived network news of its once great asset: picture exclusivity. Now, through satellites, local stations had the same access as the networks to pictures from around the world. What the networks had to do to counter this was to exploit their strengths—journalism and courage. It was no longer enough merely to *cover* the news, which used to be my mandate when I was executive producer of the Cronkite News; now the networks had to *explain* the news.

CBS News, we agreed, was suffering from the abrasions and tensions of austerity, and it would take a vigorous management to dispel the insecurities that had beset the organization. A new president had to assert his ascendancy over the high-paid talents who had been acting as if they were running the news division. Dan Rather, for example, seemed to misunderstand his role, and that might be because he misinterpreted what Bill Leonard and I had told him when he got the job as anchorman. We had told him he would be the "point man" for the whole news organization, as Walter Cronkite had been. Cronkite ran the Evening News; that was his bailiwick and he was in charge. That was all he ran. The rest of the news operation—producers, correspondents, bureaus, hirings, and firings—those were the prerogatives of management. Rather appeared to have assumed some of these prerogatives and had become a manager rather than just an anchorman, which was a full-time job. It would not work.

I told Stringer that the euphoria that was bubbling through the news organization following the ousters of the chairman of the board, Thomas H. Wyman, and Van Gordon Sauter, the news president, was unreal. Everyone was ecstatic that William S. Paley had returned from retirement and that Laurence A. Tisch was on board as acting chief executive officer. Tisch, a short, bald man, glistening with self-confidence, was head of the cost-conscious conglomerate Loew's, and now owned three times as much stock as Paley, the legendary founder of the company. Tisch was perceived by some in the news division as a Messiah, but I told Stringer the exhilaration might be premature. The problems besetting the company—a flat advertising market, keener competition from cable and other sources—would persist. In a few months some of the big-name talent who had been giving advice—great television personalities who couldn't manage a corner grocery store—would come to the conclusion that the realities of the marketplace would prevail and that miracles didn't come easily. Stringer said he knew this, but restraining the high-salaried, big-name correspondents and producers might be the most difficult task of all.

The press had been full of speculation about who would get the big job at CBS News, and I was certain that Stringer would have preferred to keep our lunch private. To his dismay, the ubiquitous television agent, Richard Leibner, who represented Dan Rather and more than a hundred other CBS News correspondents and producers, including at one time

Stringer himself, swept into the dining room and was quickly at our table.

Leibner had been a persistent hard bargainer when I was vice president and director of news during the seller's market from 1978 to 1981, a time of talent raiding and rashly inflated salaries for correspondents and producers. As he came flitting over to our table time and again with the latest jokes and gossip, Stringer became more and more unsettled. This lunch would be all over town by mid-afternoon.

When we finally left, I could not resist confirming just how badly Stringer wanted the job. "Howard, I'm afraid I have to take back what I told you at lunch. I've changed my mind. I now think I really do want the job." Stringer looked at me with disbelief. "You do?"

"Yes, I do. The lunch just reminded me how much I miss Leibner."

Six days later at a private lunch at the CBS headquarters on West Fifty-Second Street with Bill Paley and Larry Tisch, I turned down the presidency. I told them I thought Howard Stringer would make an excellent president of CBS News.

2

THE MAKING
OF A LAWSUIT

The program, *CBS Reports:* "The Uncounted Enemy: A Vietnam Deception" had been heralded with full-page advertisements in the *New York Times, The Washington Post,* the Chicago *Tribune,* and the Los Angeles *Times* on Friday, January 22, 1982, the day before the broadcast. The artist's rendition looked down at a table where eight faceless military men sat over papers as if in a hushed and furtive meeting. Emblazoned across the table, dominating the ad, was a single word, a word that would haunt CBS and the producers of the program for three years: CONSPIRACY. "Reported by Mike Wallace and George Crile," the ad prominently announced. The copy read:

CBS Reports reveals the shocking decisions made at the highest level of military intelligence to suppress and alter critical information on the number and placement of enemy troops in Vietnam. A deliberate plot to fool the American public, the Congress, and perhaps even the White House into believing we were winning a war that in fact we were losing.

Who lied to us? Why did they do it? What did they hope to gain? How did they succeed so long? And what were the tragic consequences of their deception?

Tomorrow night the incredible answer to these questions.

At last.

That the advertisement appeared on Friday was understandable. Saturday newspapers, thin in circulation, offer the least attractive day of the week for advertising. That the ad appeared at all was somewhat surprising. In the increasingly austere 1980s, networks rarely bought space to promote documentaries, especially those appearing on a Saturday night, the worst day of the week for that sort of programming. When they did, it was commonly a signal: perhaps to Washington (here is something beyond what we customarily do, say *Miami Vice*); or to alert a small but desirable community which networks covet, the so-called opinion leaders (watch this, it's important and will make news). There was another signal. The Vietnam documentary would run from 9:30 to 11:00 p.m.—ninety minutes. For those wise in these matters, this was a certain tip that the network and its news division regarded the documentary as something very special, too important to reduce to the usual *CBS Reports* time length of one hour.

As I sat home that Saturday night watching the broadcast, I was mesmerized by it. It opened with the customary "tease," a provocative introduction running from one to two minutes which producers use to entice an audience into staying with a program for the hour or ninety minutes that will follow. It is a hook, a billboard, a promise of things to come.

The Vietnam program began with the Tet Offensive of January 30, 1968, the screen exploding with gunfire and battle scenes, active footage to rouse an audience from whatever torpor had set in by nine-thirty on a Saturday night. Over the savage, cataclysmic film, expertly edited into a sequence of death and destruction, came the commanding voice of Mike Wallace:

> . . . tonight we're going to present evidence of what we have come to believe was a conscious effort—indeed, a *conspiracy* at the highest levels of American military intelligence—to suppress and alter critical intelligence on the enemy in the year leading up to the Tet Offensive.

After the tease, the broadcast went to its main title—scenes of General Westmoreland with President Lyndon Johnson at Cam Ranh Bay in October 1966. The music over the title was the familiar *CBS Reports* theme, "Appalachian Spring" by Aaron Copland.

Following the first of six commercial breaks that would divide the program into five acts during its ninety minutes, the show got down to business. Although there would be occasional bursts of action—helicopter gun ships spraying the jungles and paddies, troops in combat—it soon became apparent that this was going to be an hour-and-a-half "talking heads" show—a collection of people talking on screen with very little action to titillate the audience. In television terms, this is regarded as a curse, almost certain to drive viewers away.

The premise of the program was stated at the beginning of the first act. Vietnam was a war that cost the United States $150 billion, twelve agonizing years, and 57,000 American soldiers dead. "How could we have lost the war," Wallace asked, "when for so long we were told we were slowly but inevitably winning?"

It was a war, the program asserted, where statistics ruled supreme. General Westmoreland put the Viet Cong strength at 285,000 and said we would simply grind down the enemy. But others in the military and intelligence communities were insisting that we were fighting a much larger enemy force.

The technique that producer George Crile intended to use unfolded with the first appearance of former CIA analyst Sam Adams, the program's consultant. Adams immediately launched a series of charges against Westmoreland and his command, following which Westmoreland was confronted with them and pressed to reply.

Throughout the program, Crile would use this technique—attack and defend. He would show former military and CIA officers stating that Westmoreland's command had intentionally undercounted enemy strength, and he would then cross-cut their statements with Westmoreland denying that this was true and defending his position.

Adams was strong and persuasive. He said Westmoreland's figure of 285,000 Viet Cong made no sense: You could count enemy casualties, perhaps 150,000, and you could count another 100,000 deserters. That added up to 250,000. How could there be a quarter of a million leaving or getting killed out of an army of 285,000? "I had to ask myself," Adams said, "who the hell are we fighting out there?"

The pro-and-con pattern in the editing was thus established. There followed scenes of Westmoreland standing before a joint session of Congress on April 28, 1967, with assurances that we were winning the war of attrition in Vietnam.

What the general did not know at the time, the program asserted, was that his intelligence chiefs back in Vietnam had just discovered evidence confirming CIA estimates of a far larger enemy.

Now came important figures from Westmoreland's old command in Vietnam, high-ranking officers contradicting their former chief. Two in particular were especially firm in declaring that the enemy was stronger than the military was prepared to admit. Maj. Gen. Joseph McChristian, a West Pointer, was Westmoreland's chief of intelligence in 1966 and 1967. Col. Gains Hawkins was his chief of the order-of-battle section during those same years. They were regular Army prototypes—central casting could hardly have done better—and they were very convincing. They recounted a briefing with Westmoreland when he told them he could not send on higher enemy-strength estimates to Washington. And then came a devastating cross-cut with Westmoreland saying: "Because the people in Washington were not sophisticated enough to understand and evaluate this thing and neither was the media."

Next came former CIA officials to lend further credence to the charges against Westmoreland with direct cuts to the general denying their allegations. There were accounts of meetings during which the military adamantly refused to accept CIA studies calling for an increase in enemy-strength figures. It was charged that the Westmoreland command had dictated a ceiling for the Viet Cong of 300,000 which the military was under orders not to exceed.

In the third act, there was another damaging disclosure: Westmoreland had dropped a whole category of the enemy—the self-defense militia, a force of 70,000—from the order of battle, thus skewing the enemy-strength total. The general came on screen to defend the decision: The self-defense militia, composed of old men and teenagers, had no offensive capability, he said.

Mike Wallace's interview with Westmoreland became more and more harsh. The general, shot in extreme close-up—what cameramen call a choker, under the chin and up to the hairline—was sweating and licking his lips, the personification of a man ill at ease and growing angrier. Wallace was shot much looser, a head-and-shoulders or belt-up shot, and the visual punctuation carried a subtle message: The accused shown very tight, facial ticks and all; the accuser much looser, invariably relaxed. It is a camera technique familiar to viewers of *60 Minutes*.

When pressed by Wallace about the dropping of the self-defense militia, Westmoreland began to run out of patience:

WESTMORELAND: This is a non-issue, Mike. Well—
WALLACE: Here is the issue.
WESTMORELAND: It's a non-issue. I made the decision. It was my responsibility. I don't regret making it. I stand by it. And the facts prove that I was right. Now let's stop it.

All in all, nine former military and CIA officers were on screen to challenge Westmoreland. He had only one supporter on the broadcast, Lt. Gen. Daniel Graham, a retired officer who was on his intelligence staff in Vietnam. Graham was on screen only twice and each time very briefly.

As the broadcast neared its end, Westmoreland was reduced to angry and inarticulate replies. In one, Wallace suggested that perhaps Graham only wanted to feed him good news:

WESTMORELAND: I—I—I—I—well—no. No, no. I—no—

WALLACE: You wanted to feed Lyndon Johnson good news.

WESTMORELAND: I—I—I don't know why he would want to—feed me good news. I mean, I knew him very casually. I had never known him before.

The program ended with an epilogue of what the men in the broadcast were doing today. As the credits rolled by, I felt that I had just watched one of the most remarkable documentaries that CBS News had ever produced. That this kind of maneuvering could have happened during a war so futile and so pointless—a war I had seen first-hand during two trips to Vietnam—sickened me.

The program had a quality that I had always sought in the documentaries I had produced: Tell people what they *don't* know. Too many programs rehashed the familiar. This was news—certainly to me. It was important. It was shocking.

I told my wife that "The Uncounted Enemy" might well rank with two of the more celebrated *CBS Reports* of the past, "Hunger in America" and "The Selling of the Pentagon."

Both of these programs had been intensely controversial and were attacked, so it was a prophetic comparison.

3

THUNDERSTORM

The morning after the Vietnam program, in the huge Sunday edition of the *New York Times* there was an unusual editorial, headlined "WAR INTELLIGENCE AND TRUTH." It began: "A CBS documentary on Vietnam last night has surprising present pertinence." The program "showed that Lyndon Johnson himself was victimized by mendacious intelligence. . . . What made this report more than a matter of history is America's continuing preoccupation with guerrilla wars elsewhere, notably in Central America."

The editorial was remarkable in that the *Times* editorial page dealt only rarely with television news; in fact, the newspaper was often criticized for its cavalier attitude toward broadcast journalism. It was also uncommon for the *Times* to rush to judgment that quickly, although the paper naturally received a video cassette of the program well before it went on the air. For the producers of the broadcast, and for the management of CBS News, there could scarcely have been a more rewarding endorsement.

In the days that followed these were two other important tributes to the program. One came from a source that might have been regarded as unlikely. William F. Buckley, Jr., in his nationally syndicated column, called the program "a truly extraordinary documentary." It "absolutely establishes that General William Westmoreland for political reasons withheld from the President, probably from the Joint Chiefs, from Congress and from the American people information about the enemy."

Buckley called for a congressional investigation of the Vietnam War's "appalling conduct."

Hodding Carter III in *The Wall Street Journal* was equally enthusiastic. The Vietnam program "rendered an important public service." It "detailed the appalling lies which were fed to the upper reaches of government and to the American people about enemy strength in Vietnam in the late 1960s."

Buckley's "appalling conduct" and Carter's "appalling lies" would both be treasured by the program's producers and by CBS News management, although Carter would later have second thoughts about the broadcast that would create a major contretemps.

On Monday, you could sense the pride and pleasure that CBS News staffers felt in the aftermath of this major documentary. It has always been this way. After the notable Murrow broadcasts, after Cronkite's landmark coverage of the landing on the moon, the entire organization, from mailroom to executive suites, would bask in the company's achievement. The greatest boost for morale in television is not the memos written or the Christmas parties held but what appears on the screen. It can lift the spirits and galvanize the entire news operation. But television is ephemeral; yesterday's show soon becomes today's distant memory.

By the end of the day, I had pretty much forgotten the Vietnam program. I had just returned from a *CBS Evening News* assignment with Walter Cronkite, first in Hungary and then in Poland—a country wracked by the Solidarity turmoil and soon to declare martial law. We had been able to get both Lech Walesa and Premier Wojciech Jaruzelski to sit for interviews with Cronkite. They not only gave us a strong news report but the interviews were expanded into an 11:30 p.m. half-hour special. I was looking for another such assignment.

I was told that there had been some flak after the Westmoreland show, predictably from some of his military supporters and from conservative critics of CBS News. But everyone had expected that; it was a given when you aired that sort of material, and no one seemed overly concerned about it.

Whatever clouds were on the horizon developed into a thunderstorm on Tuesday, three days after the program aired. Westmoreland announced that he would hold a news conference at the Army-Navy Club in Washington. CBS arranged to have it piped to New York live on closed circuit. I sat alone in my office watching it.

There on camera, in a room filled with reporters, stood a grave William C. Westmoreland, wearing not the four stars of his rank in Vietnam but a dark suit—a jut-jawed, silver-haired, and decidedly angry man two months to the day from his sixty-eighth birthday. Over the years, his face had appeared three times on the cover of *Time* and once each on the covers of *Newsweek* and *U.S. News and World Report*. A reporter would later write of the general when his anger moved to a New York courtroom: "He seems to be standing at attention while sitting down."

Westmoreland was the first captain of cadets at West Point, class of 1936. By 1942, in World War II, he was an artillery battalion commander. He would fight his way from North Africa to Normandy, from the Hürtgen Forest to the Elbe River. He would be a full colonel the month after D-Day. In Korea, he commanded a paratroop regiment and by 1956, at age forty-two, he would be the Army's youngest major general. In 1960, at forty-six, he would be the superintendent of West Point. Only Douglas MacArthur had been younger when he held that post.

Flanking Westmoreland were some of his closest colleagues from those years, a decade and a half ago, in Vietnam: Ellsworth Bunker, the U.S. ambassador, ailing and soon to die; George C. Carver, Jr., head of the CIA task force in Vietnam and the boss of George Allen and Sam Adams, two of the principals in the television program which had brought them all here; Lt. Gen. Daniel O. Graham, a feisty, contentious lieutenant colonel on the intelligence staff in Vietnam who later became director of the Defense Intelligence Agency and now headed an organization supporting President Reagan's Strategic Defense Initiative or "Star Wars"; Lt. Gen. Phillip Davidson, once the top Army intelligence officer in Vietnam; and Col. Charles Morris, his deputy.

As he looked over the room, Ambassador Bunker said it reminded him of the old days in Saigon and the daily briefings called the "Five O'Clock Follies," when there were strong feelings and tough questions by reporters.

Westmoreland, his voice choked with anger, wasted no time in getting to the point:

> Last week my wife urged me to attend a movie which was my first in five years. The name of the movie was *Absence of Malice*. Although I did not take the movie literally, it did show an innocent man whose life and many others were ruined by the unscrupulous use of the media. Little did I know that within a week, a real life, notorious reporter, Mike Wallace,

would try to prosecute me in a star-chamber procedure with distorted, false and specious information, plain lies, derived by sinister deception, an attempt to execute me on the guillotine of public opinion. It was all there—the arrogance, the color, the drama, the contrived plot, the close shots, everything but the truth. . . . In essence, Mike Wallace, primarily on the basis of material provided by a former intelligence analyst for the CIA, Sam Adams, accused me of withholding and falsifying important intelligence information to the extent that generated a sinister conspiracy against the national interest. That is a preposterous hoax and will not go unanswered.

The general was just beginning to warm to his subject. If he appeared to be "excited" in the film it was because he was "ambushed." Intelligence is at best an imprecise science. "It is not like counting beans . . . it is more like estimating roaches." The theme of the program, "a Machiavellian conspiracy to show progress when in fact there was no progress," was "categorically false . . . a lie."

The general said he had misspoken about infiltration figures during his interview and had sent Wallace and Crile (which he pronounced "Creel") a letter of correction which they had ignored.

General Graham showed excerpts from the program, stopping at the end of each to claim that CBS had distorted or falsified the material. A dispute arose when one of the reporters, Robert Kaiser of *The Washington Post*, claimed that Graham himself had misrepresented an excerpt from Col. Gains Hawkins, a key accuser in the show, by eliminating qualifying words about the Viet Cong. As one former player after another in the drama rose to defend Westmoreland, the emotion in the room continued to rise; it was the sort of event television does best. In fairness, one could not watch this news conference without wondering if it did not pose some legitimate questions about both the premise and the execution of the Vietnam broadcast.

Two quotes struck me forcefully as I watched the news conference, which ran for more than an hour and a half.

GENERAL GRAHAM: Such a conspiracy would have had to involve literally thousands of government officials in the State Department, CIA, NSA, the White House and elsewhere. There would have been enough conspirators in this conspiracy to fill a football stadium.

GEORGE CARVER, JR., of the CIA: It is in my view a mistake to interpret differences of opinion—even very sharp, even very heated—as necessarily being any evidence of conspiracy. Which is what Mr. Wallace charged and my irritation at that charge is why I am here with General Westmoreland today, even though there are many aspects of the struggle with which he and his colleagues and I may not always have been and probably never will be in complete agreement.

Carver heatedly denied that there was any attempt to deceive President Johnson. Not only was the chief executive acutely aware of the military-CIA debate over enemy strength but he repeatedly told both groups: "For God's sake, can't you guys get together? Must you always disagree? Can't you find the common ground as to what the evidence dictates?"

Westmoreland asked that CBS show the other side of the controversy. "In the interests of accuracy I call upon Mike Wallace to apologize for the crude hoax he and his associate have tried to sell the American people. Mike Wallace and his boy, George 'Creel' . . . are a disgrace to American journalism."

Over the years, I had been involved with enough controversial broadcasts to know that rebuttals were not necessarily gospels, that when the ox was gored a network could be accused of a lot of things that were not necessarily true. I remembered two programs, "Hunger in America" in 1968 and "The Selling of the Pentagon" in 1971, which had vulnerabilities but were also unjustly attacked for a lot of transgressions that did not hold up. I was not involved in the production of either but got embroiled in their unpleasant aftermaths, an inexplicable habit of mine at CBS News.

"Hunger in America" was a seering look at the pockets of hunger that existed in this most prosperous of all lands, and it created a furor. The program opened at the Robert Green Hospital in San Antonio, Texas, with nurses working frantically over a dying baby, and Charles Kuralt reporting: "Hunger is easy to recognize when it looks like this. This baby is dying of starvation. He was an American. Now he is dead."

The broadcast had an enormous impact, and the predictable attacks followed immediately. The flashpoint was the dying Mexican-American baby at the top of the program; nothing else was ever successfully challenged. There was outrage in San Antonio, with the local newspaper questioning whether the baby had died of malnutrition or was born prematurely. Representative Henry B. Gonzalez of Texas bombarded

CBS with angry letters, which I had to answer, and he entered our correspondence in the *Congressional Record*. Gonzalez got a subcommittee of the House to hold hearings on the program. Secretary of Agriculture Orville Freeman denounced it. The FCC conducted a preliminary staff investigation and found no basis for proceeding further.

Whether the baby died of malnutrition or was premature was never conclusively determined. I phoned Mrs. Vera Burke, director of social services at the hospital, who had appeared in the broadcast describing cases of infant malnutrition at the hospital, and asked her if she would come to New York to discuss the matter. The trip appealed to her—more as a junket, I suspected, than to bear witness—and when she arrived in my office I knew that we had a problem. After the usual amenities, I said:

"Mrs. Burke, there's no question in your mind that the baby we showed died of malnutrition, is there?"

"I never said that," the rather formidable Mrs. Burke replied. "I don't know what that baby died of."

That was as far as Mrs. Burke was prepared to go. There was little doubt that babies from the Mexican-American community had died of malnutrition in San Antonio. Whether this baby was one of them could never be proved.

Three weeks after the program had been aired, we repeated it on a Sunday afternoon. In a postscript, Secretary Freeman attacked the broadcast as "a disgraceful travesty of facts." But elsewhere, in Congress and throughout the country, we could report on the nation's strong and compassionate response to "Hunger in America."

On "The Selling of the Pentagon," which documented some of the military's public-relations excesses, the attacks were even heavier. Assistant Secretary of Defense Daniel Z. Henkin claimed he had been misedited—several of his answers were edited together into a single statement, which they should not have been—but there was much heavier artillery. Vice President Spiro T. Agnew, warming up to his anti-press role, lashed out at the program for presenting "alleged facts which are untrue." So did Representative F. Edward Hebert of Louisiana, chairman of the House Armed Services Committee, who called it "a professional hatchet job."

Representative Harley O. Staggers, chairman of the Investigations Subcommittee of the House, demanded that CBS produce the out-takes—unused film edited out of the final version—from the program.

When CBS President Frank Stanton refused, the committee recommended that he be cited for contempt of Congress, a charge that could have brought a jail sentence. The House narrowly turned back the citation.

CBS News did not turn its back on the controversy or try to stonewall it. A month after the program was aired, it was repeated with a twenty-minute postscript which included attacks by both Agnew and Hebert along with more temperate criticisms from Secretary of Defense Melvin Laird. CBS News president Richard S. Salant then came on camera to defend the broadcast as "a vital contribution to the people's right to know." Agnew had also brought up "Hunger in America" and the dying San Antonio baby, and Salant used some of his time to defend that.

"At the time," Salant said, "we were told by a hospital official that the baby did die of hunger. Later, after the broadcast, she changed her story somewhat, and new evidence came to light. There is no way, however, for the fact to be proven or disproven with certainty at this point. But, in that area, at that time, and in that hospital, babies were dying of malnutrition."

A month later, the charges against "The Selling of the Pentagon" got further amplification. I was assigned to produce an hour with critics and defenders of the broadcast facing each other. The panel included defenders Adam Yarmolinsky and Senator J. William Fulbright, who had written a book about Pentagon public relations before CBS News ever tackled the subject. The critics were Brig. Gen. S. L. A. Marshall (Ret.) and Arthur Sylvester, former public-information chief at the Pentagon.

It was undeniably one of the dullest shows in memory, a classic soporific, live and in prime time. But CBS News had made its point on both "Hunger" and "Pentagon." When the controversies erupted, they had been aggressively ventilated.

All of these events were whirling through my mind after the Westmoreland news conference, and there was one other that I could not forget—one that epitomized the virtue of giving the other side in a controversy a fair shot. It had happened twenty-eight years before, a milestone in television journalism, Edward R. Murrow's *See It Now* broadcast on Senator Joseph R. McCarthy on March 9, 1954. The day before, Murrow had gone to William S. Paley to recommend some right of reply. Before he could say it, Paley had suggested it. And so Murrow at the top of his broadcast said: "If the Senator feels that we have done violence to his words or pictures, and desires, so to speak, to answer himself, an opportunity will be afforded him on this program."

Why would not this be the right thing to do for Westmoreland? The general had even laid the groundwork for it near the end of his news conference:

Asked, ". . . would you support a demand that CBS do a further program on this, and tell your side of the story?" the general replied: "Well, we've done a pretty good program today, if you ask me"—obviously suggesting it ought to be broadcast.

I did not know whether or not Westmoreland had a case. Some of what he and his supporters had said sounded convincing enough to make it at least a possibility. Why not let him go on the air with it, state his position, and that would be that?

I walked next door to the office of Bill Leonard, president of CBS News. Leonard, whose tenure had been extended a year before beyond the CBS mandatory retirement age of sixty-five, was in the last months of his presidency. I had worked with him for fifteen years, and we were close personally. Leonard had done it all at CBS, joining the network after serving as a Navy officer in World War II. He had been correspondent, host, producer and executive. He was a heavy-set man, white-haired, who had eclectic interests: CBS News, thoroughbred racing (from time to time he would buy horses that never ran very well), election coverage (he had pioneered CBS News coverage and vote projections), sports of all kinds, mystery novels, ham radio, expert contract bridge and good restaurants. The Vietnam program was the last documentary that would fall under Leonard's stewardship. He had screened it before it went on the air as had his successor, Van Gordon Sauter, although they saw it separately.

A documentary goes through a series of screenings before it is broadcast. When the producer is ready, he screens it for the executive producer, then for the vice president in charge of "soft" news—documentary and public-affairs programs—and finally for the news division president. It is a very difficult assignment for the top man. He may be dealing with material about which he knows next to nothing. He may in a month see four or five reports, all different and presenting different problems. Faith in the producers is essential; that and the ability to ask the right questions.

When he was news president, Dick Salant, who had never produced anything, could be particularly penetrating at these critical screenings. He would say about these sessions: ". . . the trouble with screening [a documentary] is that you don't know the questions to ask . . . until the fat's in the fire. And when it's all over, you never dream of asking one of your colleagues whether he cheated by putting in questions in advance. That's in our written standards, and I have to assume the people I pick are trustworthy. Over the years I find out whether they are or whether they aren't. The only thing I think I would have asked [on the Westmoreland program], because I asked it on all investigative documentaries, is: Is this really the best you can do for the other side? Didn't they say something more about it?"

When I went to Leonard's office after watching Westmoreland's rebuttal, Roger Colloff, vice president in charge of documentaries, was with him. Colloff, a week short of his thirty-sixth birthday, was on a fast track at CBS. A Yale law school graduate, who looks quite a bit like Senator Sam Nunn, he had been brought to CBS News by Leonard. In Washington, he had worked for Leonard in the corporate offices when Leonard was vice president and lobbyist for CBS. He had also worked for Senator Walter Mondale and James Schlesinger, then Secretary of Energy.

Leonard was seated at his desk with Colloff standing in front of it. They were obviously having a serious discussion about the Westmoreland news conference. Their conversation stopped when I entered the room.

I asked, almost as an aside and not nearly as forcefully as I wish I had, whether they had given any thought to putting the conference on the air that night.

Colloff reacted with annoyance: Oh, no . . . ridiculous suggestion . . . no need to put on anything. He said it in such a pained and disparaging way it was apparent that he regarded the idea as a personal attack, which in a way it was. He was the executive responsible for the Vietnam program; he had approved it in the penultimate screening. Leonard uncharacteristically said nothing, and I concluded they might be happier continuing their conversation without me. I left the office. That night the Dan Rather news ran a short excerpt from the news conference.

In the days that followed, I heard little about the Westmoreland program. It wound up in seventy-second place, dead last, in the ratings for the week. This was not unexpected in the entertainment blizzard of a Saturday night. Vietnam was up against two pieces of ABC kitsch, "Love Boat" and "Fantasy Island." Still, the program was seen by an estimated audience of 9,600,000, more than the combined circulations of the *New York Times, The Washington Post, Time,* and *Newsweek.*

In April, I went to Poland again for the *CBS Evening News,* this time with Bill Moyers. As far as I knew, Westmoreland had said his piece, CBS News had kept its cool, and "The Uncounted Enemy: A Vietnam Deception" could now take its place in one of the world's largest cemeteries, that limbo-land where old television programs are interred.

4

THE ASSIGNMENT

O n May 24, 1982, four months after "The Uncounted Enemy" was broadcast, the longest article in the history of *TV Guide*, the magazine with the largest circulation in the United States, hit the newstands. Emblazoned on its cover was the headline: "ANATOMY OF A SMEAR," and the subhead "How CBS News Broke the Rules and 'Got' Gen. Westmoreland."

In nine pages, staff writers Don Kowet and Sally Bedell leveled a withering indictment against the broadcast. In the CBS News offices in New York, where *TV Guide* runs a bad second to *The Economist*, the magazine was on virtually every desk and was the topic of most conversations. It was difficult to ignore a magazine—never mind that its stock-in-trade was not investigative reporting but running industry puff pieces and program schedules—which had a circulation of 17.5 million, almost twice as many people as saw the Vietnam documentary.

One of the writers of the article, Sally Bedell, was well known to me as a thorough and excellent reporter (she would join the *New York Times* shortly after the Vietnam piece appeared and, as Sally Bedell Smith, do a solid reporting job there). I had never met or spoken to Don Kowet, and still have not.

Their report had unquestionably been the product of a leak from inside CBS News; they had access to all of the uncut interview transcripts and many of the most sensitive internal documents. Their allegations about the program added up to this: The broadcast was dishonestly produced, violated many of the CBS News Standards in its editing, and began with a preconception that nothing could shake. Oddly, they carefully avoided challenging the basic premise of the broadcast, saying of their investigation, "Its purpose was not to confirm or deny the existence of the 'conspiracy' that CBS's journalists say existed."

Their major charges against the program, many of them containing detailed subcharges, ran as follows:

—"CBS began the project already convinced that a conspiracy had been perpetrated and turned a deaf ear toward evidence that suggested otherwise."

—"CBS paid $25,000 to a consultant on the program without adequately investigating his 14-year quest to prove the program's conspiracy theory."

—"CBS violated its own official guidelines by rehearsing its paid consultant before he was interviewed on camera."

—"CBS screened for a sympathetic witness—in order to persuade him to redo his on-camera interview—the statements of other witnesses already on film. But CBS never offered the targets of its conspiracy charge any opportunity, before their interviews, to hear their accusers, or to have a second chance before the cameras."

—"CBS asked sympathetic witnesses soft questions, while grilling unfriendly witnesses with prosecutorial zeal."

—"CBS misrepresented the accounts of events provided by some witnesses, while ignoring altogether other witnesses who might have been able to challenge CBS's assertions."

—"CBS pulled quotes out of context, in one case to imply incorrectly that Westmoreland was familiar with a meeting where estimates of the enemy were arbitrarily slashed—a familiarity that was crucial to proving the conspiracy."

—"CBS's own paid consultant now doubts the documentary's premise of a Westmoreland-led conspiracy."

The piece was on the newsstands at the worst possible time for CBS. Virtually all of the network's top management was in San Francisco for its annual meeting with its affiliates, the owners and managers of the more than two hundred stations that constitute the CBS Television Network.

At one time, a reporter had referred to the affiliates as a group of very rich yokels, but that was in an earlier television age when the network was dominant, and often treated its member stations like obedient vassals. By 1982, the power had shifted. The affiliates had been rich for a long time and its members now included powerful group owners who had to be courted and catered to.

In the halcyon days of the 1970s, all stops were out to make this annual conclave what the network wanted—a love-in. At one affiliate meeting in Los Angeles, the network put on a circus with everything but live elephants. At a black-tie dinner which my wife and I attended, all of the stars of the old and new entertainment shows were brought out, one after another, to parade on a big stage while the station owners and their wives broke their hands applauding them. My wife and I are, to put it generously, infrequent viewers of the network's entertainment fare, and it was like watching appearances of the stars of stage and screen from Bangladesh. Jean Stapleton, the co-star of "All in the Family," was sitting at our table, and I turned to her: "Who the hell are these people?" I asked. She smiled sweetly. "Damned if I know."

If there was a guaranteed way to cast a pall over the party in San Francisco in 1982, it was the appearance of *TV Guide* with its harsh accusations about a documentary that these affiliates had carried on their stations. For the politically conservative, bottom-line owners, it was like announcing that the food they had just been served was tainted.

In our apartment in New York that night, we had a guest for dinner, Charles Eisendrath, a journalism professor at the University of Michigan. Eisendrath, a former *Time* foreign correspondent, a knowledgeable and facile young man, mentioned the Westmoreland affair briefly and was interested mainly in my recent trip to Poland with Bill Moyers.

I had returned on the first of the month after a difficult but not earth-shaking assignment. Poland was under martial law, the nine o'clock curfew absolute, our rooms bugged, and Moyers had actually found a bug hidden in a lamp in his room. We had filed three quite good reports and working with the indefatigable Moyers had been rewarding. The story we had thought might burst upon us—another eruption by Solidarity with Soviet troops marching into Warsaw—did not happen. I told Eisendrath that I thought Lech Walesa, who was in jail, had been neutralized as a political force.

At six o'clock, as we were having drinks, the phone rang. It was Van Gordon Sauter, now president of CBS News, calling from San Francisco. He wasted no time in getting to the point. *TV Guide* was out with this disturbing piece which leveled very strong allegations against CBS

News. I told him I had read it. What we had to do, Sauter said, was to get to the bottom of these charges, who is right and who is wrong, and would I take on that assignment and conduct an internal investigation of the Vietnam documentary?

At first, I found it difficult to reply. I knew at once what this would entail. If I found the broadcast flawless, it would be a whitewash. If I found it flawed, I was a whistle blower with all that meant—damaged careers and personal attacks. I had known Mike Wallace for more than forty years—he and I were classmates at the University of Michigan— and I knew how relentlessly he would fight to maintain his considerable reputation. Crile I scarcely knew. Howard Stringer, the executive producer, had more or less been a protégé of mine.

I had given twenty-five years of my life to CBS News and without being maudlin about it, the organization meant something to me. Of course, it meant Murrow and Cronkite and Sevareid; that was easy. But more than that it meant hundreds of men and women, good reporters, producers, editors, and writers whose names were not known to the public. I thought CBS News had the finest broadcast journalists in the country, and what they stood for, and had battled for, was important enough for me to go on the line for.

My enthusiasm for the assignment was minimal, and I told Sauter that. But I agreed to take it on with one proviso. I wanted him to notify the full CBS News organization that I was doing this and to tell them that "when I speak, you're speaking."

Sauter, forty-six, had become deputy president of CBS News in November 1981, two months before the Vietnam program was broadcast. He became president after Bill Leonard retired in March of 1982. Born in Middletown, Ohio, the son of a fireman and a hat saleswoman who divorced when he was two years old, Sauter was a bushy, bear of a man—"a self-proclaimed, bearded eccentric," the writer Ron Rosenbaum had described him in *Esquire*. Nancy Collins in *New York* Magazine added this: "He has been marked for power and has operated with a blend of studied eccentricity and cool gamesmanship." It was all part of a big publicity push Sauter received from CBS when he moved to the top news job.

He had graduated from Ohio University and received a master's degree in journalism at the University of Missouri. Articulate, frequently if not shockingly profane, a good writer, he had worked for newspapers before leaving the Chicago *Daily News* to join the CBS owned-and-operated affiliate, WBBM-Radio, when it adopted an all-news format in 1968. Sauter started as a reporter, moved up to managing editor, and was promoted to New York as head of special events for CBS News-Radio. Then it was back to Chicago as news director for WBBM-TV. He tried his hand as anchorman and quickly found that was not for him or his superiors. He became Paris Bureau Chief for CBS News in 1974, a job he fell in love with, only to be moved up again as vice president, program practices—really censor—for the network in 1976. Next it was on to KNXT-TV in Los Angeles, another owned-and-operated station, as vice president and general manager in 1977, president of CBS Sports in 1980, and president of CBS News in 1981. The smile from above was obviously on Sauter, fixed and growing wider, and some said he would one day be president of all of CBS.

His eccentricities were manifold. In Chicago his office included a parrot named Sam with, in his words, "projectile diarrhea"; in Los Angeles he lived on a houseboat, drove a Jeep, and went to the office in jeans and topsiders with no socks. At CBS News his office included an old rolltop desk, a hat rack with an array of odd caps, and the framed quote of Howard Beale, the over-the-edge anchorman in the movie *Network:* "Television is not the truth. If you want the truth, go to God, go to your guru, go to yourself."

Sauter came to the leadership of CBS News convinced the networks were out of touch with the rest of the country and immediately began downplaying coverage from Washington. He was looking, he said, for "moments." They were described with a catch phrase right out of the telephone company ads: "Reach out and touch someone." Instead of Cronkite's "That's the way it is," it became "That's the way it feels." He said his attention as news president would be consumed by Dan Rather and the *Evening News,* which was stumbling in the ratings when he took over. He said, "I'm going to marry Dan Rather," and he had succeeded in moving the flagship show back to first place. He was a complex, often difficult man, and since I scarcely knew him and was a part of the old guard he seemed intent on shunting aside, I was surprised he had tapped me for the investigation.

In San Francisco, I later learned, the *TV Guide* cover piece hit Sauter and his colleagues amidships. Soon the newsstand at the Fairmount Hotel had to send out for more copies of the magazine. According to Gene Mater, a news vice president, they "talked and talked." They knew, Mater said, they had to do something; they could not ignore the story, not with a hotelful of affiliates on their hands. Sauter brought in Ralph Goldberg, assistant general counsel for CBS, and they talked some more. Someone had to look into the allegations, and who would that be? Now the meeting included Sauter, Mater, Goldberg, along with Robert Chandler and Roger Colloff, the two CBS News vice presidents. Edward Joyce, number two to Sauter, was in New York.

"When the *TV Guide* article hit in San Francisco, we were surprised," Sauter told me. "I had been led to believe that the line of questioning by Bedell and Kowet dealt with areas where we were buttoned up, that nothing embarrassing would come out. Instead, we found that it was acutely embarrassing, and I knew something had to be done."

In view of the fact that the charges were far more than anticipated, Sauter said, the question of who should investigate them was naturally dominant. They talked about CBS lawyers, outside lawyers, and someone from the inside. "I felt that journalists should investigate journalists. Goldberg spelled out the risks if a lawsuit should eventuate. Your name was the only one to be mentioned for an inside investigation."

There was some feeling that if Westmoreland sued, a lawyer's investigation might be privileged under a lawyer/client relationship. I later asked Floyd Abrams, the noted First Amendment lawyer, about this. "If a lawyer does the investigation for possible use at a trial," Abrams told me, "then his findings are privileged and not usable. If a lawyer was conducting an internal investigation for a network, then it is not so clear. Is he really acting as a lawyer or working on the journalistic side? It might be privileged but it might not."

When it was agreed that I should conduct the investigation, Sauter told me he said, "Perfect if he'll do it." He met with his boss, Gene F. Jankowski, president of the CBS Broadcast Group, who approved, and then he phoned me in New York. After the call he went forth to face the affiliates.

Gene Mater remembers that Sauter was far from his usual jovial and ebullient self when he announced that CBS News would conduct an investigation into the *TV Guide* charges. Sauter said CBS was taking this very seriously, that I would conduct the examination, and that he would be working with me. He was half right. I did conduct it but he never made any contribution, apart from asking me from time to time how it was going and when I would deliver it.

When I hung up the phone that night, I had to explain to Eisendrath and my wife what the call was all about. Sauter had urged secrecy until he made the announcement to the affiliates, and I tried to be guarded. I mentioned that the issue was the *TV Guide* article and that I might be looking into it, and let it go at that.

Eisendrath was spending the night with us, and after he went to bed I told my wife the whole story. I felt that Mike Wallace might be difficult to deal with. He was a preeminent network news figure, and I expected him to be fiercely protective of his turf. George Crile was known to be difficult, and he was squarely on the line with this show. I wondered how supportive Sauter would be and whether CBS Corporate Management would try to finesse the whole matter. And, to put it bluntly, at this stage of my life, I asked myself: Who needed this?

"Well, you've won your first raffle," my wife said. Over the years I had become addicted to contests and had wasted a lot of time mailing entries to Publishers Clearing House. I told her I had many feelings about this assignment, none of which I found amusing.

"You know," she said, "you might have been happier staying in Poland."

By noon the next day, the news that I was going to investigate the Vietnam documentary had traveled rapidly from San Francisco to New York although no memorandum from Sauter had been issued. Apparently, it moved along the gossip trail.

I was working out of a small office, next to Bill Moyers, on the second floor of the CBS Broadcast Center, the former milk barn on West 57th Street near the Hudson River. I read and reread the *TV Guide* article and added up eighteen specific charges made against the Vietnam program. I decided that these charges would constitute the framework for my report. I would investigate each one and try to ascertain whether or not it was true. I hoped to avoid such arcane subjects as how one divines the enemy order of battle or who won or lost at Tet, but I had a feeling that I would not be able to avoid them entirely. I wanted the report to deal with the two issues that were joined in *TV Guide* versus CBS: fairness and accuracy, which to me are the cornerstones of good journalism. I remembered interviewing Stanley Walker, a legendary city editor of the old *New York Herald-Tribune*, who told me this story. When a new reporter would come to the *Trib*, Walker would say to him: "Young man, I have three words of advice for you: Accuracy . . . accuracy . . . accuracy."

I knew that the press was under a lot of pressure and that a principal complaint was that the media lacked objectivity. It was my feeling that absolute objectivity was unattainable. I agreed with the writer Gary Wills, who wrote in the *Nieman Reports* in 1978: "Obviously, journalists have biases. As E. B. White has said, no man is born perpendicular."

I also agreed with John Hersey, who wrote in the *Yale Review* in 1980: "As to journalism, we may as well grant right away that there is no such thing as absolute objectivity. It is impossible to present in words The Truth or The Whole Story.

"The minute a writer offers nine hundred and ninety-nine out of a thousand facts, the worm has begun to wriggle. The vision of each witness is particular. Tolstoy pointed out," Hersey continued, "that immediately after a battle, there are as many remembered versions of it as there have been participants."

As far as my examination was concerned, I was not going to try to determine whether Messrs. Wallace and Crile had been objective. What I wanted to know was whether they had been fair and accurate.

I began getting hushed television calls and visits from other producers at CBS News. One, who worked with Moyers, expressed reservations about George Crile, the Vietnam program's producer and reporter. He urged me to see Ira Klein, the show's film editor, who, he told me, was very troubled by the broadcast and might have leaked the story to *TV Guide*. I told him I planned to see Klein. Another producer called to say Klein was working for him and I should be sure to see him. I assured him I would; I began to wonder if these calls were orchestrated. A third producer, assigned to *60 Minutes,* phoned to say he heard the interviews for the Vietnam program had been rehearsed and that they had gone back and done one of them a second time. He strongly advised me to speak with the camera crew for the program. I thanked him and said I planned to talk to everyone involved in the broadcast.

Mike Wallace phoned from the Los Angeles airport. He was on his way to Vietnam for a *60 Minutes* piece. He had heard of my assignment and said he was glad that I would be doing it. I told him, as I would tell others, that I did not see myself as judge, jury, prosecutor, or defense lawyer but as a journalist assigned to a story. And that was the way I planned to do it, as if in my earlier days as a print reporter someone on the desk had said to me: "Here's a story. Go out and see whether it's true or not."

In the fifteen-minute telephone conversation, Wallace began by insisting that *TV Guide* had made a "mountain out of a molehill," that his documentary was true, that the books in Vietnam had been "cooked." Then he began changing his emphasis, pointing out that his role in the show had been very limited due to his heavy commitments, especially to *60 Minutes*, and that he had tried to turn down the assignment when it was first brought to him. In reality, he had had very little to do with the program, conducting only five interviews, three of which were used.

He brought up his interview with Walt W. Rostow, former special assistant to President Johnson. They had filmed for three hours and used none of it, and Wallace said that Rostow had regarded the interview as an attack on LBJ, as an accusation that he and the President had colluded to keep information from the American people. Wallace told me that Rostow had flatly denied that any critical intelligence was being kept from him or from LBJ, and I asked whether that wasn't worth putting on the air. No, Wallace said, he believed the critical information Rostow got was "cooked," and that LBJ may have received his information from back-channel sources, not from Westmoreland.

Wallace said that Rostow had not heard of 20,000 to 25,000 regular North Vietnamese troops coming down the Ho Chi Minh Trail; he had said, in fact, that nothing of that magnitude could have moved down the trail. The thrust of the broadcast, Wallace declared, was whether or not there was a conspiracy, and Rostow had told them he knew nothing about any conspiracy. I told Wallace I had just started the project, and I was not read-in enough to discuss it. He said he would be back from Vietnam in about two weeks. I assured him we would talk then.

Roger Colloff, the vice president responsible for the program, phoned from San Francisco. He told me mine was a very tough assignment, and I replied that I had not volunteered for it. He said he had told George Crile to send me all of the unedited transcripts for the interviews conducted for the broadcast. I told him I would need them.

At the end of the first week, I had the research library at CBS dig out all the clips they could find about the order-of-battle controversy in Vietnam. It filled a fat folder, and I spent the weekend reading the material. There were stories from Vietnam, from the Pentagon, from the White House, and about Sam Adams and his crusade. I knew I had scarcely dented the material, which was going to be voluminous, but when I came into the office on Monday, I felt much more secure about the investigation.

I phoned George Crile. I expected a tense, perhaps even hostile, conversation, but he was gracious and cooperative. He said he was pleased they had chosen me for the assignment. I told him I would need all the transcripts, all of the memorandums and letters written during the production, and a lot of other material I could not itemize at this time. He said I would get anything I needed.

The next day I had a long-standing date for lunch with two retired CBS colleagues, Richard Salant, former president, and John Sharnik, an accomplished writer and producer. We ate in a French restaurant in the West Forties. They had not heard of my assignment, and I did not mention it. Salant was deeply concerned over the *TV Guide* article and characteristically paid no attention to what he was eating as he talked about it. He said it was the strongest and potentially the most damaging attack ever leveled against CBS News. I had a feeling that Salant, always combative and chafing at the idleness of retirement, would have loved to be back running the whole affair. He said if he were, he would assign someone he thoroughly trusted—he mentioned bringing back David Klinger, a retired vice president who had investigated "The Selling of the Pentagon"—and then have him report his findings very privately to him. He emphasized that it should be kept internal, the report going only to him and the decision ultimately being his alone.

If my investigation could be kept private and internal, I knew that Sauter would be far from displeased, but as I left the restaurant I had my doubts. Given the way the heat was building, the possibility that Westmoreland might sue, the avidity with which the press was pursuing the story, I had these questions: How internal could it remain? How private could it be? How long could it simply be one man's investigation of a single television program?

5

THE FIRST
REVEALING DAYS

In the days following, I immersed myself in the story. It quickly became apparent that what I thought was news, what CBS was revealing to the public for the first time, was not new at all. It had been unfolding for more than fifteen years. It also was obvious that the key figure in the drama was not Mike Wallace or George Crile but Samuel A. Adams, the former CIA analyst whom CBS News had hired as a consultant.

Sam Adams, forty-nine, had the right blood lines for the CIA. He was the fourth cousin, seven times removed, of John Adams, second President of the United States. His father, Pierpont Adams, who was probably named after J. Pierpont Morgan, had a seat on the New York Stock Exchange. Sam Adams went to St. Mark's School in Massachusetts, then on to Harvard, where he majored in history and was graduated in 1955. He then was commissioned in the Navy where he served for "three years, four months and eleven days." He tried Harvard Law School but gave it up after two years, then investment banking, then ski bumming, and finally he turned to the Federal Government and the Central Intelligence Agency.

That the story was not new was confirmed by a check of the *New York Times* information bank. There were thirty-six references to Adams and his work. For two years, from 1965 to 1967, he was the CIA's only analyst studying the Viet Cong full time. In one story, he quoted William

E. Colby, the CIA director, as saying: "The Agency's assessments in the late 1960s were based in substantial measure on Mr. Adams's work."

According to Adams, a captured enemy document landed on his desk at CIA headquarters in Langley, Virginia, on August 19, 1966. It revealed that in South Vietnam's Binh Dinh Province, irregular forces— both full-time guerrillas and part-time militia—numbered more than ten times the official U.S. military estimates. These were Communist forces outside the regular Viet Cong mainforce units and North Vietnamese Army formations.

The disparity intrigued and eventually consumed Adams. He began to pull together other captured documents and, assessing the information he collected, he extrapolated his data into a countrywide picture that he believed was incontrovertible proof that there were at least twice as many Viet Cong irregulars as the U.S. military command was estimating.

His passion and conviction would start him on a trail that would wind through the Pentagon Papers trial, the House Select Committee on Intelligence, the White House, the pages of Harper's Magazine, the corridors of CBS News and the Westmoreland documentary, and eventually to a Federal Court House in New York City.

In March of 1973, still a member of the CIA but isolated and frustrated, no longer involved in his Vietnam studies, Adams volunteered to be a defense witness in Los Angeles at the trial of Daniel Ellsberg and Anthony M. Russo, Jr., accused of espionage, theft, and conspiracy for copying and making public the Pentagon Papers. Adams testified that since at least some of the highly classified documents that had been initially published by the New York Times in June of 1971 were based on inaccurate and perhaps deliberately misleading information, they would be of no value to enemy intelligence officers. His position was simply this: Enemy-strength figures were rigged; they were worthless; and therefore they could not possibly violate security.

On May 17, 1973, Adams resigned from the CIA, charging that the agency was "neither honest enough nor thorough enough" in its work in Indochina. He had tried to no avail to interest the Nixon White House in his figures.

In the May 1975 issue of Harper's, Adams set forth the details of his long battle. The title of the piece was "VIETNAM COVERUP: PLAYING WITH NUMBERS." The subhead carried a portentous word: "A CIA Conspiracy Against Its Own Intelligence." The word "conspiracy" appeared nowhere in the article. The man who edited the piece for the magazine was the same George Crile who would produce the Vietnam documentary for CBS. The story made these charges:

—Since 1966 Adams had been insisting that our estimates of enemy strength, the order of battle, were too low. Instead of just under 300,000, the Communist force might be as high as 600,000.

—In January of 1967, at a conference in Honolulu, Westmoreland's order-of-battle expert, Col. Gains Hawkins, had conceded to him: "You know, there's a lot more of these little bastards out there than we thought there were."

—In September of 1967, at another order-of-battle conference in Saigon, his higher estimates were again turned back when CIA director Richard Helms caved in to the military. Col. Charles Morris, MACV's deputy intelligence chief, told Adams he was "full of shit."

Adams accused Westmoreland and his senior intelligence staff of concealing the actual enemy strength from the Joint Chiefs of Staff, the President, the Congress, and the American people. He further charged that because of the misleading indicators, our forces were surprised at Tet and suffered unnecessary casualties.

Adams was again back in the news on September 18, 1975, when he testified for two and a half hours before the Select Committee on Intelligence of the House of Representatives, the so-called Pike Committee. In pursuing his long crusade, he told the committee that the surprise at Tet resulted from a corruption in the intelligence process, the deliberate downgrading of the strengths of the enemy army in order to portray the Viet Cong as weaker than they were. He charged that the United States lost 7,000 to 8,000 men and 1,200 airplanes at Tet. In his closing remarks, he said the intelligence effort was "very haphazard, slipshod, often dishonest, prone to distort and that it did not do the job it was supposed to be doing." Anthony Lewis of the *New York Times* defended Adams in his column, writing that "his accurate intelligence estimates of Viet Cong military strength were deliberately reduced—falsified."

The controversy surrounding Adams and his allegations again surfaced in the weeks after his testimony. Walt W. Rostow, former special assistant to President Johnson, said that "Adams was confusing a debate within the intelligence community over Viet Cong strength with the question whether the United States was prepared for the Tet offensive.

. . . This debate had no bearing whatsoever" on the assessment of insurgent capabilities.

Robert W. Komer, LBJ's special ambassador in Vietnam, lashed out at Adams's "outrageous allegations." He called his charge "this piddling issue." He said it "stretches credulity it had anything to do with being surprised at Tet." John T. Morris, a former colleague of Adams, came to his support in a letter to the *New York Times* on October 18, 1975: "I can confirm the entire thrust of Sam's charges." The record "speaks of misfeasance, nonfeasance, of outright dishonesty and professional cowardice . . . a page of shame in the history of American intelligence."

The dispute continued to boil. In December, CIA director William E. Colby and Daniel O. Graham both testified before the Pike Committee. Graham had vaulted ahead in the promotion ranks since Vietnam. A lieutenant colonel then, he was now a lieutenant general and director of the Defense Intelligence Agency. Graham sharply contradicted Adams's Tet figures. Instead of 7,000–8,000 Americans dead, he made it 2,200. Instead of twelve hundred planes lost, he made it fifty-eight. He told the committee that he thought Adams had some sort of "mental problem," and suggested he had been sacked by the CIA, when he had in fact resigned.

The Pike Committee would address itself to the controversy but hardly end it. The most telling of its conclusions dealt with the word that would bedevil CBS in the months ahead—conspiracy: "The Administration's need was for confirmation of the contention that there was light at the end of the tunnel, that the pacification program was working and generally that American involvement in Vietnam was not only correct, but effective. In this sense, the intelligence community could not help but find its powers to effect objective analysis substantially undermined. *Whether this was by conspiracy or not is somewhat irrelevant*" (emphasis added).

Following his resignation from the CIA, Adams retired to a 250-acre farm in Leesburg, Virginia, where he raised cattle. He continued to work on a book about his CIA career with the working title *Who the Hell Are We Fighting Out There?*

In 1980, Adams's Vietnam crusade was revived by his *Harper's* editor, George Crile, now a CBS News producer-reporter. Crile wanted to produce a documentary on the Vietnam intelligence dispute, using Sam Adams's research, contacts, and premise, and Adams was more than willing to cooperate. Thus it was that Sam Adams found himself as a consultant, interviewee, and prime mover in the most controversial and agonizing documentary in the history of CBS News.

My preliminary research into the story had now made certain aspects evident. In itself it was not new; it had been around for more than fifteen years. But it was new to television, which in its arrogance does not believe that any story has been told until it tells it. It did have one strikingly new ingredient: the willingness of eight former CIA and military intelligence officers to go on camera to endorse it. The story was also highly controversial, with supporters and detractors in abundance. And, finally, the key figure, the prime mover, was Sam Adams, the former CIA analyst who had made this story his mission.

On May 27, I had to see Dan Rather about an unrelated news matter and went to his office adjacent to his anchor desk. I had first met Rather when he was a new, young reporter for CBS in Texas, and had watched him move ahead rapidly through London, Washington, and the White House, a publicized confrontation with President Richard Nixon, Vietnam, *CBS Reports, 60 Minutes,* and now to the most coveted job the network had to offer, anchorman and successor to Walter Cronkite on the Monday-to-Friday *Evening News* broadcasts. He was no longer the heir apparent, vying with Roger Mudd for the top job; he was the heir, the point man, the chief correspondent upon whom CBS News and especially Van Gordon Sauter had pinned their hopes.

Rather said he had heard of my appointment, and I was the only one who could do it. I thanked him although this struck me as vintage Rather, whose manner I would describe as Texas courtly. Then he said an inexplicable thing. "If you see George Crile, tell him to call me. I want to tell him I am behind him." I was put off by the suggestion and told Rather that if he wanted to reassure Crile he had better call him himself.

It became apparent that I would need research help in conducting the examination. It was a big and complicated story, and Sauter had suggested a deadline of three weeks, which I already suspected was unrealistic. I decided to go for the best person CBS News had, Toby Wertheim, the senior researcher on the Rather News. She had worked with me briefly when I was producing the news with Walter Cronkite. She was a bright, no-nonsense woman in her thirties, discreet and close-mouthed, which I knew to be essential, and I also knew she had talents beyond the demands of her *Evening News* assignment. She was then providing research for J. Anthony Lukas for his Pulitzer Prize-winning *On Common Ground*. She had previously spent a year researching his Watergate book, *Nightmare: The Underside of the Nixon Years*.

I was certain that requesting Wertheim for my staff would be awkward. She was working for Howard Stringer, now executive producer for Rather, before that executive producer for Crile and the Vietnam program. I went to see Stringer and he agreed at once to give her a leave of absence. "I hear you're the Inspector General; you can have her," he said. I thought it was especially decent of him since he had only recently taken over the Rather show. With all of the attention being focused on it, and the pressure I knew he was feeling, he might well have resisted losing a key member of his production team. He also had to know that he would be a principal in my examination of the Vietnam program.

Stringer urged me to run the twenty-seven hours of interviews filmed for the program rather than relying solely on a reading of the transcripts. "When you see them, you may get an idea of why some weren't used," he said. The suggestion made no sense to me. Was some of the film out of focus? Was some of the sound marginal? I was not being facetious, but unless there were technical problems, the essence of a television interview could be found in the written transcript. As a producer, I did run all of the "rushes" for interviews with two presidents, Dwight Eisenhower and Lyndon Johnson, and two Supreme Court Justices, Hugo Black and William O. Douglas. I did so to make certain that the film was technically right but also to look for moments of passion or emphasis that would enrich the broadcast. In my role as investigator, these considerations were no longer germane. I was interested in content: What was used, what was not used, how fairly the film was edited. I was also under severe deadline pressure, and since some of the interviews were conducted with two cameras, it would have taken longer than twenty-seven hours to get through the material. We would run no film during our examination.

Wertheim said she would join me that day on one condition. She asked for a letter from CBS News stating that if there was a lawsuit over the Vietnam program, the network would defend her and pay any legal fees. I said I would get her the letter.

Toby and I went to the Harvard Club to have lunch with Robert Shaplen, a close friend of mine for thirty-five years and perhaps the most senior of all the reporters who covered the Vietnam War.

Shaplen began as a reporter for the *New York Herald-Tribune* in 1937 and left to become southwest Pacific war correspondent for *Newsweek* in 1943–45, covering some of the heaviest action on the road to Japan. From 1945 to 1947, he was the magazine's Far East bureau chief in Shanghai and became one of the first Western journalists to visit Mao Tse-tung in the caves of Yenan. A Nieman Fellow in 1947, he joined the *New Yorker* in 1952, specializing in Southeast Asia. He was in Vietnam during a time that later correspondents would call "those days of the French" and reported the fall of their empire after Dienbienphu. In 1962, he became the magazine's Far East correspondent in Hong Kong. He wrote many books, two of which were especially notable. *A Corner of the World* (1949) was a collection of short stories about the Far East, one of which, "A Wind Is Rising," was a poignant tale of a French officer plunged into the politics of Saigon. *The Lost Revolution* (1965) was reportage, a sorrowful recounting of how the opportunities in Vietnam had been dissipated and lost.

Shaplen told us he had seen the broadcast and had hated it. He felt that to call this old story a conspiracy was ludicrous. Intelligence was a much-debated business during the war, and the estimates of the Military Assistance Command, Vietnam (MACV) were always considered less reliable than those of the Central Intelligence Agency. The question was, Shaplen said, who constituted an enemy? A man with a gun? A man with a part-time gun? A man with a night-time gun? Much of the intelligence dispute was a legitimate argument between highly trained men who had no particular axes to grind. It was not a conspiracy.

He felt that Sam Adams was obsessive. He thought well of Maj. Gen. Joseph McChristian, Westmoreland's intelligence chief in 1966–67. Shaplen mentioned other senior correspondents in Vietnam: Keyes Beech of the Chicago *Daily News*, George McArthur of the Los Angeles *Times*, Bud Merrick of *U.S. News and World Report*, and Malcolm Browne of the *New York Times*. He doubted that any of them would buy the conspiracy theory that CBS News had propounded. He urged me to call McArthur, whom he considered to be one of the best informed of the correspondents.

I phoned McArthur in Washington, the first of several conversations with him. He had just read the *TV Guide* article and shared Shaplen's feelings about the use of the word "conspiracy." "CBS treated the story as if it was new," he said. "It wasn't new; it was old." McArthur said that Ambassador Ellsworth Bunker placed no credence at all in the figures he was getting from MACV. "Military historians to this day do not know what the correct enemy-strength numbers are."

In 1982, as I was beginning my investigation, a new book, *On Strategy: A Critical Analysis of the Vietnam War*, written by an Army historian, Col. Harry G. Summers, Jr., appeared. Summers dealt with the numbers dispute succinctly. "The problem in Vietnam was not the numbers; it was the policy."

And so the issues were beginning to be joined, the differences more sharply delineated, the old animosities and disputes rising to the surface. Our principal job was not to answer all of the abrasive questions the war had posed but rather to determine how fairly and honestly the Vietnam documentary had dealt with its material. That would be the main focus of our efforts in the days ahead.

On Friday, May 28, 1982, the end of my first week of research, Edward M. Joyce called me to his office. Joyce was executive vice president of the news division, second only to Sauter. In fact, the two men had vied for the top job when Bill Leonard was retiring, and Sauter had won it. Sauter and Joyce worked closely together; at times they seemed to be cloned. Sauter, who had a weight problem, drank endless cans of Tab in his office and soon so did Joyce, who had no visible weight problem. Around the newsroom, they were swiftly known as Tab One and Tab Two.

In some ways, they were an odd, unlikely couple. Sauter, heavy-set, full-bearded, would stride through the halls, bear-hugging favorites and greeting subordinates, both tall and short, with "Hi, big guy." When he entered a room, he filled it. He left no doubt—he was the boss. He was changing CBS News by shedding what he called "the yesterdays," the older employees who had been prominent in the past, and CBS News was going to be reshaped into his mold.

Joyce, forty-nine, was much more laid back, but it was a mistake to confuse his deceptively bland manner with softness. He was as tough and determined as Sauter. There were reports of flareups between the two—none ever witnessed by me—but that was predictable. Black Rock had picked one and made the other number two, and in corporate America that inevitably produces tensions.

Sauter and Joyce reported to Gene F. Jankowski, president of the CBS Broadcast Group, who reported to Thomas H. Wyman, president and chief executive officer of the corporation. At one time, the news chief reported directly to the president of CBS, and Richard Salant for a time was a member of the board of directors, but those days had passed.

Joyce would occasionally say things that got him in trouble. He would lash out at the agent Richard Leibner, and agents in general, saying: "I am determined not to let the flesh peddlers affect the caliber of our broadcasts." It was widely reported and not helpful in future negotiations. He would tell a press junket that CBS has "the only world-class anchorman" and that NBC was peopled with "fifty-two guys named Irving." It was a thoughtless remark and some felt it was anti-Semitic.

When I came to his office, Joyce was in shirt sleeves, wearing red suspenders, his usual dress. He has a pleasant, mellifluous voice, a product of his early days as a radio reporter. He had been instrumental in establishing all-news radio in New York before he moved into television as general manager of the CBS-owned stations in Chicago, Los Angeles, and New York.

We reviewed the situation on the Vietnam broadcast as I knew it at that early date. Joyce freely conceded that he was troubled by the whole situation. He said CBS News ought to have regular sessions, as the stations division had, reviewing the news standards for correspondents and producers. He said he thought I would be best off by confining my examination as much as possible to the *TV Guide* allegations and resisting any broadening of the investigation. I told Joyce I was worried about time pressures. There was no way I could complete the assignment in the three weeks I had heard Sauter mention. He said he was certain I would be given enough time.

That afternoon I received a phone call from Edward M. Fouhy, a former colleague at CBS, who was then the bureau chief for ABC News in Washington. "It's a dangerous assignment," Fouhy said, "and you could get hurt." I asked him how. I was past ambition and what could they do—make me retire? "Okay," he said, "but what if they ask you to water down your report?"

I told Fouhy that would be easy. I'd just retire sooner.

The Vietnam program I was now going to investigate reminded me of a parable which circulated around the Pentagon at the height of the Vietnam War. As the story went, it was decided to put into a computer all of the data on North Vietnam and all of the data on the United States—gross national products, size of the armies, size of the air forces, size of the navies, logistical capabilities, comparative weaponries and manpower available to each side. Some keys were pressed and the machine was asked when the United States could win the war.

The answer came back quickly: 1964.

The problem was the year was 1969.

6

ENTER
THE HEAVIES

The office of Gene F. Jankowski, president of the CBS Broadcast Group, is on the thirty-fourth floor of the corporation's headquarters at Fifty-second Street and the Avenue of the Americas. An understated, gray-honed-granite building, somber and brooding, it was the last designed by Eero Saarinen and is known throughout the trade as Black Rock. There are only two floors above Jankowski's: the thirty-fifth, which understandably accommodates the highest brass, at that time William S. Paley, the founder and chairman, and Thomas H. Wyman, the president and chief executive officer, along with their corporate staffs; and the thirty-sixth, which incomprehensibly is home for the company lawyers. I always felt that placing the lawyers at the very pinnacle was oddly foreboding.

The purpose of the meeting that I came to attend on Wednesday, June 2, was obvious, and it had now been reduced to shorthand: The Westmoreland Show. We gathered in Jankowski's rectangular conference room around a large table that could seat as many as twenty persons. Next to the conference room was his private dining room, and next to that his office.

Jankowski, forty-eight, a husky, athletic, incurably optimistic man, held one of the most important jobs at CBS; the Broadcast Group was the principal source of the company's revenues. Born in Buffalo, a graduate of Canisius College, he went on to get a graduate degree in communications art at Michigan State, served in the Navy, and joined CBS

Radio as a salesman in 1961. He moved quickly up the corporate ladder, through sales and finance, and in 1977 was elevated to his present job, which over the years has been one of the most volatile at CBS. He had survived the ousters of two presidents and a good many other high-level executives.

The meeting, the first of several, lasted into the afternoon. It began in typical CBS fashion: relaxed; peppered with a little gossip here, a joke there; grace under pressure; the unflabbable, Tiffany-of-the-networks image incarnate. Present were Van Gordon Sauter, president of CBS News; Edward Joyce, executive vice president; Gene Mater, vice president in the Broadcast Group; and Ralph Goldberg, assistant general counsel for CBS. Jankowski was in and out of the room during the day, stopping at one time to inform me that I would see Tom Wyman the next day. The Westmoreland affair had risen to the top.

Yet the atmosphere—free of panic or raised voices—did not surprise me. No jobs were on the line, as far as I could determine. Sauter and Joyce, while discomfited by the program they had approved, were not mortally threatened by it. Mater and Goldberg were as uninvolved in its production as I was. Jankowski was far above the fray; he probably had never heard of the program until a few days before it aired.

I had expected to receive very sharp and specific marching orders for my investigation, but instead I was given a list of general suggestions. They recommended a two-pronged examination with the obvious first consideration being journalistic—the paramount issues of accuracy and fairness. Second, I would have to address myself to the matter of the CBS News Standards, the guidelines formulated over the years which delineate quite specifically how CBS News is expected to conduct its business. Did the program violate these guidelines as *TV Guide* had alleged, and if so, how and why?

They felt I should see no outsiders at this time and should confine the examination to those within the organization. They included as insiders Sam Adams, the program's consultant, and Alex Alben, its researcher, who had left CBS News for the Stanford Law School. They said that interviews with Generals Westmoreland and Graham and with Walt W. Rostow, LBJ's special assistant, were beyond the scope of the examination. Since I had already seen an hour and fifty-four minutes of Westmoreland and his supporters at his news conference, I thought I could live with that.

In addition, they did not think it wise for me to contact Lt. Gen.

Phillip Davidson, Westmoreland's intelligence chief during the Tet Offensive, or Davidson's physician, Dr. Mauro Gangai, director of the urology clinic at Brooke Army Medical Center in San Antonio. That gave me a problem. Mike Wallace had told both Westmoreland and Graham during their interviews that Davidson was on his deathbed. This became the excuse for not having him on the broadcast. *TV Guide* had checked out the story and found it flat-out wrong. Both Davidson and his doctor had told the magazine that the general was in good health. I decided to ignore the instructions, and we had no trouble reaching Davidson, who told us he had recovered from the bout with cancer he had suffered in 1974 and had just remarried.

Ralph Goldberg, a CBS lawyer, had drawn the unenviable assignment over the years of keeping the network out of trouble and extricating it when it got into trouble, which was not infrequently. He had been in the trenches during such trying experiences as "The Selling of the Pentagon," and the "Winner Take All" tennis program, in which a CBS Sports broadcast described a tennis match in Puerto Rico as winner take all. It was not, and the FCC got into the case. The network managed to escape with a slap on the wrist.

Now Goldberg had the Westmoreland matter on his plate—I was certain it gave him no pleasure—and I listened carefully to his advice. He put the heart of the allegations this way: That we were out to get Westmoreland, and that we would not let the facts get in the way, which suggested willful intent on the part of CBS. "Your job," he said, "is to find out whether the allegations are true." In all of the advice, notwithstanding the low-keyed meeting that had just ensued, I could sense an unspoken concern: The fear that Gen. William C. Westmoreland was going to take his case to the courts and sue CBS for a lot of money.

Back at my office later that day I decided to look into the matter of Sam Adams's consultancy. Was he a consultant or a *paid consultant,* and if he was the latter, which I assumed he was, how much was he paid? I phoned the CBS News vice president for Business Affairs, Arthur Sekarek, and got this breakdown of payments to Adams:

February 13, 1981—$4,000	June 2, 1981—$5,000
April 10, 1981—$8,000	June 16, 1981—$5,000

Later, another $3,000 was authorized by a note from Vice President Roger Colloff. The total fee was thus $25,000, with an additional $400 to

$500 still to be decided. Adams also had received $4,904.69 in expenses. The significance of these payments was that while Wallace would say in his narration at the top of the broadcast, "A former CIA analyst, Sam Adams, introduced us to this evidence, and he became our consultant," he never revealed that Adams was a *paid* consultant. Since Adams was also interviewed on camera by Wallace, not revealing that he was being paid was a violation of CBS News Standards, which states that

> Appropriate payments may be made, of course, to informants, consultants, and others who furnish liaison, information or contact services. If, however, any of these are interviewed in connection with the broadcast on which they are being paid for such services, we must identify them in the broadcast as having worked as paid consultants.

Adams had been given more roles than any consultant I had ever seen at CBS News. His research and contacts shaped the story; he was interviewed on camera and so became a part of the story; he functioned as an associate producer from time to time, sitting in on several interviews with people he had helped persuade to appear, and was in and out of the cutting rooms and at various production meetings.

The paid-consultancy clause doubtless stemmed from the news division's long standing aversion to any kind of checkbook journalism, its determination not to pay for news. In those few cases where it was permissible to pay for some unique expertise, the rules were clear: Make sure your audience knew precisely what you had done. In the past, CBS had paid for interviews with former Presidents Eisenhower, Johnson, and Nixon. It had also paid for one with H. R. Haldeman that was roundly criticized as inappropriate, especially after Haldeman sat there for an hour saying nothing. Over the years, however, the network had pretty well held to its no-payment policy.

The guideline frequently gave us problems in filming interviews with important figures in Britain. The BBC routinely pays for these interviews, and we were often turned down by prominent persons who could not understand why if the impoverished BBC could pay, big, rich CBS could not. The traditional CBS News position was: We don't do this except in unusual circumstances. Over the years, it kept the network out of a lot of trouble.

On Wednesday, June 2, I went to the thirty-fifth floor of CBS for the meeting with Tom Wyman. As I walked down the hushed, heavily carpeted corridor to his executive suite, I wondered how this intense and cultivated man, who had been with the company for only two years, was reacting to the stir over Westmoreland. Paley had brought him to CBS from a business that could not have been more different—Pillsbury and its subsidiary, the Green Giant Company. When he was appointed, I thought to myself: Wait until he finds out how jolly this giant is and how important the green is at Black Rock.

Since Frank Stanton's forced retirement in 1971, Bill Paley had appointed four presidents. In nine years, two had been fired, one had died in office, and Wyman was in place. In spite of Paley's enthusiastic endorsement of Wyman—he told the press he had finally found the man to succeed him—there had to be unease on the part of anyone who was the designated number two at Black Rock.

Wyman was cordial and businesslike as the meeting began but left no doubt that he was deeply concerned about the Westmoreland matter, as was his board of directors. Fifty-three years old, he was a soft-spoken man and sometimes I had to strain to hear him. He had qualities that would attract Paley. He had graduated *magna cum laude* from Amherst, where he wrote his senior thesis on Yeats, played on the tennis team, and was an excellent golfer as well. He had studied in Switzerland and worked for Nestlé there, had then returned to the United States for an important post at Polaroid. He was said to have substantial management skills. In all respects, Tom Wyman impressed observers as a man of taste and intellect, two qualities which CBS had always coveted in its public image.

Jankowski, Sauter, Mater, and Goldberg were invited to the Wyman meeting, and I outlined how I planned to proceed. The investigation would be journalistic, not judicial. I was assigned to a story and would try to get to the bottom of it. I told them, as I had told others, that I did not plan to be judge or jury, prosecutor, or defense attorney. I would conduct the major interviews face to face but would not use a tape recorder, which I thought might be inhibiting. It was agreed that the way I chose to operate was the way to proceed, and few suggestions were offered.

The meeting with Paley followed, and only Wyman, Jankowski, and Sauter were asked to join. I found this instructive—the rigid pecking order in the corporate world, those invited and not invited. At the outset, a major question arose: Should an outsider, such as a journalism dean or an eminent lawyer, be brought in so that the investigation would not seem to be totally inside CBS? Paley mentioned "that fellow who was involved in the Watergate case"; he could not remember his name. I told him I would have no problem with an Archibald Cox or someone like him. As a matter of fact, I wanted him to know that I would not feel deprived at all if they turned over the entire investigation to a person of that sort. I said I had not sought the job nor did I covet it. Wyman said they knew that and as quickly as it was brought up, the matter was dropped.

It was apparent to me that the concern over the Westmoreland affair on the thirty-fifth floor of Black Rock was palpable. Watching the top players now—Paley, Wyman, Jankowski, and Sauter—I sensed that there would be other meetings at the summit after I had gone. That the law department would be involved was unquestionable, and I suspected the CBS outside counsel, Cravath, Swaine & Moore, was certain to be brought into play. Wyman had said he would keep the board of directors informed, and I thought of one director who certainly would be interested—Roswell Gilpatric, former deputy Secretary of Defense and also a Cravath partner.

Wyman asked me how long it was going to take to finish the investigation, and I said I hoped to finish it in three weeks, a naive estimate on my part. It would take me six weeks working long days and weekends. As I left the thirty-fifth floor, I began to think, angrily, how easily this whole exercise could have been avoided. Had they put Westmoreland and his news conference on the air on that Tuesday night in January, the general would be back in Charleston, licking a few lingering wounds perhaps, but mollified, the incident forgotten.

Jankowski and Sauter told me that they were going to Phoenix where about a hundred television critics would gather for an annual meeting arranged by the CBS press department to promote the network's wares. Jankowski said they would tell these critics exactly what we were doing so that the CBS side got to the press directly.

On June 10, Van Gordon Sauter stood before the critics in Phoenix and said: "The eighteen allegations in that [*TV Guide*] article are serious and troublesome. They require a response predicated on an examination of our records and of people, internally and externally, who were involved in the broadcast. . . . What is most troubling to us as a news organization is the allegation relating to the violation of CBS News Standards and improper journalistic techniques."

Sauter said that he and I would be doing the investigation and would complete it in about three weeks. Asked by a reporter why anyone should believe what CBS came up with, he replied: "We are going to be thorough, objective and zealous. I trust my own efficacy and I certainly trust Bud Benjamin's [Sauter and most of my colleagues always used my nickname] based on his record and my knowledge of him. We both have a significant vested interest in the ongoing credibility of CBS News, and there is no protective attitude that can stand in the way of that."

Sauter then made a point which seemed odd to me and still does. If the CBS investigation "leads to the conclusion that you're not guilty, then you'd better get some outsider to come in and look at it, too—so they'll say you're not guilty." It made it sound as if they would only believe me if my conclusion was "guilty."

Asked whether *TV Guide* got the story through a leak from a disgruntled CBS employee, Sauter said he didn't know but that "it could have been prompted by leaks from a source who simply cared about good journalism."

Some reporters expressed skepticism about *TV Guide*, whose publisher was Walter Annenberg, former Ambassador to the Court of St. James's, close friend of Presidents Nixon and Reagan. Annenberg's conservative preferences were well known, and he had recently used his magazine to outline his aversion to "adversary and advocacy journalism." This skepticism about Annenberg's influence would recur throughout my investigation in spite of denials by *TV Guide* reporters Kowet and Bedell, and their editors, that the publisher had had any input into the story.

The toughest analysis of the Jankowski-Sauter visit to Phoenix came from Tom Jicha of the Miami *News:* ". . . the charges are too serious and the stakes too high for an extended in-house probe to suffice. The public deserves answers, independently arrived at answers, and it deserves them the day before yesterday. The credibility of all tv documentaries and news magazines, perhaps most especially CBS' blockbuster hit *60 Minutes*, stands to be caught in the fallout of this sordid episode. . . ."

Jicha's column concluded: "Sauter defended his probe by saying: 'it really comes down to whether the company trusts me.' I disagree. It comes down to whether the nation trusts CBS."

The aggressive questioning by the reporters might have been expected. Many of those covering television tend to be hostile toward the medium—"blow-dries with pancake makeup earning too much money," one veteran reporter called television journalists not long ago. I doubt that any of them were expressing concern that CBS's problems might dampen investigative reporting in their newspapers. They are inclined to view television as "them" and print as "us"—not in the same boat. As Eric Sevareid complained when television was attacked on a press issue and newspapers were standing aloof: "We're both in the same boat, and my end is sinking."

As Sauter wrestled with the case in Phoenix, I was in New York wading through the material. The timing of my investigation, it seemed to me, could not have been more inauspicious. Derelictions by the press—the prestigious and respected press—had been a disquieting part of the news in recent months. *The Washington Post* in 1981 had been jarred by the Janet Cooke scandal. It had been revealed that its story about an eight-year-old heroin addict was a fake, and the paper had to turn back in humiliation a Pulitzer Prize its reporter had won for it. The same year, the *New York Times Magazine* had been stung by a partly plagiarized, partly fabricated story written by a reporter who had described a month-long journey in 1981 with Cambodian guerrillas.

I hoped, fervently hoped, as I worked that weekend in New York, that CBS News was not about to make this a troika.

7

THE TIP OF
THE ICEBERG

During the first week in June of 1982, more and more material descended on our cramped offices at CBS News, much of it sent over by George Crile, producer of the Vietnam program. There were five books of uncut transcripts representing twenty-seven hours of interviews, and we would study these with particular care: How did the film that was used in the program correspond to the film that was shot? Did the excerpts selected accurately reflect what each of these people had said? Had the film been edited fairly in accordance with the applicable CBS News guidelines?

There were also a thick volume, referred to as the Crile White Paper, which was about the size of the telephone book in his hometown of Cleveland. Prolix and resolutely defensive, it was an augury of the cascade of paper that would be a legacy of the Vietnam documentary. It indicated at the outset the unease felt by Crile and Mike Wallace over the *TV Guide* investigation into their work.

The White Paper included a twenty-eight-page single-spaced rebuttal to the "Anatomy of a Smear" article, with transcript excerpts from the interviews with Generals Westmoreland and McChristian and an insistent defense from Crile that he had treated them fairly. There were two letters to the *TV Guide* writers from Crile and Mike Wallace which had expressed concern about the proposed article well before it was scheduled to appear on May 29.

On March 25, Wallace had written a three-and-a-half-page Dear-Sally letter to Bedell, and on April 9, Crile had followed with an eleven-page, single-spaced, Dear-Sally-and-Don letter. Both Wallace and Crile had urged the writers not to rush to judgment. There were other letters—exchanges between General Westmoreland and Crile, replete with once-secret documents, and several letters from Walt W. Rostow. Wallace had interviewed Rostow for three hours and Crile had chosen to leave all of the interview on the cutting-room floor.

There was also a predictable five-page, single-spaced letter from Reed Irvine, self-appointed watchdog for the conservative press watchers known as Accuracy in Media, requesting time under the Fairness Doctrine to reply to the Crile documentary. Crile had drafted a twelve-page reply, condensed by Bill Leonard to a page and a paragraph turn down.

In addition, Crile had prepared a fourteen-page rebuttal to the critical Westmoreland news conference of January 26, full of handwritten editing revisions and demonstrably written under the guns.

There were generous excerpts from books which Crile believed supported the premise of the broadcast—one from Thomas Powers's book *The Man Who Kept the Secrets: Richard Helms and the CIA*, another from David Halberstam's *The Best and the Brightest*. Crile always referred to them as Pulitzer Prize winners, which indeed they were, but not for the books he was citing. Halberstam, then with the *New York Times*, had won the prize for international reporting from Vietnam in 1964, and Powers, then with United Press International, for national reporting in 1971.

Sam Adams's original *Harper's* article of May 1975 was also enclosed, along with a nine-page, double-spaced article by Col. Gains Hawkins, one of the key on-camera supporters in the broadcast. It was titled "Musings on Vietnam—On a Latter Day."

Throughout the White Paper it was apparent that the producers had anticipated trouble as soon as the broadcast was aired and had been assiduously mounting a defense in depth. In addition, there were documents written well before the documentary was even completed which reflected certain tensions on the part of both the producer and his chief correspondent.

On May 11, 1981, four days before Westmoreland would sit before the cameras in a West Fifty-Ninth Street hotel in New York, Crile had written to Wallace:

Mike:

We're on for Westmoreland next Saturday morning. I read him the letter yesterday, and he didn't complain about any of our proposed areas of interest. He puzzles me—seems not to be all that bright. . . .

We have certainly covered our asses, technically at least. But I am a bit worried that he just doesn't understand that we are going to be talking to him about American intelligence, military intelligence during the Vietnam war. I just don't want to have him sit down and refuse to answer questions on the grounds that he can't remember certain things and that we hadn't told him what we were up to. So I think I will give him another call later in the week and try to bring him a little further along without hitting him over the head with a sledge hammer.

I've redone the questions. There are now less of them and better focused with comments at front of each section. They're being typed now—will be sent up this morning. Would like to go over them with you when you can.

George

The letter that Crile had read to Westmoreland on the telephone on May 7, as mentioned in his note to Mike Wallace, listed five main points that the interview would cover. The real subject, the controversy between the military and the CIA over military-strength figures, was not listed first but fourth in the letter.

1. Did American intelligence adequately predict the Tet offensive and the nature of the attack? Were those with a need to know adequately alerted? Were we surprised by the scope and timing of the attacks?
2. Was the Tet offensive an American victory or defeat? Why did so many Americans consider it a defeat when most military men claimed it was a major victory? How should we think about this critical event?
3. Did the press present a reliable picture of the enemy we faced and the state of the war?
4. *What about the controversy between CIA and the military over enemy strength estimates?* (Emphasis added)
5. What about the differing views of the enemy and progress in the war as seen by Lyndon Johnson, Dean Rusk, Robert McNamara, Richard Helms, Walt Rostow, and of course General William Westmoreland?

Why Crile had read the letter to Westmoreland instead of sending it to him in the mail was something I would have to determine. In an earlier phone conversation with Wallace and Crile before consenting to the interview, the general had asked whether this was going to be a "*60 Minutes*-type program." He said Wallace had replied: "Oh, no, it'll be an educational and objective type of program." I would also learn that the afternoon before the interview in New York, Crile had his secretary, Carolyne McDaniel, try to hand-deliver the five-point interview letter to Westmoreland at the Plaza Hotel, but the general had not yet checked in. She left the envelope at the front desk.

Mike Wallace's lengthy, harsh interview with Westmoreland took place on May 15. Present along with the producer, correspondent, and two camera crews were associate producer Joseph Zigman and Grace Diekhaus, a staff producer for CBS News.

Two women, Diekhaus and Judy Crichton, had been co-producers with Crile in his previous efforts. This was the first time he had produced a documentary alone, and he had invited Diekhaus, a close friend and confidant, to be with him for the critical Westmoreland interview. Diekhaus had been his co-producer on his last *CBS Reports*, "Gay Power, Gay Politics." She had been a producer for *60 Minutes* and was now the executive producer of an afternoon spinoff, *Up to the Minute*. After that show folded, she would again be a producer at *60 Minutes*. She had not been assigned to "The Uncounted Enemy"; she was helping Crile on her own; and no one in CBS management knew she was there. She was frequently with him in the editing rooms during the production.

The Westmoreland interview was quintessential Mike Wallace— the questions tough and unrelenting. The camera angle on the general was kept ultra-tight, a closer angle than even *60 Minutes* normally features. "It wasn't just a close-up," an observer said later. "It was a close-up of his pores."

Two exchanges that made the final cut and were in the broadcast typified the scene—the probing Wallace and the beset Westmoreland. In the first, Wallace asked whether dropping the irregulars and self-defense militia from the order of battle was based on political considerations.

WESTMORELAND: No, decidedly not. That—that—
WALLACE: Didn't you make this clear in your August 20th cable?
WESTMORELAND: No, no. Yeah. No.

WALLACE: I have a copy of your August 20th cable—
WESTMORELAND: Well, sure. Okay, okay. All right, all right.
WALLACE: —spelling out the command position on the self-defense con-
troversy.
WESTMORELAND: Yeah.

Wallace then read excerpts of the cable to him. "We have been projecting an image of success over the recent months . . ." Wallace left out the next three words: *"and properly so."* Also, the August 20 cable was not sent by Westmoreland; it was sent by Gen. Creighton Abrams, second in command. Westmoreland did sign off on it. Wallace then quoted further from the cable, which explained that the self-defense militia had to be removed, "or the newsmen will immediately seize on the point that the enemy force has increased . . . drawing an erroneous and gloomy conclusion."

WESTMORELAND: Well, sure. They would have drawn an erroneous conclusion because it was a non-issue. It was a false issue. It would
have totally clouded the—the situation, which would have been
detrimental. But the fact is that since it was wrong, since it was
not accurate, since it was not sound, would have brought about
that impact, yes.

Later, Wallace quoted a question he had asked Col. George Hamscher, a man Westmoreland had never heard of—not a member of his command but with the Defense Intelligence Agency in Hawaii. Wallace had asked the colonel whether he had not sat back in amazement at an intelligence meeting "when you watched this performance of arbitrarily cutting certain numbers out of units?" He asked Westmoreland about that.

WESTMORELAND: I didn't do that.
WALLACE: No, I know you didn't.
WESTMORELAND: I didn't do that.
WALLACE: Well, you—people in your command did.
WESTMORELAND: I didn't do that. Now—
WALLACE: It was on your watch, sir.
WESTMORELAND: —I—well—

As the questions grew tougher, the general grew testier. This retort to Wallace did not make the broadcast:

WESTMORELAND: See, I happened to be in Vietnam. I don't know where in the heck you were, but I was in Vietnam.

During the interview, sweating under Wallace's barrage, Westmoreland kept licking his lips nervously. Later, he would say that the harsh lights dried them out and it wasn't until his wife acquainted him with "that wax stuff you put on your lips" that he would know how to handle this in the future. He was so innocent about television that he thought this interview was like a live appearance—when Wallace was speaking, his camera would be on and the camera pointed at the general would be off. He was not aware that when you shoot film, both cameras are running all the time, and any lip-licking, perspiration-wiping, and unease are recorded. He would also say that he was upset during the interview when he looked over his shoulder and saw Crile holding up cue cards with questions for Wallace.

When the Westmoreland interview ended, the general stormed out saying he had been "rattlesnaked." He was later asked why, when Mike Wallace unloaded his first broadside, he didn't get up and walk out, giving the audience a protracted view of his backside. The general replied he feared it would have been an admission of guilt, but he came to understand that had he done so, and then blasted CBS for its interviewing technique, the program would have been scrapped.

Three days after the interview, Crile wrote to Wallace:

> Mike:
>
> The interview was a classic. It keeps growing in my mind. I don't think you could have possibly done a better job; I certainly know no one else who could have. It was wonderful having you as our champion.
>
> Now for the reaction. I can't imagine Westie taking this lying down. I'm sure he has already called Danny Graham [Lt. Gen. Daniel Graham, his former intelligence officer] which is fine and to be expected. I think we should call Graham ourselves and line that interview up for you right away.

In Crile's White Paper, the preponderance of material dealt not with what happened before the broadcast but after it. Now TV Guide was on the case, and both producer and correspondent were obviously concerned. Two months after the broadcast and two months before the magazine would publish "Anatomy of a Smear," Crile and Wallace both sat for disturbing interviews with Kowet and Bedell.

It was these interviews that generated the letters from both the producer and his correspondent to the two writers while they were still working on their piece. Wallace's letter to Bedell declared that those who were now criticizing the Vietnam program—"the old boy military network, mainly"—were unwilling "to confront its main thesis: That there was a concerted effort to keep a 'cap' on the enemy order of battle in order to prove 'progress' in the war, and to that end, junior officers were forced to 'cook the books,' to manipulate figures, so as to keep those numbers down."

Wallace mentioned a part of the interview that was troubling him: "Sally, the thrust of your questions last Friday seemed to indicate that you felt we had not done enough to get differing views on what went on . . . that we simply took at face value what was offered by those opposed to Westmoreland et al, and failed to follow up sufficiently. Not so." He said Crile's notes were voluminous and clear on this.

Speaking candidly, Wallace went on: "By no means am I suggesting that we put together the perfect errorless documentary. But little so far presented in your questions to me, nor in George's reports to me on what you have put before him, lead me to believe that the documentary was less than faithful to the facts." He concluded by praising Crile: "not the kind of individual to 'cook' a story to follow some pre-determined line. He's a good, devoted reporter, just as you are. He is an honorable man who produced what he . . . and I . . . genuinely believe was faithful to our understanding of what went on back in 1967 and 1968. And it wasn't pretty."

Crile's letter a week later was more impassioned and much longer. In its eleven pages, it was alternately imploring and sternly resistant. Concerning an interview Kowet had conducted with Col. Gains Hawkins, a key supporting witness, Crile wrote: "Hawkins may not have been totally forthcoming with you, Don, because he was taken aback by what he thought were peculiar questions from you. He even called me afterward to ask if you were indeed a reporter from *TV Guide*. He had an unfortunate experience many years back when Sy Hersh kept calling his wife pretending to be working for military intelligence." (Seymour Hersh, a nationally known investigative reporter, told me that he never made any such calls.)

Under "Some Final Observations," Crile wrote: "You told me that from the standpoint of the story you are working on, that you are not interested in whether the charges made in that documentary are right or wrong. I said I couldn't believe you were disinterested in this question. You finally acknowledged, Sally, that you were not convinced that MACV had suppressed evidence of greater enemy numbers. That took my breath away . . . I would urge you to read your own words and see if you feel comfortable that they reflect the kind of probing objectivity that ordinarily accompanies a reporter's consideration of official statements and actions."

In his concluding paragraph, Crile pleaded with the two writers:

> I realize this is an unusual thing to do—writing this kind of letter. I do so because of your reputation for thoroughness and fairness. My concern is that due to what may be certain preconvictions you may rush to judgment and in some instances base your conclusions on incorrect premises. It is your choice, of course, but I still think it would be useful for you to share your central criticisms with Mike and me. All we can do is give our best explanations. If they are unpersuasive, you can leave them on the cutting room floor.

Once the *TV Guide* article appeared, during that fateful May weekend when most of the network brass were courting their affiliates in San Francisco, Crile was back at his typewriter with a fifteen-page, single-spaced rejoinder. He began by stressing "one critical point." The authors had not challenged the central premise of the broadcast, that enemy-strength figures had been intentionally undercounted. The testimony of the military intelligence officers who supported this allegation "has not been challenged. General Westmoreland has personally called several of them and suggested that they might like to make public statements saying their words had been taken out of context. They have refused."

Crile denied he had "turned a deaf ear" toward contrary evidence. "As in any investigative report," he said "there was, of course, an operating thesis." He vigorously denied that his paid consultant, Sam Adams, had been rehearsed, and presented a statement from Adams backing him up. He admitted that he had twice interviewed former CIA man George Allen when he did not like the first interview and had shown Allen interviews of other supporters. "This kind of screening is not standard practice at CBS News," he wrote, "and I should not have done it. . . ."

He insisted he had not thrown soft-ball questions at friendly witnesses while "grilling unfriendly witnesses with prosecutorial zeal." He denied that he had been guilty of unfair or deceptive editing. He said he had interviewed a great number of people beyond those who appeared in the broadcast. He maintained that he had not deceived General Westmoreland in advance about what his interview would cover.

What Crile had put forth was a point-by-point denial of the charges made by *TV Guide*. It was now up to me to determine who was right.

There were two aspects of the Vietnam broadcast that critics seized upon—the program was out of balance and those supporting its thesis were treated much more kindly than those opposing it. The lineup of those who appeared on camera broke down this way:

Supporting Adams Thesis	*Opposed*
Sam Adams	Gen. William Westmoreland
Col. Gains Hawkins	Lt. Gen. Daniel Graham
Maj. Gen. Joseph McChristian	
Lt. Richard McArthur	
George Allen	
Col. George Hamscher	
Col. Russell Cooley	
Joseph Hovey	
Cdr. James Meacham	

This amounted to a nine-to-two equation—eight supporters for Adams and one for Westmoreland. And General Graham, the lone Westmoreland supporter, was given exactly twenty-one seconds on screen. In total, Westmoreland and Graham spoke for five minutes and fifty-nine seconds in the broadcast. Adams and his eight supporters spoke for nineteen minutes and nineteen seconds.

While no producer is expected to weigh the two sides on a scale and come up with a precise balance, a fundamental question had to be asked about the Vietnam broadcast: Was there fairness and balance, the essence of the CBS News Standards, in terms of people or time on camera?

After his interview, and understandably still bruised by it, General Westmoreland wrote to Wallace and Crile on June 9, 1981:

> If it is your purpose to be fair and objective during your quest which I assume you intend to be, I suggest that you interview:
>
> Ambassador Ellsworth Bunker

Mr. Robert Komer
Lt. Gen. Daniel Graham
General Walter Kerwin, Jr.
Mr. George Carver, (former CIA) and
Mr. William E. Colby.

Westmoreland also suggested "a colonel who was associated with Col. Hawkins whose name I believe was Morris." He was referring to Col. Charles A. Morris, a MACV intelligence officer. From the above list, only one man, General Graham, found his way on camera.

As I began to read through the transcripts, the contrast in tone between the interviews conducted with Generals Westmoreland and Graham and LBJ's special assistant, Walt W. Rostow, on the one hand, and those supporting the Adams-Crile position on the other, became more and more pronounced. The hostile witnesses were questioned by Mike Wallace, perhaps the most able and certainly the most tenacious interviewer in television. Sam Adams was also interviewed by Wallace, but his eight supporters were questioned by George Crile and the difference was striking. Instead of the vigorous interrogations that Westmoreland, Graham, and Rostow sat through, the approach was friendly and supportive, more like prompting than like journalism.

In my report, I would characterize the two kinds of interviews as Harsh and Coddling.

HARSH

Gen. William C. Westmoreland, *Commander, U.S. Military Assistance Command Vietnam, 1964–68*

We have seen some of the stern questions which Mike Wallace asked the general and which were used in the program. There were others that wound up in the outtakes which further reflected the spirit of the interview.

In one case, Wallace brought up Maj. Gen. Joseph McChristian, MACV's intelligence chief, a fellow West Pointer whom Westmoreland had praised. Wallace asked Westmoreland about differences between him and McChristian about removing the self-defense militia from the order of battle.

WESTMORELAND: I don't remember everything that I talked to Joe McChristian about. If he has a vendetta because he didn't get promoted, well, I'm sorry. But that seems to be the case. These village defenders had no offensive combat capability, and neither did the defenders of the Vietnamese. This is a non-issue, Mike. I made the decision. It was my responsibility. I don't regret making it. I stand by it. And the facts prove that I was right. Now let's stop it.

Later, Wallace pursued the matter of enemy troop strength, suggesting that the Viet Cong may have had as many as half a million men. Then he got to the key premise of the broadcast. If that were so, he went on, "you were going to be in trouble. You couldn't ask for more troops, therefore you couldn't let the enemy be perceived as larger."

WESTMORELAND: Well, that is absolutely fallacious. It has no validity whatsoever. I'm absolutely amazed that you would come out with a statement like that.
WALLACE: It's not a statement; it's a question.

Perhaps the most hostile question in the interview came during an exchange about Tet. Wallace brought up Sam Adams. He said he had told Adams this: Westmoreland has called Tet a great military victory and said it proved that his command had really overestimated, not undercounted, the enemy. Then he quoted Adams's reply:

WALLACE: He still thinks you're nuts, Adams. He still thinks that you're dead wrong. Were and remain dead wrong. Forgive me, sir, for what I'm about to say. Adams said, he's a liar. I know so much now about what General Westmoreland has done behind the scenes that I know General Westmoreland is lying. . . .
WESTMORELAND: . . . I never saw Adams in my life. Adams made his pitch to the authorities in the CIA. They shot him down. They did not agree with his pitch. Where Adams is I don't know now. I never met the man. He's never met me to the best of my knowledge. He is in no position to make a statement of that type, and he is absolutely dead wrong.

What the interview succeeded in doing was to put Westmoreland on the defensive and confuse him. He declared angrily that he had not prepared himself for this kind of an interview, dealing with events and decisions that happened fifteen years before. "I can't remember figures like that," he told Wallace at one point. "You've done some research. I haven't done any research. I'm just reflecting on my memory."

Lt. Gen. Daniel Graham, *Chief of Current Intelligence and Estimates Division, Vietnam 1967–68*

At the Westmoreland news conference General Graham accused Crile and Wallace of breaking their word to him. "When Mr. Wallace asked me for an interview," Graham said, "I said I would do so on one condition—that I be allowed to state the facts, which he could check out easily, that the size of the enemy attacking force in the all-out Tet offensive was under 100,000 and this made MACV's estimate of 285,000 look a lot better than Adams's estimate of 600,000. That he, Wallace, would leave that in my interview after editing. He agreed to do so, but he did not honor that agreement."

Both Crile and Wallace denied that they made any such agreement. They conceded that they had promised to ask the question but had never said they would use the answer. Roger Colloff later wrote to Graham: "both Mr. Wallace and Mr. Crile indicate firmly that *no* assurance was given that this subject would be included in the final broadcast. Such an assurance would have been contrary to CBS News Standards."

The question was the first posed to Graham in his interview. "All right, the point you wanted to make about Tet. Why don't you make it right off the top?"

Graham replied that if only 84,000 of the enemy attacked at Tet, then his strength figure of 296,000 was not too low but too high. If the enemy had a larger force—the kind of numbers Adams and his supporters were pushing for—they would have thrown many more men into the Tet Offensive.

The remainder of the interview was much more pointed and occasionally acerbic. Graham lashed out at Sam Adams, who had obviously been his *bête noire* for a long time. "He tried to get me court-martialed ... I think he's got a hangup that verges on a mental problem over people refusing to accept his number at the time of the Tet Offensive. I think it's a mental problem."

Wallace minced no words in dealing with the general. "Honesty is what we're talking about; not that you set out to lie. Some of your former officers who compiled this report, this very report for you, say it's an unreliable report. They say in effect, you, MACV's intelligence chiefs, had begun dictating to them what the strength estimates were going to be, and that it was left to them to manipulate the evidence to fit the figure."

WALLACE: It's your report.

GRAHAM: No that's not my report.

WALLACE: It's your estimate. Take a look at it.

GRAHAM: No, it isn't. No, that's not an estimate. That's so bloody precise. That's no estimate.

Graham insisted that the military had "guys all over the districts trying to find out how many guerillas there were. That is better than a guy sitting in Washington looking at old captured documents. The military estimates were the best."

Adams extrapolated, he said, and he was wrong.

None of this made the final broadcast. Only two extracts from Graham's lengthy interview found their way on the air. The first extract, or sound bite, dealt with an allegation that he had blocked infiltration estimates from going through.

GRAHAM: I never blocked any reports.

WALLACE: Who did?

GRAHAM: Nobody that I know of blocked any reports. If anybody had blocked information going forward, it would have been me. But I never blocked any information going forward. I'm not that dumb.

The second charge by an intelligence officer was that Graham had ordered that the staff's computer data base be altered.

GRAHAM: Oh, for crying out loud. I never asked anybody to wipe out the computer's memory. I don't know what he—I honestly haven't got an idea what he's talking about.

That was it for General Graham. He got twenty-one seconds to issue two denials—suppressing enemy-strength estimates, altering the computer data.

Walt W. Rostow, *Special Assistant to President Lyndon B. Johnson, 1966–69*

Rostow, who was interviewed by Mike Wallace for three hours— none of which was used—tried hard to convince the correspondent that the White House knew all about the numbers argument and that this dispute was not critical to the kinds of decisions that had to be made. "This tortured debate about order of battle and whether it was manipulated," Rostow said, "should not be confused with the range of information on which President Johnson made his assessments—before Tet, during Tet and after Tet."

Rostow and Wallace knew each other and there was some banter midway in the interview:

ROSTOW: Now, Mike, let me remind you what the history is, which you know as well as I do.
WALLACE: Not as well as you do. Don't patronize me, you son of a bitch. Go ahead. (CHUCKLE)
ROSTOW: All right. No, you do. You've worked hard on this and much more freshly than I have.

Beyond that, it was hardly a light-hearted interview. Wallace kept pressing Rostow about the order of battle and the "cooking of the books," Rostow kept insisting Wallace had his history wrong.

ROSTOW: Now there you are wrong. He [LBJ] absorbed all of this intelligence.
WALLACE: This intelligence didn't come to him.
ROSTOW: You're quite wrong. It did get . . . You're wrong, Mike. Don't keep saying things that are not so.

ROSTOW: Now, let me just . . . No, you've really got to take this seriously because you're going to do great damage to the country, and you're going to get it wrong.

WALLACE: You're a historian.
ROSTOW: Yes, sir.
WALLACE: History is owed an explanation for this. Why this effort has been made to cook the figures?
ROSTOW: The . . . if . . . Mike, you . . . you know, you've got to get to the bottom of this. You've got to listen to all sides.

CODDLING

The attitude toward the friendly witnesses, who supported the Adams thesis that George Crile had adopted as the linchpin for his documentary, was nowhere more apparent than in the double interview of George Allen, the senior CIA official in Vietnam. Allen was interviewed in New York on May 26, and when Crile found the result disappointing he was interviewed again on June 29.

Allen, one of the most respected intelligence figures of the war, had spent more than fifteen years studying the conflict in Vietnam. His interviews were filmed in different locations but Allen was asked to wear the same suit, which would have made it possible to intercut the two sessions although this was not done. What was used in the program all came from the second interview. The questions asked in the two were virtually identical.

The double interview was a violation of CBS News Standards, which explicitly state: "Interviews which are not spontaneous and unrehearsed are prohibited unless specifically approved by the President of CND [CBS News Division]." It was implicit that a second interview could be neither. Furthermore, before the second interview Allen was shown excerpts from interviews with Gen. Joseph McChristian, Col. Gains Hawkins, and CIA analyst Joseph Hovey, all supporters of the program's premise. No one from the opposing side, Westmoreland, Graham, or Rostow, was afforded an opportunity to see other interviews. Sam Adams was at Crile's side when he interviewed George Allen, Col. Gains Hawkins, Col. Russell Cooley, Col. George Hamscher, Cdr. James Meacham, and the CIA's Joseph Hovey.

In his White Paper, Crile took issue with the *TV Guide* charge that sympathetic witnesses had received preferential treatment. "This totally misrepresents the character of those interviewed and the nature of the questions put to them," he wrote. "None of the military officers . . . were eager to grant interviews. All of them would have preferred to let this chapter in their lives remain buried. Invariably it was an agonizing experience for them to have to admit to being part of a process that they believed to be dishonest and against the best interest of their country."

How Crile went about getting the information he wanted is shown in the following excerpts:

Sam Adams, *Former CIA analyst, Vietnamese affairs, 1966–70*

Mike Wallace's interview with Adams was fairly straightforward, with some pressing questions at the end about his preoccupations and possible obsessions. It was a far cry, however, from the severe questioning given to General Westmoreland.

WALLACE: You know, this sounds almost too pat, Mr. Adams.
ADAMS: Yeah, okay.

WALLACE: Wait. Okay. Come back to that question I asked a little while ago in which I said, you know, Sam Adams is there. He's Paul Revere. He's the only man who knows all of this.
ADAMS: Yeah.

ADAMS: I'm not doing this very well.
WALLACE: Oh, no. No. No. You were perfect. Don't say that. You're doing it just right.
ADAMS: Okay.
WALLACE: Keep it up. Pick it up. Go.
ADAMS: Okay. I was getting confused. Now . . .

WALLACE: Sweet shit. You—what happened to your career? What happened to your career at CIA?

WALLACE: This is perfect. All right. This is going to be good. That's really what you want.
ADAMS: Okay.

WALLACE: Why is this such a preoccupation of yours, almost a mania to get to the bottom of it?
ADAMS: I suppose because it was, you know, I figured I had this big thing going. I felt very strong about it, and—
WALLACE: It's an obsession with you.
ADAMS: An obsession with me? That's a strong word, but I suppose you could say that's a case, but it's a hell of an interesting subject. I mean, if you got to be obsessed, it's not a small obsession.

George Allen, *Senior CIA officer in Vietnam, 1964–66. (Allen was with Army intelligence from 1949–61; with the Defense Intelligence Agency, 1961–63; and with the CIA, 1963–79.)*

First Interview

At both Allen interviews, Sam Adams was present. From time to time, Allen turned to him for help.

CRILE: George—let me—don't worry about it. I know exactly what you're doing as I recall the way you told it first . . .

CRILE: George, if you were George Orwell trying to give a sense of how we went about thinking about the enemy in Vietnam, how would you characterize the use of language and the thinking that went into our intelligence reporting?

ALLEN: I'm not sure what you have in mind, George.

CRILE: George, would you please help your old protege, Sam Adams, here in some way?

CRILE: All right. Then what happens to his findings?

ALLEN: What happened, Sam?

CRILE: I don't mean to pin you down, George.

CRILE: If you can't answer this one, it's fine. We just go on to the next one, but I really would love some insight into the dimensions of the problem.

CRILE: It strikes me that you were in a reasonably peculiar position here. George Allen, the . . . perhaps the government's greatest expert on Vietnam.

CRILE: Well, I'll quote you. The real reason the numbers were such a big deal is that once you questioned overall strength estimates, you are challenging the premise of U.S. involvement.

ALLEN: Did I say that?

CRILE: You did, but you can take it back.

ALLEN: No, that's pretty good. I must have . . . I was only drinking beer that day, too.

CRILE: Make it simpler, George.

ALLEN: I'd like to make it simple.

CRILE: Not simple, simpler.

ALLEN: Simpler. I'm just grasping here for a simple expression.

CRILE: Come to the defense of your old protege, Sam Adams.

Second Interview

CRILE: We're going to keep going at this until we get it right.

CRILE: There was more to it than that as you have explained it. Remember?

ALLEN: No I don't remember. Refresh me.

CRILE: I'll refresh you.

ALLEN: Is it really kosher to go over this?
CRILE: Oh, this is what we do.

CRILE: George, if you . . . keep your enthusiasm, you're on the right side.
ALLEN: It's getting late. (BACKGROUND LAUGHTER)

ALLEN: This isn't good either.
CRILE: It's beautiful. It's wonderful.

CRILE: We've done it before but tell me. Why was it the most difficult assignment you ever had?
ALLEN: I'm sorry, George. I don't know what you want me to say. I don't know what you're expecting me to say.

ALLEN: Oh, George, I still don't have an answer for that one.
CRILE: Is there an answer for it? Paint the best face on it you can.
ALLEN: I'm going to have to come up for another interview, George. (LAUGHTER) . . . I've got to think about that. That's where you lost me last time.

Maj. Gen. Joseph McChristian, *Chief of Intelligence, Vietnam, 1966–67*

In the interview, McChristian decried attempts to falsify intelligence reporting. Crile followed this with a statement that established the tone for their exchange.

CRILE: The reason we are interviewing you, sir, is because you represent a different tradition than the one that is being alluded to. And I'd like just to read to you part of a letter from Gains Hawkins, who is your old order of battle chief. And this is him writing about you. He says, "General McChristian is your . . ." and you'll have to pardon Gains Hawkins because he may be engaged in hyperbole here, but forgive him. He says, "General McChristian is your white knight serene, impeccable and untouchable."

Col. Gains Hawkins, *Chief, Order of Battle Section, MACV, 1966–67*

The interview with Colonel Hawkins was equally friendly and supportive.

CRILE: Could I help?

HAWKINS: Yes.

CRILE: When you talked to Sam Adams a few years back, you described it this way.

HAWKINS: He expressed concern with the impact of these new figures being so much higher than the figures we had carried in the order of battle. I hate to—

CRILE: No, that's fine.

HAWKINS: —to put words in a man's mouth.

CRILE: Let me not, let me not. But the way I said it was approximately the way you remember it?

HAWKINS: Yes.

Col. George Hamscher, *Intelligence staff officer, Commander in Chief Pacific, Hawaii, 1966–67*

Colonel Hamscher attended an intelligence meeting at the Pentagon that wrestled with the order-of-battle question. He was based in Hawaii and was not part of Westmoreland's command. He referred to his junior status at this meeting; he was then a "light colonel . . . an elbow man . . . not a moving force." He told Crile he was just monitoring the events—sitting on the sidelines—but was "aghast" at the manipulation of enemy-strength numbers.

HAMSCHER: This isn't how it ought to be done, this is how you are taught it should be done. On the other hand, when you have spent maybe a quarter of a century in the Army—

CRILE: C'mon, sure. Don't pull away from that.

HAMSCHER: There is no real moral issue involved as you see it at the time. You do what you are told. At least, I do.

CRILE: C'mon, go back to who you are. You represent something when you are a colonel in the Army at time of war. You have some set of values. You are sitting in the Pentagon. Isn't it right next to the Joint Chiefs of Staff, that room?

HAMSCHER: I don't remember honestly. There are a lot of small rooms in the Pentagon.

None of this made the program. In the broadcast, Crile sought to get Hamscher to say that the Pentagon meeting was engaged in faking intelligence estimates. Hamscher held back from that.

HAMSCHER: That's your characterization, and that's too strong for me. My misgiving was that we were faking it. There was manipulation, yeah.

Joseph Hovey, *CIA analyst in Vietnam, 1965–68*

Hovey was a young intelligence analyst in Vietnam. According to the program, he had predicted the Tet Offensive.

CRILE: You are 28 . . . you're probably the man in Vietnam who knows as much about the Viet Cong as any other American. The CIA analyst watching them . . .

CRILE: Well, you must be something of a hero at this point. You've predicted the biggest event of the Vietnam war.
HOVEY: Well, I don't know if hero is the right word. But I feel that I did the job I was sent there to do. I—
CRILE: Well, let's just think back in terms of what happened to you and your career. You had authored an extraordinarily predictive intelligence report. It's like having predicted Pearl Harbor.
HOVEY: Okay.

Cdr. James Meacham, *Senior Intelligence Officer, MACV, 1967–68*

Commander Meacham, now military editor of *The Economist,* was interviewed by Crile with Adams assisting in London on March 2, 1981. The thrust of the interview involved a series of letters Meacham had written to his wife during the war, letters highly critical of American intelligence operations in Vietnam. Alone among the friendly witnesses, Meacham resisted many of Crile's questions and was a difficult interview.

CRILE: (referring to letters to his wife): They're your words. "Lying." In other words, we will lie. "We're mesmerized in our lies. Some day it will come out." (Later) . . . they're about lying. They're your words.

MEACHAM: Well—well, I mean—so what? What do you want me to say about them?

CRILE: Well, I was trying to have you put some light on it.

MEACHAM: Well, I'm not sure I can. I mean we've been over this several times . . .

CRILE: . . . you wrote that [letter to his wife].

MEACHAM: Well, so what?

CRILE: So aren't you saying that you were manipulating figures to come out with preconceived notions as to what the estimate should be? Faking intelligence?

MEACHAM: No, no. I'm not saying that at all.

CRILE: You say, anyhow: "We are winning the war and now I can prove it, having received sufficient, adequate guidance from my leaders."

MEACHAM: Well, we certainly weren't faking any intelligence. Nobody that I have any connection with ever faked any intelligence.

CRILE: Well, please—please help me, because it's not a mystery.

MEACHAM: I mean, you're trying to get me to say that we all falsified intelligence. I'm not going to say it because we—I don't have any sense of having done that.

CRILE: What do you have a sense of having done?

MEACHAM: I don't know how to answer.

CRILE: Are you proud of your performance, of MACV's performance?

MEACHAM: Well, of course not. But I mean—I don't see the connection.

CRILE: Do you understand that the—I mean, what Sam and I are both trying to say right now?

MEACHAM: I understand perfectly well what you're trying to say.

CRILE: And . . .?

MEACHAM: I don't agree with it.

CRILE: Well not—not that—agree with it. It's a question of whether there isn't some way to reach a—Well, I would love to have you present this history with some perspective which would be—

MEACHAM: Well, I've done the best I can do. I'm sorry that it's not satisfactory to you.

The double standard that a reading of the transcripts demonstrated, the harsh treatment of some, the coddling of others, was hardly reassuring. My next task would be to see how fairly the material had been edited.

Toby Wertheim persuaded me that we needed additional research help, and I was able to add Barbara Pierce to the staff. A calm and measured woman, who had worked in print before coming to CBS News, she was exactly right for the assignment—close-mouthed and energetic. My staff now consisted of three: Wertheim, Pierce, and Shari Lampert as research assistant. Lampert, genial and industrious, had worked with me when I was vice president of news. She would help with the research and run the office.

I began to worry about leaks and called a staff meeting, the first and last we would have. All of us knew that CBS News was a human sieve; it sustained TV gossip columnists all over the country. I cautioned that we must be ultra-discreet. In what had to be a first, there would not be a single disclosure during our six-week examination. Our investigation might or might not prove to be important, but the fact that nothing ever leaked would be historic.

8

A MATTER
OF STANDARDS

If one were to search for an inflammatory word, a spectacularly inflammatory word, it might well be "conspiracy." It was a word that the Vietnam documentary used only once (interestingly enough, just as it had been used only once in Sam Adams's 1975 *Harper's* article, not in its text but as a subhead). In the CBS program, it was used in the so-called tease, the introduction to the broadcast.

Inevitably, the word "conspiracy" was going to be a critical issue in assessing the program, and I addressed it in the most direct fashion available. I looked it up in several dictionaries:

conspiracy [*Webster's Third New International Dictionary*]: 1a: An illegal, treasonable, or treacherous plan to harm or destroy another person, group, or entity. . . . 2: a combination of persons banded secretly together and resolved to accomplish an evil or unlawful end. . . .

conspiracy law [*Random House Dictionary of the English Language*]: An agreement by two or more persons to commit a crime, fraud, or other wrongful act. . . .

In the *TV Guide* article, Crile had been quoted as saying: "Conspiracy . . . was a characterization which we agreed to use in the script at the very end, after reviewing everything in the show." In his White Paper, Crile went on:

My thinking and I think everyone else's was quite simple. Evidence was

74

systematically suppressed, reports altered and blocked, officers instructed to argue for estimates they knew to be indefensible. These actions were carried out in order to conform to a command position which called for indefensibly low estimates of enemy strength. It was not a single act; it was a series of actions, often calling for a great deal of coordination and boldness. It took place over a number of months involving a large number of intelligence officers. The word conspiracy is strong, but we could not figure out what other word described the activities that we had documented. I still cannot.

Roger Colloff would later write to Van Gordon Sauter that "conspiracy" was not a word that he and other executives had taken lightly. They, too, had turned to a dictionary, *Webster's New World*, which carried these definitions:

> 1: a planning and acting together secretly, especially for an unlawful or harmful purpose, such as murder or treason 2: the plan agreed on; plot 3: the group taking part in such a plan 4: a combining or working together.

According to Colloff, "we agreed that the use of the word 'conspiracy,' while tough, was warranted by the facts presented by the broadcast and the underlying research." He said this was accepted by those who were at the screenings: George Crile, Howard Stringer, Andrew Lack, Mike Wallace, Margery Baker (a CBS News vice president), and Bill Leonard.

In defending the use of the word "conspiracy," Roger Colloff would quote Wallace's critical phrase from the broadcast with a truncated dictionary definition: that a conspiracy ("a planning and acting together secretly") existed at the highest levels of American military intelligence. Missing from his parentheses was the rest of the dictionary's definition—"especially for an unlawful or harmful purpose, such as murder or treason." I did not find this persuasive.

The word "conspiracy" should have come as no surprise to any of George Crile's superiors at CBS News. On November 24, 1980, fourteen months before his program would be broadcast, Crile submitted to management what is known as a Blue Sheet, a proposal for the documentary he wanted to make. Producers routinely send these not only to outline but to protect their ideas; if two producers come up with the same idea, it is usually first in, first out. Crile's Blue Sheet was unusual: it ran for sixteen single-spaced pages. Most producers find a single page, or at most two pages, sufficient. In Crile's lengthy proposal, the word "conspiracy" was used twenty-four times and the word "conspirator" five times. The finished program would indeed parallel what Crile had promised in the Blue Sheet, and when criticism began to mount he would point this out in a June 1982 memorandum to his correspondent, Mike Wallace:

> Throughout that Blue Sheet were references to "conspiracy." . . . As Bill Leonard said: "these things either happened or they didn't; if they happened it was a very important story and we should run it." My commission was to go out *with* Adams and prove on film that these people would testify to what Adams told us they had told him. So I did. And CBS News with its eyes wide open, looked at the interviews, decided to commission the documentary, hire Adams and sent us on our way to complete the work as spelled out in the Blue Sheet. The documentary they got is the documentary they commissioned.

Management did not give Crile a full-fledged approval. Instead, they told him to go out and present evidence on film, rather than on paper, to support his proposal. They authorized a conditional budget of $25,000 and told him to film some of the former military officers and CIA men who, he maintained, supported the Adams-Crile thesis. He interviewed Col. George Hamscher, Lt. Richard McArthur, Col. Gains Hawkins, Maj. Gen. Joseph McChristian, Cdr. James Meacham, and Joseph Hovey of the CIA. A Mike Wallace interview with Marshall Lynn, a CIA analyst, was scrubbed.

It was after seeing excerpts of the filmed interviews, excerpts carefully selected by Crile, that CBS News gave the producer a firm go-ahead. For the first time, he would be the sole producer of a major documentary. He was given a budget of a quarter of a million dollars to complete the program.

One aspect of the program puzzled me. Why had Crile not made reference in his script, however briefly, to the final report of the House Select Committee on Intelligence that was issued in 1976? The committee, known as the Pike Committee after its chairman Otis Pike, said some things that would have fortified Crile's case considerably.

Although the committee could not help him much on conspiracy (as mentioned, it had said that whether or not there was a conspiracy was irrelevant), it had some other things to say that would have been useful. It accused Westmoreland's command of creating "false perceptions" of enemy strength that gave policymakers "a degraded image of the enemy." It cited "pressure from policymaking officials to produce positive intelligence indicators." It said the Vietnam "numbers game" prevented "perhaps the President, and certainly members of Congress, from judging the real changes in Vietnam over time." On the dropping from the order of battle of the enemy's Self-Defense and Secret Self-Defense forces, the S.D. and S.S.D. irregulars—who, Westmoreland said, were made up of black-pajamaed men, women, and children with no capacity to fight—the Pike Committee said: "As foot soldiers realized at the time, and as different studies by the Army surgeon general confirm, the destructiveness of mines and booby traps, which irregular forces set out, was increasingly responsible for American losses."

I considered writing in my report that by not using any of the arsenal available in Pike, the program had missed a great opportunity to counter its critics. One paragraph of narration by Mike Wallace quoting from the report would have helped. I decided to resist the temptation. My mandate was not to assume the role of producer but to analyze where the program might have gone wrong. I had already determined that there was a strong disparity in the way opponents of the thesis and those friendly to it had been treated.

The next question was: How was the material itself handled? Had it been edited fairly, in accordance with the standards CBS News had established over the years? Here again, my staff and I were in for some surprises.

One of the great advantages that print journalism has over television is the ellipsis, a mark or marks such as —, . . . , or *** to indicate the elimination or suppression of words or phrases. When a reader comes across a paragraph with one of these symbols, he assumes there has been a jump in what the person quoted has said.

For example, a newspaper might quote Mr. Jones as saying: "My position on protecting the tankers in the Gulf has not changed. . . . It is the right policy and I support it."

To save space, the reporter used four dots to shorten the quote. Mr. Jones had said more in his interview, and what the dots eliminated was: "Most Americans may not have heard of Kuwait, Bahrain, Qatar, or the United Arab Emirates, but they are vital to our national interests." The reporter decided that was excess verbiage and the four dots took care of that.

Television has no such ellipsis. When a jump is required in an answer, the usual technique is to cut away to a listening shot of the interviewer while the subject continues his reply. (In a one-camera interview, the listening shot is usually made after the interview is over, sometimes after the subject has left the room.) To the viewer, the uninterrupted answer, punctuated only by a listening shot of the reporter, plays as a single, direct reply. The listener is unaware that a cut has been made.

Some fitful attempts have been made to clarify this confusion—a fast dissolve of the picture of the subject may indicate to some there has been a passage of time, but this device is infrequently used. Another device, much clearer, is to have the reporter record a narration line: "He would also say . . ." which is inserted between two disparate answers. To this day the ellipsis is a problem that troubles television news producers.

The core of the predicament is that reporters are not stenographers. Their job is not to present an unevaluated transcript of what a person says; if they did, newspapers would read like the *Congressional Record*. Reporters fling a wide net, select the most pertinent statements, and compress these into a coherent story. Their job is to illuminate with precision and fairness. The raw data goes into the reporter's notebook; the finished abridgment goes into the newspaper.

In television, the extract used of what a person says is called a sound bite; the unused portion is an outtake. The print press and television over the years have fought hard in the courts and in Congress to keep reporters' notebooks and outtakes privileged, generally with success.

A landmark example was the refusal of CBS President Frank Stanton in 1971 to turn over to a House committee outtakes from an explosive documentary, "The Selling of the Pentagon." The sanctity of outtakes was threatened again in 1979 when the Supreme Court ruled in *Herbert* vs. *Lando*, a case involving a Mike Wallace report on *60 Minutes*, that outtakes were necessary to determine a reporter's "state of mind." Today, newspapers and television continue to oppose attempts by judges and legislators to get into their notebooks or outtakes.

The filmed interviews conducted for the Vietnam program ran for a sprawling twenty-seven hours. When cut down by Crile, they totaled twenty-five minutes and eighteen seconds. This was a ratio of more than fifty to one, which might seem profligate and excessive but really was not all that unusual. In television, the greatest eater of film is the interview. It would not be a question of length or overkill that would be a consideration in my examination but whether the material had been selected and used fairly.

Fairness can never be completely codified; it is something that resides in a producer's mindset and heart, perhaps even in his genes. Over the years, the CBS News Standards had tried to help. It is a document prepared by management, evolutionary in that many of its clauses could be traced directly to past transgressions. Whenever the network got into serious trouble over a practice that had developed, a clause or section would be added to the Standards proscribing it in the future.

A good example was "The Selling of the Pentagon." In that otherwise excellent broadcast, Roger Mudd had interviewed Assistant Secretary of Defense Daniel Z. Henkin. Answers to different questions were edited together into a single uninterrupted reply. To the viewer it appeared to be one question, one answer. Henkin complained that he had been edited unfairly and the Standards address this directly:

> If the answer to an interview question, as that answer appears in the broadcast, is derived, in part or in whole, from the answers to other questions, the broadcast will so indicate, either in lead-in narration, bridging narration lines during the interview, or appropriate audio lines.

In the Vietnam program, I would find that this provision had been violated continually. Two Westmoreland answers to two separate questions were edited into one answer, as were three George Allen answers, two Sam Adams answers, and three Richard McArthur answers. None did violence to what these people said, but they were still violations of the guidelines.

I would have more serious problems with Crile's editing decisions during the production, which I felt distorted some of the interviews that had been filmed.

In one case, accounts of two separate meetings about enemy-strength estimates were cut together so that they appeared to be one meeting. Both meetings were in Saigon, the first in April of 1967; the second in August of the same year.

Present at the first meeting were:

General Westmoreland.
Maj. Gen Joseph McChristian, intelligence chief.
Col. Gains Hawkins, order-of-battle expert.

Present at the second meeting were:

General Westmoreland.
Ambassador Robert Komer, LBJ's special envoy.
Colonel Hawkins.

The pattern Crile used in editing this sequence was: first meeting; straight cut to the second meeting; straight cut back to the first meeting. The distortion was this: Westmoreland began talking about an April meeting; Hawkins's response was about an August meeting; and Mc-Christian followed him talking about the April meeting again. When you read the following excerpt, you will see how the sequence played out. Remember it goes: first meeting, second meeting (in italics), back to first meeting, and it all ran in one uninterrupted block.

WESTMORELAND: I do recall a session with Hawkins, yes, but I was very suspicious of this particular estimate. And the reason was, you come to a shade of grey. You get down to the hamlet level, and you've got teenagers and you got old men who can be armed and can be useful to the enemy and who are technically Viet Cong—

WALLACE: Right.

WESTMORELAND: —but they don't have any military capability of consequence.

HAWKINS: *There was no mistaking the message.*

CRILE: *Which was?*

HAWKINS: *That there was a great concern about the impact of these figures, that—they're being higher.*

CRILE: *They didn't want higher numbers.*

HAWKINS: *That was the message.*

WALLACE: This is the way General McChristian remembers Westmoreland's reaction to the briefing.

MCCHRISTIAN: And when General Westmoreland saw the large increase in figures we had developed, he was quite disturbed by it. And by [the] time I left his office, I had the definite impression that he felt if he sent those figures back to Washington at that time, it would create a political bombshell.

Later in the broadcast, this happened again—separate meetings cut together so they appeared to be one meeting. The first meeting was a National Intelligence Estimate meeting at the Pentagon in August of 1967. Westmoreland was not there. The second, chaired by Westmoreland, was a meeting in Saigon in September of 1967.

The sequence began with Col. George Hamscher, the officer from Hawaii, talking about the Pentagon meeting. Then via a straight cut to Westmoreland talking at a totally different meeting in Saigon (italics). Then back to Hamscher still talking about the Pentagon meeting.

HAMSCHER: It was a lousy strength estimation. It was shoddy. But we did it.

WESTMORELAND: *Now, who actually did the cutting? I don't know. It could have been my—my chief of staff. I don't know. But I didn't get involved in this personally.*

HAMSCHER: This boils down to another one of the uncomfortable little jobs that you do for your commander. And these vary in degree.

To the viewer, it all played as one meeting. Westmoreland, as edited, was put in the context of talking about a meeting he did not attend in a colloquy with an officer, Hamscher, he had never met.

There was more selective editing in a section dealing with President Johnson. Wallace asked Westmoreland whether LBJ was "a difficult man to feed bad news about the war." Crile cut a critical portion of the general's answer. As it played in the broadcast, the viewer had to assume that LBJ hated bad news and the Saigon command spared him from a lot of it. But that was not what Westmoreland said. His full answer follows; only the boldface portions were used.

WESTMORELAND: **Well, Mike, you know as well as I do that people in senior positions love good news,** and they don't like bad news, and after all, it's well recognized that **supreme politicians or leaders in countries are inclined to shoot the messenger that brings bad news. Certainly he wanted bad news like a hole in the head.** He welcomed good news. But he was given both the good and the bad, but he was inclined to accentuate the positive.

Later in the interview, Westmoreland was even more cogent in describing what was sent to the President. This exchange was not used in the final broadcast.

WALLACE: You told me the President didn't want to hear bad news.

WESTMORELAND: Well, who does? But that doesn't mean we didn't give him bad news. We did give him bad news.

The Vietnam program maintained that the enemy count in the war was seriously skewed in 1967 when the Viet Cong irregulars—the old men, women, and children in their black pajamas—were eliminated from MACV's order of battle. Sam Adams and his supporters pointed out that this seemingly insignificant force was hardly benign. They set mines and *punji* sticks, razor-sharp bamboo spikes, tipped with human excrement, which they would camouflage on trails and in the jungle. The stakes could pierce a military boot, wounding and causing infections, and they resulted in many American casualties. Estimates of the size of this force, the so-called Self-Defense and Secret Self-Defense, ranged from 100,000 to 200,000. Westmoreland's position was that these people had no real military capability. Furthermore, since we did not count the old men, women, and children on our side, why should we count them on the enemy side?

Nine times in his interview with Wallace, the general said this as forcefully as he could. Some sample quotes leave little doubt about the point he was trying to make:

> . . . if you're going to do that [count the enemy irregulars] you have to have the counterpart group with the Government of Vietnam troops, which we never included. They had no military competence. . . .

> In order to include a lot of teenagers and old men, village defenders who could prepare *punji* stakes in the enemy order of battle, we had to also include the counterpart in the order of battle of the South Vietnamese. The fact is that these village defenders had a minimum to do with the outcome of the war. . . .

> . . . the defenders of the South Vietnamese villages, those under control of the government and with allegiance to Saigon, they also put in *punji* stakes. They defended their villages. They put in mines. But these people had no offensive combat capability. . . .

> I come back again: if you're going to include people defending a village in the order of battle of the enemy, you've got to include them in the order of battle of the GVN, the Government of Vietnam.

The general may have been right or wrong, but his point—we don't count ours, why count theirs—got lost. The program also implied there was something secret or furtive in the elimination of these forces, but it did not go unnoticed by the press in Saigon.

On November 24, 1967, the *New York Times* published in an inside page a story from its correspondent in Saigon, Tom Buckley, which gave the details. It stated that total enemy strength now numbered 223,000 to 248,000. This was a sharp reduction from the old figure of 297,000. Gen. Winant Sidle, the military command spokesman, explained that 75,000 to 85,000 officials such as hamlet chiefs, tax collectors, and propagandists would no longer be carried in the order of battle, nor would 30,000 to 50,000 of the irregulars in the Self-Defense and Secret Self-Defense forces, whom he described as "essentially low-level fifth columnists used for information collecting."

There had to be something of a Catch-22 about this. They were there, then they were not there, but they were still there.

There were revealing editing decisions made in the interview with Maj. Gen. Joseph McChristian, who in 1966–67 was Westmoreland's chief of intelligence. McChristian told George Crile that in 1967, he brought new enemy-strength estimates, showing a large increase, to Westmoreland, who was disturbed by them. He asked McChristian not to send the estimates along but to leave them so he could review them. "Shortly thereafter," McChristian said, "I left the country, and I don't know for a fact actually what happened to that message."

The program charged that McChristian's estimates were suppressed by Westmoreland and suggested that this had led to McChristian's transfer from Vietnam. Although prodded repeatedly during his interview, McChristian never came out flatly and said this. He described his transfer this way: At the end of his two-year tour, Westmoreland asked him to stay an additional year as chief of intelligence, but he wanted to command a division in combat, which meant in Vietnam, the only combat the United States was then engaged in.

"I didn't want to remain just an intelligence specialist," McChristian told Crile. He said Westmoreland agreed that he had earned a combat command and that he would support his request. Later, Westmoreland showed him a Pentagon cable which said that extending general officers in Vietnam for a third year "was not favorably considered at that time." But he would get command of a division at Fort Hood.

Crile pressed McChristian on the transfer. He quoted a Jack Anderson column of November 30, 1967 (Crile revealed to the general that he was working for Anderson at the time), which said that McChristian had been transferred "for reporting higher estimates than the Pentagon liked."

"Do you think you were transferred out because you were reporting higher estimates than were wanted at the time?" Crile asked the general.

MCCHRISTIAN: I can't answer that question.

CRILE: Possibly?

MCCHRISTIAN: I don't know. Possible—yes, it's possible, but I don't know whether that's a fact or not. In fact, the column that you refer to was the first indication that ever came to my attention that I was moved out of Vietnam. I had just assumed it was normal Army transfer policy orders.

None of the above was used in the final broadcast.

Crile continued to pursue the matter with McChristian. He returned to another Jack Anderson column, written in 1975, and asked the general about "your suspicion that you had been transferred because of some connection to trying to raise the figures." McChristian's reply was still ambiguous: "It has made me feel that perhaps I was very naive at the time and more than likely I was moved out of Vietnam to get me out of the way. But I don't know that for a fact." This also was not used.

The portion that was used required a highly selective edit. First, the broadcast used a brief sound bite of Westmoreland expressing admiration for McChristian but saying that he and his staff disagreed with his findings. Then Mike Wallace said: "Consider Westmoreland's dilemma. If he accepted his intelligence chief's findings, he would have to take the bad news to the President. If he didn't, well, there was only General McChristian to deal with."

There followed a misleading edit of McChristian's reply to still another Crile attempt to nail down the sequence: Was he moved out of Vietnam "because you would not keep the numbers down—the estimates?" (The section in boldface was used in the final broadcast.)

MCCHRISTIAN: No, because nobody ever asked me that, because I reported it as I saw it and **evidently people didn't like my reporting because I was constantly showing that enemy strength was increasing.**

Although McChristian was pushed hard in his lengthy interview, he never conceded that his reports were "suppressed." Yet Wallace ended the sequence in the final broadcast with this narration: "Shortly after Westmoreland suppressed his intelligence chief's report, General Joseph McChristian was transferred out of Vietnam. . . ."

There was another aspect of the McChristian interview that troubled me—the hypothetical mode. Crile started it with this question (not used), which set the stage:

CRILE: If I could ask you to be what amounts to an expert witness here as to procedure, and this did not happen under your regime, under your command, but if you had been chief of MACV intelligence, and if a commanding officer had come to you and said that he wanted to put a ceiling on all enemy-strength estimates, and he did not want you to allow the estimates to rise above that, even if you believed they should, what would you have done?

There followed an array of hypothetical questions, none of which dealt with any specific actions or decisions by McChristian. Questions like: ". . . if you could put yourself in the shoes of a loyal staff officer who has just been instructed by a general to go to Washington, to a National Intelligence Estimate meeting and argue for figures that he knew in his heart to be wrong. . . ."

The next two hypotheticals elicited strong McChristian answers, and they were used in very specific context in the broadcast.

CRILE: To put a ceiling on enemy-strength estimates, to tell an intelligence operation that it is not permitted to report enemy-strength estimates over a certain number—

MCCHRISTIAN: Uh—hmm.

CRILE: —what does that constitute, sir?

MCCHRISTIAN: From my point of view, that is falsification of the facts.

CRILE: Are there statutes in the Uniform Code of Military Justice that would speak to that situation?

MCCHRISTIAN: Not that I'm aware of. But there's something on a ring that I wear from West Point that the motto is: "Duty, Honor, Country." It's dishonorable.

This provided a highly dramatic ending for the second act of the program. "The Uncounted Enemy" then went to a commercial.

Col. Gains Hawkins, the former order-of-battle chief, was and would continue to be a staunch supporter of the Adams-Crile thesis, but the editing of his interview was also open to question. In an early part of the program, Adams had described to Mike Wallace a 1967 meeting of the National Intelligence Estimates Board at the CIA in Langley, Virginia. Hawkins was there to represent MACV and to Adams's surprise was defending the military's lower enemy-strength figures. The Hawkins sound bite was edited from his long interview with Crile. The sequence began with Sam Adams saying that Hawkins looked sick as he sat there endorsing the MACV's figures. Then it went to Hawkins with a critical deletion (boldface used):

HAWKINS: Now prior to this when we had the old figures that we inherited from the South Vietnamese forces, **there was never any reluctance on my part to tell Sam or anybody else who had a need to know, that these figures were crap. They were history. They weren't worth anything.**

Hawkins had called the old South Vietnamese figures "crap." As used in the broadcast, the MACV figures at Langley became "crap."

Another aspect of the interview was Hawkins's repeated disagreement with a key premise of the program—that information had been kept from the President of the United States, Lyndon B. Johnson. Twice Hawkins said that he doubted that. None of what follows was used:

CRILE: How much did General Westmoreland know?
HAWKINS: Knew everything as far as I'm concerned. President Johnson knew everything.
CRILE: Let me stick for the moment . . .
HAWKINS: No one fools the commanders.

CRILE: Yes, but why should we think that President Johnson knew about this controversy?
HAWKINS: Because President Johnson had his special representative in Saigon, Mr. Robert Komer, who was at . . .
CRILE: Ambassador Robert Komer.
HAWKINS: Ambassador Robert Komer, who was acutely aware of every figure that was being presented, every figure that was being rejected or not approved. Thoroughly, completely aware. And you must assume he was reporting . . .
CRILE: Back to the White House.
HAWKINS: To the White House. Else why was he there?

There were other Hawkins quotes which wound up on the cutting-room floor. Among them:

On his relationship with his commander: "I have no direct relationship with General Westmoreland other than in two intelligence briefings."

On Westmoreland ordering the MACV representatives to hold to an enemy-strength ceiling of 300,000 at the National Intelligence Estimates meeting at Langley in 1967: "I'm not familiar with that instruction."

On who was the villain in all of this: "I'm not going to point a finger at anyone."

On intelligence estimates: "When you get down to it, who the hell can prove one figure is better than the other figure? You don't have that two plus two equals four in this business."

I had now gone over the transcripts with my staff as carefully as possible. The next step was obvious: We would confront, face to face, those who had been responsible for the Vietnam program.

9

THE INTERVIEWS
BEGIN

Ira Klein, *the film editor*

He came striding into our office on Thursday, June 3, 1982, the first of my face-to-face interviews. Before I finished, I would interview thirty-two people, fourteen in person (twelve of them CBS employees) and eighteen by telephone. As agreed, I never used a tape recorder. Wertheim, Pierce, and I would take full reporter's notes, then combine them into a single transcript. My office was barely large enough to accommodate the three of us and the subject.

Some film editors develop what I call a cutting-room stare, which comes from too many hours in too many windowless cubicles, eyes fixed on images they have rerun a hundred times. It is a job that demands intense concentration, a visual sensitivity, considerable hand-eye coordination and, among the better practitioners, a strong story sense and intellectual input. It is a lonely, confined life, and it is not uncommon for film or tape editors to seem preoccupied and withdrawn.

Ira Klein seemed neither; he was only thirty, perhaps too young to have fallen victim to some of the occupational burdens of his craft. He is of medium height with dark, curly hair and brown, friendly eyes. He was wearing the trappings of his trade—open-collar shirt, jeans, and a bush jacket.

Klein was born in Queens, attended Forest Hills High School, and majored in film at Ohio University. After graduating in 1974, he worked on several low-budget features as an assistant film editor, the bottom rung in the editing room. He came to CBS News as a free-lance assistant in the documentary unit in 1978. He was well thought of and a year later was promoted to full editor. Although he had never worked on a documentary that ran longer than eighteen minutes, two years later, in December of 1980, George Crile offered him what loomed as his greatest opportunity—editor of the ninety-minute Vietnam program. Klein seized the assignment and began in April of 1981.

As soon as we started the interview in my office, it became apparent that Klein was a man who wanted to unburden himself. While not especially articulate, even laconic at times, he spoke with passion and pent-up anger about what had happened during the production of the Vietnam program. I would have to weigh whether his embittered account was based on fact or on personal animus.

Klein agreed that the program was what television producers call a "talking head" film. Of the 74,000 feet of 16-millimeter film that was shot, it was all interviews, someone talking, except for a brief scene of Sam Adams and Mike Wallace walking together at the Adams farm in Leesburg, Virginia. The rest of the program was composed in the main of library footage from the Vietnam War.

Klein was bitter about the procedures followed during the production. He had hired an assistant film editor, Phyllis Hurwitz, and, since he was busy completing another documentary, it was she who edited the "selects," the preliminary interviews with General McChristian, Colonel Hawkins, Commander Meacham, and others. CBS News executives had ordered Crile to shoot these interviews in order to convince them that his Blue Sheet witnesses would deliver their indictments on film. The excerpts were screened for Roger Colloff and Howard Stringer in Klein's editing room on a Steenback, an editing console with a television-size screen. Although the film ran for only twenty minutes, the presentation took an hour, with Crile starting and stopping the machine to provide narrative for his two superiors. Klein had never seen the material before, and it was after this show-and-tell that a firm approval was given by management for the Vietnam program.

I asked Klein how deeply Mike Wallace was involved in the broadcast. He said: "Wallace was only peripherally involved with the project from start to finish. He was not involved at all in the editing; he was never in the editing room. He'd be around for the big moments. When we screened the selects for Colloff and Stringer, when we got around to screening the show for Bill Leonard and Colloff, then Mike was there. And when arguments started to break out about the show, Crile would call Wallace in and Wallace would make a decision one way or another."

This confirmed what Wallace had told me on the telephone, that he had not played a heavy role during the program's production.

For the interviews conducted by Wallace, two film cameras were used, one on the subject, one on him, so that the questions were the actual ones used in the interview. On those where Crile was the questioner, only one camera was used, and "reverses" were filmed—questions repeated for the camera by Crile after the interview was over. This was hardly a departure from normal CBS News practice. Two cameras meant two crews and was quite expensive, usually a perk reserved for the elite correspondents, a small group which certainly included Mike Wallace.

Klein thought the lighting used in the show was designed to create a mood, an ominous mood. That was not apparent to me; the lighting was undistinguished, flat, close-up lighting, free of any nuance that I could see.

Klein first got to know Sam Adams in April of 1981 when he started working on the film. "I would attend chronology sessions with him in Crile's office. Sam carried around a briefcase full of chronologies, his handwritten research on the Vietnam dispute, and he would read from these and Crile would sit there taking notes."

Klein said he was present at half a dozen of these meetings and after one of them, he claimed he told Crile that Adams seemed obsessed. He asked Crile: "Can you trust the information and accuracy of what Sam is telling you?" Crile said that he knew about Adams and cut off the conversation.

Later, Klein said, Crile told him he did not want Adams around when the two of them were editing. Crile even resisted having Phyllis Hurwitz, Klein's assistant, in the editing room at these times although her technical assistance was important. Neither Joseph Zigman, the associate producer, nor Alex Alben, the researcher, was encouraged to participate in these editing sessions.

The editing room was open, however, to two women who frequently were there behind closed doors with Crile. Throughout the production, Grace Diekhaus, his former documentary associate, would join Crile to offer critiques of sequences that had been edited. Another woman who began to appear was Susan Lyne. Klein found out she was living with

Crile (they were soon to be married). Lyne was managing editor of *The Village Voice* from 1979 to 1981.

Lyne came with increasing regularity, going over the film with Crile and working on the script. One Saturday, Klein said, he was in his cutting room after a screening with Crile, Sam Adams, and Alex Alben. After Crile left, the three of them were having a frank discussion about the film when Susan Lyne entered. She listened for a while and then left. The next day, a Sunday, Klein was in his cutting room waiting for Crile when the producer phoned. According to Klein, Crile said, "Don't listen to Sam and Alex." He said he had heard that Adams and Alben had been "bad-mouthing" the broadcast.

Klein said he told Crile he didn't want Lyne in his editing room again, but the producer was inflexible. At eight-thirty one morning, the day of an important screening, Klein said he arrived to find Crile and Lyne running the film on his editing console.

Before Sam Adams's interview, one that would be critical to the program and its thesis, "he was definitely rehearsed," Klein told us. "It was in Alex Alben's office and Crile, Alben, and Joe Zigman were in there with Sam. I was in and out of the room. Crile was going over the questions with him. They rehearsed him all day long. Mike Wallace was not there or possibly even aware that this was going on. When the interview took place, Wallace was handed the questions that had been rehearsed."

Klein's charge would be strongly denied by all who were allegedly involved—Adams, Wallace, Crile, Zigman, and Alben. No one disagreed that there were long meetings with Adams before his interview, but they said this was to get him to focus on his material. He was so full of information they were worried about long, windy answers.

Klein would buy none of this. "Adams was rehearsed," he insisted during my interview with him. "And he wasn't the only one. There were long, elaborate discussions with Colonel Hawkins before his interview that sounded like a rehearsal to me."

The film editor's relationship with Crile became more antagonistic as the program went into full production. "Crile was totally disorganized," Klein told me. "He would disappear. In August he was involved with another story—a report for the *Evening News* on hired assassins. He was making plans to do another show on drugs in November."

Klein said he asked Crile: "Why are you doing this? It's unrealistic. How can you work on other projects at the same time as you work on this?" He said Crile apologized but did not change his schedule. "He'd be gone all day," Klein told me, "and then he'd come into the cutting room at six o'clock at night and begin pressing the crew to get going. ·

"Here we were with all of this material and not a line of Mike Wallace's narration recorded or laid down, and he was pressing us. George is difficult to work with and incapable of taking responsibility. It's always someone else's fault."

Before the production was completed, Klein would say that he couldn't stand to look at Crile. He conceded during the trial which followed that he had called him "devious and slimy," "a social pervert."

His rancor did not embrace others involved in the production. "Sam Adams," he said, "was a wonderful man but obsessed." George Allen, the CIA's Vietnam expert, was "an honorable man, very loyal. He almost backed out of the show." Klein liked Joe Zigman, the veteran associate producer who, in the hierarchy, was the man he reported to and often confided in.

The double interview of George Allen created the most heated exchange between Crile and Klein. After the first session, Crile brought Allen to the editing room and told Klein he wanted to show him film of his interview and samples from some of the others who supported the program's premise. Klein said he looked at Crile as if he were out of his mind. "You're compromising me and jeopardizing the project."

"Don't worry," he said Crile replied. "Everything will be okay."

The next day Crile again brought Allen to the editing room and everyone but Klein was asked to leave. "Don't worry," Crile told Klein. "George Allen is an old CIA man. This won't go any further."

"I was stunned," Klein said, "but I ran the interviews for him."

Klein told me he was also troubled at the way Crile was cutting the Westmoreland interview. "Here this old man comes up—I doubt he ever read the letter they dropped off at the hotel—and they ask him questions about things that happened fifteen years ago and Crile doesn't give him a chance to speak. He didn't want Westmoreland to speak of women and children in the Self-Defense and Secret Self-Defense forces not belonging in the order of battle. All he wanted was yes and no. He didn't give him a chance in the cut."

By September, after reading the full transcripts of all of the interviews, Klein told us he was also bothered by the Hawkins interview. Crile did not plan to use the statement by the colonel that LBJ had to know what was going on in the order-of-battle dispute that was boiling over in Saigon. Klein said when he was unable to persuade Crile that this belonged in the broadcast, he went to Joe Zigman. He told us Zigman looked at him and said: "Ira, don't get involved."

In September of 1981, believing the program to be in disarray and drained by late hours and weekends of work, Klein said he insisted they add another film editor to the staff. Others would dispute that it was Klein's idea; some would say he resisted the change. But Joseph Fackovec, an experienced staff editor, was taken on and would cut the last two of the five acts. Klein said Crile told him: "Joe is just a pair of hands."

Klein said he told Crile he must get Howard Stringer involved with the show and urged a screening by October 1. The last two weeks of September, Klein said, "were murder for the staff. Seven-day weeks and some all-night work." Several rough-cut screenings were held for Stringer. "There were lots of questions and some battles," said Klein. "There was one cut of Westmoreland that Stringer thought was too short—didn't give him a chance to say his piece. Crile objected to lengthening the cut and called Mike Wallace in. Wallace agreed with Stringer, and we added a few lines to the cut."

In December, Van Gordon Sauter, the president-designate of CBS News, asked to see the program. The day before the Sauter screening, Roger Colloff decided he wanted to check the film once more, and during this screening another battle erupted between Crile and Klein. It had to do with enemy-infiltration figures and a November 1967 appearance by General Westmoreland on *Meet the Press*.

The full exchange with Lawrence Spivak, the moderator of that program, was as follows (what Crile used is in boldface):

SPIVAK: **What about infiltration? A year ago you said they were infil-trating at the rate of about 7000 a month. What are they doing today?**

WESTMORELAND: **I would estimate between 5500 and 6000 a month.** But they do have the capability of stepping this up.

At the Colloff screening, the sound tracks had been split and Klein was sitting at a panel manipulating knobs that controlled the volume. The unused portion of Westmoreland, "But they do have the capability of stepping this up," came out loud and clear. Apparently, it got by Colloff, but after the screening, according to Klein, Crile went into a frenzy. "Why is that line in there?" he asked Klein. The editor explained it came with the *Meet the Press* film and would be dialed out in the final sound recording. Crile was still furious.

When Sauter, Colloff, and Ed Joyce came for their screening the next day, Crile stood up behind them during the *Meet the Press* sequence and gave Klein a big hand signal to cut the sound so that Westmoreland's last few words would not be heard. None of the others noticed this or were aware of the deletion.

In the final broadcast, Westmoreland was asked to explain the contradiction between the infiltration figure of 20,000 a month that he gave Mike Wallace in the *CBS Reports* interview and the 5,500 to 6,000 a month he had given Lawrence Spivak in the 1967 *Meet the Press*.

WESTMORELAND: Sounds to me like a misstatement. I—I don't remember making it. But certainly I could not retain all these detailed figures in my mind.

Back at his home in South Carolina after the interview, the general had some time to reconsider his answer. On June 9, 1981, seven months before the program would be broadcast, Westmoreland had written a "Dear Mike-and-George" letter about the matter. With his letter, Westmoreland had sent seventy-two pages of documents consisting of cables, declassified reports, intelligence estimates, and the like. Twenty-seven pages into the package, a letter was buried. It read in part: "As of November 1967, infiltration (probable plus possible) was carried on the running tabulation as 5900. Hence my estimate given to Larry Spivak was generally correct."

What the general was saying was that he was right the first time on *Meet the Press,* and wrong the second on the *CBS Reports* interview. It would have been a lot clearer if the letter had been the top page of the package and had stated unequivocally: "I hereby ask for a correction." That would have been hard to ignore. Crile assured Mike Wallace there was nothing new in Westmoreland's package and filed away the letter. Westmoreland would later say: "Why should I write a letter if I didn't intend a correction?"

Klein knew none of this as he was completing his editing, nor was it entirely clear to him why Westmoreland's line about the enemy having the ability to step up its infiltration had agitated Crile so much, but the episode made him more suspicious about the program.

After the screenings for the outgoing and incoming CBS News presidents, Bill Leonard and Van Gordon Sauter, the Vietnam program had secured its final approvals and crashed through the Christmas and New Year's holidays toward final completion. They now had an air date: January 23, 1982. Instead of sailing into those final days as many programs do—the worst is over and only technical details have to be completed—controversy and editorial problems continued to beset the unit.

On Wednesday, January 13, ten days before air, Klein had recorded all of his sound onto a single magnetic track and the negative for the film had been cut and printed into air and standby reels.

Crile was in Washington to screen the finished show for Don Oberdorfer of *The Washington Post*. Oberdorfer told me that his reaction was: "It was a nice piece of journalism, it was a good job of portraying the numbers controversy, but it had nothing to do with Tet." (Peter Braestrup in the *Washington Journalism Review* in May of 1982 had quoted Oberdorfer as calling the program "ambush journalism." Oberdorfer denied to me that he had said this.)

Back in New York, all that remained to be done was relatively routine—transfer picture and sound to videotape, which is what the networks transmit when the program is broadcast. But now an agonizing problem arose.

Sam Adams had read the final script that was about to be distributed to the press and had found two errors. There was a line in the script about Gen. Phillip Davidson that was inaccurate. More serious and difficult to deal with was a Mike Wallace question to General Westmoreland which misquoted a letter the former intelligence officer, Cdr. James Meacham, had written to his wife during the war. Picture and sound for the program were wrapped up, the negative cut, and to make changes now would be an intricate and exacting business.

Adams immediately brought the two mistakes to Carolyne McDaniel, Crile's secretary, who was shaken by the news. She rushed to tell Terry Robinson, the unit production manager, and Klein. Klein told us that he advised McDaniel, who was an intense woman, known to panic, to calm down, phone Crile in Washington, tell him about it, and let him look at the film and provide an explanation. She made the call and Crile said he would deal with it the next morning.

When Crile arrived on Thursday, January 14, he discussed the two problems with Sam Adams. He then told Klein to remove the inaccurate General Davidson line. The misquote in the Westmoreland question was no problem, leave it.

That night, Crile summoned Klein and told him there was a problem with the Westmoreland line and the way they would fix it was to change the *picture*. They would cut from Wallace reading the Meacham letter to Westmoreland to a shot of the general listening. The sound track, which contained the misquote, would remain the same.

Klein told us he said to Crile: "There's no way I'm going to participate in that. If the track has an error in it, what good is it to change the picture?" Klein said Crile walked out of the room.

The next day, when the film and sound were to be transferred to videotape, Klein said Crile walked by his office and said everything was okay. "No, it's not okay," Klein replied. Crile said he had spoken about both changes to Roger Colloff, the vice president in charge of the production, and had his approval. "If that's an executive decision," Klein replied, "I'll do it, but I do think Colloff should see it."

On the following day, according to Klein, Terry Robinson went to Andrew Lack, the senior producer of the program, and told him of the picture switch in the Westmoreland interview. That night, the show was transferred to tape.

On Sunday, January 17, there was more tape work to be done. It was at that point, Klein told us, that Robinson came to him and said: "You're not going to believe this but we have to make a change. Colloff, Lack, and Crile met on Saturday and the inaccurate line has to be taken out."

Crile arrived at the studio a few minutes later. Klein said when Crile spoke to him, he made no eye contact: "We have to make a change. Roger says we have to make a change if it is not too much trouble." He then left the room. Klein said he and Terry Robinson just looked at each other.

That night Klein said he happened to meet Lack outside the CBS News Broadcast Center on West Fifty-Seventh Street and asked him: "You know what's going on?" According to Klein, Lack said Crile had lied to him. Crile had only spoken to him about the routine Davidson change, not the Westmoreland error. Lack said Crile had asked him whether Klein had been the whistle blower and had come in through the back door to tell him about the problem.

On Monday, Crile called Klein into his office and said they definitely had to make the change. He would record a line of narration from Wallace to cover the mistake and for picture use a shot of Westmoreland listening. Klein found a listening shot from the first act and inserted it into the sequence, which was in the fifth act.

Thus, when he was interviewed, Westmoreland was responding to a question that had an inaccuracy in it. When the inaccuracy was deleted, it changed the question. Westmoreland's response remained the same. So in the finished broadcast the general was not answering the same question he had been asked in his interview.

Lost in the flurry over the last-minute corrections was another problem which Klein told us he found deeply disturbing. He said Sam Adams had informed him earlier that week that Lt. Gen. Phillip Davidson, the former intelligence chief who was supposedly on his deathbed, was in good health. In a taxi the next night, Klein had passed this on to Crile, but the producer said nothing. The information got buried during the frantic days before air.

General Davidson was there when Gen. William Westmoreland and his supporters issued their angry rubuttals to the Vietnam program at the Army-Navy Club in Washington on January 26, 1982. Crile, Klein, Sam Adams, Grace Diekhaus, and Carolyne McDaniel watched by closed circuit in an office at the Ford Building, across the street from the CBS Broadcast Center. When Westmoreland brought up what he considered to be a correction letter about enemy-infiltration figures, Klein said he mouthed silently to Crile: "What's this all about?" He described Adams as slumped in his chair as if to say: Why is he doing this?

According to Klein, Adams came to his cutting room the following day and said: "We have to come clean. The premise is not accurate. Westy is overburdened in his role in the film. He was not concealing evidence. LBJ had to know."

"It's a little bit late," Klein said he told Adams. "Didn't you discuss this with Crile?" Adams replied: "Yes, I discussed it with him all along. We are involved in a cover-up while we are accusing others of a cover-up."

It was at this time, Klein said, that he felt he had a professional responsibility after ten months on the program to speak with Andrew Lack, the senior producer, "Instinctively," he told me, "I knew you cannot suppress the truth." On February 24, he went to Lack's office for a three-hour meeting. The editor expressed his concerns: the Westmoreland documents; the failure of Crile to interview former CIA man, George Carver, who had said at the news conference that it was he who had resolved the order-of-battle controversy with Westmoreland; and Sam Adams's expressed doubts about the program's premise. Klein said that Lack asked him: "Why the hell didn't we interview Carver?"

Klein said he told Lack: "There is a potential problem here, and we must address it with some kind of dignity." Lack said he felt that Klein should discuss the matter with Crile. "What good would that do?" the editor replied. "He has lied to me in the past. I don't trust him." He told Lack to look at the documents in the program's files and give him his interpretation.

The summit meeting was held in Lack's office—Crile, Lack, and Klein. Crile called Mike Wallace and asked him to join them. According to Klein, Wallace looked at the Westmoreland documents and said to the editor: "You know I was only a cosmetic factor in the show." Klein replied: "Yes, I understand."

"When did you see these documents?" Wallace asked him. "Why didn't you come up with them earlier?"

"I didn't know they existed until last week," said Klein.

Wallace thumbed through the documents again and according to Klein said, "Well, Westy has lied. He's lied before." Then, Klein said, he turned to him: "I respect your opinion, but this sort of thing happens all the time on *60 Minutes*."

Shortly after the meeting, Klein went on a two-week vacation. When he returned, he was told by Lack that he had spoken with Sam Adams, who denied saying the program's premise was wrong. Lack said he saw no sense in conducting any kind of inquiry since it would take at least a year.

In March, Klein received a call from Sam Adams, who invited him to visit him at his farm in Virginia. Again Klein went over what he considered to be the program's inadequacies. He told us that Adams agreed the program had oversimplified the story and put too much of a burden on Westmoreland.

Klein said he thought the decent thing to do was to tell Crile about his meeting with Adams. "Let's you, Sam, and me get together," he said Crile told him. "By the way, are you the guy talking to *TV Guide?*" It was then that the magazine was concluding its investigation of the Vietnam program. Klein said he had never spoken with anyone from the magazine but he had talked about the show with colleagues at CBS.

At the end of April, Wallace said he wanted to speak with Klein. Wallace asked who was leaking to *TV Guide*. Klein described him as accusatory and angry. Klein asked him whether he believed in the film. Wallace said he had been reading transcripts and talking to people. Again he said to Klein: "You know what my role was," and walked out.

Later, in Crile's office, Klein said Wallace told him: "I'm not going to leave Crile dangling."

Klein said he replied: "What about all of us, our careers?"

We had spent four hours with Ira Klein and would spend another at his request with him and his assistant, Phyllis Hurwitz, who confirmed his story and had no new information. One question we did not ask either of them was: "Did you leak the story to *TV Guide?*" Klein was a prime candidate, but he had denied it, and we were not persuaded that the question of who leaked was important to our inquiry.

Ira Klein's accusations were detailed and damning. Our job in the days ahead would be to hear the story from others, especially those he had accused of mismanagement and shoddy journalism. Was Ira Klein engaged in a vendetta or had he told us the truth?

Alex Alben, *the researcher*

On June 8, he came into our office, a short, squarely built young man in his early twenties, preppy in his dress and at first somewhat guarded in his answers. He had left the Vietnam unit before the program was completed and entered the Stanford Law School, not an easy admission. He was obviously bright and, as soon became apparent, inexperienced in television journalism. We would interview him again on June 10.

Alben said he had heard of the issue of undercounting enemy strength in Vietnam when he came to the project but did not know Sam Adams nor had he read his article in *Harper's*. At first, Alben felt unclear about the direction he was supposed to take as researcher. He read about the Vietnam War and went through the Pentagon Papers. He still did not understand what the progression of the program would be.

Did he know from the outset what the premise of the show was? "Not exactly. Crile gave me bits and pieces of what I was supposed to do but not the big picture. There was some element of secrecy about the project. Others on the unit told me that's the way things worked on *CBS Reports*."

About a month into the assignment, Crile let him read the Blue Sheet after what he called "some misdirected and unproductive work." Then he told Alben to focus on President Johnson's visit to Cam Ranh Bay in October of 1966.

Was the premise of the program logical? "This was a paradox I grappled with. Given Westmoreland's desire to increase manpower, why would he underestimate enemy strength in Vietnam? The paradox remained with me as long as I was on the show, and I believe it was a concern of Crile's, too."

Did he believe they made the right selection of people to appear on the program? "General Davidson should have been contacted, but Sam told us he was ill. In a perfect world we would have had him and also Col. Charles Morris. The multiple roles of George Carver of the CIA could not be conveyed in a documentary. But no one was ever afraid that an interview with him would blow the entire thesis out of the water."

Why not try to find library footage and let LBJ speak for himself? "I called the LBJ Library in Austin and they told me they didn't have any outtake film of him. I was unable to get transcripts of the LBJ interviews that CBS News had done."

I knew a good deal about the Johnson interviews, which had been conducted by Walter Cronkite. I was executive producer of the series. I also knew that one episode, "The Decision to Halt the Bombing," filmed in 1969 and broadcast on February 6, 1970, was in house with all of its outtakes and readily available. I checked the transcript and found that President Johnson had made these points:

—We were ready for Tet. My advisors told me in the late fall that a substantial move by the North Vietnamese was underway. The troop deployments, captured documents, information available to us said it was coming but we didn't think they would do it exactly at Tet, a religious holiday.

—Westmoreland cancelled leaves so as to be prepared.

—On the presidential trip to Australia, I said we were going to get an all-out kamikaze attack.

—Tet was a military victory for us.

—General Westmoreland called it.

—The North Vietnamese took very heavy casualties.

It could certainly be argued that some of these statements by the President of the United States might have been useful to include in the broadcast.

What about the interviews conducted for the program? Alben said: "I read all of the raw interviews. At first I thought we used them well.

Then I began to feel we should have used more complete statements. Perhaps it was inexperience. I didn't understand how to do this."

What about the three-hour interview with Walt W. Rostow, LBJ's special assistant, none of which was used? "I agreed with the decision not to use any of Rostow. I pulled Rostow memos from the LBJ Library and came to the conclusion that, given Rostow's view of the war and his relationship with the President, it would have given us too much trouble explaining his position. It would have been good to get someone else from the White House. I began to pull 1968 campaign footage to underscore what Westmoreland meant by political pressure coming from Washington, but there was not enough time."

Was Sam Adams coached for his interview with Mike Wallace? "He was not and I told Sally Bedell [of *TV Guide*] that when she asked me. There were two sessions of a couple of hours each, broken by lunch. I was there most of the time and so were Joe Zigman and Ira Klein. We were trying to get Sam away from his chronologies and get him to talk to camera. Crile was concerned that Adams would talk of his experiences and not talk of what he learned as a reporter. I was giving Adams feedback but never shaping his answers editorially."

Alben said Crile wrote out the questions for Mike Wallace to ask Adams. Alben said he submitted some questions but 90 percent of those on the list were Crile's.

What about the Westmoreland "correction" letter? "When it came in, Crile asked me: 'What is this?' I told him it was documents I already had. That was all he asked."

What about the letter to Westmoreland, delivered the night before the interview, with the five points to be covered in his interview? "I was with Crile when the letter was drafted. I wanted to be more explicit. I felt the real subject of the interview, American intelligence and the order-of-battle controversy, should have been higher up. Crile probably did not tell Westmoreland what we were covering. His letter may have hidden our real goal."

And what about the word "conspiracy"? "The word was not freely bandied about. I did not use it. In retrospect, it was a mistake to use the word 'conspiracy.' "

Alben told us he did not find Crile to be intransigent. "He respected people's opinions and would listen. You could argue with him over points."

Alben said he spoke to Crile by phone from California after the *TV Guide* article appeared. He said Crile told him there would be an investigation of the show.

Carolyne McDaniel, *the secretary*

On June 11, George Crile's secretary and part-time researcher walked nervously into my office as if she were being followed. A full-blown woman in her twenties, about five-seven with black, shoulder-length hair and glasses, she aspired to be an opera singer and seemed physically right for the role. Klein told me she sometimes practiced arias in an empty office at the production center.

"Crile was anxious for me to see you," she said. She told us she had been a social worker, was new at CBS, and had no interest in a career in television or journalism.

Her attitude toward Crile was decidedly ambivalent. She would damn and praise him in virtually the same sentence. "He is a manipulator," she told us, "yet he has the ability to get people to work their tails off for him. The project was disorganized from the beginning. Crile is the most disorganized person I know. Sometimes I could not figure out his desk.

"I told him in a cutting room one night, for someone in communications, you have the worst skills in communicating. I think this helped things a bit.

"At a certain point, I hated Crile. He would ask you to come in early. You show up and he calls an hour late to say he just woke up. He was not considerate of other people's time. He expected me to do research, to get food for the staff, and to do personal errands for him. But there are also lots of good things about George.

"He's a brilliant man and reporter, but I think he does not like to be alone. He needed the confidence of someone at his side like Grace Diekhaus and Susan Lyne. That caused extra problems. I found that when Grace and Susan got involved, we were on the outside.

"Crile had few friends in our area. I was told he did not get along well with other people he had worked with. On our unit the troops began to be against Crile. I am ashamed I behaved that way."

She said Howard Stringer was aware that Crile drove people crazy and was disorganized but at the same time he was confident of his ability. She quoted Stringer as saying: "Crile is not here for his weaknesses."

McDaniel was scarcely flattering about Ira Klein. "I believe there was an ego problem between Ira and Crile. George would come and talk to me, then Ira would come and talk to me. They weren't talking to each other, and I would become the go-between. It was as if I was the in-house social worker.

"Ira and George always had different accounts of the same conversation. Crile would say one thing and Ira another. Ira felt he was part owner of the show. This feeling grew and became too large. After a while, it seemed to me that Ira wanted to make his own film.

"The attitudes on the show were bad. Ira, Phyllis Hurwitz, and I would trade Crile stories in the cutting room—not things of substance, small things. I am not proud of my feelings then. I was fatigued, but I realized I could not leave the show in the middle."

When Alex Alben left the unit to enter law school, McDaniel said she was given research responsibilities although she readily conceded she did not know much about journalism. "I did not have a good handle on this intelligence thing. It did not interest me," she told me.

Crile, she said, told her to go to the CBS News library and read back issues of the news magazines from the Vietnam War period. She said he wanted colorful passages describing the war that would be useful to him in writing the script for the program. She also went through transcripts of the *CBS Evening News* for the period, searching for stories that were relevant, but she could never find the videotapes she needed. She was also told to research the political climate of the time. She said Ira Klein told her that some of the people on the unit resented her being elevated into research.

"George allowed me to go into the cutting room," she told me, "but he did not want Alex Alben there. He said the chemistry was not right. Alex wanted too many facts and figures in the broadcast. He said I had a more visceral, gut reaction."

After she became involved in research, she said she told Crile that perhaps the notion of conspiracy was simplistic. "I told him that from what I had read, I did not believe LBJ did not know what was going on. Crile said to me: 'You're probably right, but it's not important to the essence of the show.' I told Sam Adams the same thing, but everyone seemed wishy-washy on this issue."

It was McDaniel who tried to phone General Davidson, then supposedly on his deathbed. She said she tried many times during the normal work day but could not reach him. She never tried him at night.

She told Crile and wondered why Davidson was not at home. She said Crile's answer was that Davidson was in a hospital dying, but he did not tell her what hospital.

McDaniel said she was shaken by the Westmoreland news conference. She told Sam Adams she did not believe LBJ did not know what was going on in Vietnam, and he tended to agree with her. Adams told McDaniel he had spoken to Crile about this but they did not have the evidence to prove the point. He said he had no doubt Westmoreland was the ringleader. McDaniel then went to Ira Klein and told him about her conversation with Adams.

"Telling Ira was probably wrong. All it did was fuel the fires. At that point everyone was angry with Crile, and no one knew how to vent his or her anger."

A couple of days later, she said Klein came her desk to say that Sam Adams had come to him and told him that he now believed the premise was wrong. "LBJ had to know. We've got to come clean on this."

McDaniel said she didn't believe Klein; he was simply repeating what she had told him. "Sam is very low-key. I don't believe he would come to a person on that level to complain."

Some final emotional and confusing observations from McDaniel:

"I won't cover up for anybody. . . ."

"People were cowards. They were afraid to complain. . . ."

"There was confusion and fear after the Westmoreland news conference. I was afraid of what the *TV Guide* story would do to CBS now. . . ."

"Westmoreland was a lousy general. I would have liked to see more time for the other side."

In all of my years at CBS, I could not remember seeing a production unit in the kind of disarray that had afflicted this one. I knew that the production of a ninety-minute documentary, to be run in prime time, was no easy assignment. There are abrasions, petty irritations, and personality clashes in every unit. The producer is especially vulnerable. In one ephemeral evening, a year's work and a quarter of a million dollars are squarely on the line. His reputation, indeed his job, may be riding on a single program.

I had seen my share of tensions at CBS News. I remembered one producer who never could sit through the final screening with the news division president. He would invariably have to rush to the men's room and throw up.

But when I thought of this unit, it had no parallel: A producer, George Crile, who conceded he was often disorganized, engaged in his first major effort alone; another producer, Grace Diekhaus, secretly working with him; a close friend of the producer, Susan Lyne, not on the staff of CBS News, involved in the production; an experienced associate producer, Joe Zigman, not allowed to participate fully; a film editor, Ira Klein, so antipathetic toward his boss he could not stand to be in the same room with him; a consultant, Sam Adams, immersed in a fifteen-year crusade, wandering in and out of cutting rooms and going on location; a researcher, Alex Alben, not familiar with documentary production; and a star correspondent, Mike Wallace, with little time to devote to the project at hand.

The documentary is a quintessential form of group journalism. I had seen other units beset, but they had managed to coalesce, rise above the irritations—petty and severe—and develop the necessary intellectual give-and-take and essential esprit to get the job done.

Our research and our first interviews had produced a catalogue of allegations about the broadcast and about its producer. We would now give George Crile an opportunity to reply to those charges.

10

FORGET PROCESS

Over the years, George Crile III has been called a zealot, a martyr, and a patrician. He has been described as brilliant, tenacious, ambitious, brave, arrogant, wrongheaded, combative, uncompromising, trusting, naive, and stubborn. He came to my office on June 15 for an interview that would last for six hours. A week later at his request there was a second, two-hour interview.

A self-assured man from the right side of the tracks, Crile had joined the network in 1976 and was thirty-five years old when CBS News assigned him to "The Uncounted Enemy." He was attractive to women and two had been co-producers in his previous productions. Judy Crichton worked with him on two: "The CIA's Secret Army" in 1977, which won an American Film Festival Blue Ribbon, and "The Battle for South Africa" in 1978, which won the George Foster Peabody Award and an Emmy. Bill Moyers was the correspondent for both, and the two programs ranked among the better documentaries produced by the news department over the years. Crile was known to tackle very difficult subjects, dig at them with unrelenting persistence, and come up with material that was often startling and news-breaking.

Grace Diekhaus was his co-producer in 1980 on a show called "Gay Power, Gay Politics," which was something less than a triumph and drew intense criticism from homosexual groups in San Francisco.

The program had accused the gay community of exerting pressure on politicians for its "special interest"; it suggested that San Francisco politics was controlled by the city's large homosexual population. A critical editing transgression was uncovered in a sequence showing Mayor Dianne Feinstein apologizing to a large group from the gay community for critical remarks she had made about them in a magazine interview. In the film, her apology was followed by cheering and clapping by the audience. Actually, the applause did not come until later in Mrs. Feinstein's speech. Moving it up made it appear as if she had been forgiven by the homosexual group.

Mayor Feinstein demanded an apology. She got one from CBS News after the now-defunct National News Council, responding to a complaint by three San Francisco groups, voted eleven to two that the documentary "exaggerated the political concessions to homosexuals and made those concessions appear as threats to public morals and safety." The network also confirmed that the applause in the Feinstein speech had been tampered with.

In writing about Crile in *The Washington Post*, Eleanor Randolph quoted a friend as saying he had been born into an extraordinary family, full of money, power, and immense amounts of energy. His grandfather and his father were prominent doctors in Cleveland. His grandfather, George Washington Crile, was a surgeon who established the Cleveland Clinic, today a massive medical complex which draws patients from all over the world. His father, Dr. George (Barney) Crile, Jr., also a distinguished surgeon and ahead of his time, was once censured by the Cleveland Medical Association for opposing radical mastectomy as the only choice for women suffering from breast cancer. When his first wife died, Barney Crile married Helga Sandburg, daughter of the poet and biographer, Carl Sandburg.

After graduating from Trinity College and a stint in the Marine Corps, George Crile III turned not to medicine but to journalism. He began his career as a reporter for the syndicated columnist, Drew Pearson. In 1970, according to Eleanor Randolph, he met Walter Ridder, the publishing executive, at the Washington home of his aunt, Kay Halle, and asked him for a job. Ridder hired him as a reporter on his Gary *Post-Tribune*. It proved to be a stormy and inauspicious relationship.

In Gary, Crile had access to the publisher and could circumvent the working editors. This did not contribute to his popularity. He wrote a long piece about the city's tax assessor, accusing him of taking bribes. He turned it in to Ridder, and it was ignored.

In 1972, Crile was promoted to the Washington bureau but he

would not let go of the Gary tax assessor investigation. He had shown his story to a Ralph Nader staff member, who began to leak it to a small weekly paper that had started up in Gary. When Walter Ridder found out, he promptly fired Crile. Another reporter for the *Post-Tribune* continued to pursue the investigation and found that Crile was on the right track. With new sources this reporter broke the story and the tax assessor went to jail. Crile, who had joined *Harper's*, also wrote an account of Gary and the tax assessor for the magazine and had some unkind things to say about the Ridders.

According to Eleanor Randolph, Ridder is still bitter. "I wouldn't publish a thing he produced without triple-checking it," the publisher told her. "He drove me crazy because he would come up with stories that were so fantastic, and he was so stubborn. If you didn't believe him or agree with him, he got angry."

Ridder's wife, Marie, called Crile's failure "in some ways sad. . . . If George had been more accurate or careful with his figures, he would have done so much better. He was not too far off the track."

In Washington in 1968, Crile had married 18-year-old Anne Patten, a descendant of John Jay, daughter of Susan Mary Alsop and stepdaughter of the columnist, Joseph Alsop. It was one of the fancier weddings of the season in that socially-inclined city. Among the guests were Robert S. McNamara, president of the World Bank; Paul H. Nitze, deputy secretary of defense; and Walt W. Rostow, national security adviser for President Lyndon B. Johnson. Ironically, sixteen years later in a courthouse in New York, all three were to testify against Crile in "the libel trial of the century"—General William C. Westmoreland, plaintiff, against CBS Inc., et al., defendants.

It was during that trial that the columnist, the late Joseph Kraft, an old friend of Crile's, would write of him: "Crile is a brilliant journalist of extraordinary tenacity who emerged from school in the late 1960s. Like many of his generation, he abhorred the war and was prone to look for conspiracy in its genesis and unfolding."

Later in his column, Kraft would ask this question about the documentary Crile had produced: ". . . how did CBS, with one of the best professional news organizations in the world, become so imprudent in editing a program that tilted so sharply on such a complex question?"

Crile seemed tense when he came to my office on that June day in 1982. He had phoned me when he first heard of my assignment, saying he

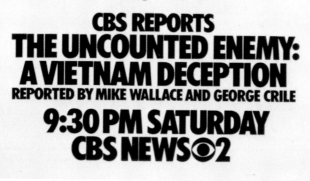

CONSPIRACY

CBS Reports reveals the shocking decisions made at the highest level of military intelligence to suppress and alter critical information on the number and placement of enemy troops in Vietnam. A deliberate plot to fool the American public, the Congress, and perhaps even the White House into believing we were winning a war that in fact we were losing.

Who lied to us? Why did they do it? What did they hope to gain? How did they succeed so long? And what were the tragic consequences of their deception?

Tomorrow night the incredible answer to these questions. At last.

CBS REPORTS
THE UNCOUNTED ENEMY:
A VIETNAM DECEPTION
REPORTED BY MIKE WALLACE AND GEORGE CRILE
9:30 PM SATURDAY
CBS NEWS ⊙2

1. The CBS advertisement preceding the broadcast.

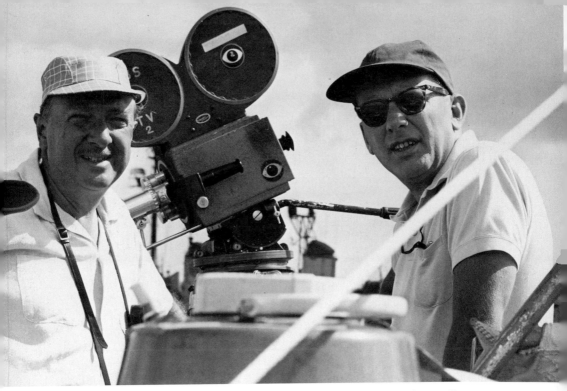

2. The author and Walter Cronkite on the aircraft carrier *Coral Sea* off Vietnam, shooting for the *Twentieth Century* broadcast "Air Rescue," 1965.

3. Cam Ranh Bay, October 26, 1966. Johnson awarding a medal to Westmoreland during visit to troops.

4. Westmoreland and the President reviewing strategy at the White House.

5. General Westmoreland, President Johnson, General Nguyen Cao Ky (Prime Minister of South Vietnam), and U.S. Ambassador Ellsworth Bunker, December 23, 1967.

6. Westmoreland meeting with reporters, January 26, 1982, demanding an apology from Mike Wallace. "It was all there, the arrogance, the color, the drama, the contrived plot, the close shots, everything but the truth."

7. Howard Stringer.

8. Edward M. Joyce.

9. Van Gordon Sauter.

10. Federal Judge Pierre Leval, who heard the case.

11. Westmoreland, with his lawyer Dan Burt, arriving at U.S. District Court, October 8, 1984.

12. George Crile, with CBS attorney David Boies on the right, outside the courthouse.

13. Retired Army Lt. General Daniel Graham, who now heads an organization supporting President Reagan's "Star Wars" program.

14. Walt W. Rostow arriving at Federal Court, October 14, 1984, ready to testify for Westmoreland. Rostow was National Security Adviser under Lyndon Johnson.

15. Mike Wallace at the federal courthouse.

16. CBS attorney David Boies outside the courthouse.

17. Westmoreland arriving to testify at the trial, November 15, 1984.

18. Sam Adams leaving the court-house, January 9, 1985.

19. Dan Burt talking to reporters in New York.

20. Major General Joseph A. McChristian leaving the courthouse, February 5, 1985.

21. George Crile leaving the courthouse after testifying, February 6, 1985. Crile accused Westmoreland of "not being candid" when he was interviewed for the broadcast.

22. Colonel Gains Hawkins arriving at court. Hawkins was chief of the Order of Battle branch. He testified he had arbitrarily reduced enemy strength figures and said: "I consider this to have been a coverup."

23.-24. The news conference following settlement of the suit, February 18, 1985. Above: Westmoreland with his wife, Katherine. Below: Westmoreland and his attorney Dan Burt.

25. Van Gordon Sauter at the news conference.

26. Mike Wallace answering questions during a CNN interview after the out-of-court settlement.

27. Pham Van Dong, Walter Cronkite, and the author at the old French Governor's Palace in Hanoi, February 26, 1985, shooting for *CBS Reports*: "Honor, Duty, and a War Called Vietnam," which aired April 22.

28. Westmoreland walking across the Brooklyn Bridge at the start of a parade honoring Vietnam war veterans, May 7, 1985, the largest tickertape parade in the city's history in terms of the number of marchers.

was pleased I had been selected; he was certain I would be fair. I wondered now whether he had spoken with Alben and McDaniel and had been warned that the questioning might be sharp and uncomfortable. He had a knapsack, filled with documents, which he put on the floor, then he took off his jacket. I introduced him to Wertheim and Pierce, and the six-hour session began. There would be a brief interruption for lunch—the two researchers and I going to the CBS cafeteria, Crile leaving rather hurriedly to go off on his own.

At lunch, I told Wertheim that I thought he had been forthcoming and direct in his answers. I had expected him to turn stubborn or combative, but so far he had been low-keyed and was answering questions without any apparent evasion. I asked her what she thought. She said she agreed and the only thing she had noticed was that when he left our small, hot office, he was wringing wet. I didn't read too much into that; so was I.

The interview broke down into these areas:

Theme

How would Crile define the premise, the thesis, the theme of the program? I asked him. *TV Guide* had stated it this way:

> The evidence amassed by CBS seemed to prove the U.S. military's intelligence operation in Vietnam, led by General Westmoreland, conspired to deceive President Lyndon Johnson, the Congress and the American public. Beginning in 1967, the documentary charges, Westmoreland had systematically underreported to his superiors the size and strength of the enemy, in order to make it appear he was indeed winning the "war of attrition."

Crile maintained the way the magazine had set up the premise was misleading.

"What happened in 1967 was that evidence became available to indicate the enemy size was much bigger than was previously reported or understood. The CIA was at a disadvantage. They didn't have the vast number of analysts that the military command had. The CIA had Sam Adams poring over captured enemy documents. . . .

"Either the military was looking through rose-colored glasses or cooking the books. Our evidence showed that on higher numbers the military came to the same conclusion as the CIA, but instead of passing this on, the military commenced to suppress that information. *TV Guide* reduced this to an argument over whether this shadowy group—the Secret Defense militia—should be included in the order of battle. That misrepresents what the show was about."

I told Crile there was another definition of the show's thesis in his White Paper and perhaps he liked it better:

> That in 1967, American military and civilian intelligence discovered evidence indicating the existence of a dramatically larger enemy than previously reported . . . that instead of alerting the country, U.S. military intelligence under General Westmoreland commenced to suppress and alter its intelligence reports, *in order to conceal this discovery from the American public, the Congress, and perhaps even the President.*

Crile: "Now that I look at it, I would put a period after the word "reports" and eliminate the rest of the sentence (his suggested deletion is in italics).

Conspiracy

What about "conspiracy," used only once in the script, but the word that had become the most critical allegation in the program?

"Oh absolutely, the word is properly used," said Crile. "Yes, it was used in the Blue Sheet, but I never dreamed I would use the word 'conspiracy' in the script until I had talked to everyone. It was the only word that worked for me to explain the pattern of events. I saw this as official misconduct by a variety of people. It was a violation of the code of military justice."

"I understand the dynamics of the Blue Sheet," I said to him, "but the word 'conspiracy' appears twenty-four times and the word 'conspirator' is used five times in that document. One would have the impression your mind was made up."

"The program was not sold on the basis of a conspiracy but on the basis of Sam Adams," he replied.

"How about the print ads for the show—CONSPIRACY in big type right across the middle?" (The ad had been prepared at Black Rock by the advertising department and had been approved by Van Gordon Sauter and Ed Joyce. Crile had had no input in this.)

"The ad bothered me. I never saw the ad before the program. It gave me the heebie-jeebies. The ad was not to my liking."

The 9–2 Equation

Was the program out of balance? On one side, there was Sam Adams and eight former military and CIA officers supporting his thesis. On the other side there was Westmoreland and General Graham, who got twenty-one seconds on camera.

"It wasn't a question of for or against," Crile explained. "I don't consider McChristian, Hawkins, Cooley, Hamscher, and Meacham as partisans. They weren't expressing opinions. They were stating what happened as analysts."

Still with ninety minutes of air time, was there no room to include some of the people who disagreed with Adams—George Carver and General Davidson, for example?

"In Act I, the show covers the discovery of a much larger enemy. The source was Westmoreland. There was really no one else to talk to."

Graham could have gone on the air to argue that the enemy-strength figures were not undercounted.

"The show in my mind was a presenting of evidence. It starts with McChristian and Hawkins on Westmoreland's decision not to pass on higher enemy-strength figures. I interviewed the entire MACV delegation. There was no controversy."

"Are you saying that the broadcast was not controversial? That Sam Adams makes no charges?"

"I don't see Adams delivering charges. It's not Adams's thesis. This is important. Sam developed it, but I don't think it needs to be his thesis any more. The people we had on camera were bureaucrats with no interest in going on the air. They simply said what happened. In general, these were admissions by people of things they personally did. It wasn't whistle blowing."

"I understand these people on camera said they did certain things," I said. "But weren't there people who said it wasn't true? How could it not be controversial, given history and the impact of television? The ratio was in effect nine to two. You think this was fair and balanced?"

"What I'm really saying is we were dealing with people, working people, who had hands-on evidence . . . I rightly or wrongly was laboring under the impression that we were presenting unchallengeable facts—what people say happened."

"Five times Westmoreland says it makes no sense for a commander to downgrade the size of the enemy in time of war. Did you ever consider letting him say that?"

"Sure, you could have done a lot of things in fairness to Westmoreland. I never expected Westmoreland to say on air that he blocked numbers. What he said was that he was not accepting numbers and that meant blocked or suppressed to me."

Coddling Friendly Witnesses

Crile strongly disagreed with the charge that friendly witnesses had been coddled while those opposing the program's thesis had been treated harshly. I read for him excerpts from the Sam Adams transcript—"Sam Adams is there. He's Paul Revere" . . . "You were perfect . . ."

"I ask you, George, is that normal? Words have been used for this—coached, leading questions, soft questions. Here you have a man who literally, it appears, was taken by the hand."

"Oh, Bud. If you look at transcripts of other shows—60 Minutes, CBS Reports—you'll find the same thing."

"I don't see any of that in Westmoreland, Graham, or Rostow."

"On Adams, I could not dictate to Mike. He ran off with his own speculative questions with Sam. It was not to my liking."

"Did you give Mike the questions in advance?"

"Oh yes."

"Well, that's not a first."

"Not a first! It's always done that way. In Bill Moyers's "The CIA's Secret Army," I did all of the questions for him. In the South Africa piece with Moyers, I did all of the questions. For Ed Bradley, he always gets the questions. . . . If I didn't hand the correspondent the questions, we wouldn't have a show. Especially when it's as wildly complicated as this one was. . . . Overall, Moyers and Wallace are most actively involved with producers."

"Do they do their homework?"

"Most of the time."

Crile said Wallace had never heard of Sam Adams before they did the interview. They made an odd couple: Adams, who did not watch television, had never seen Mike Wallace on the air. Crile said he had spent a great deal of time with Wallace trying to brief him and bring him up to snuff.

"What Mike does is totally unprecedented. What he does with a producer—he rattles them, he shakes them."

I had heard that Wallace could be demanding and dictatorial with his producers on *60 Minutes*. As he often said: "It's my face hanging out there." I had worked with him only once—not on location but as the executive producer in New York. In 1967, I assigned him to go to Israel to report "How Israel Won the War." It was an account of the smashing Israeli victory in the Six Day War. Wallace was still relatively new at CBS News; it was a year before the launching of *60 Minutes*, and he could not have been easier to work with or more cooperative.

What about Adams being present at some of the interviews and actually participating by throwing questions and coaching?

"Coaching?" Crile replied. "As far as I understood it, we were dealing with interviews, trying to get on the record something that's not controversial."

"Not controversial?"

"These were building blocks, not areas of speculation."

"What adversarial interviews were there? Westmoreland, Graham, Rostow. Three. Correct me if I'm wrong."

"There is a place for an adversarial interview, but why do you want to go adversarial if a person is confessing?"

The Two Allen Interviews

I asked Crile why George Allen had been interviewed twice, once on May 26 and then again on June 29, 1981, both times in New York.

"There was nothing basically wrong with the first interview," he said. "This was a personal thing with me. Allen was particularly concerned about ratting on the CIA. He looked like hell, looked guilty, on those questions about the CIA. He was concerned about looking like a whistle blower. When it came to questions as to why the CIA caved in [to MACV], he looked very bad although it was good theater."

Did he tell his superiors about the double interview?

"No, I didn't tell Andy Lack or Howard Stringer that I did the interview twice. I don't know if they knew. No, I didn't know this was a violation of CBS News guidelines. Why was it?"

"How could it be spontaneous and unrehearsed if you interviewed him twice?"

"I honestly was not aware of it being a violation of the guidelines."

Why did he bring Allen to Ira Klein's editing room and show him interviews of others filmed for the program?

"For the same reason as the second interview. I know it's against the sensibilities of everyone here . . . I don't think what I did there was right. Allen was caught in stage paralysis. He felt badly about doing the interview . . . I said to him: 'Look, George, you shouldn't feel alone. Come on, I'll show some others to you.' "

Two years later, at the Westmoreland-CBS trial, Crile was asked whether Westmoreland had been given an opportunity for a second interview. "No," Crile replied, "he didn't request one."

Westmoreland

Crile said it was not difficult to get Westmoreland to agree to appear on the program, but that it was hard to get through to him what they were talking about—intelligence under his command.

"He has always had a good cover story. . . . We told him we were doing the documentary on the role of intelligence using Tet as a jumping-off point, and were we alert to enemy strength?"

In one telephone conversation, after reading Westmoreland the five areas he wanted to discuss, Crile said they spoke about the CIA and the general brought up Sam Adams and his story but never asked him: "Is this the Adams theory?"

Why did Crile find it necessary, after reading the letter with its five points on the phone, to hand-deliver it to Westmoreland at the Plaza Hotel the night before the interview?

"I wrote the letter to get on the record and spell it out to Westmoreland. . . . Short of spelling out the accusations, I did everything I could."

"He seemed ill-prepared."

"There's something more fundamental here. This was the commander of U.S. forces talking on a critical issue of the war. We were dealing with a very disturbing report which he blocked. . . ."

"I had the sense that he didn't understand why he was here, that he was not well informed."

"I have to get back to this. He was wearing the mantle of MacArthur and Eisenhower. These are serious charges."

"Do you think Westmoreland was somewhat inept?"

"Yes. He seems stupid."

"Well, if he doesn't come off well, maybe you should have got someone else to defend him."

"Westmoreland was not the show."

"He came out as the heavy, George."

Just before the interview, Crile had written a note to Mike Wallace: "Now all you have to do is break General Westmoreland and we have the whole thing aced." Later in trial testimony, Crile would explain that the term "break" was "obviously a hyperbole." He was referring to the large challenge that Wallace faced in view of "General Westmoreland's continued practice of stonewalling and denying that there had been this fundamental contradiction within his own command. . . ."

I asked him whether Westmoreland had said after the interview that he had been "rattlesnaked"?

"Something like that," Crile replied.

What about the *Meet the Press* excerpt involving enemy infiltration just before Tet and Crile's deletion of the line "But they do have the capability of stepping this up"? Why was he so incensed that the line had been left in?

"I didn't want the line in there. It was contradicted a page before in the *Meet the Press* transcript."

He looked in his knapsack for the page but did not have it.

He did not respond when I asked him: "If it was contradicted on the page before, how did you know which statement was correct?"

What about the big hand signal to Klein to lower the sound so that the line could not be heard during the Sauter screening? He said that Joe Fackovec, the second film editor, had cut the line from the piece and Ira Klein had put it back in. "That's what made me mad."

What about the letter from General Westmoreland of June 9, 1981, in which he told Crile and Wallace that the infiltration figure of 20,000 which he had given in his interview was in error and the figure of 5,500 to 6,000 stated in 1967 on *Meet the Press* was "generally correct"?

"I didn't see it as a correction letter," Crile told me. "He never phoned to say I erred on the 20,000 figure. The cover letter never mentioned a correction or asked for one. What I believe is that Westmoreland remembered the facts and forgot the cover story."

After receiving the Westmoreland letter, Crile wrote to Wallace: "Westmoreland doesn't bring anything to our attention that is particularly relevant. Certainly nothing that causes concern and requires a new look at anything we have been asserting."

Rostow

The former special assistant to President Johnson was interviewed by Mike Wallace for three hours; none of what he said was used.

Rostow knew before the broadcast that he would not be included. Crile informed him of this by letter on January 15, 1982. He explained why: The broadcast was essentially evidence that General Westmoreland's command had suppressed and altered critical intelligence on the enemy during the year preceding Tet, and Rostow had told them he knew nothing about it. Therefore, he was not in a position to comment authoritatively about the premise of the broadcast.

On January 27, 1982, four days after the broadcast, Rostow wrote an angry letter to Crile which began:

> As the enclosed indicates, I accepted the high cost of losing a cheerful Saturday night to see what you and Mr. Wallace made of the VC order of battle struggle. Evidently, I was disappointed. And my final question is honest. I can't for the life of me, figure out why you would use expensive, prime time at this point in the nation's history to produce something as grotesquely distorted and misleading as that. . . . On the other hand, I am too old and have been around too long to try to assess other people's motives.

Rostow went on to say that no apology was necessary for dropping him from the program.

> I accepted your invitation to participate because I felt it to be a duty as a former public servant. I was also impressed by the seriousness of the research you and your staff conducted. On the other hand, I was, frankly, appalled by the ignorance and crudity of some of the propositions put to me in New York and realized that I was under some risk of having extracts from what I said used in contexts which I might not approve—in the best of faith from your perspective.

Rostow denied he had ever pressured the CIA. ". . . as an old intelligence officer, I would never do it. I would hope and expect Helms [Richard Helms, CIA director] would raise hell with me and the President if I did."

Rostow followed up with a letter on February 7 to the *New York Times* stating that the program's conclusion that "Lyndon Johnson himself was victimized by mendacious intelligence [before the Tet Offensive] is false and those who produced the documentary know it is false."

Crile replied to the *Times* a week later that in his letter Rostow had not challenged "the testimony of the former intelligence officers who appeared in the documentary." Crile then went on to emphasize another point. *TV Guide* had quoted him as saying that if Rostow had said in his interview what he said in his *Times* letter, he would have used him in the program. Crile declared that the magazine had misquoted him. They had confused Rostow's letter to the *Times* with a Rostow "Memorandum for the Record," which Crile said he had written to the LBJ Library on January 25.

Comparing the two, I found that all of the points in the *Times* letter had been made by Rostow in his interview with Wallace. One key point in his "Memorandum" had not been made in the interview: that the enemy-infiltration rate may have been higher than 25,000 a month. Rostow wrote: "This background is required to understand the grotesque Crile-Wallace misrepresentation of the pre-Tet North Vietnamese infiltration rate. What was happening in the autumn of 1967 was not an 'increase in infiltration'; it was a quite massive invasion by fresh, regular North Vietnamese units. . . . The 'infiltration rate' may well have been *higher for a few months than 25,000* [emphasis added]. Everyone concerned, including President Johnson, knew this."

This was in direct conflict with Rostow's interview statements:

WALLACE: . . . The MACV analysts were reporting upwards of 25,000 North Vietnamese coming down the Ho Chi Minh Trail each month and all of their reports were blocked.

ROSTOW: This is something I don't know but what I can tell you is that's not what President Johnson was looking at.

Later in the interview, Rostow added: "I'd like to see the evidence. I don't know what the evidence is because they didn't mount that kind of order-of-magnitude attack."

In the interview with Wallace, Rostow did make these points which the producer considered and then elected not to use:

—Rostow had informed LBJ that there was a debate going on between MACV and CIA about enemy-strength figures.

—Helms would tell LBJ at the Tuesday luncheons that there were various estimates of enemy strength—"on the one hand there are these views, there are those views, this is my personal view."

—CIA gave one figure, MACV another. CIA's was higher. The President was fully informed about this.

—He had not heard of Westmoreland "blocking" higher enemy-strength estimates.

"I agonized over whether to use Rostow," Crile told me. "I finally had to drop him for time. . . . The problem was Rostow was contradictory and in some places unresponsive. . . . No one has ever accused Rostow of being a liar but people do say he filtered information to LBJ. . . . He was considered intellectually dishonest in the academic community, which is why he wasn't able to get any positions with Northeast universities. The Rostow interview was a colossal problem for us to cope with."

Carver

Crile interviewed George A. Carver, Jr., on January 11, 1982, at Georgetown University's Center for Strategic and International Studies in Washington, where Carver was a senior fellow. No cameras were present; it was twelve days before air and the Vietnam program was locked up. Carver remarked to Crile that "the program must be in the can," and in his words, Crile "did not disagree."

Carver was the CIA's deputy director of Vietnamese affairs from 1966 to 1973 and was George Allen's boss. It was Carver who went to Saigon in early September 1967 to carry on the difficult negotiations with General Westmoreland over the enemy order-of-battle figures. It was Carver who had sent CIA director Richard Helms a famous cable on September 13, 1967, when he and Westmoreland came to an agreement: "Circle now squared . . . we have now agreed on a set of figures Westmoreland endorses." According to Sam Adams, the phrase "we have squared the circle" came from an essay by the English philosopher Thomas Hobbes about whom Carver had written his Oxford dissertation. "I took it to mean we had done the seemingly impossible," said Adams.

The deal that was hammered out provided an estimate of enemy strength of 224,000–249,000 plus 75,000–85,000 in the political cadre, for a total of 299,000–334,000. The controversial Self-Defense forces, those black-pajamaed irregulars, would not be counted in the order of battle but would be described verbally in the estimates sent to President Johnson. It was noted they had run as high as 150,000.

Crile made notes of his meeting with Carver, some of which the former CIA officer would claim were inaccurate. I asked Crile why he had not put Carver on camera. "Would you say that Carver was articulate?"

"He's brilliant. It was going to be Carver or Allen all along."

"Allen is so tight on camera, you say, so inhibited. And his boss is so articulate."

"Allen was the most honorable, spoke with force and integrity. Carver was identified by Joe Kraft and others as Rostow's man at the CIA. He had a willingness to think intelligence was the piece of paper that can get through the bureaucracy. I felt that the ability to get Allen to come on camera was a major coup. If Allen had not come on, I would have felt compelled to have Carver on. But Carver was in a terrible position having caved in."

"Wasn't that good to have on the show?"

"The CIA story wasn't the story in the show. It was a judgment call. Carver's position was firmly etched in documents in my file. He caved in; his position flip-flopped. I could have turned the tables and tried to roast Carver."

"Couldn't you have let Carver tell his story and let the audience decide, which we often do around here, George?"

Morris

Another officer who was interviewed late and off camera by Crile was Col. Charles A. Morris, who was in charge of intelligence estimates and evaluations for MACV in 1967 and 1968. A memo to me from Crile said the interview took place by phone in December 1981, "about a week or ten days before we locked up the show." *TV Guide* had charged: "Crile says that Morris confirmed the documentary's story, although Crile cannot explain why he left this important information until it was too late to include it." (Morris denied to us that he supported CBS's allegations.)

In the notes of his conversation with Morris, Crile wrote: "I tell Morris that Westmoreland had told us the infiltration figure was about 20,000 a month in the fall of 1967, and Morris replies: 'That's on the conservative side' but agrees that that was roughly the size."

As to the statement by General Westmoreland on *Meet the Press* that enemy infiltration in late 1967 ranged between 5,500 and 6,000 a month, Crile quoted Morris as saying: "Westmoreland knew better at the time, and you've got to remember one little thing. Westmoreland was a pawn of LBJ." Crile also quoted Morris as saying that there was terrific pressure from the White House concerning the so-called crossover point. This was an analysis championed by then Lt. Col. Daniel Graham, which claimed that a point had been reached where U.S. Troops were knocking out more of the Vietnamese than they could replace.

Crile pressed Morris on what he regarded as an inconsistency. How could the enemy be suffering a net loss and at the same time be beefing up its forces?

"Why have you just said he's no longer able to sustain this rate of infiltration," he asked the colonel, "and then say they're building up?"

According to Crile's notes, Morris replied: "The only way of answering this is to say we screwed up and we didn't want to say it."

Crile's notes then concluded: "He agrees with the premise that the American public was misled."

At the Westmoreland news conference directly after the program was broadcast, Morris had taken a different position: "Had General Westmoreland told me to lie about figures, I would have resigned my commission, taken the consequences and left. I swear to you that no such thing was ever done. Nor did General Westmoreland ever approach me or anyone else and say we cannot exceed a certain figure in the order of battle."

Crile phoned Morris again on January 30, a week after the broadcast. At first, he had told us he had no telephone tapes. Then he acknowledged that he had taped this conversation with Morris and gave us a copy. I did not ask whether he had told Morris he was taping him.

Crile asked Morris about his statement in their first conversation that "we screwed up." Morris replied: "We did screw up. There's enough bad we did over there to where if we just tell exactly what happened as best we can reconstruct it, we'd still be entitled to a knock on the wrist. But it was honest. There was nothing surreptitious about it. And that's what I really resent about the whole thrust of the program is that you said that Westmoreland and Phil Davidson, whom you people didn't even bother to contact, and Charlie Morris, Danny Graham were involved in a conspiracy. That's your word, I believe. Your program's word. A conspiracy to deceive, and that couldn't have been further from the truth."

"And God knows," Morris told Crile later, "if you had just done to us what we're entitled to, why, we wouldn't have had a leg to stand on.

But I just really am not at all interested in getting more information in your hand than I have time to sit down and give measured replies to."

Morris concluded: "I'll tell you for sure I wouldn't go on your program under any condition unless I had a legally binding contract and the right to edit it in the future."

Toby Wertheim phoned Colonel Morris on June 21, 1982. He told her: "I don't think I'd like to confirm anything. I was taken out of context by Crile. I might not want to say anything because I'm afraid this might wind up in court. The only thing I am willing to say on the phone is that Crile didn't use the general tenor or specifics of our conversation. The major thrust of our conversation [of December 1981] was misrepresented by him. Even the way the *TV Guide* story is written can be taken two ways. I deny that the original Crile story was correct."

Morris was right, of course, in predicting that the matter would wind up in court. As a witness for Westmoreland, he was asked whether he believed his superiors were under political pressure. After a long pause, the colonel replied: "I'm going to say yes, there was a certain amount of pressure. I just sensed it was an unpopular war and we had to get on with it. Like General Westmoreland said, no one likes bad news."

Graham

Lt. Gen. Daniel Graham, who as a lieutenant colonel was Westmoreland's chief of current intelligence and estimates, was interviewed by Mike Wallace for more than an hour, and two sound bites totaling twenty-one seconds were used. This was a judgment call on the part of Crile; in any documentary there are hundreds of such calls.

Among the statements General Graham made in unused portions of his interview were:

—He thought the MACV enemy-strength estimates were not too low but too high, 30 to 40 percent too high. They were getting all this pressure from the CIA to raise the figures.

—Adams extrapolated, and he was wrong.

—Despite the "crossover memo," he nevertheless agreed with General McChristian that "the enemy could still continue for an indefinite period of time."

—He denied that MACV had put a 300,000 cap on enemy-strength figures in its negotiations with CIA. "Where would the order have come from except from me, and I gave no such order. . . . Nobody told me there was some figure I couldn't go over or under."

—Westmoreland was wrong in his interview when he gave Wallace the figure of 20,000 for enemy infiltration. "You managed to confuse him, Mr. Wallace."

The matter of General Graham and his very brief appearance on the program was a question for Crile:

"Should you have used more of Graham?"

"Graham was not being candid. He was being demonstrably untruthful."

"Then maybe Graham was the wrong man to interview on camera. Why not Godding? [Gen. George Godding was head of the MACV delegation to the National Intelligence Estimate meeting at CIA Headquarters in Langley, Va., in 1967.] There was your horse's mouth."

"You can't underestimate the power of the Hawkins interview. He did state he received instructions [to maintain a ceiling] on paper during the meeting."

"The 300,000 ceiling was really pivotal?"

"I think so."

"We'll call Godding on the ceiling figure and see if he was refused permission from General Davidson to increase the figure."

We spoke with Godding on June 20, 1982. He told us he spoke with Crile four or five times but never quoted any number to him, and he said he would not quote any numbers to us. He said before leaving Saigon for the meeting at the CIA, he explained his numbers to Westmoreland and General Davidson, who felt "they were the best we had." Godding said the biggest problem with the CBS program was that people don't know the difference between information and intelligence. "Intelligence is taking information and evaluating and synthesizing it," he said.

At the Westmoreland trial two years later, General Godding ran into trouble. First, he contradicted his own sworn deposition concerning the composition of enemy forces. In his deposition, he had said the Secret Defense irregulars were included in the enemy count. At the trial he said—no, they were excluded and put in a special category. Second, under vigorous cross-examination, he conceded that the enemy-strength figure he was carrying to the CIA meeting at Langley could not be exceeded without permission from Saigon. In spite of all the semantics, it certainly appeared that there was a ceiling or cap dictated by MACV, as the Vietnam program had asserted.

Tet

The program had made much of the size, scope, and ferocity of the Tet Offensive in 1968. It had made the point that General Westmoreland had called Tet a major defeat for the Viet Cong. I asked Crile whether he reflected adequately the view held by a good many Vietnam experts that Tet was a military victory for the United States.

"If you're talking about a war of attrition, it was a terrific victory for our side . . ."

"The implication was that it was a goddamned disaster."

"It was a political disaster."

"Is it fair to indicate it was a total disaster?"

"It's such a controversial point, whether Tet was a victory . . ."

"That's exactly my point. It is a controversy."

"I have to acknowledge something. Given the comments following the broadcast, I wish I had a line in that in a war of attrition this was a terrific military victory."

Editing

Throughout the interviews conducted for the Vietnam program, there were violations of the CBS News guidelines which prohibit combining answers to several questions into single, uninterrupted answers. A question would be asked, an answer given, but that answer was actually a reply to two or three questions. "My understanding," Crile said to me, "is that as long as you begin the answer you can jump if it's the same subject."

Told that the guidelines specifically forbid this, Crile replied: "Number one, I was not aware of it. Two, I believe other people would be surprised. And three, I don't think it should be part of the guidelines."

I asked him whether he thought the guidelines should be revised for documentaries: "I think the guidelines have to be rethought if they make it so goddamn difficult to get the essence of a person on air."

Apart from the guidelines, there was a careless edit in the program that was more embarrassing than substantive. It dealt with the CIA meeting at Langley and Col. George Hamscher, an officer who attended but by his own admission had a clearly subordinate role. Mike Wallace began the sequence with narration:

WALLACE (NARRATION): *CBS Reports* has learned that Colonel Hawkins was in fact carrying out orders that originated from General Westmoreland. Westmoreland says he doesn't recall these orders. But the head of MACV's delegation told us that General Westmoreland had, in fact, personally instructed him not to allow the total to go over 300,000.

CRILE: Wasn't there a ceiling put on the estimates by General Westmoreland? Weren't your colleagues instructed, ordered, not to let those estimates exceed a certain amount?

HAMSCHER: "We can't live with a figure higher than so and so"—

CRILE: Three hundred thousand.

HAMSCHER: —Is the message we got.

WALLACE (NARRATION): Colonel George Hamscher was one of several members of the military delegation troubled by having to carry out General Westmoreland's command position.

HAMSCHER: I was uneasy because of the bargaining characteristics. This is not the way you ought to do it. You don't—you know, you don't start at an end figure and work back. But we did.

The juxtaposition of Mike Wallace's lead and then Hamscher coming up on screen gave the impression that the colonel was the head of the MACV delegation. When I questioned Crile about it, he replied that it was made clear by Wallace's narrative bridge eight seconds into the sequence—"Colonel George Hamscher was one of several members of the military delegation . . ." It did not seem clear to me. Would not the head of the delegation also be one of its members?

Crile was not reluctant to speak about the personal tensions that existed during the program's production and in its aftermath. On Ira Klein, his film editor: "The situation with Ira was so extreme. It was Ira's first hour show. . . . When he took it on, he was properly ambitious; he felt it would be a good show. It was difficult for him because so much was determined by my presence. This was hard for him. There was a lot of starting and stopping. I'm apparently a very difficult person to work with—in some respects disorganized.

"When I went to Florida to work on another show, I didn't make it clear to Ira. He was angry. He realized he couldn't do it all by himself, and we needed another editor due to the time pressure. I felt Ira went on a sit-down strike. There was a crunch when I came back. I tried a *mea culpa*. I may even have told Howard Stringer about it. Ira never got over it."

On Howard Stringer, the executive producer for the program: "He totally confused me. He didn't call me after the program went on the air. I sent him a letter after the show. No answer. I told him that *TV Guide* was making accusations . . . and I'd like to know your position. No call. The article came out. No call. When I put my White Paper out, I wanted Stringer to read it. I called him at home and told him I really wanted him to read it. He said he would. I complained to Roger Colloff that Stringer had not read it. I began to hear that Howard said that if he had been on the show and not at the *Evening News*, the show wouldn't have gone on the air.

"Last night," Crile said, "Howard called me. He was angry. He had heard something. He said he had been defending the show. He didn't need to read the White Paper. He knew me. He trusted me. He had a keen sense of what I did. . . . He said had he been there he could have defused it—the whole business of leaks."

In 1984, Crile's account of the Stringer conversation would become a matter of bitter irony and intense controversy. Don Kowet, one of the reporters for *TV Guide*, was expanding his article into a book to be called *A Matter of Honor*. It was a decision that had got him fired by the magazine in 1983; his editors said they wanted to "adopt a neutral stance" in the CBS-Vietnam matter.

Kowet had interviewed Stringer and secretly taped their conversation, much of which the CBS News executive had designated as off the record. The tape surfaced in 1984 when Kowet, his book completed, released the tape to General Westmoreland's lawyers. Kowet said that because Stringer and other CBS officials were attacking his book, "that gentleman's agreement with me is void." It was an unconscionable act and the quotes, five months before the Westmoreland trial began, were devastating.

"As you may have gathered," Stringer told Kowet, "we have our own suspicions about George Crile anyway. . . . He's been my nemesis for some time. . . . It [responsibility] does devolve on me, because I should never have hired him to do it in the first place. I should have known I wouldn't get fair journalism off him."

The incident was especially embarrassing to CBS News. About the time that Kowet was clandestinely taping Stringer, it was revealed that during the production of the Vietnam program, Crile had also secretly recorded telephone conversations, some of them off the record, with former Secretary of Defense Robert McNamara, former Under Secretary of State George Ball, former Army Chief of Staff Gen. Matthew B. Ridgway, and former Supreme Court Justice Arthur Goldberg. Westmoreland's lawyers had heard about the McNamara tapes from Ira Klein and had subpoenaed them. Crile said they had been lost or erased but eventually he found and produced them.

Although Crile had not used or broadcast any of the material, the recording of telephone conversations without the prior approval of the president of CBS News was a direct violation of network guidelines. When Westmoreland's lawyers released the tapes to the press on June 15, 1983, Crile was suspended with pay by CBS.

11

MIKE WALLACE
TAKES
QUESTIONS

On June 17, 1982, Mike Wallace, the Grand Inquisitor of *60 Minutes*, came to my office in an unaccustomed role. He would be taking, not asking, the questions. The interview would last for six hours.

Toby Wertheim and Barbara Pierce, my researchers, asked to be excused from the session, a decision I thought strange but did not press them on. Their only explanation was that they might be working with Wallace in the future and so found it awkward to be a part of the interview. It gave me no real problem except that I would have to take all of the notes.

I certainly had no inhibitions about confronting Wallace alone. We had been classmates at the University of Michigan more than forty years before. He was then Myron L. Wallace from Brookline, Massachusetts—I never heard anyone call him Mike. The college yearbook shows him looking much the same as he does now: a thin-faced young man with black hair and dark, probing eyes, staring with faint suspicion at the camera.

The yearbook listed his activities over four years: He had tried out for the track team as a sophomore and as a junior with unnoticed results; had been chairman of the student finance committee; had been involved with play production for three years and with the Men's Union for two.

His greatest achievement went unrecorded; he was the runaway star of the tiny student radio station. His supervisor, Professor Waldo

Abbot of the speech department, thought Wallace had the greatest natural voice he had ever heard. It was an opinion shared by many of us, including the station's student engineer, Jerome Wiesner, who became better known as president of M.I.T. and President Kennedy's science adviser.

Wallace's penetrating and resonant voice, so familiar today, needed little tutelage. He changed his major from English to speech, and we all felt that he was every bit as good as the voices we heard on network radio from New York.

When we both graduated in the depression year of 1939 and went our separate ways, Wallace immediately landed a radio job in Grand Rapids and it took me more than a year to find a newspaper job in Cleveland. At radio station WOOD in Grand Rapids, Wallace handled all of the chores expected of a young announcer in those austere days. He did the news—"rip-and-read" copy off the station's wire-service machine—and read commercials. After ten months, the move up the ladder began when he was hired by WXYZ in Detroit, a quantum and impressive jump. Here, along with news and commercials, he narrated two network favorites, "The Lone Ranger" and "The Green Hornet." In 1941, it was onward and upward to Chicago where, except for two years as a naval officer in the Pacific, he would spend the next decade.

In Chicago, Wallace launched a talk show with Buff Cobb, granddaughter of the humorist Irvin S. Cobb, that quickly caught on. His first marriage to Norma Kaphan, a class behind him at Michigan, had ended in divorce. (Ironically, she would in 1957 marry Bill Leonard, who later became president of CBS News and Wallace's boss.)

In 1949, Mike Wallace and Buff Cobb were married. In 1951, their show, "Mike and Buff," moved to New York and to television. It languished, as did their marriage, and in 1955 he would be married for the third time to Lorraine Perigord, an artist he met in Puerto Rico.

In New York, Wallace did the rounds, including a stint on Broadway in the comedy *Reclining Figure,* in which he played an art dealer. In 1956, he and Ted Yates, a gifted young producer from NBC News, launched "Night Beat" on Channel 5, the Dumont station. It was an interview show that proved to be a groundbreaker. It gave Mike Wallace considerable recognition and provided the public image for the rest of his career—the bulldog interrogator asking the most probing and outrageous questions.

The show was so simple and yet so ingenious that it became an immediate hit. The set was a black velour drop; a hot white light shone on the guest; the camera angle was an extremely tight close-up, unusual in those early television days. And Mike Wallace, cigarette in hand *à la* Ed Murrow, just sat there and asked questions that were tough, unadorned, and often embarrassing. One interview still remembered was a dismemberment of the cartoonist Al Capp which seized upon his habit of giggling after each answer and left him limp and destroyed.

ABC, a bad third among the networks, persuaded Wallace and Yates to join them in 1957, but it was never the same. The network was hardly prepared to take the heat generated by Wallace's tougher interviews. Two particularly nasty sessions helped end the association. In one face-to-face session with Wallace, the gangster Mickey Cohen attacked the police chief of Los Angeles and his deputy in such strenuous terms that the president of ABC had to go on the air and apologize. The network still had to pay minor damages. In another, the columnist Drew Pearson told Wallace that John F. Kennedy had not written *Profiles in Courage;* one of his staffers had ghosted it. That was about all ABC could tolerate.

Wallace tried a variation of the show on another independent station in New York, but it never worked as well as the original "Night Beat." He did some documentary work for David Wolper and for Westinghouse, but what was paying much of the overhead were his commercials for Parliament cigarettes. What he longed for—and was prepared to suffer financially to get—was a network news job. In 1963, as he was about to accept an anchor post at an independent station in Los Angeles, he got the call he wanted. It came from Richard Salant, then president of CBS News, and it resulted in Wallace's being hired as a correspondent at a very spare $40,000 a year. Two decades later it would be a million dollars a year.

As a CBS News correspondent, Wallace could not go on the air while his Parliament cigarette commercials were running all over the country. Joseph Cullman, president of Phillip Morris, agreed to pull them off the air. Wallace's reception at CBS was rather cool; some of his colleagues still regarded him as a shill for cigarettes, not as a journalist. It took him only a couple of years of good, solid work to change his image, although even when he became a superstar, some traditionalists never really accepted him.

The decisive and providential moment in Mike Wallace's career came in 1968 when producer Don Hewitt persuaded CBS News to put on the air his new idea for a television news magazine program, which he called *60 Minutes*. There would be two reporter-hosts on the series, Harry Reasoner and Mike Wallace. When his assignment was announced, Wallace sent me a piece of sculpture, an Eskimo whalebone snow goose, to thank me for supporting his bid for the show. It was generous, as I told him, but he had misunderstood the power structure at CBS News. I had indeed backed him for the job, but I was down in the echelon. Three men had made the choice: Richard Salant, Bill Leonard, and Don Hewitt.

When Mike Wallace walked into my office that June day in 1982, he was one month past his sixty-fourth birthday. His third marriage to Lorraine Perigord was about to break up. In 1986 he would take as his fourth wife Mary Yates, widow of Ted Yates, his collaborator on the old "Night Beat" series, who was killed covering the Six Day War in Israel. She had once reported to me when she produced the Sunday interview program, "Face the Nation," for CBS News. I knew her as a good journalist and a woman of style and generous spirit.

I did not know quite what to expect from Wallace, whether he would be confrontational, which was his forte, or withdrawn and uncommunicative. He was neither.

If anything, he was disarming. One of the first things he said was: "I am not entirely blameless in this whole affair. Things went on I didn't know anything about."

Wallace said that George Crile and Grace Diekhaus had approached him about doing the program several months before the Blue Sheet pitching the idea to management was written.

"I had heard of the story vaguely. One of my *60 Minutes* producers, Barry Lando, had some interest in it. Lando had met Sam Adams but the show decided to pass on it.

"I was impressed with Crile. I had seen 'The CIA's Secret Army,' which impressed me. I thought George had taken a bad rap on the 'Gay Power, Gay Politics' show. Crile wanted to become a correspondent. I like him. I thought, if I can help this young man get ahead, I'll do it."

Wallace went to see Robert Chandler, then a CBS News vice president, who confirmed that they would like him to do Crile's show. Wallace said: "I told him: 'I don't know when I'll be able to do all this work.' I had an appetite to do it but shouldn't have had. I was doing *60 Minutes* and two other series, *Mike Wallace Profiles* and *Up to the Minute*, at the same time."

Wallace said he continued to have misgivings about his involvement. He was no innocent. He knew that management wanted him not only for his talent, especially in conducting the major interviews, but as a showcase. Shortly before his scheduled interview with Sam Adams, Wallace went to Roger Colloff, then the news vice president responsible for documentaries, and asked to be taken off the show.

"I told Colloff, 'I'm busy. I have a full plate. It's George's story. You've seen what he can do. I like his pieces. I like the story. It's just the pressure of work.' But Colloff persuaded me to stay. He said they wanted me especially for the Westmoreland interview."

Wallace said he could sense that Crile did not want him to do any of the subsidiary interviews. He preferred to do those himself. "These people would be leery of sitting down with me," Wallace said. "They would be afraid to talk, afraid that the interview would become adversarial." The first interview that Wallace conducted was regarded as sort of a warmup for him. It was with Marshall Lynn, a young military intelligence analyst, and it was scrubbed.

Wallace met Sam Adams before their interview in Virginia. "I read his *Harper's* piece. I did not read the Pike Committee Hearings nor did I know about his testimony at the Ellsberg trial. There was no question in my mind that the subject we were doing would be highly controversial. I made some handwritten notes before the interview, but I told Crile: 'I'm up to my ass. You have to fill me in' "

Wallace did not agree that the nine-to-two equation on the program, Adams plus eight supporters on one side, Westmoreland and Graham on the other, was wrong. "Adams is a whistle blower, not an adversary," he said.

He agreed that there should have been other points of view expressed. He mentioned LBJ's special ambassador in Vietnam, Robert Komer; the CIA's George Carver, Jr.; and William Colby, who succeeded Richard Helms as CIA director, as three who should have been interviewed. Another was Arthur Goldberg, former Supreme Court Justice and U.N. representative. "I wanted Goldberg on the show. I mentioned him as somebody they ought to get."

Wallace emphasized that he was never in the mainstream of the production. He never saw the Blue Sheet, never went into the editing rooms unless called down by Howard Stringer or Andrew Lack, never got a research report or a finished script. He did not know that Sam Adams was a regular visitor to the editing rooms and was on location for some interviews. No one told him that General Davidson was not terminally ill, nor did he know that General Godding was the head of the MACV delegation to the CIA Langley meeting. He knew nothing of the Westmoreland phrase that had been dropped in the *Meet the Press* interview, nor of Crile's anger when the line could be heard in one of the screenings.

He agreed that the introduction he had narrated to Col. George Hamscher, which made him sound like the head of the MACV delegation to Langley, was "imprecise." He did not know that in the final broadcast, separate meetings in Saigon and at the Pentagon had been combined so that they appeared to be a single meeting. He winced when I told him about it.

Wallace said the way he worked on the Vietnam program was in sharp contrast with his method of operation on *60 Minutes*. "On *60 Minutes*, I ask my producers: 'Is it true? Can we prove it?' On this broadcast I thought these questions would be asked by Colloff, Stringer, and Lack."

He conceded that the tone in his interview with Sam Adams was much softer than the tone in his interview with General Westmoreland. "Adams was our employee, our consultant. My job was to be a funnel for him."

As to the controversial Westmoreland statement about enemy infiltration being 20,000 a month before Tet, Wallace said he went back to the question again and again to give the general an opportunity to correct himself. He was right; our research showed that Wallace brought up the matter no fewer than fifteen times in the interview.

Wallace rejected the idea that Westmoreland was not prepared. "This man was a four-star general, a West Point graduate." Nevertheless, Wallace revealed that after the interview, when an angry Westmoreland had departed, he had an argument about the major premise of the program with George Crile and Grace Diekhaus.

"I told them it didn't make any sense to say that Westmoreland had intentionally undercounted enemy troop strength. Why would he do it? Why would he degrade his enemy? No general does that. I expressed skepticism about the whole story."

In the weeks ahead, Wallace's doubts were somehow assuaged, and he went ahead with the two remaining interviews that Crile had scheduled for him—Lt. Gen. Daniel Graham and Walt W. Rostow. Wallace dismissed General Graham's statement at the Westmoreland news conference that he had agreed to be interviewed only because Crile and

Wallace had guaranteed they would ask him a question about Tet and use his answer.

"An untruth," Wallace said. "We did say we would ask a question as to whether Tet was a military victory or defeat for the United States, and I kept my promise. I started the interview with it. But we never agreed to use his answer."

On the Walt Rostow interview, three hours filmed and none used, Wallace said he was not consulted. After completing the session in New York, he went back to his vacation house in Martha's Vineyard and then went to China for *60 Minutes*. "I kept asking: Let me see the assembly on Rostow, but I never saw it. I was under the impression that Stringer and Lack had screened it."

Wallace made it clear, however, that he supported Crile's decision not to use Rostow. "Rostow and LBJ were not our story. Our story was that the books were cooked. . . . The broadcast was basically accurate."

I quoted two excerpts from Rostow:

—. . . this tortured debate about the order of battle and whether it was manipulated and so on should not be confused with the range of information on which President Johnson made his assessment—before Tet, during Tet, after Tet.

—All I can tell you is the story of the order-of-battle debate and whatever was done with these categories, did not distort President Johnson's assessment of the war.

I asked Wallace whether he did not believe that either of those quotations was worthy of inclusion in the broadcast. He did not. "Rostow would say that," he said.

I read Wallace the definitions of the word "conspiracy" that I had found in two dictionaries. He conceded it was a tough word, but he did not agree that it should not have been used. Later, in his pre-trial deposition, he would call my interpretation "a very narrow and, in my mind, a wrong definition." Wallace said the definition of "conspiracy" he preferred was: "Two or more individuals acting together to achieve a wrongful end."

Wallace had no input into the print advertisement or the on-air promotions for the program. In his deposition, he would say that headlining the word "conspiracy" in the advertisement gave him problems ". . . playing the word 'conspiracy' as broadly as it does, is not consistent with the way the word 'conspiracy' was played in the broadcast itself."

As the session was about to end, I asked Wallace whether he thought my interview had been fair. He replied: "A hundred percent."

As I thought about it that night, I was persuaded that Wallace had leveled with me. There was no doubt in my mind that the interview had troubled him. He had learned first hand just how many things had gone on that he had not known about. Yet, in spite of his stated misgivings, his frank admission that his role had been peripheral, he continued to hold doggedly to the premise of the broadcast—that "the books were cooked." He kept returning to the phrase again and again. I was convinced that he would never retreat from that position.

The next morning, Wallace phoned me. He told me that he had had "problems sleeping last night." He also said that George Crile was distressed because he had shown me a letter the producer had sent to him a few days before.

During the interview, Wallace had first mentioned and then let me have an emotional letter to him from George Crile. It was a direct attack on the examination I was conducting. In it were lines like these: "Bud [Benjamin] has a conceptual misunderstanding of the show. It is not that old Sam Adams story as Rostow, Westy and Graham say. . . . Bud has an unshakable idea: it is Westy vs. Adams . . . I am not impugning Bud's fairness or integrity but remind him of the realities of the business. . . ."

Crile's letter began:

Mike:

I meant what I said the other day—that I can't apologize to you for getting into this mess. I can't do it because I believed in the show then and still do believe in it. It doesn't mean that I don't feel badly seeing you dragged unfairly through all of this. You sounded so depressed on the phone.

For what it is worth, I want you to know how much I have valued and depended on you these last few weeks. I have never known anyone to act with the strength and character and fairness that you have in your dealing with me.

I really would do anything for you, win, lose or draw in this contest. You have a dedicated friend for life.

But that is the future and there is the spectre of a hangman's knot to deal with first . . . I just don't think we can sit back and expect divine justice from the CBS internal review. . . .

I am convinced that CBS is not acting in its own self-interest, that it is making an enormous mistake by not addressing itself now to the specific

questions of whether or not it stands by the broadcast. It is a simple
question. Forget process. Does CBS believe in the substantive points and
accusations made in the show or not?

It seems to me that management has fallen into a trap by accepting
TV Guide's ground rules. Bud and Sauter have gone underground to consider the eighteen accusations about process. Meanwhile, the real battle
in everyone else's mind is over substance, over the *TV Guide* cover that
says we smeared Westmoreland. Our silence is viewed as an admission of
guilt. There are charges of cover-up. And the impression that we are worried about the thrust of the show is indeed untrue. . . .

I think we should move heaven and earth to get the powers-that-be
to make up their minds about this as soon as possible. . . . I really think
it's worth talking to Dan [Rather] about this. It seems to me that it is a
clear cut question of what's in CBS's best self-interest and he could be of
help. . . .

So what am I saying? I'm saying I don't want to be the bureaucracy's
fall guy here. And I know full well that your reputation has also become
tied up in the outcome of this investigation in a very fundamental way.
And I don't want you to indirectly become a fall guy either. This is a show
that the news division commissioned with its eyes wide open. It was given
exactly what it was promised. . . .

If anyone was clearly at fault in the way the show came out, Crile
had a prime candidate: Howard Stringer.

As far as I'm concerned, everyone did their job on the show, except Howard. And I think you ought to tell Bud that if he has criticisms about the
documentary that the person who was primarily responsible for overseeing
the show and making sure it was both fair and accurate was Stringer. I say
that, Mike, simply because it is (1) true and (2) because Howard is apparently making mischief. And I believe with all my heart that Bud and everyone else ought to know very clearly that there are a lot of people involved
in this. If there were failings here—in this explosive documentary which
we all understood was going to be controversial—the man who was supposed to protect all of us and watch out for the reputation of the news
division was Howard Stringer. And he is bad-mouthing the show and apparently even refuses to read my White Paper.

When Mike Wallace called to tell me that Crile was dismayed that
he had shown me the letter, I suggested he tell Crile that it certainly
would not influence my findings. Yet I must confess I found the episode
fascinating. It took the letter to remind me that this was a high-stakes

game and some of the players had their careers on the line and might play very rough.

I had expected that I might have to ward off a lot of high-level pressure as I pursued the investigation. I would not have been surprised by a summons from Black Rock for that corporate euphemism—an interim progress report: How does it look? Are we in trouble? Who did what to whom? None of this ever happened. On two occasions, Sauter did phone to ask how I was doing. When I said just fine, he seemed more than satisfied, asked no details, and let it go at that.

In this rather civilized atmosphere, it was a shock to realize that I had not yet written a word of my report, and it was already under attack.

12

SAM ADAMS
AND
THE CIA

I was an actor in the controversy. I was probably one of the prime actors." That was Sam Adams's answer in my office on June 21, 1982, when I asked him the first question: "How did you understand your role?"

Samuel Alexander Adams, one week to the day past his forty-ninth birthday, blue-eyed, his brown hair showing the first flecks of gray, was described by a woman friend as looking like "a rustic Paul Newman." He was wearing a rumpled tweed sport coat, worn slacks, and boots that had seen the mud of his Virginia farm. He was carrying an old shoulder knapsack bulging with the handwritten notes, the precious "chronologies" he had accumulated during his CIA studies of the Vietnam War.

Adams had been collecting notes and documents since 1966 when he was an analyst for the CIA. By 1969 he had gathered a number of CIA documents dealing with Vietnam order-of-battle matters. He put them in plastic leaf-bags, stowed the bags inside an old wooden box, and buried them in a field near his farm in Virginia. He had put red thumbtacks on three trees so that he could triangulate the location of the box.

In 1973, he dug up the leaf-bags and found they had sprung a leak, water had seeped in, and worms had eaten away some of the documents. Most were still legible, and he had turned over some of them to Representative Paul N. McCloskey, Jr., a Democrat from California, with whom he had been in contact and who shared his views on Vietnam. He said the CIA had not authorized him to pass on the documents, but since McCloskey "had the highest level of clearances" and he wanted to make certain the material was preserved, he saw nothing wrong with doing it.

To his critics, the documents were one more example of Adams's obsession about Vietnam. (During the trial, Westmoreland's lawyers were quick to label them "purloined documents.") Mike Wallace had asked him during their interview whether he was obsessed, and I asked him again.

"What is obsessed?" he replied. "I'm very interested in the subject. I explain how we lost the war. If this is obsessed, so be it."

I must say that Sam Adams, who came to my office for a four-hour interview, did not behave like a man obsessed. He lacked the intensity of one driven by a cause. He was relaxed and detached, rarely raising his voice. But when you got into the Vietnam story and the strength of the enemy, he left no doubt that he was absolutely convinced he was right. He could be patronizing if challenged. He could also be stubborn and inflexible. After all, this was a man who had tried to get Gen. William C. Westmoreland court-martialed, who had tried to get CIA director Richard Helms fired, and who had no compunction about going out of channels to the White House and Capitol Hill to wage his lonely campaign. Obsessed or not, he was not one you would choose lightly as an adversary.

George C. Carver, Jr., the agency's special assistant for Vietnam affairs and Adams's boss, praised Adams's "energy, enthusiasm and imagination. . . . He did the donkey-work chores others might shy away from." But Carver also said Adams was "prone to jump to conclusions and was very intolerant of people who did not share the conclusions to which he jumped." Carver said he had rebuked Adams in 1967 for "going off half-cocked" when the young analyst sent a memo over Carver's name criticizing U.S. Army enemy-strength estimates in Southeast Asia.

R. Jack Smith, a deputy director of the CIA while Adams was there, saw two sides to Adams—the cultivated man in a social situation and the driven analyst at work: "Sam is a very charming man, extremely persuasive, and it never fails to surprise me how people who only know him socially get their impression of him. Our impression in the agency was rather different."

Clinton B. Conger, retired from the CIA, told me that when Adams wanted something, he would plunge after it, blinders on, red flags flying. "I wrote a memorandum for the director once that Sam was unhappy about. He not only followed me into the men's room complaining about it, I practically had to push him out of a stall."

When Adams resigned from the CIA in 1973, he impugned the agency's honesty in dealing with intelligence in Vietnam and Cambodia. "Since 1967," he wrote in his resignation statement, "I have submitted complaints about the integrity and completeness of research to the Inspector Generals of the CIA and the U.S. Army, to the National Security Council and to the President's Foreign Intelligence Advisory Board. My criticisms were met with evasion, delay and sometimes threats. As far as I can determine, they were largely fruitless."

In spite of his vendetta with the agency, Adams declared he was still a strong supporter of the CIA. He said he thoroughly enjoyed working there and that if asked he would very much like to go back.

Adams had met George Crile through a mutual acquaintance. He told us he had written some pieces for the *New York Times* and *The Wall Street Journal* and said he had spoken with Patrick Sloyan of *Newsday*, who had written stories based on information he had given him.

"After the Pike Hearings, which were Mickey Mouse, I called lots of people—about three hundred. I was an actor and researcher. As a researcher, I helped convince these poor fellows [former CIA and MACV intelligence officers] to tell their stories on camera."

For the Vietnam program, he boiled down his list of names to sixty prospects. "How about those who didn't appear?" I asked him. "The Carvers, Komers, and Rostows."

"In the selection of people we asked, we had so many to support me that we had to slice the list of supporters. For the infiltration story, we used [Lt. Col. Russell] Cooley, but we could have had several other sources."

In his chronologies, Adams had compiled a list of all those who played a part in the order-of-battle drama in Vietnam. After each name he had analyzed how they might be used in the program. This was what he had to say in those chronologies about the men who failed to make the final broadcast.

Lt. Gen. Phillip Davidson, *MACV intelligence chief, 1967–69*

"He is said to have cancer. A deathbed confession? Doubt it but may be worth a call. I plan to check with him prior to final draft."

I asked Adams how he knew Davidson was ill. "I thought the bastard was on his last leg."

Should we have talked to him? "No. We had so damn many people, he was just another."

Adams said he thought Col. John Lanterman had informed him that Davidson was terminally ill, but now he was not sure who told him. (Lanterman denied to us that he had ever mentioned Davidson to Adams, or even knew about the state of the general's health.)

When did he find out Davidson was not on his deathbed? "Well before the broadcast, around December."

"You told Crile?"

"I told George, 'Holy Cow!' I don't know if he tried to get hold of Davidson."

Gen. Maxwell Taylor, *Army chief of staff, 1955–59; chairman of Joint Chiefs of Staff, 1962–64; and U.S. Ambassador to Vietnam, 1964–65*

"I prepared for my interview with Taylor [previous interview not connected with broadcast] for upwards of a month and in our hour-and-a-half talk got nothing, save one. . . . Referring to the press, Taylor exclaimed angrily: 'Well, you had to do something to beat down those 'lying sons of bitches.' Would he repeat that for the tube? Who knows? My predilection is that if Taylor repeats quote [about the press], CBS ought not to get self-righteous about it. Many people share Taylor's distrust for the press, including me."

Ellsworth Bunker, *U.S. Ambassador, Vietnam 1967–73*

"Bunker was in on all this although it's problematical how much he knew of the fakery. . . . But he's awfully old now, and CBS might look like it's hounding an old man to his grave."

Robert W. Komer, *Special Assistant to President, Vietnam, 1966–67; Deputy to Commander, MACV, 1967–68*

"God knows what Komer knew about the lowering of infiltration statistics at this point. . . ."

"Read Komer the Meacham letter to his wife. ("Never in my life have I assembled such a pack of truly gargantuan falsehoods.") CLOSE-UP of his face. Maybe Komer'll pull it off. He's an impressive man."

"*[Or] start with Komer. Get him to denounce McChristian. . . . This would get McC to reply.*"

I asked Adams whether he felt now that Komer might have been useful to have on camera. "He would have been a damned interesting interview," Adams told me. "This is what Komer would have said: 'Of course, we did that stuff. The goddamn lying press. Of course, we did that. We had to.'"

"Might have fortified your case," I said to him.

"Yes," he replied.

Walt W. Rostow, *Special assistant to President Johnson, 1966–69*

"*Would he finger LBJ?*"

Rostow was interviewed, and he certainly did not finger the President he had served so dutifully. I asked Adams whether he thought any of the Rostow interview should have been used:

"I had the least to do with this one. I wasn't persuaded there was anything in the Rostow transcript but it wasn't my decision."

Gen. George W. Godding, *MACV Director of Intelligence Production, 1967. Head of Army delegation to MACV-CIA intelligence meeting at Langley, Virginia, in 1967*

"*He got instructions from Westy to stay under 300,000 [for enemy strength]. . . . Basically an honest guy but a strong Army type. Doubt he'd talk but might be worth a try. . . . Problem: He might not realize what putting the ceiling on meant.*"

Arthur Goldberg, *Secretary of Labor, 1961–62; Supreme Court Justice, 1962–65; and Ambassador to the United Nations, 1965–68.*

"*He'll doubtless talk, perhaps endlessly.*"

I asked Adams whether he had thought further about Goldberg, who was a member of the group known as the Wise Men, prominent Americans summoned by LBJ in 1968 to advise him on the war that was going so badly.

"The Wise Men were interesting, but they wouldn't have told you a hell of a lot. The best one was Goldberg. He is the only one who took notes. Crile said, and I agreed, that we had so many people we didn't need one more."

Clark Clifford, *Secretary of Defense, 1968–69*

"Danger with Clifford would be his tendency to pontificate and retell the story of how he stopped the war. . . ."

In the *TV Guide* article, the magazine had charged that "CBS paid $25,000 to a consultant on the program without adequately investigating his 14-year quest to prove the program's conspiracy theory."

George Crile in his White Paper had denied that the program had simply taken Adams's research at full faith and made a film out of it. "CBS did not . . . rely on Mr. Adams's personal testimony to document the central thesis of its report. Any review of the documentary clearly shows that the critical charges were all made and supported by key military officers from MACV intelligence. . . . It was their testimony and not that of Mr. Adams that documented the accusations made in the documentary."

The statement understated Adams's role. He was the paid consultant who had immersed himself in the story; he was the in-house encyclopedia for the broadcast. It was Adams who persuaded the disaffected and often reluctant MACV and CIA officers to bare their souls on camera. It was Adams who held their hands at some of the key interviews, who cheered them on and helped sustain them when they faltered. If the broadcast had a father, it was Crile; if it had a godfather, it was Adams.

TV Guide had also charged that "CBS violated its own official guidelines by rehearsing its paid consultant before he was interviewed on camera." Crile vigorously denied this: "Anyone who has talked to Mr. Adams will confirm that there is no way to dictate or manipulate his statements or opinions about this subject."

The all-day Crile-Adams session before his interview, which Ira Klein, the film editor, claimed was definitely a rehearsal, was nothing of the sort according to Crile. ". . . I decided to try to confine the questions Mike would ask and answers Adams would give to those areas where he had been a direct participant in the story we were reporting. I felt it was unwise to have Adams making accusations in the documentary based on information he had learned as a reporter after the fact."

"Did you consider your interview with Mike Wallace to be a probing interview?" I asked Adams. "The kind of interview Mike Wallace is famous for."

"I'm so familiar with it, it's hard to probe. I didn't feel he was an adversary. He asked a couple of embarrassing questions like 'Why are you so obsessed?' I had to come up with some lame answer. When I ran off on a subject he waved his hand to stop me."

I read him a couple of puffball statements from the interview. ("Sam Adams is there. He's Paul Revere. . . . You were perfect. Don't say that. You're doing it just right.")

"I guess that's an example of coaching—okay, cheerleading. There was one answer I gave four or five times. But there was no session with George when he ran the questions by me."

The most serious allegation by *TV Guide* was this one: "CBS's own paid consultant now doubts the documentary's premise of a Westmoreland-led conspiracy." This would seem to have come from Ira Klein, who had told us, and apparently others, about Adams coming into his editing room after the broadcast and saying: "We have to come clean. The premise is not accurate."

Adams had issued a denial right after the magazine hit the newsstands:

> The *TV Guide* statement indicates that I am uncomfortable with the premise of the documentary. This is simply untrue. First of all, I am convinced that there was a falsification of estimates of enemy strength; second, that there was a conspiracy; third, that General Westmoreland was responsible for directing these actions. My sole reservation concerns my suspicion— based on circumstantial evidence but no smoking guns—that the White House either ordered or condoned the faking of official estimates. This suspicion was reinforced by Walt Rostow's memo to the LBJ Library after the broadcast aired in which he said the President was aware of the massive increase in enemy infiltration in the months prior to Tet. To suggest, however, that this sole reservation in any way reflects a lack of belief in the reporting and thrust of the documentary completely misrepresents my basic convictions.

Using his statement as a framework, I asked Adams a set of questions about the program and his involvement.

What about the premise of the show?

"I didn't say the premise was wrong . . . I went in and said something to the effect that if I had a problem with the show it was that it hung the rap too much on Westmoreland and not enough on White House involvement . . . I wouldn't say the premise of the show is that Westmoreland is the perpetrator. . . . There were a lot of premises—conspiracy, Westmoreland up to his ears but not acting on his own hook."

What about his statement to Ira Klein—"We have to come clean. The premise is not accurate"?

"Ira was in a state of agitation, God knows over what. He was sort of leading me into it. I said this a million times, we should have shifted the emphasis higher. I don't recall this as a big event in my life. This was something I felt from the beginning. Crile was never adverse to it. We never had the goods on who gave the orders to Westmoreland. From the Rostow memo, we now know that LBJ knew. Klein went to Andy Lack and said the premise of the broadcast was wrong and that's when Lack called me. . . . When I got the final script, I found some factual errors which Crile corrected. . . . I didn't point out LBJ again. I felt I had lost that battle already."

What about the use of the word "conspiracy"?

"There is no doubt in my mind that there was a legal conspiracy. I don't intend to use the word in my book. What happened was so complex. I look at the damn thing as more of a tragedy myself. It was unlawful. No one was being a traitor. I thought early on that 'conspiracy' was too strong a word. It didn't imply evil or treachery. These people weren't traitors to their country or evil. They did falsify statistics without evil intent. The ad for the show was overblown. I didn't have anything to do with the ad. It implied plotters whispering together. 'Conspiracy' is not a word I normally use. It's a much more tragic story."

What about the Blue Sheet? Had he seen it?

"I must have."

"The word 'conspiracy' was used twenty-four times."

"At one point I said, 'Oh, for Christ's sake, George, come off it.' "

Adams was obviously not present when General Westmoreland was interviewed. That would have blown the whole game plan and it was doubtful that the general would have sat still for the first question had he seen the man he regarded as his nemesis on the set. I asked Adams if he had seen the confusing Westmoreland letter, buried in a mass of documents, in which he told Crile that he had misspoken about enemy infiltration before Tet—that it was not 20,000 a month as he had said in his interview with Wallace but 5,500–6,000 a month as he had said on *Meet the Press*.

"Yes, I saw the letter. . . . My problem with that is that he is lying and I had others to disprove what he was saying."

"If he says that he wants to pull back from his statement, is that ethical?" I asked him. "He said, in a sense, 'I misspoke.' We didn't give him a chance to go on the record with what is or is not the truth."

"There you go. To me the man is so clearly lying."

"Did you see the Westmoreland transcript?"

"Yes."

"Was he ill-prepared?"

"I don't think he was expecting what he got."

"There were five categories of questions listed and the essence was number four."

"That doesn't bother me a bit. The key one is number four, but the others are related. The fact that we ambushed him a little doesn't bother me. The nature of the ambush—I agree there was one—is we had talked to all of his subordinates. My own feeling is why should we tip our hand to someone who gave the order?"

Sam Adams's research documented some of the love-hate relationships that swirled through the corridors of MACV and the CIA during the Vietnam War. One involved two colonels at MACV—Charles Morris, the chief of intelligence production, and a subordinate, Everette S. Parkins, chief of order-of-battle studies.

The Vietnam broadcast said that Parkins, a 1951 West Point graduate, had been "fired" by Morris when he became "so incensed at MACV's refusal to send on the reports of enemy infiltration at 25,000 a month that he lost his temper and shouted at his superior." Lt. Col. Russell Cooley, who was not in the room at the time but says he heard it from Parkins, then described the incident on camera for George Crile.

At the Westmoreland news conference, Morris denied the story. He said the argument, which took place on November 15, 1967, was over an order he gave Parkins to try to get "a better handle on relating reported killed in action to actual killed in action, or wounded in action. . . ." Morris said they had a wealth of captured documents, and he asked Parkins "to see if he could detect a pattern between what our people had reported on those operations" and what the enemy documents said. Morris said Parkins told him it couldn't be done and he wouldn't try. "Now, no officer in combat tells me he won't try," said Morris, "and for that he was fired."

Cdr. James Meacham told Crile and Adams when they interviewed him in London that Parkins was fired because "you don't yell at the old man."

"I am terribly familiar with the Parkins story," Adams told me. "It was well known at the time at MACV headquarters. I got it directly from Parkins around 1980 over a three- or four-hour interview. . . . The talk was in high decibels. . . . Morris says you've been a troublemaker all along." Adams said he had several sources for his account, although none of the people had been in the room when the incident took place.

In his interview with Westmoreland, Wallace recounted the story for the general, who said he knew nothing about it.

We had spoken by telephone to Parkins a week before our interview with Adams. He told us he and Morris had had a personality conflict for a long time, but he would not confirm or deny any version of the story. He said he was acting on the advice of counsel.

Parkins was to testify for Westmoreland at the trial in New York, and he would not be a very persuasive witness. He confirmed that he was relieved of his duties after a final run-in with Morris, whom he "disliked intensely," and who "more than reciprocated" the feeling. Then he told a rather incongruous story of how the confrontation was touched off. He wanted to use the unit's only Jeep to go to the PX, which would have been a problem, so he first dropped off his enemy-strength figures to justify the use of the vehicle. It was an ill-fated diversion, for when he arrived at intelligence headquarters with his figures there was Colonel Morris to receive them, and the confrontation followed.

At first, Parkins said he did not think he was fired for delivering higher enemy-strength figures. Then he said he was only a messenger, and when hammered on that, said, "It was not a hundred percent clear that we were arguing about numbers . . . I do not know exactly what inflamed Colonel Morris." His testimony was less than helpful to General Westmoreland.

As for Sam Adams and love and hate during the intelligence battles of the Vietnam War, he had a candidate in each category—Col. Gains Hawkins and Lt. Col. Daniel Graham.

Hawkins was a man whom Adams vastly admired. He considered him to be the finest order-of-battle officer of the war. His esteem and affection were reciprocated.

"I had met Sam Adams in February, 1966," Hawkins wrote shortly after the broadcast. ". . . His brilliance and intensity of purpose were recognizable. In subsequent months, I learned to respect and admire him and sometimes to wish that he would go away."

Three days before the broadcast, Adams wrote to Hawkins: "I'd appreciate any comments you have on the documentary. Overall, I think it's reasonably good, but, as I mentioned before, there's a major problem. The documentary seems to pin the rap on General Westmoreland when it probably belongs higher than that."

The major problem that Adams referred to certainly sounded as if he had some doubts about the premise of the broadcast.

Adams's feelings toward Colonel Hawkins, who was to become a key CBS witness at the trial, were in sharp contrast to the visceral antipathy he felt for then Lt. Col. Daniel Graham.

"How did Graham, only a lieutenant colonel then, get so much influence with Westmoreland?" I asked Adams.

"He picked up the ball and ran with it. You have to understand the MACV organization. Graham's office was in headquarters near West-moreland. Westmoreland would come to see Graham almost every day. When Hawkins left, Graham assumed more responsibility."

Had he read the Graham interview—more than an hour filmed, twenty-one seconds used?

"Yes. I read the entire interview. Tough one to use because the guy lies constantly. When you use something, you have to explain why he's lying. He's done this for years."

At the Westmoreland news conference, Graham had said of Adams: "He has made wild claims that are readily proved to be lies."

I said to Adams: "Graham says you have it all wrong. That instead of underestimating enemy strength in Vietnam, they were actually over-estimating it."

"He is lying."

Near the end of the interview I asked Sam Adams about Tet. Was it a victory or defeat?

"This is too complex a question to answer. The broadcast did well by it. My view is that it was clearly a political defeat in the sense that the American people no longer believed what the administration and MACV were saying. A military defeat? Well, what the hell is a military defeat?"

I said I had heard that after Tet you could drive around Saigon like a beltway. The enemy was gone.

"That's horse shit," said Sam Adams. "Two months after Tet we had our highest casualty rate."

With that, he began stuffing his chronologies into his knapsack and said if we had any more questions to be sure and call him at his farm in Virginia. As he walked out of the office, there was no doubt in my mind that Sam Adams felt he had the answers to any questions I, or anyone else, might ask.

13

LAST OF
THE INTERVIEWS

There were four more interviews to be conducted, each of them with men well up in the hierarchy of CBS News, all of whom had played various roles in the drama of "The Uncounted Enemy." When the corporate shakeups had erupted in 1981—Van Gordon Sauter in as news president, Bill Leonard out—each of the four men had been affected. Three had moved sharply up, and one had moved sideways and out of the main stream.

The three movers, who in varying degrees also proved to be shakers, were Roger Colloff, Howard Stringer, and Andrew Lack. The shunted-aside executive was Robert Chandler, who was replaced in February by Colloff as vice president in charge of public-affairs programs. It was a significant executive switch. Chandler, who had given George Crile his first conditional approval, was a veteran known as a fine editor who asked probing questions of producers when he screened their programs. He was moved into administration, out of the creative mix, and he would have no input into the Vietnam program. He was never invited to a screening nor were his opinions ever solicited.

Colloff, a fast-track executive, a lawyer by education, had virtually no production experience. Very bright and quick, with no lack of ambition, he rode herd on Crile and devoted more time to the program than was normal for a vice president. Into his lap fell all the woes of "The Uncounted Enemy."

The rising star, Howard Stringer, was the executive producer of the program, reassigned two months before it went on the air to the Dan Rather News and quickly consumed by its problems and faltering ratings. During the most acute decision-making time, Stringer was a lost asset.

Lack, younger than Stringer and equally aspiring, did not get involved with "The Uncounted Enemy" until November, much too late to comprehend either its complexities or its burgeoning problems. He was an outsider who had no time to get inside.

By now, the vulnerabilities in the Vietnam program had become apparent to me and to my staff. In my separate interviews with these four men, I would ask them virtually the same questions. Their answers, in juxtaposition, provide insight into the problems which beset the program and their perceptions of them:

How do you assess the performance of George Crile and what was your role in the production of the program?

CHANDLER: George came in to see me with his proposal in the fall of 1980. The basic thrust was that these very respectable and senior people from the military and the CIA believed that such a conspiracy existed and for the first time they would be willing to talk about it publicly.

My position was that if these people truly would go public and would say on camera what they had told George in person, it would be a hell of a broadcast. I was skeptical that they would, but it certainly was worth a preliminary investment. I said, Okay, we limit this as preliminary based on your success on getting these people to talk on camera. You won't be the correspondent. You'll do some interviews but Mike Wallace will be the correspondent.

I told him after he collected the interviews, we would decide whether to go ahead or not. Late in the year, I reviewed with Mike the ground rules and his participation. Then I got out. I never screened anything.

STRINGER: Like many investigative reporters, George Crile is excessive and slightly flaky. He is one of those investigative reporters, not unlike others, like Sy Hersh for example, who always get obsessive. George had to convince me over and over. I did ask him whether there weren't others who challenged the broadcast. In fairness, I think George got an almost unfair level of skepticism on this show.

I think I made an error in thinking he had made the transition to producer. I knew his strength was in digging out information. Fifty percent of the *CBS Reports* producers can do it all. The rest, including Crile, need help. That's why I put Joe Zigman into the project as associate producer. Joe is so honest, but George wears you out a little bit and he may have worn Joe down. But George will tackle subjects that others won't. Investigative reporting is a dwindling form. . . . I thought I could catch George if he did anything wrong.

Before I left the show to go to the *Evening News*, I told Colloff I'd go over the transcripts. But I never did. That's the point. It wasn't Roger's fault. I was lying awake nights worrying about the *Evening News*.

COLLOFF: There was no doubt my involvement was going to be heavier due to the nature of the broadcast. There was no doubt it was going to be a controversial broadcast, and George had had a run-in the previous year with the News Council on the gay show. I knew about it. It was a combination that meant I'd be heavily involved. I probably spent more time on this broadcast than on three other documentaries.

Let me say one thing. It sounds like self-justification but it's true. I had in many conversations spoken in general terms with George and with Howard Stringer and George about editing precisely because George had been in trouble with the News Council. I couldn't have been more clear to Crile. We would be going over this broadcast with a fine-tooth comb, and he damn well better be in the clear.

LACK: You need someone who knows how a documentary was shot. People who come through the discipline and know how stories are put together. That is not a judgment on Roger Colloff professionally or personally. If you're not a writer or producer, you don't bring to it the same eyes and understanding. That's not to say you can't know where there's something gone awry. But it's more difficult.

Crile? I'd be pretty involved. He's a fairly familiar quantity as a producer. I'd be asking who are you interviewing and why? What are you getting? I wouldn't be in the editing room. But I'd be getting an understanding of how it's taking shape.

What about Crile's sixteen-page Blue Sheet with its twenty-four mentions of conspiracy?

STRINGER: That was George trying to sell an extremely reluctant executive producer. The length of the Blue Sheet reflected a massive amount of skepticism on my part.

What about the use of the word "conspiracy"?

CHANDLER: I wasn't particularly upset about the word. If these people would say on camera what George said they would say that fits the definition of conspiracy pretty easily. Obviously, the other part is conspiracy against whom? Crile said they would develop that later.

STRINGER: I didn't want to use the word. I saw an alternative lead for the show that Mike Wallace wrote. It did not use conspiracy but read something like this: "This is a mystery story . . . about Duty, Honor, and Country." It was later dropped. In George's defense, I've always been skeptical of investigative pieces. They always give me trouble. I usually end up by saying, "So what?"

COLLOFF: We talked about it at Leonard's and my screening. Is the use of the word justified? We concluded that it was. Had Crile made up his mind? That's a valid question. Was it more than a working hypothesis? I don't know. George clearly had strong feelings about it.

If I had to do it again, of course, I wouldn't use it. The reason is, frankly, it wasn't worth the hassle.

LACK: I never studied the broadcast or picked it apart. Three weeks after it had been on the air, I said to Mike Wallace that the word "conspiracy" feels wrong, particularly after all the criticism.

Do you think fairness and balance apply in a broadcast like this?

CHANDLER: Yes, fairness and balance apply, but this was a peculiar kind of show because it dealt with a set of accusations. You lay out the accusations and you lay out the responses. It's not your average story.

STRINGER: Crile was told about the guidelines umpteen bloody times on this show.

LACK: When I first saw the show, I did not think it was fair and balanced. My immediate concern was whether Westmoreland was edited fairly and given the full opportunity to express himself. I raised it publicly with Stringer and Crile, and then Mike Wallace was called in. There were two examples where I said it sounds like an upcut, and we went to the transcript and added material to those two places.

What about Sam Adams and his role in the broadcast?

CHANDLER: Adams was going to deliver these people. I was told we couldn't get these people on camera without Adams's help. I felt it was only fair to reimburse him for his time since he was working for us on this program and it was time away from his book.

Should the script have described Adams as a paid consultant?

Yeah.

Would you agree that Adams was not only a consultant but a principal adversary?

Absolutely.

Do you have problems with having Adams on location and the coaching of friendly interviewees?

I have problems with that.

STRINGER: We had a number of meetings with Sam Adams before the show was even approved. He was in and out of the office. His consulting fee went up in stages. Originally, it was $10,000. The reason was that Sam, who often looked disheveled, apparently didn't have a lot of money. It became absurd for this man, who was obviously obsessed with this issue, not to have his expenses covered.

Initially, George indicated there wouldn't be such an extended period with Adams. We were dealing with a fait accompli in effect. George didn't know we would need Sam Adams so much. But there was so much paranoia among those to be interviewed that we needed Sam along. . . . In essence, everybody was a reluctant witness. I don't think there was a vast body of knowledge that was expanded by Adams after a few months.

I knew Sam was in the cutting room from time to time. I

knew he went to London for the Meacham interview. The reason, as I was told, was that George had tried to get people to speak, and they wouldn't without Sam.

COLLOFF: I didn't have all that much contact with Adams. I talked to him a number of times. I thought the *TV Guide* story was off the mark here, as in a lot of other areas. Adams did not carry the show. . . . The only reason we went forward with the broadcast was that there were a large number of people adding to or confirming the story.

LACK: I never met Adams. I didn't know who he was before air. I wasn't familiar with the *Harper's* article or his testimony before the Pike Committee. I have problems with his being a consultant, reporter, and adversary. Too many hats.

What about Mike Wallace and his role in the broadcast?

CHANDLER: I did have trouble getting Wallace to do the documentary. He was busy with *60 Minutes* and a new show called "Mike Wallace Profiles." He said: "Jesus, I don't have to tell you what *60 Minutes* takes out of me." At the same time he said he found the thesis of the broadcast very compelling.

Are big-name correspondents over-used—cut too thin—given more assignments than they can handle?

Sure.

Are their names used to increase audience size?

Absolutely.

STRINGER: I agree correspondents are cut too thin and used to showcase a piece. But part of the attraction of having Mike Wallace is he's tough, not just in interviews but on producers.

COLLOFF: Mike's role was minimal but that's not unprecedented. With Westmoreland, he did his homework. When you read through the interviews, Mike was not a puppet on a string. He got into some back and forth and held his own.

Are top correspondents given too many assignments?

A close call on this one. There is no problem, say, in taking advantage of Charles Kuralt's name by having him narrate a noncontroversial subject. On a broadcast of this sort, it's a lot more troublesome.

LACK: My impression is that Mike Wallace was terribly involved. He knew why he was interviewing, and he was heavily involved in the writing of the script. He's not the kind of guy to walk in and read the script.

Wallace had told me he didn't see the transcripts.

I think that is a bit disingenuous on Mike's part. He should have had ample opportunity to read the transcripts and know what the broadcast stands for.

Was General Westmoreland fairly treated in the broadcast?

STRINGER: I didn't know that it came down to the wire in getting the interview areas to him in writing. I don't know what they might have been afraid of by letting him see this in writing earlier. It's not clear to me how much you're obligated to tell a person about a pending interview.

I saw the Westmoreland news conference. It made me nervous. It wasn't Westmoreland but the presence of all those other people that made me nervous.

COLLOFF: I think Westmoreland should have been prepared for his interview. If George was any more clear, it would have been a violation of standards. If Westmoreland wasn't more aware, I don't know what you can do. He could have canceled.

I never saw his "correction" letter until he held his news conference after the broadcast. A good case could have been made that we put in a line: "Subsequent to our interview, Westmoreland reversed his position." Frankly, I wish I'd have known about the letter. I didn't.

LACK: I told Crile and Wallace I would have handled Westmoreland's letter differently. I would have included a line about the letter in the broadcast: "Westmoreland wrote us again after the interview . . ." I think Mike agreed with me. He had some doubts about the way it was handled.

What about the two interviews with George Allen?

STRINGER: I did not know that Allen was interviewed twice.

Did he know that he was coaxed and coddled so much he finally asked Crile: "Is this kosher?"

(Shakes head.)

That he was asked the same question eleven times with Crile telling him: "You can do this better"?

Oh, shit.

COLLOFF: When Sally Bedell was writing her article for *TV Guide,* Crile called me and said: "Roger, I've got some bad news for you." He told me about Allen. He was very agitated. I was upset. No, I didn't know at the time that Allen screened other interviews.

LACK: I did not know Allen was interviewed twice.

A violation?

First, I would ask why it was done a second time.

What about spontaneity?

If you go back a second time to ask additional questions, that is okay."

What if you don't like the way it looks?

I don't buy that.

What if I say I'll screen some of the material for you?

(Shakes head).

What about turmoil in the production unit?

STRINGER: One of the problems was the location of the editing room. It was away from the rest of the operation so it was hard to detect bad vibes. And in December and January, when I was not there, there were apparently vibes all over that place.

COLLOFF: As for Ira Klein, I was at screenings that he was at but I'm not sure I'd know him.

LACK: Klein came to me several weeks after the broadcast. His first concern was that we were not fair to Westmoreland in a particular cut. I asked if he had discussed it with Crile. He said no. I thought he had an obligation to talk to Crile first. Klein said he was upset by the Westmoreland news conference. I made sure all of them got together.

How about Adams disagreeing with the premise of the show?

I called Adams. He said he didn't know what Klein was talking about.

STRINGER: What makes me particularly angry is that Grace Diekhaus was on location. It was those kinds of things that really pissed me off. I said to George: "I gave you a fair amount of trust, and you didn't share these things with me."

LACK: I would have asked why she was on location. I'd probably ask what it is she's contributing. Is it personal or professional? If just personal, I'd have no objection. If professional, I'd like to know about it.

How about the print advertisement for the show?

CHANDLER: I was bothered by the way the word "conspiracy" was used in the ad, splashed all over that piece of art. The ad people prepared one version. Van Sauter didn't approve it. Conspiracy was in the body of the text, but there wasn't a bold conspiracy headline. Sauter sent it back. He felt it wasn't a good strong ad. The second time it came back with the conspiracy thing. Van and Ed Joyce approved it.

They played all kinds of game with the art. In the first version, Johnson and Westmoreland were standing together, but it was thought that was taking it a little too far. The second version was the generals seated around a table. They considered shooting a still of their own people dressed up in uniform.

I said: "Wait a minute. I have serious problems with that— staging something we don't know took place." Van agreed that we shouldn't stage a photo.

I was still disturbed. I thought the drawing of the generals sitting around a table was too realistic, too much like a real picture.

I didn't have very many troubles about the copy. But there was a question in my mind whether the word "conspiracy" in the headline was too strong.

COLLOFF: The ad gave me a problem and I said so.

Looking back at the show, how do you feel about it now?

CHANDLER: When you commission a documentary, you never know what you're going to get.

Dealing with producers as an executive is an act of faith. Ninety-eight percent of it is faith. Do you trust them? The documentary area will not be a driving, forceful operation unless you let them do their thing. It is a matter of integrity, ethics, and professionalism. If you as an executive get too much involved, you destroy what you're trying to create.

STRINGER: If all the standards for fairness had been followed, it would not have changed the outcome of the broadcast.

COLLOFF: I'm prepared to answer for my involvement. But it is hard to answer for others. . . . It is not fair to the broadcast or to me to say it was leaderless.

I felt I walked right up to the line of what I could do in a management job. I read the Graham, Westmoreland, and Rostow transcripts to be sure we were representing that point of view accurately. I went back over them after the screenings with George, stopping and starting and asking for sources to satisfy myself. . . . He answered everything to my satisfaction.

LACK: The last month of a documentary is for the management screening and a period of checks and balance when you take the hardest look at what's being done. I think, though there's no joy in saying this, that most executive producers take the last three weeks as a time where you can stop a runaway locomotive. You turn the editing room upside down. Clearly, this didn't occur. I don't know why. Whether everyone thought Roger was doing what Howard was and vice versa. Maybe there wasn't enough communication between them.

George Crile phoned and asked if I would speak with David Halberstam, who had won a Pulitzer Prize in 1964 for his reporting from Vietnam for the *New York Times*. I know Halberstam reasonably well and said I would be glad to talk to him. During my investigation, I had tried to be responsive to Crile or to anyone involved in the broadcast if they asked me to see or speak with someone they considered to be important.

I reached Halberstam in Nantucket. He told me he had not seen "The Uncounted Enemy" but had read the *TV Guide* article. Later, after he had screened the program and in an affidavit for the Westmoreland trial, he would strongly support the broadcast.

"It was crucial then to rig information," Halberstam told me. "It was probably done unconsciously, and therefore the word 'conspiracy' is too strong." (Halberstam would later change his mind about this and call the usage "reasonable and appropriate.") "We created a vast lying machine starting in Washington with parallel parts in Saigon.

"The standards and tone were set in Washington. They let Saigon know what they wanted to hear. Saigon would report to Washington, and Washington, pleased with what it got, would say: 'Isn't that wonderful!'

"George Romney's brainwashing statement was really brilliant. Everyone had been had. Everyone was victim of the lying machine.

"Walt Rostow manipulated information. Information became highly politicized. LBJ said it was a small war and then we had four to five hundred thousand men there. The stakes were much higher than we admitted. This was not like World War II or Korea where you held land, attacked, and held land. It was completely a matter of judgment here. Here you can jiggle information. If the information is accurately reported, based on the numbers, the war cannot be won.

"I believe Westy is a sort of decent man, not smart, and he is politicized. He didn't understand the war. He thought you had to hold territory. He and LBJ had a skillful relationship. Westmoreland got almost all he wanted. The understanding was he wouldn't blow the whistle on LBJ. Therefore, he consciously or unconsciously rigged information. Westy was a Boy Scout. He knew he had to play with LBJ.

"The enemy could absorb enormous losses. We were fighting the birth rate of a nation. Westmoreland didn't understand the war. He was caught up in the technological success.

"Tet a victory? Bullshit. There is no such thing as a military victory and a political defeat. You can't separate the two. If they were ever straight with the American people, then Tet wouldn't have been a surprise. If they didn't disingenuously believe and give the public the wrong picture, the people wouldn't have been so surprised. Until Tet, no one believed people like me, Morley Safer, and Ward Just.

"It was a vast lying machine. Everyone was a victim. Rostow manipulated information. Carver was making a career. He was pleasing people in Washington. George Allen is very shrewd, terrific. He understood Indochina. He knew the institutional bias.

"The essential core of the broadcast, as I understand it, was that crucial information was withheld, they underestimated the North Vietnamese, and there was false optimism. I believe it began with LBJ. They misled themselves, and they misled the country."

With Halberstam, my interviews for the investigation had reached an end. There were two aspects to "The Uncounted Enemy" that would now have to be addressed.

First, the program itself: I was persuaded that the basic story, the premise, that George Crile and Mike Wallace had presented to the

American public could not be dismissed or, as *TV Guide* had done, ignored.

Second, the way the program had been produced: My inescapable conclusion after an examination that I had tried to make as thorough and fair as possible was that, in its execution, "The Uncounted Enemy: A Vietnam Deception" was seriously flawed.

14

THE MESSAGE
IS DELIVERED

For eleven days after completing the last interview, I worked on writing my report. It was to go only to Sauter and Joyce, and while it had all been very low-key—neither applying any inordinate pressure—both had told me that they were anxious to get it as soon as possible.

My staff and I worked through the Fourth of July holiday and followed a simple, cross-checking procedure. I would write a page on yellow copy paper and give it to Toby Wertheim and Barbara Pierce. "I don't want this checked only line by line," I told them. "I want it checked word by word. One trivial mistake—a wrong date or even time of day—will be seized upon."

Later, there would be plenty of people picking away at the report but no one ever caught us with those kind of corrections. There would be the usual complaints about interpretation and some bitter attacks on me personally, but that was to be expected.

A spate of letters to Sauter supporting the broadcast began to descend upon us. They came from former CIA officers Sam Adams and George Allen; former military officers Gains Hawkins, Richard McArthur, William Corson, and George Hamscher; Representative Paul N. McCloskey, Jr; Richard M. Moose, a former special assistant to Walt W. Rostow; Greg Rushford, an investigator for the Pike Committee; and Thomas Powers, author of the Richard Helms biography. I had a hunch the campaign had been orchestrated by George Crile, and I decided to put all of these letters in the appendix to my report. Some of the excerpts:

From Col. Gains Hawkins: " . . . none of the information stated by me during my two or two-and-one-half hour interview with George Crile was taken out of context. Indeed, I was amazed at the skill of the documentary editors in preserving the text and flavor of my remarks."

From Sam Adams: "I do not have, nor have I ever had, serious reservations about the CBS documentary. . . . On the contrary, I think it was a service both to United States Intelligence and to the American public."

From George Allen: "That the show itself became controversial should surprise no one; no treatment of the Vietnam war is likely to escape that fate. . . . I believe 'The Uncounted Enemy' was a reasonably fair and accurate depiction of the 1967 controversy over the enemy 'order of battle' . . . despite my early misgivings about participating in a public airing of some rather 'dirty linen,' I'm glad that I did."

From Lt. Richard McArthur: " . . . all statements made by me in the telecast were absolutely accurate. . . ."

From Col. George Hamscher: " . . . as far as I'm concerned the documentary was produced as well as the events and people under examination would or will allow. I have no complaint about George Crile's conduct or his product, which is more than I can say for Don Cowet [sic]. . . ."

From Thomas Powers: "I think CBS's documentary made an important contribution to the integrity of the intelligence process, and I hope you will express the unreserved pride in your reporters which their work deserves."

In addition to the supportive letters—there were ten in all—I added two that were critical. Ironically, that was almost the same pro-and-con ratio as that in the broadcast. Gen. Phillip Davidson, at Westmoreland's request, sent Sauter a letter he had written to the *New York Times* on March 8 which the paper had elected not to publish.

In it, Davidson claimed that the military men who supported Sam Adams's numbers thesis were "relatively junior officers, preselected by Mr. Crile to support his charge of a massive conspiracy to lower enemy strength figures. While the junior officers themselves did not use the terms 'manipulated, suppressed and altered'—those are Mr. Crile's words—they did say they could not get their figures accepted by the senior officers for whom they worked. This statement is far different, however, from alleging a conscious and organized conspiracy. . . ."

Rostow's letter, which I extracted from the Crile White Paper, was written on January 27, four days after the broadcast, and included his memorandum for the record to the LBJ Library. He called the broadcast "grotesquely distorted and misleading."

Whether orchestrated or not, the ringing support of the "friendly" witnesses who appeared on the broadcast—Hawkins, Allen, Hamscher, and McArthur—would be important to Crile. Television news producers grow accustomed to complaints from those who appear on their programs: They were edited unfairly; their most important statements were left on the cutting-room floor; or they were used out of context. None of these men had these complaints. All of them were generous in their praise for the program, for its producers, and for CBS News.

On Thursday, July 8, I delivered my report to Sauter and Joyce. It ran fifty-nine pages, and I thought they were a bit stunned by its length. Perhaps they had been expecting a memo! I was still worried about a leak and made only one extra copy which I locked in my desk. I assumed that the copying machines in Sauter's office were working overtime and that he would be distributing the report. There might well be a leak but it wouldn't be coming from me.

The report I turned in was as factual and unadorned by adjectives as I could make it. The three principal findings, the ones that would lead all of the press accounts, were stated without equivocation:

- While the premise—that we had undercounted the enemy in Vietnam—was persuasively supported by former military and CIA analysts, the program was out of balance. There were others, equally impressive and knowledgeable, who disagreed with this premise, and they had not been fairly represented.
- A "conspiracy," given the accepted definition of the word, had not been proved.
- The friendly witnesses had been coddled in their interviews, while those opposing the thesis—Westmoreland and Graham—had been treated harshly.

All of the other findings that I had found fault with were listed: the double interview and screenings given to George Allen; the flaws in the editing; the failure to identify Sam Adams as a paid consultant; and the lack of journalistic enterprise in trying to locate General Davidson.

The severity of the report gave me no joy. When I had taken on the assignment, I had secretly hoped that whatever shortcomings were uncovered would be minor and that I would be able to endorse the broadcast with only minor reservations. "Forget process," George Crile had urged me. But more than process was involved here. What was involved was the essence of good journalistic practice—fairness, accuracy, balance.

I was critical of *TV Guide* for its cavalier decision not to deal with the premise of the broadcast. It seemed indefensible for the magazine in the longest article in its history, splashed all over its cover, to say of its investigation: "Its purpose was not to confirm or deny the existence of the conspiracy that CBS's journalists say existed." That seemed at best like a cop-out. It was certainly possible that the premise was true, and a group of prototypical Americans, hardly fringe people, had gone on camera to support it.

I wondered whether the report would inhibit the news division in the days ahead. There were those who would say: Don't hold your breath until CBS does another controversial documentary; the heat from this one will last for a long time. If that were true, if caution and fear were to be the enduring legacy of my investigation, then it would have been a thoroughly depressing exercise for me. I wasn't asking for caution; I was asking for care.

I also had to wonder about the reaction of my superiors in the news division and at Black Rock. The hands-off policy they had followed while I was conducting the examination was admirable and welcome. But now the deed was done and their impassive civility could easily be replaced by an eruptive, critical reappraisal. How did we get into this? We asked you to look into the *TV Guide* allegations and tell us where, if at all, we went wrong. And now you have delivered to us this damning, fifty-nine-page document that the press will be clamoring for.

The next day Sauter phoned. He called the report "a remarkable piece of work." Joyce called a few minutes later and said much the same thing. Gene Jankowski, president of the Broadcast Group and Sauter's boss, called with congratulations; Tony Malara, president of the television network, wrote a thoughtful note of approval. The most extravagant praise came in a phone call from Thomas Wyman, president and chief executive officer of CBS: "Everyone has a hero at one time or another. You are my hero. It was a difficult and thankless job, and you did it brilliantly." It was kind of him, although I found the words a bit purple for my taste.

I was certain there were a few folks ranging through the corridors who were not about to describe my report in quite the same terms. Among them would be George Crile, Mike Wallace, Roger Colloff, and Howard Stringer, and I gathered that both Sauter and Joyce were waiting for them to come thundering into the executive suite. I was certain they would try to pick the report apart and to soften it. I figured that would be Sauter's problem. My job was done. I had seen my role as reporter, and I had filed my story.

I discovered rather quickly that I was being naive. Sauter phoned in the afternoon to tell me that there would be an all-day meeting on Sunday at Gene Jankowski's house, and that I was expected to be there. I was to drive to Sauter's house in Redding, Connecticut, join him and Joyce, and then drive to nearby Weston where Jankowski lived.

When I arrived at Sauter's modern, glassed-in house, he and Joyce were in the living room watching the CBS program *Sunday Morning*. The *New York Times* was spread between them on the floor and as if on cue, whenever a commercial came up or a story on screen began to bore them, they would begin thumbing through the papers. I found it fascinating—they seemed to watch and read in synch. They said little to me; there was no talk of an approach or game plan for the impending meeting.

When we left to go to Jankowski's, Sauter and Joyce drove together and I followed them in my car. Jankowski lives in a handsome white clapboard house in Weston, and the meeting was held on his back terrace overlooking the pool and the tennis court. There were six of us— Jankowski, Sauter, Joyce, and myself, and two CBS Broadcast Group vice presidents, Gene Mater and David Fuchs, both upper-echelon executives knowledgeable in matters of public information and policy. Fuchs had moved between the news division and Black Rock. He had not shown much as a producer but became a highly regarded executive. He knew the business and the dynamics of television, and Jankowski valued his opinion. Mater, tough-minded and often dour, specialized in the Washington scene and the intricacies of the Federal Communications Commission and had good media contacts.

The hot, sun-drenched July day, the inviting pool and tennis court, struck me as an oddly inappropriate setting for the painful meeting that was about to begin. No voices were raised; there was no acrimony. That was not the CBS style. It was unpleasant, serious business, and even the normally buoyant Jankowski seemed subdued as he listed the areas that had to be addressed.

—*News standards:* What violations were there and what can be done to see that this sort of thing doesn't happen again?

—*Disciplinary action:* What should be done? "Roger Colloff ought to be fired," Mater said.

I told Mater I thought he was wrong. "Colloff," I said, "had been thrust into an impossible situation." It was one of the few times during the day when I spoke out. With its managerial overtones, the meeting was making me increasingly uncomfortable.

—*Public statements:* What should be said to the press and to the public?

—*What should be done on the air?* Should we do a broadcast on this whole affair?

—*Internal.* What should be said to the staff of CBS News?

—*Legal.* What legal problems are there? What lawsuits are possible? Our lawyers will be reading my full report.

Van Gordon Sauter spoke next, and he made these comments:

—We stand by the premise of the broadcast. It was legitimate in its basic facts, that these former MACV and CIA people did confess to "cooking the books."

—The CBS News Standards were violated. There should be regular meetings at our bureaus in New York, Chicago, Los Angeles, and London. Every employee should get a copy of the Standards. Every new employee should sign for one.

—In its execution, the broadcast was out of balance. It barely stands up.

Gene Mater said that the thrust was all right but the use of the word "conspiracy" was wrong. Any errors by *TV Guide* should be pointed out. We should put a program on the air with Westmoreland and his friends getting twenty minutes and Sauter replying for ten minutes. Mater thought the idea of appointing an ombudsman for the news division was a good one.

The meeting went on until mid-afternoon with a short break for a buffet lunch near the swimming pool. Jankowski wound it up by telling us that they would write a statement giving the gist of my report on Monday. The lawyers would go over it on Tuesday. The Board of Directors of CBS would read it on Wednesday, when it would also be shown to Crile and Wallace. On Thursday, July 15, the expurgated report would be made public.

At last, I thought, I was finally out of the mix. Again, I was wrong.

Monday was a waiting-for-the-storm day. Sauter was in his office with Joyce preparing the statement he would release on Thursday, and from time to time I was called down to read some of the copy he had written. What I feared, and what I was prepared to take a strong stand on, including going public, was an attempt to soften or whitewash what I had written. Sauter was writing his drafts on a vintage typewriter he kept in his office, and nothing that he showed me indicated any inclination to undercut my report.

On Tuesday, I spent all day in Gene Jankowski's conference room at CBS headquarters as a group of executives tried to thrash out the statement that Sauter would issue. Present were James Parker, senior vice president and general counsel for the corporation; Ralph Goldberg of the legal staff; and from the Sunday meeting at Jankowski's, Mater, Fuchs, Sauter, and Joyce. Jankowski moved in and out of the meeting during the day. The unstated question, one that concerned me deeply, was how forthright they were going to be about my findings.

To my mind, there were three essential elements that could not be finessed. The use of the word "conspiracy" was unwarranted; the broadcast was out of balance in reflecting the opposing sides; and the CBS News Standards had been violated repeatedly.

As for the substance of the broadcast, that enemy strength in the Vietnam War had been intentionally undercounted, nine former military and intelligence officers, on their own volition, had made that allegation, and none had recanted. I was convinced that if opposing views had been given more time, which they were entitled to, the thrust of the program would have remained the same, and it would have been a stronger broadcast.

Sauter was doing most of the writing, and he was having more trouble than he had anticipated. There were endless debates over phrases and words, not to mention lofty digressions into the philosophy and mission of CBS News. It was a prototypical example of group think, so familiar in large corporations, during which very little gets accomplished. I had the feeling that if they had put Sauter in a room alone, he could have knocked out the statement in an hour.

The meeting spilled over into a second day with Sauter grinding out versions for the others to criticize. In one he wrote: "CBS News regrets that this broadcast aired with violations of its news standards." He changed "regrets" to "apologizes." Neither would make the final cut. The flat statement that would be released was the standard news organization declaration: "CBS News stands by this broadcast."

In one version, Sauter wrote: "There was a good story here, but CBS News did not cover it with a broadcast by which we wish to be judged." This was changed to: "There was a good story here and we should have done better by it." Which became: "There was a good story here, and it deserved from us a less vulnerable production."

On the use of the word "conspiracy," there were several permutations. " . . . the credibility of the broadcast has been marred, in our opinion, by the use of the word conspiracy" was changed in the next version to " . . . it would have been more effective without the word conspiracy," and finally came out as "would have been a better broadcast if it had not used the word 'conspiracy' . . . a judgment of conspiracy was inappropriate."

Lines like this were dropped: " . . . when one begins a story with the assumption that the 'Truth' is known and obvious, there is a compelling moral obligation to seek out those who differ and to fully consider their position." The final statement would say that it would have been a better broadcast "if it had sought out and interviewed more people who disagreed with the broadcast premise. . . ."

In one version, Sauter said: "Tomorrow night, I will give a brief summary of this study in a special report on our television network." This was abandoned for reasons that were never made clear to me.

A rough draft of Sauter's report was sent one flight up, to the thirty-fifth floor, to be read by Bill Paley and Tom Wyman. That afternoon, Jankowski, Sauter, Joyce, and I went to Wyman's conference room to discuss it. It started flatteringly enough with both Paley and Wyman commending me.

After those amenities, the meeting became tense. Wyman left no doubt as to what he wanted: a very tough statement. Paley to my surprise did not seem to be as overwhelmed by the situation, and he began to reminisce about other trying experiences that had beset CBS in the more

THE MESSAGE IS DELIVERED   169

than fifty years since he founded the company. I was sitting next to Wyman, who could scarcely restrain himself. He began to mutter, so softly I could barely hear him, but words like "nonsense" and "ridiculous" came through. His body language—head down, hands clenched, face reddening, a continual twisting in his seat—was even more eloquent. He never raised his voice but his final orders were categorical: Sauter's statement must reflect the toughness of my report.

We went back to Sauter's office, where he began to pound out more drafts on his old typewriter. At nine that night, he had an eight-page statement that I felt satisfied Wyman's directive and accurately reflected my report. It dealt with the conspiracy and imbalance questions, although not as strongly as I had. I had said that a conspiracy had not been proved. Sauter said it would have been better broadcast without the word. I was not inclined to argue over that. His draft dealt straightforwardly with the George Allen double interview, with Sam Adams not being labeled as a "paid consultant," and with the editing transgressions.

On the Westmoreland "correction" letter, Sauter pointed out that the letter requested no correction and it was "a judgmental decision whether a Westmoreland memorandum included within these documents would have served to clarify the General's position." He said that "greater diligence" would have revealed that Gen. Phillip Davidson was not terminally ill. He took the position that the decision not to use any of Walt W. Rostow was a "judgment call."

Sauter called unwarranted TV Guide's accusations that Sam Adams was rehearsed or had backed away from the premise of the broadcast. He denied that any deal had been made with Lt. Gen. Daniel Graham to use his answer about Tet. He said there was an "honest disagreement among the three of us" whether "sympathetic witnesses had been given more gentle treatment in their interviews." I was the one who disagreed. I did not see how you could read the transcripts, which to my knowledge neither Sauter nor Joyce had, and not come away with the conclusion that Crile had played soft ball with those who supported him.

Sauter announced that an ombudsman would be created with the title Vice President, News Practices, to field and evaluate future complaints, both internal and external. He also revealed plans for a future broadcast on the issues treated in the Vietnam program.

He concluded by writing:

As we emerge from this episode, there will be no diminishing of our appetite for the controversial story or documentary.

The greatest asset of CBS News is its credibility. Protecting that credibility is the most important thing we at CBS News do as individuals and as an organization, and it is the most important aspect of our service to the public.

On the night of July 14, Sauter held a closed-door meeting with Mike Wallace, George Crile, Roger Colloff, and Howard Stringer. I was not invited. From accounts that I have heard, it was an often stormy and bitter affair which carried over into the next day.

I have been told that the four men, especially Crile and Wallace, were intensely critical of my report, but the only substantive change in Sauter's statement was one of positioning. The sentence "CBS News stands by this broadcast" had been on the second-to-last page of his statement. It was moved up to the second page. It became the first conclusion, following a page and a half of introduction.

At 4:00 p.m. on July 15, Sauter's statement was released to the press. Sauter was closeted in his office taking press calls. I took none.

15

THE HUE
AND THE CRY

If I had had any doubts that the press and the country had a consuming interest in how CBS would reply to the complaints about its Vietnam documentary, they were dispelled on the morning of July 16 with the release of Sauter's eight-page statement.

It made a front-page story in the *New York Times* under the head-line: "CBS CRITICIZES DOCUMENTARY BUT STANDS BY IT." Reporter Jonathan Friendly called the Sauter account an "unusually frank and critical memorandum."

Friendly quoted Mike Wallace as saying he had spent three weeks on the show while Crile spent fifteen months. Wallace said he was busy with *60 Minutes* and other specials and acknowledged a need for procedural reform that would require correspondents to take a more active role.

George Crile told Friendly that the double interview with George Allen was "not something I would do again." He also said that the Westmoreland "correction" letter "went right by me and Mike."

The *Times* also reached General Westmoreland in South Carolina. He called the Sauter statement "an incredible piece of whitewash," which had concentrated on procedural matters. The general said that he had expected me to contact him during my investigation "as a matter of courtesy," but that he never got a call.

Jonathan Friendly would call me about this the next day. It was the first time I had spoken with a reporter since beginning the investigation.

I told him that I had repeatedly screened and studied the text of West-moreland's one hour, fifty-four minute press conference cataloguing his complaints about the broadcast, and that I felt this had presented his arguments pretty thoroughly.

Not all of the reactions to my investigation were favorable. Tom Shales, the influential and caustic critic of *The Washington Post*, wrote: "CBS has done more apologizing for an outstanding documentary on Vietnam than Richard Nixon ever did after Watergate."

George Crile, who had been under orders to remain silent during the investigation, was now free to speak and told Shales: "Mainly, I'm happy that CBS stands by the broadcast, and I am now free to defend it as fully as it deserves to be defended. I have been frustrated by not being able to use my own voice." In the weeks ahead, his voice would be raised against both me and my report, but I would elect not to make any public response.

Three days later, Shales in fifty column inches unloaded more heavy ammunition. The headline—"CBS' LAVISH APOLOGIA"—accurately reflected where he was coming from. The text began:

> Killing, or at least impugning, the messenger who arrives with bad news is an old tradition, but you don't often find the messenger bopping himself over the head. Instead of dispelling the cloud that had formed over the program, CBS News all but seeded it for rain. . . .
>
> If they're going to be sheepish and equivocating about investigative reporting, maybe CBS News should also start apologizing for "Harvest of Shame," "The Selling of the Pentagon," "The CIA's Secret Army" [produced by Crile] and "The Defense of the United States."

The most astonishing, and to me revealing, phrase in the Shales story was this one:

[The CBS statement] "stood by the story but found it guilty of five violations of CBS News 'standards' and had other *quibbles* over such details as use of the word 'conspiracy' in describing the scandal being exposed" (Emphasis added).

In my six-week investigation, I had heard the word "conspiracy" interpreted and dissected. This was the first time anyone had dismissed my doubts about the use of the word as a "quibble."

In the days ahead, Shales's own paper would disagree with him on its editorial page. On July 24, *The Washington Post* wrote of the investigation and of Sauter's statement: "We think it's journalism that is self-confident enough to be self-critical. That is the only credible kind."

A *Wall Street Journal* editorial of July 20 praised CBS: "It is the first time we can recall that a major network has openly and seriously responded to charges against such a program." It then went on to deride the program. "The mistake of Crile and Wallace," the paper wrote, "was covering the story as a two-bit cover-up when it was a Greek tragedy. Most participants in this episode, one of them told us, were struck most of all by the sheer laughability of the thesis that 'Lyndon Johnson was Westmoreland's dupe.'"

In its issue of August 7, *TV Guide* tried hard and barely succeeded in suppressing its glee at the way things had turned out. Calling the CBS response "a touch of class," the magazine whose article two and a half months before had launched my investigation wrote on August 7:

"It's never easy for a respected news organization to admit errors. . . . *TV Guide* took no joy in criticizing CBS News. . . . We are pleased, however, that our article may have contributed, in some measure, to the network's moves to insure its credibility."

My own feelings were summarized best in the *Columbia Journalism Review* of September 10:

Being journalists, the makers of "The Uncounted Enemy" conceived the program almost exclusively in journalistic terms—specifically, in the ex-posé style popularized by *60 Minutes:* The credible and intelligent prose-cution witnesses, the sweating and less-credible villain (Westmoreland), and the conclusion of "conspiracy," a term that the network later dis-avowed. The conventions of neo-muckraking, moreover, forbade acknowl-edgement that the information was anything but new and exclusive. . . .

Viewing history in terms of conspiracy and betrayal invites the pre-sumption that journalism is seeking its own kind of retribution and is en-couraging the public to seek revenge as well. Good journalism should place itself above and beyond such presumptions.

The extensive coverage given the abbreviated version of my report surprised me, although I should have expected it. The print press has a persistent fascination with television, and the revelation that CBS was finding fault with itself was obviously going to receive considerable at-tention. I could not help but be pleased with the job I had done, al-though I took no personal satisfaction out of it. I told my wife I would much rather have produced a blockbuster documentary than a critique of CBS News. I spent the next few days warding off requests from friends and bare acquaintances for a copy of the full report. To my astonishment, it still had not leaked.

Within two weeks, the inevitable lull set in as the press turned elsewhere in its computerized, satellite-driven quest for instant news. Westmoreland and CBS moved off the front pages, out of the television columns, and, as many had predicted, began its inexorable journey into the data banks. But the lull was deceptive; a firestorm was building. Its center was in Charleston, South Carolina, home of Gen. William C. Westmoreland, and it would soon burst onto the front pages of America in what would be called "the libel suit of the century."

In August of 1982, I was given a new assignment. It was as far away from investigating someone else's work as I could get and that delighted me. I rejoined Walter Cronkite as executive producer of his documentary unit. Our first project, one that interested me considerably, was a one-hour *CBS Reports* titled "1984 Revisited," marking the fortieth anniversary of George Orwell's epic, predictive novel. It would be an Orwell biography, but more than that it would pose the question: How close are we to the apocalyptic world of Big Brother, Newspeak, and Double Think that Orwell foresaw?

The documentary took ten months to produce, and along with extensive shooting in the United States, we went to Britain, Denmark, Spain, and Switzerland. When it was broadcast on June 7, 1983, to praising reviews, I would be reminded again that the Westmoreland affair was unshakable.

Tom Shales, a hard critic to please, would write in *The Washington Post* that the hour was "engrossing, instructive and inventive," and then went on to say: "there's the nagging impression that the show was produced according to the directive, 'Give us something that couldn't in a million years cause us any trouble.' It happens that the executive producer is Burton Benjamin, previously a CBS News administrator and the author of the in-house report on the hot-potato 'CBS Reports,' 'The Uncounted Enemy: A Vietnam Deception.'"

I told Andy Rooney how I felt about my new eminence. After nearly thirty years at the network, after producing more than four hundred documentaries and eight hundred editions of the *CBS Evening News,* if I got hit by a truck, the modest obituary would probably carry the headline: "REPORT AUTHOR SUCCUMBS."

As we were gearing up for the production of "1984 Revisited" in September of 1982, the decision that some said would never be made and others said was inevitable was finally taken: General Westmoreland sued CBS. His lawsuit, calling for $120 million in compensatory and punitive damages, was filed in U.S. District Court in Greenville, South Carolina. The general said that if he won, as he expected to, he would donate the money to charity.

Named in the suit were Van Gordon Sauter, who was subsequently dropped; Mike Wallace; George Crile; and Sam Adams. Westmoreland had rejected a CBS offer of fifteen minutes of unedited air time at the beginning of a proposed program to reexamine the issues of enemy troop strength raised in the documentary. Instead, the general had asked for forty-five minutes in a presentation to be approved by him.

My reaction to the lawsuit was dismay and bewilderment. Dismay because it reopened the Westmoreland episode, which I had hoped was closed, and I knew I would now once more be involved. Bewilderment because I honestly had never believed that Westmoreland would sue. It was not the amount of damages sought, which seemed astronomical, but the legal burden he faced. As a public figure, he would have to prove that the statements CBS made about him not only were false and harmful to his reputation but were also made with "actual malice"—that is, with knowledge that they were false or with reckless disregard for their truth.

The general reportedly had been advised not to sue by two prominent Washington lawyers, Edward Bennett Williams and Clark Clifford, and by Senator Barry Goldwater, but he had gone ahead anyway.

On September 13, at the Army-Navy Club in Washington, the same place where he had held his new conference after the Vietnam program, an angry Westmoreland made his announcement:

"I am an old soldier who loves his country and have had enough of war . . . I have been reviled, burned in effigy, spat upon. Neither I nor my wife nor my family want me to go to battle once again.

"But all my life I have valued 'duty, honor, country' above all else. Even as my friends and family urged me to ignore CBS and leave the field, I reflected on those Americans who had died in service in Vietnam. Even as I considered the enormous wealth and power that make CBS so formidable an adversary, I thought, too, of the troops I had commanded and sent to battle, and those who never returned."

Standing next to Westmoreland was his lawyer, Dan M. Burt of the Capitol Legal Foundation, a public-interest law firm in Washington. Burt, forty two, a short, scowling, hyperactive man, called the CBS offer of fifteen minutes of air time for his client "dignifying a lie." He pointed out that the conspiracy charge in the broadcast was a crime punishable by imprisonment and fine.

The lawyer for CBS would be David Boies, forty-three, of the prestigious New York law firm, Cravath, Swaine & Moore. Boies had been a key lawyer in Cravath's successful defense of IBM in a thirteen-year Justice Department anti-trust suit. Neither Boies nor Burt had ever been involved in a libel action.

Both men had received their law degrees from Yale but they had little in common. Burt, perpetually combative, called himself "a short, foul-mouthed Jew from the streets." Boies, relaxed and laid back, liked to tell people that he bought his suits at Sears. His somewhat casual demeanor was misleading; he had shown himself to be a tough and adroit advocate.

Burt was taking the case on a *pro bono* basis, but he would receive financial backing from four conservative foundations—Richard Mellon Scaife, Olin, Fluor and Smith Richardson.

On November 18, the lawsuit was moved from South Carolina to New York City. A U.S. district judge ruled that the general's home state was not the proper venue since all of the defendants lived in New York. A CBS spokesman said: "They were looking for a friendly jury."

I was traveling at the time for the "1984" documentary and did not learn of the switch until a week later.

George Crile was finally, in his words, free to speak, and he mounted a spirited attack against my report. He wrote a thirteen-page memorandum which he wanted CBS News to issue defending virtually every phase of his production. News executives and lawyers were given copies to analyze, and I was handed one for my comments.

He emphasized how many people he had interviewed for the program—139 in all. He listed people like Paul Warnke, former Vietnamese Premier Nguyen Cao Ky, Arthur Goldberg, George Ball, and Gen. Matthew Ridgeway—none of whom had appeared in the broadcast and to my way of thinking had little to do with the issue at hand.

When he decided to use the word "conspiracy," he said he had in mind "conspiracy to deceive not to violate the law." This is not quite how the dictionaries define the word.

He made much of my failure to take cognizance of the Pike Report, just as I was critical of him for not alluding to it in the broadcast. It might fairly be asked why he never chose to interview former Representative Otis Pike, who was alive and well and living in Long Island. Perhaps he was prescient. Some months later, Pike wrote a column in *Newsday,* and his reaction to the documentary would have given Crile a lot of trouble had he put the former congressman on camera:

> Our committee report said, ten years ago, that the estimates of enemy strength had been massaged, worked over and reduced for the purpose of encouraging the American people to believe that the war in Vietnam was going triumphantly, and that these optimistic reports certainly contributed to the shock felt in America when the enemy was able to launch its huge Tet offensive.
>
> Well, the CBS broadcast said all these things, too, and I watched it with great interest, seeing familiar faces saying familiar things. In my opinion, it was unfair. Not inaccurate or libelous, merely unfair.
>
> Our committee and the committee staff had argued over the word "conspiracy." The liberals, who had hated the war in Vietnam, thought there had been a conspiracy to deceive the American people. The conservatives said that Westmoreland was trying to win a war, and morale on the home front is always a vital factor. In the end, we finessed the word, saying whether there was a conspiracy or not was irrelevant.
>
> CBS said there was a conspiracy.
>
> Conspiracy is a bad word, connoting criminal activity in the minds of most of us. CBS made Gen. Westmoreland appear evil, and he was not evil. He may not have been either the best or the brightest, but he was doing the best he could for his country and he deserved better than CBS gave him.

Only in his "Conclusion—A Personal Statement" did Crile offer any sort of *mea culpa*. He wrote: "I have never questioned CBS's right or need to conduct such an investigation. And I do not want to leave the impression that I dispute the fact that certain, internal CBS guidelines were violated. Mistakes were made, lessons learned. . . ."

On this, Crile and I were finally in agreement.

I was tempted to reply to Crile point by point, but I knew I would just be getting into a paper chase, and I was about to go to Europe for the "1984" documentary. Before leaving I sent Bob Chandler this memo:

> George Crile's "Statement on the Benjamin Report" is quite vulnerable and obviously if I have to testify, which seems likely, I will be obliged to point out the vulnerabilities.

Madrid is a city where you go to dinner at eleven o'clock. On Thursday evening, January 27, Walter Cronkite and I with our wives had taken a chance and tried a restaurant at nine-thirty. Not to our surprise, we found that it would not be ready to serve us for half an hour. As a matter of fact, they were still vacuuming the floors.

We had hoped for better. We had spent a long and thoroughly unpleasant day shooting at the laboratory where a scientist was carrying on behavior-modification experiments with cats and monkeys, foreshadowing what George Orwell had said would happen to humans in 1984. The scientist had implanted electrodes in the animals' brains and was stimulating them with radio waves. I could not shake the sight of those cages with the palsied cats and the terrified, red-eyed monkeys. I don't know how he managed it, but when we finally got to eat, Cronkite ordered wild boar. After the day we had spent, I selected the most bland entrée on the menu.

We returned to our hotel, the Ritz, at twelve-thirty. I had just fallen asleep when the phone rang. It was 1:00 a.m. Of course, it was only 7:00 p.m. in New York, an ideal time to phone if the world had one time zone. We used to call it the flat-earth syndrome. It was Bob Chandler on the phone, and he told me that George Crile's statement had been cut to four pages; could he read it to me for my approval? I told Chandler that, no, he could not, and if he gave me some time to compose myself I might have some interesting suggestions about what Crile could do with the statement. I certainly was not going to listen to four pages of criticism at one in the morning after which I was expected to put my imprimatur on it. I told him to call my lawyer, Raphael Scobey, and read it to him. I heard no more about it.

We returned to New York and our documentary began to take shape. For the next two months, I immersed myself in it and was told virtually nothing about William Westmoreland, George Crile, or Vietnam.

On one night, Thursday, April 21, two events brought me abruptly from a novelist's 1984 to the actuality of 1983. The first took place in the Federal Court House in New York City; the second took place on nationwide television over the Public Broadcasting Service.

Responding to intense pleas from both sides, the judge in the Westmoreland case, Pierre N. Leval, ordered CBS News to give the general the full copy of my report. The decision, which the *New York Times* carried on its front page, was said to pose an issue novel in journalism law.

As Jonathan Friendly reported: "News organizations frequently investigate their own stories if questions are raised about them, but they have not been required to tell a libel plaintiff everything that such an investigation finds."

Judge Leval, a Harvard Law School graduate, appointed to the bench by President Jimmy Carter, said that CBS had waived any privilege of protecting my report when it released the Sauter memorandum.

"The Sauter memorandum," the judge wrote, "implies that the Benjamin Report supports its conclusions." He went on to say that if it did not, it could be "important evidence of the necessary element of malice."

Judge Leval also said that because my report studied the making of the documentary, it "may well lead to evidence of degree of care for accuracy, concern for truthfulness, and possible bias, prejudgment or malice."

"[CBS] has not treated the Benjamin Report as a confidential internal matter," said Leval. "It has relied in public statements on the fact of the Benjamin investigation and on the conclusions expressed in the report for public justification of its broadcast. . . .

"CBS cannot at once hold out the Benjamin Report to the public as substantiating its accusations and when challenged, decline to reveal the report, contending that it is a confidential internal study utilized solely for self-evaluation and self-improvement. . . ."

Dan M. Burt, Westmoreland's lawyer, greeted the release with a statement that CBS had been trying to cover up the *TV Guide* allegations but "Bud Benjamin told the truth and then they had a problem." My reaction at the time was that this was a compliment I could have done without.

The second event of the day might have been called the conversion of Hodding Carter III. On his PBS series analyzing the press, Carter moved 180 degrees in his appraisal of the Vietnam program. After it had been broadcast, Carter wrote in *The Wall Street Journal* that it had "rendered an important public service." On PBS, Carter offered a radically different conclusion:

> History may yet decide there was indeed a conspiracy in Saigon to fake the numbers. But at this point the evidence is less compelling, the witnesses more contradictory and the possible conclusions less obvious than the documentary suggests.

If you're going to make a case that there was a conspiracy at the highest levels of American intelligence, then you have to go to the highest levels and allow the chief conspirators to talk.

CBS is entitled to its opinion. But we're entitled to a more balanced presentation. Even if you're sure of guilt, there's a vast difference between a fair trial and a lynching. It's a distinction that was badly blurred when CBS made "The Uncounted Enemy: A Vietnam Deception."

George Crile appeared on the broadcast and later complained about its editing. He said the show had done to CBS what it claimed CBS had done to Westmoreland. Carter had announced that Mike Wallace was "not available to our cameras," and that created another brouhaha. Wallace vehemently denied that he had refused to appear. "Carter never tried to get in touch with me," he said.

Hodding Carter also noted in the broadcast that *TV Guide*'s "Anatomy of a Smear: How CBS News Broke the Rules and 'Got' Gen. Westmoreland" had recently been honored by the Society of Professional Journalists, Sigma Delta Chi. It granted its Quill Award to Don Kowet and Sally Bedell, which so infuriated CBS News that Sauter wrote a letter of protest to the Society.

There was another fallout that was fascinating to media watchers. It involved a 700-word story about Hodding Carter's broadcast in the *New York Times* and an Editor's Note that was printed the next day. Frank J. Prial had written the story, which was not a review but simply an account of what was in the show. The next-day's Editor's Note said that the Prial story had been "too long and too prominenty displayed," since Hodding Carter had turned up nothing "fresh, substantive or otherwise newsworthy."

All sorts of ominous theories were voiced about the note and its repudiation of its own report, including the allegation that Mike Wallace had complained about the Prial story to his friend, Abe Rosenthal, executive editor of the *Times*. Rosenthal scoffed at this and said it was nothing more than a part of the new self-policing policy of the *Times*. It was one more footnote to a story that was continuing to build rapidly.

As the CBS duplicating machines churned out copies of my investigation that night, I sat in my office, concerned not so much with how the report would be received as with what its release would do to me. It was obvious that try as I might to work in the Orwellian world of 1984, I was going to be thrust into the reality of a lawsuit in 1983.

16

FROM FOLEY SQUARE TO HANOI

We are about to see the dismantling of a major news network." The words were those of Dan M. Burt, lawyer for General Westmoreland, when he was delivered, by court order, a copy of the Benjamin Report on April 26, 1983. His statement was exaggerated and intemperate, reflecting an impetuosity that would be manifest in the courthouse in Foley Square in the months ahead.

Burt told Tom Shales of *The Washington Post* that he found the report "devastating" and "very harmful" to CBS news. "Obviously," he said, "I don't think it's a document CBS is happy to have other people have." He thought the report would make his case "substantially easier."

"If they had published the results of the Benjamin Report and come clean," Burt said later, "we wouldn't be in court today."

The release of the report received considerable press coverage, but oddly was not carried on the *CBS Evening News with Dan Rather* in its Tuesday, April 26, broadcast. "It was a news judgment, right or wrong," Rather told *The Washington Post's* John Carmody. He said a senior producer had informed him that the report was consistent with Sauter's earlier memorandum and therefore did not make a story. It did seem curious to media watchers for CBS to ignore a story involving its own network. NBC covered the release of the report the first night and ABC, claiming a producer misread the embargo date, carried it the following night.

The report was generally well received, although it was not without

181

its detractors. The Associated Press called it "thorough and thoughtful"; *Newsweek* called it "a stunning critique." Joshua Muravchik in the *New Republic* would write that I was "the one person who emerges a genuine hero" and "gave evidence of no interest other than getting at the truth," and might be seen "to represent all those journalists who welcome being held to, and having their news organizations held to, the highest standards of their profession." The conservative columnist James J. Kilpatrick said my report was "a model of fair and balanced coverage."

I was pleased to have the sensible Jack Kilpatrick, who had worked with CBS News as a commentator during political conventions, endorsing the report, but in the months ahead I found myself gaining some right-wing supporters who made me uncomfortable. Reed Irvine, head of Accuracy in Media, had been clamoring for my report to be released, and he was one ally I could have done without. Irvine had been unrelentingly critical of CBS News over the years and had recently suggested that Walter Cronkite might be soft on communism.

If there was any danger of an inflated ego during the post-report period, critics wasted no time in rectifying that. Ben Brown of *USA Today* wrote:

> While it ends up wringing its hands over the future of investigative journalism, the Benjamin Report's nit-picking specifics will scare most reporters. Few stories calling for interpretation of complex evidence could stand up to this kind of probing of methods and motivations. There is always someone else to talk to, another point to admit.
> . . . We should all be grateful that, while we take our turns judging both Westmoreland and CBS, Burton Benjamin isn't peeking over our shoulder taking notes.

Reuven Frank, the president of NBC News, had this to say:
"I'm afraid [the release of the report] will have an inhibiting effect. It means that people in charge of large news organizations can't look into what's being done in their own house without fear that their internal procedures and findings will become a matter of court record to be used against them."

Jonathan Z. Larsen in *New York* Magazine called my report "almost prosecutorial in its harshness." He said Westmoreland's supporters were "bedeviling the world's largest network. . . . The Pentagon Papers have become the Benjamin Report."

In their book, *Vietnam on Trial*, Bob Brewin and Sydney Shaw would write: "Benjamin's single-minded devotion to CBS and its traditions could be likened to religious fundamentalism."

An unceasing critic of me and of my report was Connie Bruck of the magazine *The American Lawyer*. She lost no opportunity to praise George Crile and his program and to disparage me.

In the September 1983 issue of the magazine, she wrote:

> Benjamin, who came to CBS in 1957 and is best known as the executive producer of Walter Cronkite's "Twentieth Century" series and of the "Evening News" during the seventies, has never produced the kind of controversial, ambitious piece that "The Uncounted Enemy" was; his forte is historical documentaries. Even his friends describe him as "purist," "literal-minded" and "fundamentalist." Benjamin is also more fervent than most; for him, friends say, CBS is almost a religion.

Bruck said David Boies, the Cravath lead lawyer, had told her he thought "a lawyer would have done a 'more sensible' report."

On August 23, Boies wrote her a letter about the statement:

> This is the only quotation you attribute to me that I think is completely inaccurate. As you know, I disagree with a number of the conclusions of the Benjamin Report. However, as I also told you, there are a number of its statements with which I agree, and I believe Mr. Benjamin did a credible job at a very difficult, and not particularly pleasant task—a task which, I also pointed out to you, he did not seek. I have no reason to believe, nor did I say, that Mr. Benjamin was not "sensible" or that a lawyer would have been "more sensible."

Bruck did not let up. In another piece, a year later, she referred to me as an "old-time newsman" who had elevated the CBS guidelines to "a canonical level; indicted Crile for misdemeanors in a tone that suggested that these acts were capital crimes; and, though Benjamin had undertaken no real study of the show's substance, nonetheless cast doubt on its soundness."

I decided not to respond to any of her pieces. Her personal criticisms annoyed me, but she had the typewriter and the magazine and that's what the press is all about. I was tempted to send her a list of so-called controversial documentaries I had produced, including a couple dealing with Vietnam, and jotted down ten that qualified. I thought about it and threw the list away. I considered telling her that if you cherish controversy, try producing the *Evening News* for three years. In that job, you are apt to deal with a controversy a night.

With the full report released, George Crile continued to defend his program. He told the Associated Press: "There's no way I can justify sitting back silently. A reporter has to defend his work. But I was so convinced that CBS was going to attack *TV Guide* and blow them out of the water that I agreed not to talk. . . . A narrow attack on the process alone got misconstrued as an attack on the substance of the broadcast."

Crile began to work the talk shows in face-to-face shouting matches with Don Kowet, who had expanded his *TV Guide* article into a book. They were on Cable News Network twice, the first time with Sandi Freeman, the second on "Crossfire" with Tom Braden and Pat Buchanan.

On the Freeman program, Crile was joined by David Boies and Kowet by David Dorsen, one of the Westmoreland lawyers. In the supercharged, watch-the-clock atmosphere of the talk show, Crile was a strong advocate who defended his case very well. He understood the logic of these appearances—that the tyranny of time often dictates who will prevail, that the more you talk, the less you will be asked. He had his facts and his arcane order-of-battle statistics firmly in hand, and while he occasionally patronized Kowet in flashes of arrogance that were familiar to those who knew him, he was a persuasive witness.

The months ahead were among my most productive at CBS News. The Cronkite documentary unit was increased in size after we broadcast "1984 Revisited," and over the next two years I would be the executive producer of six *CBS Reports*, virtually all that the news division produced.

They included a report on the impact of high technology on the nation's changing economy; an analysis of the rising threat of terrorism; a retrospective on the legacy of Harry Truman; Hiroshima plus forty years—the Bomb then and now; and a return to Vietnam ten years after the war. I would also produce a live ninety-minute program called "The Great Nuclear Arms Debate" with Cronkite which was ambitious and worthy but misfired. We had a reasonably good mix: Henry Kissinger in New York, Paul Warnke in Florence, and government officials in London and Bonn. It was a technical tour de force that unfortunately went nowhere.

With Cronkite, I went to Normandy for the fortieth anniversary of D-Day and to London for V-E Day plus forty years. At Pointe du Hoc, where American Rangers under intense fire had scaled the sheer cliffs on the beach with grappling hooks, we broadcast live for the *CBS Morning News*. President Reagan was there, and Cronkite was granted an exclusive interview, which was nicely timed by the White House with the presidential election campaign only five months away.

I also recycled a famous Fred Friendly documentary, made twenty years before, with President Eisenhower and Cronkite returning to the Normandy beaches. We had to cut the original broadcast from ninety minutes to an hour, and we built an effective new opening with Cronkite at Portsmouth in the original decision room for the D-Day invasion. We opened with Cronkite and Eisenhower in the black-and-white original interview at Portsmouth, then dissolved to Cronkite alone in color in an exact match. The program got an enthusiastic reception.

At this time, the Westmoreland affair seemed comfortably in the past, but of course it was not. The heavy legal guns were preparing for a trial that would begin on October 9, 1984. Two months before I was to go to Normandy, I was told to expect a subpoena from the Westmoreland side to give a deposition. It arrived, and I had to pull myself out of the news and documentary world and return to an investigation that I had all but forgotten.

Over the years, I have been fortunate enough to avoid legal proceedings and court rooms. As a young newspaperman in Cleveland, I occasionally had to cover police courts, but that was hardly an environment in which to gain sophistication about the law. In New York, except for signing a will and assuming a mortgage, my only involvement with lawyers and court rooms was as a juror. Now suddenly I was in the impressive law offices of Cravath, Swaine & Moore in Chase Manhattan Plaza conferring with an agreeable young lawyer from the firm named Randy Mastro. And he was briefing me on the intricacies of giving a deposition.

I found the experience unsettling because the technique involves a rather unforthcoming posture in which you are urged to supply as little as possible. I told Mastro that this might be easier than he suspected; it had been two years since I wrote the report. I had not looked at it since and given the production load I was carrying at CBS News, I had not thought about it. This news seemed to please him.

Mastro gave me a short course on depositions which he had obviously done many times before:

—Answer only what you are asked. Give them short answers. "Make them peel the onion," was the way he put it.

—You are talking for dictation as you would to a secretary or a dictating machine. You are not carrying on a conversation.

—Don't seem eager to answer. Pause as long as you like. A transcript does not indicate pauses.

—Beware of flattery. They may try to set you up as a great expert. Don't let them.

—If you get a tough question, ask them to repeat it. It gives you more time to think.

—If the questioner paces, don't follow him with your eyes. Just look straight ahead or stare at the stenographer.

—If you make a mistake, say, "Let me begin again." Don't say, "Excuse me" or, "I'm sorry."

—Don't let their lawyer interrupt. Say, "May I finish?"

—Emphasize: "My report speaks for itself." Don't go beyond it.

I told Mastro that I found the exercise fascinating and henceforth I would be able to watch the court-room dramas on television with new comprehension. I added that I planned to answer all the questions that I could, and if my memory failed, which I suspected it might, I'd say so.

There was one unpleasant meeting a few weeks later when a lawyer from CBS began to talk about the lawsuit as a challenge to CBS and to CBS News and to emphasize that loyalty was very important. My lawyer, Raphael Scobey, was with me and cut off the exchange rather sharply. I told Scobey after we left that I was glad he had interceded. He had spared me getting up and walking out.

If I ever had the idea that I would be a pivotal witness in the case, I was disabused when I was deposed on May 15. The entire proceeding, including a short recess, took only an hour and forty-five minutes. In contrast, George Crile's deposition was taken over fifteen days and ran more than nineteen hundred pages. General Westmoreland's was equally long. Howard Stringer's deposition ran for five days. I must confess I had indulged in a bit of Walter Mitty before the deposition—the key witness, days of testimony, lawyers wrangling. But it was all so perfunctory.

I had expected to be deposed by the contentious Dan Burt, and frankly was looking forward to it. Instead, I was examined by David

Dorsen, an experienced litigator. I found him to be courteous and straightforward.

Reading my testimony after the deposition, I was disappointed. I had told the truth, of course, but I was so caught up in the new game I had been taught—deposition giving—that I came on as too laconic. It did not sound like me, and I thought I had done poorly. The Cravath people said I had done fine, which heightened my misgivings. I resolved that if I was called to testify at the trial, I would forget court-room strategies and just be myself.

Dorsen uncovered an embarrassing omission in my report. He asked me if I remembered that Sam Adams had told me that he had informed Crile a month before the Vietnam program was broadcast that Gen. Phillip Davidson was not terminally ill and could be interviewed. I told him I had no recollection of that. Had I known it, I would certainly have put it into my report.

Dorsen then went into my Adams interview notes and read this excerpt:

BB: Did you tell Crile?
ADAMS: I told George. I said "Holy Cow." I don't know if he then tried to get hold of Davidson.

He was absolutely right, of course, and the exchange should have been in the report. I conceded it was a mistake that I could not explain. I had simply forgotten to include it. Dorsen without changing his expression asked me if I had ever heard of Col. Edward Hamilton. I said I had not. I later learned that it was Hamilton who told Adams that he had seen Davidson at a West Point class reunion at Myrtle Beach, South Carolina, and the general seemed to be in excellent health.

I told Randy Mastro after the deposition that given its brevity, I would bet that I would never have to testify. He said I was flat-out wrong. I was certain to be one of the early witnesses, as a matter of fact I might be the first witness. I told Mastro if that happened, they would never find me. I planned to be in Hanoi.

The trial began on October 9 and received predictably heavy coverage in the press and on television. The Cable News Network sought to report live from the court room, which is forbidden in all federal courts. Although he conceded he had some sympathy for the idea, Judge Pierre N. Leval was obliged to turn them down. Television had to resort to its customary way of covering trials: arrivals and departures of the principals with on-camera statements in the street or hallways when possible and sketch artists in the court room.

The trial would last for eighteen weeks, and I did not attend any of the sessions. Rumors persisted that I would be an early witness, but my name kept dropping off the list.

George Crile and Sam Adams were regulars in the court room. Mike Wallace was there from time to time, and there were flash visits by Sauter, Joyce, and Dan Rather. One juror indicated after the trial that the presence of the two superstars, Wallace and Rather, did not go unnoticed in the jury box.

I was now spending much of my time in a frustrating effort to secure visas for Cronkite, a production unit, and myself to get into the Socialist Republic of Vietnam so that we could produce a *CBS Reports* marking the tenth anniversary of the end of the war. The producer, Brian T. Ellis, CBS News bureau manager in Saigon when the war ended, had excellent contacts and was sophisticated about the Vietnamese, but our progress was glacial. He would be assured that everything was set and then be told there was a "little problem" in Hanoi.

I began to despair that we would ever get in, and one evening tried some personal persuasion at the apartment of the Vietnamese mission to the United Nations in Waterside Plaza on the East River. My contact was Tran Trong Khanh, a young second secretary for press relations, enigmatic but pleasant, and he ushered me into the apartment which had a striking view of the river but was almost barren of furnishings. He introduced me to their U.N. Ambassador, Hoang Bich Son, who spoke no English and listened to the translation of my pleas for visas with the impenetrable reserve so common among Communist functionaries. I spoke for nearly two hours about Walter Cronkite, the most trusted man in America; CBS News, the premier broadcasting network in the United States; and why it was vital to their national interests that we be permitted to do this documentary.

The ambassador assured me that they were honored that Mr. Cronkite and CBS wanted to come to their country, but it was very difficult, very hard to get answers from Hanoi, all Americans suddenly wanted to come to Vietnam, and they would continue to try. I began to suspect that the message was "Don't pack." "And, by the way," the ambassador asked, "were there any officials Mr. Cronkite particularly wanted to interview?"

"Yes," I replied, "certainly his excellency, the prime minister, Pham Van Dong."

Even the imperturbable ambassador seemed startled by that suggestion, but he quickly smiled and said that would be very difficult. The prime minister was an old man now and did not grant interviews, but they would tell Hanoi of our interest. Anyone else?

Suddenly, I was thrust back into the Westmoreland case and the courthouse. There was one man who ought to have the definitive answers for all of the questions being argued in Foley Square.

"The honorable general, Vo Nguyen Giap," I said.

If there was anyone who ought to know all about the communists' order of battle it would be the legendary Giap, hero of Dienbienphu and defense minister during the war. Imagine—I fantasized—getting a breakdown from Giap and bringing it back to New York to resolve the trial with one swift coup. They smiled. "That will be very difficult, too," Ambassador Son said. I brought myself back to reality and left, convinced that we were were not likely to get into Hanoi in the foreseeable future.

On December 13, 1984, any hopes that General Westmoreland's lawyers may have held that the Benjamin Report would destroy CBS and become a pillar of their cases were abruptly destroyed. Judge Leval so restricted the use of my report that it ceased to become a major weapon for the plaintiff.

"The fairness of the broadcast," the judge ruled, "is not at issue in the libel suit. Publishers and reporters do not commit libel in a public-figure case by publishing unfair one-sided attacks. The issue in the libel suit is whether the publisher recklessly or knowingly published false material. The fact that a commentary is one-sided and sets forth categorical accusations has no tendency to prove that the publisher believed it to be false. The libel law does not require the publisher to grant his accused equal time or fair reply. It requires only that the publisher not slander by known falsehoods (or reckless ones). A publisher who honestly believes in the truth of his accusations (and can point to a non-reckless basis for his beliefs) is under no obligation under the libel law to treat the subject of his accusations fairly or evenhandedly."

What Judge Leval said in unmistakable language was that as far as libel was concerned, news organizations do not have to be fair.

During the trial Leval repeatedly underscored this position. "My view," he told Boies and Burt at sidebar during Crile's testimony, "is that the fact that CBS may have had a guideline that prohibited this practice, so far as I can see, has no bearing on whether Crile or other defendants broadcast what they broadcast either recklessly as to the truth or falsity or with knowing dishonesty. . . . [The] fact that there is a rule at CBS that says 'Don't do it' in no way adds to the issue of whether there was knowing falsity propagated in the broadcast."

Leval addressed the matter of coddling friendly witnesses and treating harshly the unfriendlies during Westmoreland's testimony. He told the jury:

". . . Mr. Burt suggested that you should compare the tone of questioning of General Westmoreland during his CBS interview with the tone of questioning employed by CBS while questioning General McChristian.

"Now, I instruct you, you may consider tone of questioning only if you find that it bears on an element of truth in the plaintiff's case. The tone of questioning of persons by CBS is not an element in the lawsuit. There are many legitimate reasons why the tone of questioning may vary from witness to witness. A news organization cannot be held liable for the tone it uses in questioning a person.

"The issue is not whether CBS used a hostile or aggressive tone when conducting one interview, and a friendly, encouraging tone in another interview. The defendant may not be held liable for any such use of tones in questioning.

"The issue is whether defendants made false, defamatory statements either believing them to be false or recklessly as to their truth, and you may consider tone of questioning only insofar as you find it bears on that issue."

The judge also dismissed the matter of bringing George Allen into a cutting room and showing him excerpts from other interviews. At sidebar during Ira Klein's testimony, he told Boies and Burt:

"Well, I have previously ruled that if CBS had a guideline or a rule that prohibited the showing of interviews to a potential witness, the fact that there was such a rule and the fact that such a rule was broken, if it was broken, is not relevant to the issue whether the defendants knew they were putting on a false broadcast or were reckless with respect to a likelihood of falsity of the broadcast. And for that reason, that was part of the reason that I ruled out large portions of the Benjamin Report which discussed those rules."

The judge did permit the Westmoreland side to use statements made to me by defendants Crile, Wallace, and Adams, and by other CBS employees. But much of the report was out of bounds. For example, Dan Burt in his examination of Crile would not be allowed to mention the Benjamin Report unless Crile raised the subject first—an exceedingly unlikely prospect.

On February 17, 1985, I was at the Hôtel de la Tremoille in Paris waiting for Walter Cronkite to arrive. Momentous meetings were taking place in New York between the lawyers from CBS and General Westmoreland, but I had no way of knowing this. I had in my pocket a document I had been trying to get for six months—a visa for Vietnam. I had gone to the Vietnamese Embassy early that morning and after the usual deadening amenities, tea, and small talk, an embassy official stamped the visa in my passport.

Brian Ellis and the camera crew had been given their visas in Bangkok and were already in Hanoi. With them was John S. McCain, then a congressman from Arizona, now a senator. During the war as a Navy lieutenant commander, McCain had flown off a carrier in an A-4 Skyhawk and been shot down by a SAM missile. He had ejected from his plane and parachuted into a lake in Hanoi, suffering a broken leg and two broken arms. The son of the admiral who was then Commander of U.S. Naval Forces in the Pacific, he had been a prisoner of war for five and a half years. Now we were returning McCain to the scene of his anguish—the lake where a monument had been erected to celebrate his capture on October 26, 1967, and to the small cellblock where he had been beaten and tortured.

As I sat waiting for Cronkite in the hotel lobby, I began to worry that there would be a hitch and his visa would be denied. Our experience with the Vietnamese had been so maddening that the prospect did not seem absurd. But Cronkite arrived late that night, and early the next morning with Marthe Schurman of the CBS News Paris bureau, we went to the Vietnamese Embassy. I sat uneasily as we went through tea and small talk again. We were booked on a noon flight to Bangkok. Finally, Cronkite's passport was stamped and for the first time, the production was set. We rushed to the airport for the fourteen-hour flight to Thailand, which would be followed by a two-hour layover and another two hours to fly to Hanoi.

At Gia Lam Airport in Hanoi, capital of one of the world's most underdeveloped countries, we were met by the producer, Brian Ellis, and David Green and Andrew Stevenson, cameraman and soundman. When we passed through immigration at the airport, we had to put our money on the counter so that it could be counted; it would be counted again when we left. In addition to my pocket money, I was carrying $5,000 in cash in a money belt which I did not put on the counter.

Everything in Hanoi has to be paid for in U.S. green; credit cards or traveler's checks are useless. The government provides the transportation and logistical help, and it gets paid each day in cash. I gave my money to Ellis, who turned in the dollars for Vietnamese dong at some improbable official rate and doled out the worn bills in stacks during the trip.

We stayed at the Victory Hotel, the *Thang Loi*, built by the Cubans after the war and one of the few buildings in Hanoi bearing some semblance of modernity. An inexpressibly dreary place, its facilities were primitive—leaking plumbing, bug-ridden rooms, and atrocious food that was made more intolerable by the sight of rats scampering across the dining-room and kitchen floors. The lobby featured caged monkeys which added just the right ambience and odor to the hotel.

The sequence with John McCain retracing his experiences as a POW was unusually poignant. At the lake where he had parachuted from his downed plane, our camera crew drew a crowd of old men and women and some children. Our interpreter pointed to the monument with McCain's name and then to McCain, and the Vietnamese suddenly realized: This was the U.S. Navy pilot who had been shot down. They gathered around him, smiling and shaking his hand. McCain smiled back and exchanged small talk through the interpreter.

I thought McCain might have difficulty maintaining his composure when we went to the prison compound in the center of Hanoi. He walked unhesitatingly through the bleak courtyard and went directly to his former cell, no more than ten by twelve feet, where he had been held in solitary confinement. The emotions of the moment were manifest but McCain described the scene quietly and evenly, as if he were returning to some innocuous scene from his past.

To our surprise, we were granted an interview with Pham Van Dong. The frail and obviously failing prime minister, then seventy-nine, had been Ho Chi Minh's closest associate. We saw him at his official residence, a palatial yellow house out of the French colonial past. The press office in Hanoi had been unenthusiastic about the idea and wanted to know what Cronkite would be asking the prime minister. We gave them some vague areas we planned to cover and proceeded to start taping in a huge, dark room on the main floor.

The interview was a disaster. It is never easy when you have to go through an interpreter, but this was perhaps the most frustrating session I had ever been involved with. No matter what Cronkite asked, Pham Van Dong had his pre-set answer, as if memorized. The problem was that he was not always answering the question that had been asked. When we finished, we knew we had just accumulated a lot of tape for the trash basket, and Cronkite asked Pham if they might take a walk together around the palace grounds. The old man agreed.

Brian Ellis set the camera on a balcony to get a high shot of the walk, and Pham, Cronkite, and an interpreter began their leisurely stroll. Now the prime minister, unencumbered by his briefing book, was lively and interesting. He talked freely about MIA's, Cambodia, and normalization of relations with the United States. I realized that with the distant camera we were not recording any sound, so with an audio tape recorder in my hand I joined the group and managed to pick up most of the conversation. The story was used on the Rather News a week later.

Since we had been granted an audience with Pham Van Dong, I was certain we could interview anyone in the government we chose. I asked the press officer if we could now see General Giap. I was all ready with my questions about his order of battle during the Vietnam War, which I would then take back to New York to settle the unseemly legal quarrel that was taking place in Foley Square; at least, so I thought. "General Giap? Oh, yes, General Giap. We are sure that will not be possible but we will check." The next day, the predictable response: "General Giap is not here. He is on vacation." I was about to reply: "Where, in Cambodia?" but I knew that would be foolish.

Before McCain left us, he met with Col. Nguyen Van Cok, whom they introduced as their air force ace. They told us he had shot down twenty-one American planes during the war, a statistic I had some skepticism about. The colonel, they said proudly, is known throughout Vietnam as "Hero Cok." He sat with McCain, the two pilots using their hands to pantomime airplane maneuvers just as they do in the movies.

We then went to Army headquarters to meet Gen. Van Thien Dung, who was chief of staff during the war and in a sense was Westmoreland's counterpart. It was Dung, a protégé of Giap's, who led the final assault on the South in 1975. Two exchanges between Cronkite and the general were especially meaningful in view of the legal battle that was being waged in New York.

CRONKITE: General Westmoreland and some later historians say that we won a military victory in Tet by causing you extreme casualties, admitting that you won a psychological victory. But they claim that we won a military victory. What do you answer to that?

DUNG: I think this question has been dealt with in many tables and books. You know our war was a people's war. And it was an all-out war. Victory has to be measured politically, diplomatically as well as militarily. The general offensive . . . and concerted uprising of 1968 was an attack from our side not only in the military field but also in the political field and leading to the diplomatic field. And its end was to defeat the will of the United States administration. You know the political repercussions of the attack and the psychological effects were both great.

CRONKITE: General Westmoreland said that if he had been given a few more troops after Tet that your army was so badly mauled in the Tet offensive that we could have won the victory.

DUNG: He's a military man so it is likely that he only thinks of the number of troops. I'm also a military man, but I strongly believe that had he been given another hundred or two hundred thousand troops, the war would have ended the way it did with the defeat of the United States.

As we got ready to leave, General Dung gave Cronkite what was easily the most tasteless gift he had ever received: a spittoon made out of B-52 parts. We had done several sequences around the downed bombers which lay undisturbed in Hanoi, like ghostly victory memorials, and that had been disturbing enough. The Vietnamese general managed to top that.

We drove to Haiphong, crossing the Paul Doumer Bridge which during the war had supposedly been destroyed by American planes. There was no doubt it had been badly hit; ten years later, the damage could still be seen. Part of the bridge roadway had wooden planking and we had to inch our way across. Halfway to Haiphong, we stopped to tape an incredible scene: A huge throng, perhaps ten thousand men, women, and children, were building a new road virtually by hand. It was reminiscent of the heroic communist films of Stalin's time. The women and children were carrying the dirt and rocks in sacks on their shoulders and heads. The swarming mass of humanity epitomized, more than anything we had seen, just how primitive and impoverished the country was. Cronkite's report was also used on the Rather News.

Haiphong, bombed repeatedly during the war, was a cheerless city with many buildings still in need of repair. The harbor, the one we were always going to mine, was filled with merchant ships. On the streets, there were many children playing. The most popular street sport seemed to be, of all things, badminton.

We flew to Ho Chi Minh City on Air Vietnam, which is known to handle over-booking by having the extra passenger sit in the lavatory with the door open during the trip. Cronkite, Ellis, and I, who had been there when it was Saigon, were all eager to see the city once again. I remembered the first time I had seen it in 1963, before half a million Americans had arrived, when it was still the charming Frenchified city that had justly been called "the Little Paris of the East." And I remembered, too, the second visit in late 1965 with the buildup under way—the streets choked with Jeeps, families sleeping on the sidewalks, bar girls and prostitutes everywhere, children begging and clinging to you until you gave them money.

In 1963 I had left with some rather hawkish feelings; we were right to help the South Vietnamese preserve their freedom. When I came back two years later, one event started to turn me around. Cronkite and I went to a base camp south of Saigon where a brigadier general, obviously awed by the famous anchorman, briefed us in his tent. He was a bantam-rooster of a man and as he paced back and forth describing the Viet Cong, he suddenly said: "You know, those little bastards are yellow."

I thought it was an ethnic slur and I was tempted to reply: "Yes, and those Nazi bastards were white." Then I realized he meant yellow as in cowardly. "Why don't they come out in the open and fight like men?" the general asked, and it suddenly all seemed so hopeless. He was fighting the wrong war—a linear war like World War II or Korea with battle lines drawn and an enemy you could count in front of you. Cronkite was equally depressed. When we left, he said he wondered how many generals were as blind as the one we had just seen.

There was a group of Polish tourists on the plane from Hanoi, led by a large and loud man who was drinking vodka out of a bottle at seven in the morning. Whenever he spoke, which was often, his voice filled the plane and his companions burst out laughing.

Memories flooded back as we landed at Tan Son Nhut Airport. Physically it had not changed much, but now it was a virtually abandoned relic. The old ticket counters were empty; the swarm of Vietnamese customs and immigration officials and porters was gone. There were no taxis lined up in front. The revetments on the tarmac, built to protect U.S. fighter planes, lay empty and overgrown. There was a damaged U.S. transport plane near the terminal which, I was told, the Vietnamese were considering converting into a nightclub. And, of course, there were no Americans. I remembered the joyous faces of those who were departing, leaving the war behind them, and the sad, sullen faces of those who were arriving to take their places.

We checked into the old Majestic Hotel, now the *Cuu Long*, along the Saigon River. The woman at the reservations desk was startled to see Brian Ellis; she had once worked at the CBS News bureau in Saigon. She reached out, as if to embrace him, and then pulled back. An embrace in a lobby watched by the secret police would have been foolish on her part. I took the faltering elevator to my room and to my surprise recognized the only other passenger. It was the vodka-drinking Pole from the plane.

"Deutsch?" he asked me.

"No, American."

He motioned for me to draw closer and whispered. "Russians— shit." He threw me a smile and a half salute and got off the elevator.

Saigon had not only changed its name to Ho Chi Minh City but it had been transformed in many ways. The bar girls and prostitutes were nowhere to be seen, sent off to reeducation camps. There was no begging on the streets. A pall seemed to have settled over the city, once so clamorous and chaotic. Shopkeepers on Tu Do Street, who used to smile and try to entice you into their stores to buy green ceramic elephants or other artifacts, sat impassivly in their doorways ignoring the passers-by.

We walked up the block to the Caravelle, now the *Dong Khoi*, the Uprising Hotel, and asked if we could visit the suite where we had housed our bureau. It was on the second floor and was now occupied by the consul general of Indonesia. He was out of town and the room was locked. We went up to the roof garden, which has a sweeping view of the city, to shoot some on-camera sequences with Cronkite. During the war, this was where you would find the correspondents, exchanging stories of visits to the front and the latest non-stories from the daily MACV briefing, the "Five O'Clock Follies." Now it was empty and forlorn.

We went back to the old American Embassy which I had last seen on television on April 29, 1975, when helicopters were landing on the roof to evacuate the remaining Americans from Saigon before the North Vietnamese troops entered. We stood at the gates which thousands of South Vietnamese had tried to scale in a frantic effort to get out. The massive complex, so obviously an American transplant, had become the headquarters of the Oil and Gas Administration.

It was a wrenching moment for Brian Ellis, who stared briefly at the building and then turned away. On that April day in 1975, he had been in charge of the evacuation of the American press contingent and in the darkness was the second to last person to leave the roof by helicopter. The last man to leave was the U.S. Ambassador, Graham Martin.

The place I wanted to visit more than any other was Westmoreland's former MACV headquarters, near the Tan Son Nhut airport. I thought of my investigation and of the trial that was unfolding in New York. I was haunted by the echoes I would hear in its corridors: the voices of Westmoreland and Joe McChristian as they conferred about enemy-strength figures; a visiting Sam Adams in muted conversation with Gains Hawkins; the click of Danny Graham's heels as he walked down the corridors assuring everyone that his order-of-battle numbers were right; Charley Morris shouting at Everette Parkins. But it was not to be. We were told that the headquarters had been demolished but we were not permitted to confirm that first-hand.

My hotel room was dirty and dispiriting but had a fine view of the Saigon River. The junks and sampans were still flitting noisily about and in the early morning the riverfront park was alive with activity. A group of perhaps fifty Vietnamese men, women, and children would gather to engage in an exercise similar to the ancient Chinese system, *T'ai Chi Ch'uan*, bodies frozen, arms uplifted, then gracefully moving into a new position and freezing again. As they stood motionless, etched against the river, you felt as if you were looking at an eleventh-century Chinese painting.

There was one group in the streets that I had never seen during the war—the Amerasian children. We had not only left our blood in

Vietnam; we had left our genes. These were the children of American servicemen and Vietnamese women, and now they ranged in age from twelve to eighteen. It was obvious that some of their fathers had been black, and we knew that they were having the most difficult time of all.

They must have an underground transmission belt, for they found out immediately that there were Americans at the hotel. Each morning as we left with our camera crew, they were waiting for us. Our conversations with them were furtive; they were terrified of the police. Whenever a green uniform appeared in the distance, they would dart away in fear, only to reappear later in the day or the next morning. They all had pictures they said were of their fathers; some gave us letters to take back to the States. These children gnaw at you: they implore you to help them. One young woman who said she was seventeen and whose father had obviously been black told us her mother needed money for medicine. We gave her a few dollars although we had been warned to be suspicious of stories like hers. I found the plight of these Amerasian children, many of whom are no longer children, the most trying experience of the journey.

We had to fly back to Hanoi for our exit from Vietnam. We had a few pickup shots to tape there, and before we left our hosts made certain that we saw three of their historic landmarks. We were taken to the compound where Ho Chi Minh lived during the war, now a national shrine, and to the mausoleum where Ho is interred much as Lenin has been in Red Square. The top of Ho's coffin is glass, and you look down at the face of a thin, wispy-bearded man in repose, preserved for all time as the hero of his nation.

We were then escorted to the Museum of the Army in Dienbienphu Street. When we entered, it looked like a U.S. Army depot trying to dispose of surplus equipment. Made-in-the-U.S.A. weapons, half-destroyed tanks, and airplane parts were dispersed in the courtyard. Inside the museum, the first thing you saw was a giant blow-up of a captured U.S. pilot, a heavyset and thoroughly cowed man, being held at gunpoint by a fifteen-year-old girl. It set the tone for an exhibit which understandably trumpeted their victory and our defeat.

Gia Lam Airport: We were leaving Hanoi after nine days in Vietnam. With the help of a man from the foreign office, we had moved smoothly through immigration and customs and were waiting to board our Thai Airways flight to Bangkok. The plane arrived each Wednesday at 12:40 in the afternoon, stayed on the ground for exactly one hour, and then hurried back to Bangkok. I was told that the crew rarely got off during the layover.

There was a problem today, however, that threatened the departure of two of the passengers. A young British member of the Agency for International Development (AID) group in Vietnam had married a Vietnamese. For a year, he had been trying to get her an exit visa, and it had finally been granted. Now immigration and customs were subjecting the young woman, who was strikingly beautiful and close to tears, to a brutal examination. Every bag, every case, all of her clothing was pulled out of suitcases and thrown on the counter. A suitcase would be opened, examined, closed, and then reopened again for another inspection. We were told to board the plane, and as we left I saw the couple, half the woman's clothes still on the counter, trying to reason with the guards.

"Unless she gets on, I'm not going," Cronkite said. I persuaded him that his refusal to board would not have the same impact in Hanoi that it might at JFK in New York, and reluctantly we went up the steps into the plane. We knew the Thai pilot would not stay beyond his departure time and we kept our eyes on the windows, hoping to see the couple.

About two minutes before we were scheduled to leave, they came flying out of the terminal and raced aboard. The flight attendant shut the door and the pilot began to taxi. The passengers stood and cheered and two of them, whom we learned also worked for AID, cracked a bottle of champagne and quickly passed glasses to the passengers. When we were airborne, I asked the young woman where she was going.

"To the Oriental Hotel in Bangkok," she said, "and I know just what I'm going to do. I am going to get in a bubble bath and soak. Maybe for three days."

To move from the *Thang Loi* in Hanoi to the Oriental in Bangkok might be compared to moving from a flophouse to a penthouse. I felt like soaking, too, but when I got the news from New York, I was too startled even to unpack.

The Westmoreland case was over. The general had withdrawn his lawsuit the day we had flown into Hanoi. It had been virtually impossible for us to receive telephone calls or telex messages from the States, and if anyone had tried, the information never got to me.

Some of my CBS News colleagues were in Bangkok, trying to get visas for Vietnam, and they were able to fill me in. Within a few hours, I had most of the story.

On February 18, 1985, after two and a half years of litigation, half a million pages of documents, thirty-six witnesses, and sixty-five days in court, General Westmoreland had agreed to abandon his $120 million lawsuit against CBS, one week before the case was to go to the jury. Each side would pay its own legal expenses—CBS $10 million, all but $100,000 covered by insurance; Westmoreland's side, $5 to $7 million.

Dan M. Burt, Westmoreland's lawyer, said that four words from the bench—"clear and convincing evidence"—had made his case impossible. On February 15, Judge Leval had ruled that the jury in deciding whether the Westmoreland documentary was false would need "clear and convincing evidence," rather than "a preponderance of evidence," which Burt had hoped for. Given this instruction, the jury could have ruled that the broadcast was true, and Burt said: "If he loses on truth, it will kill the old man."

Westmoreland got no apology and no money from CBS. He issued a statement expressing esteem for CBS's "distinguished journalistic tradition." In its statement, CBS said it "never intended to assert and does not believe, that General Westmoreland was unpatriotic or disloyal in *performing his duties as he saw them*" (emphasis added).

Those words moved Alistair Cooke to say in his "Letter from America" that the phrase "can be said of any unlucky, or defeated, or even incompetent soldier. It can be said admiringly of Napoleon, of Robert E. Lee, of Erwin Rommel. It has been said disparagingly of very many generals in many wars."

"Performing his duties as he saw them" also angered Adm. Thomas H. Moorer, the former chairman of the Joint Chiefs of Staff and a staunch conservative supporter of Westmoreland. "You could have said that about Hitler," the admiral said.

Although the word "apology" could be found nowhere in the CBS statement, Westmoreland told Ted Koppel of ABC News that he dismissed the suit because the language, to his thinking, constituted an apology. "If they had thrown in the word 'apology' I certainly wouldn't have objected to it," the general said, "but I interpreted their language as something that cleared my name." Some observers likened this to a recommendation by the late Senator George Aiken of Vermont on October 19, 1966, that the way to end the war in Vietnam was to declare a unilateral victory and get out.

Late in the afternoon, I was having a drink at the Oriental with Lance Morrow and Dirck Halstead of *Time*. They were trying to get into Hanoi and were still unable to pry loose visas from the Vietnamese. They were asking me about our trip—where to go, what you could see, how much free movement was allowed. I was telling them that it was a hard ticket, that the power was in Hanoi, and that they were keeping a pretty tight lid on the country, when Derek Williams of CBS News in Bangkok came to the table. He said he had a long telex for me from New York.

I told Williams I doubted it was for me; I had already spoken with my wife, who was in London, and had been assured that she and my family were well. "It's from Ed Joyce," said Williams. "It's for you with copies to the whole CBS News organization."

As I began to read the telex, I wondered for a moment whether Cronkite or Ellis had framed it as a gag. It was extremely flattering, even fulsome, and it had to do with my investigation of the Westmoreland documentary.

> You didn't volunteer for this assignment, but I recall your telling me that you took on this burden because "nothing was more important than CBS News." How fortunate we all are that an individual of such unblemished integrity was willing to accept this kind of responsibility.
>
> As painful as it was to acknowledge the flaws in our broadcast, I believed then and I believe now it was right to do so.

I turned to Derek Williams: "You know, I'm tired as hell but I feel all right. This sounds like something from an obituary."

Morrow and Halstead had more questions, and we returned to the story in Vietnam. I put the telex in my pocket and the next day sent Joyce a cable thanking him.

Some days later, I was to get a further perspective on what might have been behind Ed Joyce's message to me and why he made it public. After the trial had ended, CBS and Cravath threw a celebratory party at Regine's, the flashy Park Avenue disco-restaurant.

More than a hundred people attended—lawyers, CBS executives, witnesses, and some of the reporters who had covered the trial. They danced to recorded music and took advantage of the open bar, especially the champagne, and a buffet dinner. Edwin Diamond of *New York* Magazine described the evening as "tasteless" and "dancing on the grave of Westmoreland." Mike Wallace, Dan Rather, George Crile, Van Gordon Sauter, Sam Adams, and Col. Gains Hawkins were among the guests. Ed Joyce arrived and made a U-turn, staying for only a few minutes. He apparently agreed with Diamond, and his message to me, *Broadcasting* Magazine wrote, was "reminding the rejoicers that the broadcast at issue had been flawed."

When it was all over, I thought Stanley Karnow, author of *Vietnam: A History,* wrote the most telling epitaph for the broadcast: "They were both losers from the beginning. CBS did a lousy program, and Westmoreland never understood what the war was about."

Early the next morning, Cronkite and I boarded a Lufthansa flight to Tokyo. It was always nice traveling with Walter; you usually sat in the front of the bus, in first class. In that way, as the fiction went, you had an opportunity to "talk" and "do business" on the trip. Cronkite got the usual deferential treatment, so familiar to me after nearly thirty years of travels with him. The pilot, whose English made him sound like the Red Baron, came back and told us how honored he was to have Mr. Cronkite on his flight. Since his regular route was New Delhi to Tokyo and return, I wondered how he had managed to hone his expertise on American anchormen. To me, it was Marshall McLuhan's "Global Village" personified.

I succeeded in annoying the two other passengers in first class by bringing out my portable typewriter and typing up the scripts for the two reports from Vietnam that we had prepared for the Rather News. I would have no time to do this in Tokyo; the next morning we would be flying out again.

For the life of me, I don't know why it struck me as amusing—black humor, perhaps—but after Westmoreland, after Vietnam, our next destination seemed perversely appropriate.

We were going to Hiroshima.

EPILOGUE

What has happened to the principal players in *General William C. Westmoreland* vs. *CBS Inc. et al.?*

Gen. William C. Westmoreland: Since the trial, the general has returned to his home in South Carolina but has not faded away, as he suggested he might. He has resumed his public life and receives more requests for speaking engagements than he can accept. He attended a large rally at the Vietnam Memorial in Washington and received a warm reception from his fellow veterans, whose treatment he has called "shabby." He has also been urging that the National News Council be revived.

George Crile: Contrary to what some observers said after the trial— "George will never be heard of again"—Crile is still a staff producer at CBS News. He joined *60 Minutes* as one of Mike Wallace's producers and from all reports it has been a mutually satisfactory relationship. The first story Crile produced for Wallace dealt with a semi-invalid who was reported to be the brains behind Senator Jesse Helms, the man who had threatened to take over CBS so that he could become "Dan Rather's boss." Crile married Susan Lyne and continues to maintain, whenever he is asked, that except for some technical violations, which he regrets, there was nothing wrong with the Westmoreland broadcast.

Mike Wallace: As he moved into his seventieth year, Wallace is still the lead correspondent for *60 Minutes,* the only one of the five reporters on the show who has been with the series without interruption since it began in 1968. He seems as indefatigable and energy-charged as ever, traveling throughout the world on a back-breaking schedule. He has done no documentaries since the Westmoreland program.

Howard Stringer: In September of 1986, Laurence Tisch invited Stringer, then acting head of the news division, to take a Metroliner ride with him to Washington for a meeting that was to introduce Tisch to staffers at the news bureau there. It would give them a chance to chat and get to know each other better. For Stringer, the leading and most active candidate for the news presidency, the train ride was apparently a success. In October, he was named president of CBS News. While financial austerity still prevails at the network, Stringer has managed to recapture the morning news, which had been turned over to the entertainment division, and has been given a weekly prime-time hour for a new series called *48 Hours*.

Thomas H. Wyman: On September 10, 1986, Wyman was removed as chairman and chief executive officer of CBS after a tense board meeting. Convinced that Laurence Tisch was achieving a takeover of the company at bargain prices, Wyman urged the board to consider other buyout offers and it was revealed that he held conversations with one suitor, Coca-Cola, without telling Bill Paley and Larry Tisch about it. Wyman descended from his plush aerie on the thirty-fifth floor of Black Rock by golden parachute. His ouster agreement included more than $1 million in salary and bonus, a lump sum of $2.7 million or ten installments worth $3.8 million, and $400,000 a year for the rest of his life.

William S. Paley: With the Wyman ouster, Paley moved out of the limbo he had been relegated to and stepped back into the chairmanship of CBS. The octogenarian founder of the company has become active again, especially in the area of programming. He owns nearly 2 million shares of CBS, more than 8 percent of the outstanding common stock, and as the price has risen under the Laurence Tisch regime, he has become an even wealthier man.

Laurence A. Tisch: He became acting chief executive officer after Wyman, and in January 1987 dropped the "acting" and became president as well. It is said he is fascinated by CBS and has no immediate plans to search for a successor. The Tisch family holds a 25 percent stake in Loew's Corporation and Loew's holds 24.9 percent of CBS, some 5.8 million shares. The common stock, purchased at an average price of $127 a share, almost doubled in price before tailing off in late 1987. Tisch has turned CBS back to its original business, broadcasting, selling off its records division (to Sony for $2 billion), its educational and music publishing operations, and its magazines.

Van Gordon Sauter: In September of 1986, the day after Wyman was fired, Sauter was asked to resign as president of CBS News. His parachute, if not pure gold, was gold-plated. He will receive his $300,000 annual salary and 50 percent of his bonus payments through 1990. He moved back to Los Angeles and for a short time was a news commentator for Fox Broadcasting's KTTV. He has been writing occasional columns on urban affairs for the Los Angeles *Times*. Sauter's latest project is to co-produce a syndicated show with the title "Group One Medical," described by its backer, Metro Goldwyn Mayer/United Artists, as "infotainment" and by others as a medical version of "People's Court." According to its sponsors, the show will "feature three real family doctors dealing with real medical situations that will both educate and entertain . . ."

Edward M. Joyce: He was replaced as CBS News president in December of 1985 by Sauter, who returned to the news division after being elevated to an executive vice presidency in the CBS Broadcast Group. The ridiculed performance of the *CBS Morning News* with Phyllis George, who had been hired by Sauter, mounting internal dissension in the news division, and a fallout with Dan Rather led to Joyce's departure. He was offered a job as vice president of CBS's World Wide Services, which sells CBS programs overseas, but quit and left the network. He reportedly received a $250,000 advance from a publisher to write a book about his stormy two years as president of CBS News. It is scheduled for publication in 1988.

Roger Colloff: He has had three job shifts since Westmoreland. In 1983, he was moved to Black Rock as a vice president with the CBS Television Stations division; three months later he was moved to policy and planning for the CBS Broadcast Group; and two years after that became vice president and general manager of WCBS-TV, the network's flagship station in New York.

Andrew Lack: He became executive producer of the CBS News series, *West 57th*, which has been in and out of the network prime-time schedule. The program finally regained a regular spot in 1987, Saturday nights at 10:00 p.m., considered by many to be disastrous scheduling for a program of this character.

Ira Klein: He continued to work as a free-lance film editor in New

York. He was hired by Bill Moyers for his *Walk Through the 20th Century* and did some editing for NBC News. He is currently working free lance, cutting whatever comes along from documentaries to commercials. He has not worked at CBS News since the Westmoreland program and many would be surprised if he worked there in the foreseeable future.

Sam Adams: He now lives near Purcellville, Virginia, eight miles from the 250-acre farm in Leesburg, his home until 1985. That year, after twenty-three years of marriage, he was divorced from his first wife and married Anne Cocroft, a free-lance reporter for *The Washington Post*. They have a two-year-old son, Abraham. His first wife lives at Leesburg with their son, Clayton. Adams filed a libel suit against Renata Adler for her book *Reckless Disregard*, a critical account of the CBS defense in the Westmoreland trial, but dropped it two months later. "I basically didn't have the heart to go through another three years of lawsuiting. I'm not a rich man. I think I could have raised the money but I just wasn't up to it." He is still working on his own book, *Who the Hell Are We Fighting Out There?*, dealing with the numbers controversy in Vietnam, but no publication date is set. He says it will not treat Westmoreland harshly. "He is a nice old man. I like him. He was in a terrible spot in that war."

David Boies: He moved from the Westmoreland case to representing Texaco in a multi-billion-dollar lawsuit by Pennzoil. He has received wide praise for his legal sagacity in the defense of CBS. The *New York Times Magazine* favored him with a cover piece which called him one of the great litigators of the country. In spite of an annual income reported to be in excess of $1 million a year, he says he still buys his suits at Sears.

Col. Gains Hawkins: The former order-of-battle chief, whose testimony for CBS and against Westmoreland was critical during the trial, lived in West Point, Mississippi, where he was administrator of a nursing home and chairman of the Clay County Republican party. In 1986, he had a lung removed because of cancer. On February 26, 1987, according to county authorities, he died of a gunshot wound "that was apparently self-inflicted." He was sixty-seven.

George Allen: Retired from the CIA after twenty years of service, Allen has been using "The Uncounted Enemy: A Vietnam Deception" at the agency as a teaching tool. It is screened in a professional development course for senior CIA officers as a case study in ethics and intelligence. The CIA acknowledges that Allen shows the documentary, but says it is "used purely as a training device to show one side of a complicated intelligence problem and doesn't represent official advocacy of that version of history."

Burton Benjamin: In April of 1985, David A. Englander of the Bronx wrote a letter to *New York* Magazine in which he made this comment about the Westmoreland affair: "As for whistle-blower Burton Benjamin, now that he's received a letter of praise from CBS News president Ed Joyce, he'd better start inquiring about a job at Columbia University."

Mr. Englander was prophetic. In March of 1986, I did indeed go to Columbia University on a fifteen-month fellowship from the Gannett Center for Media Studies. My project: To write this book.

INDEX

ABC (American Broadcasting Corporation), 129, 181
Abrams, Creighton, 56
Abrams, Floyd, 29
Accuracy, 30–31, 45, 164
Accuracy in Media, 53, 182
Adams, Samuel A.: Benjamin's interview of, 137–48; charges of, 11, 111; chronologies of, 90, 137–39; coaching of others by, 66, 142–43; and the conspiracy theory, 35–36, 144; Crile's relationship with, 36, 37–38, 139; Crile's views about the interview of, 111, 112; and the Davidson illness, 97, 187; and editing problems, 79, 86; and errors in "Uncounted Enemy," 95; *Harper's* article by, 35–36, 53, 74, 131; included in the internal investigation, 45; involvement in "Uncounted Enemy" of, 34, 38, 47, 110, 113, 153–54; and Klein, 90, 91, 92, 97, 98, 104, 142, 143, 144; named in Westmoreland law suit, 175; and the nine-to-two equation, 60; obsession question about, 40, 67, 90, 92, 105; as a paid consultant, 25, 46–47, 59, 142, 153, 164, 169; personal/professional background of, 34–35, 37, 139, 206; and the Pike Committee, 36, 139; and the premise of the broadcast, 25, 97, 98, 104, 143–44, 147, 156, 169; rehearsal of, 25, 59, 91, 101, 142, 169; screenings for, 91; and the selection of people for "Uncounted Enemy," 139–42; supports "Uncounted Enemy" broadcast, 161, 162; and the Tet Offen-

sive, 36, 147–48; tone of interview of, 66–67, 112, 132, 143; *TV Guide's* allegations about, 25, 142, 143; Wallace interview of, 11, 66–67, 79, 101, 111–13, 132, 143; and the Westmoreland news conference, 97; and the Westmoreland trial, 188; as a whistle blower, 111, 131. *See also* Adams, Samuel A.—perceptions about; Adams, Samuel A.—views of; CIA/military estimates
Adams, Samuel A.—perceptions about: of Alben, 101; of Carver, 138; of Chandler, 153; of Conger, 138–39; of Graham, 63, 146, 147; of Hawkins, 36, 146–47; of Klein, 90, 92; of Rostow, 36–37; of Shaplen, 40; of Smith's (R. Jack), 138; of Stringer, 153–54; of Wallace, 131; of Westmoreland, 17, 62, 114
Adams, Samuel A.—views of: about Bunker, 140; about Clifford (Clark), 142; about Davidson, 139–40; about Godding, 141; about Goldberg, 141–42; about Graham, 146, 147; about Hawkins, 36, 146–47; about Komer, 140–41; about Rostow, 141; about Taylor (Maxwell), 140; about Westmoreland, 144–45, 206
Advertising, 9, 74, 110, 133, 144, 157
Affiliates/local stations, 6, 25–26, 29–30
Alben, Alex, 45, 90, 91, 99–102, 103, 105
Allen, George: Adams present at interviews of, 66, 67–69; Colloff's reaction to interviews of, 155; Crile's views about the interviews of, 59, 113–14; double interviews

More Critical Praise for *And Then I Danced*

"Mark Segal has for decades been a pathfinder for LGBT journalists of all stripes. We're indebted to him for his years of radical activism, helping to foster a movement for change that has had a dramatic and positive impact for millions."
—Michelangelo Signorile, author of *It's Not Over: Getting Beyond Tolerance, Defeating Homophobia, & Winning True Equality*

"Mark Segal's ideas run from the alpha to the omega. Sometimes I think there's got to be more than one Mark Segal: he has done way too much for one lifetime. I highly recommend this book. If you can't get to meet Mark in person, this is the next best thing!"
—Michael T. Luongo, editor of *Gay Travels in the Muslim World*

"Before there was Ellen, Will, Grace, Rosie, Andy, and Anderson, Mark Segal was the squeaky gay wheel of American television, pulling stunts that forced the medium to open its closet door. If Walter Cronkite were still alive, he'd say: 'Not *HIM* again!' And that's the way it is. And was. Read all about it."
—Bruce Vilanch, two-time Emmy Award winner

"Mark Segal has taken the LGBT aging world by storm, and in the process has made a remarkable difference for our community's courageous pioneers. We've all learned so much from him."
—Michael Adams, executive director,
Services and Advocacy for GLBT Elders

"Mark Segal has been a courageous and eloquent leader of the LGBT community and cause for longer than many lifetimes. His efforts have indisputably changed important elements of broad public importance, leaving a permanent mark on the world. His life story is as compelling as it is important, and this rendering of it is as delightful as it is provocative."
—Michael Pakenham, former editorial page editor
of the *New York Daily News*

AND THEN I DANCED
TRAVELING THE ROAD TO LGBT EQUALITY

A MEMOIR BY

MARK SEGAL

OPEN
LENS

Published by Akashic Books
©2015 Mark Segal

Hardcover ISBN: 978-1-61775-410-4
Paperback ISBN: 978-1-61775-399-2
Library of Congress Control Number: 2015902762

Second printing

Open Lens
c/o Akashic Books
Twitter: @AkashicBooks
Facebook: AkashicBooks
E-mail: info@akashicbooks.com
Website: www.akashicbooks.com

To Jason Villemez, who each day tells me there is more I can do and encourages me to dream and follow that vision; my parents Marty and Shirley Segal, who encouraged their son to be who he was; and Fannie Weinstein, suffragette and civil rights supporter, who taught her grandson well.

Acknowledgments

As a newspaper publisher, my knowledge of book publishing was nonexistent. A project of this scale does not get done without those people who have the expertise and believe in it to the point that they encourage you to make yourself vulnerable. Marva Allen, my copublisher, is a legend in the African American literary community who was one of the first women to break that glass ceiling. Upon our first meeting she told me simply, "You have a story to share and we will get this done." She soon introduced me to her colleagues Marie Brown and Regina Brooks at Open Lens, and to the folks at Akashic Books, which hosts their imprint. Again at first meeting they gave me the encouragement I needed since the endeavor frightened me. After all, up until this project, I only wrote a 500-word weekly column, not an entire book. Thanks too to my actress friend Sheryl Lee Ralph, who introduced me to my future publisher.

After the first draft, we invited the talented editor Michael Denneny (*The Mayor of Castro Street: The Life and Times of Harvey Milk* and *The Band Played On*) to work on the project. He took it on and explained to me that this was history that had to be recorded. He also took a book that was full of flashbacks and showed me how to put it in a mostly chronological order. I believe his special sense of history and enthusiasm for this book made me fully realize that it had to be completed.

I must thank my close friends and family, who were aware of the manuscript and kept it quiet knowing that I wanted to be able to abandon it at any time, and understood that they would read it only when it was published. Also, Richard Aregood, former Pulitzer Prize editorial writer for the *Philadelphia Daily News*, who helped me shape the early version of this book.

I have a new sense of appreciation for LGBT historians who assisted with getting me the hard facts needed to underscore issues in the book, especially Sean Strub, author of *Body Counts* and founder of *POZ* magazine, who read my chapter on AIDS to assure its accuracy.

Thanks to my family at *PGN*, who allowed me the time away from the office to do my various projects and who fill me with pride by delivering award-winning journalism each week.

Many writers forget the work our editors do, and my editors had a special task in teaching me to put my passion into words, and then into a weekly column. To Al Patrick, Pattie Tihey, Sarah Blazucki, and Jen Colletta—thank you.

Finally, thank you to those who lived this history with me and are still with us, and to those gone pioneers and friends who inspired and worked with me. To my sisters and brothers in Gay Liberation Front New York who were my teachers, especially Jerry Hoose, who in true GLF fashion debated with me many parts of this book. (Jerry lost his battle with cancer before it was completed but his spirit lives in these pages). To my Gay Youth New York family, who allowed me to learn to lead. To my friends in LGBT media, who fight each day to inform our community. And to my friends in mainstream media, who taught an activist how to become a publisher.

Table of Contents

Introduction

The rights that the LGBT community have gained and continue to gain, from marriage equality to employment nondiscrimination, are the result of decades of hard work from individuals who in the early days, most of the time, lived off the kindness of friends. In the 1960s, being a gay activist was not a profession; it was an unpaid job for those dedicated to LGBT equality. When the newly energized gay movement sprouted from the Stonewall riots of June 1969, there was no organizational support with deep pockets, bailing people out of jail. Those of us in the riot didn't have any best practices or contingency plans to fall back on. The only gay person I knew who was receiving a modest stipend was Reverend Troy Perry, who was building the gay-friendly Metropolitan Community Church.

Thanks to the early activists, today the LGBT community is represented in every segment of American society: from Fortune 500 CEOs, to leaders in education, labor, public safety, and politics, including at the White House. The Obama administration has appointed out LGBT individuals in almost every capacity at the highest levels of government.

We were able to get here because of the tireless work of pioneers such as Frank Kameny, Barbara Gittings, Harry Hay, Del Martin and Phyllis Lyon, Randy Wicker, Reverend Troy Perry, Martha Shelley, Marty Robinson, many of my brothers and sisters in New York's Gay Liberation Front, and so many others, including a man named Henry Gerber, who in 1925 created the first LGBT organization in the nation in Chicago.

Since we had no funds, we had to be creative in our efforts to change individuals' minds about who we were. This is my story but it is also an American story, one that illuminates and documents the historic LGBT struggle for equality. In most cases, I've kept to a chronological narrative, but sometimes, as is typical for me, I go off and explore issues that deserve further discussion and attention.

Chapter 1

The Boy from the Projects

I was an outsider from the beginning. When I was born in 1951 to Martin and Shirley Segal, my father was the proprietor of a store in South Philly, one of those neighborhood groceries that were once common throughout the big cities; in New York they are called bodegas. His proprietorship was short-lived. Against the backdrop of row homes and big Catholic churches, my father's store was condemned by eminent domain to be replaced by a housing project. My parents, with two little boys and no work, were provided for by the city. At some point, we moved to nearby Wilson Park. There, as a member of the only Jewish family in a South Philadelphia housing project, I got an expert lesson in isolation. Kids who lived there said that we were from the other side of the tracks, and it was a reality since the housing project was sandwiched in on one side by an expressway and on the other by the 25th Street railroad bridge. We were, literally, across the street and an underpass away from a middle-class, mostly Catholic neighborhood.

We were poor, which in the Jewish community is almost a sin against God, or in our case a sin against the rest of the family. To them, living in a housing project was almost unimaginable. Our relatives either turned up their noses at us or pitied us. We were the lowest rung of the family. I was ashamed of my address, 2333 South Bambrey Terrace, of wearing the same clothes until

they wore out, of our lack of money, and of every other charac-
teristic of being poor.

Our new neighbors were hardly welcoming. I still remember
the first few days of kindergarten when Irish and Italian kids
would say to me, "You killed our Christ," or the one that always
stumped me, "You're a devil with horns." Somehow I became a
deformed six-year-old murderer. For a while I'd subconsciously
touch the top of my head, waiting for the horns to grow, and I
wondered, *How could I possibly comb my hair with horns?*

The only support system I had were my parents, whom I
adored and who adored me. They followed the Jewish tradition, knowing that their central obligation as parents was to
love their children and to tell them they're the greatest people
in the world. They did that well. I knew I was loved and I knew
I was smart. I also knew that I could face the world armed with
those two gifts. After all, what else did I have? They gave me the
strength to persevere.

My father taught me to be quietly modest, although I occasionally (note: always) broke that rule. I knew my father had
been in the war, that he had a Purple Heart, and that his plane
had been shot down over the Pacific. That's all I knew until
he died and I went through his papers. He was a war hero who
would only say to us, "I have a fake knee, it's platinum and it's
more expensive than gold. When I die, dig it out and cash it in."
Neither he nor my mother would talk much about those times
or about their grandparents, my great-grandparents, who died
in the Holocaust.

One time my mother went to my grade school to defend
me because the teachers had demanded that I sing "Onward,
Christian Soldiers." In those days there was still prayer in public
schools, and they had us sing Christian songs. I didn't know why
I didn't want to sing that song, I just didn't. My teachers couldn't,

or more appropriately were unable to, force me to utter a word. Hence, my mother's first of many trips to the school. Of course, that made everyone in Edgar Allen Poe Elementary—students, teachers, and principals—hate my guts. The compromise on the hymn was that I was to stand and be silent while everyone else bellowed out that they were "marching off to war." So I knew discrimination from a very young age—from my affluent extended family, from the people around me in school, and even from the poor people in the project where I lived, who had their own noneconomic reasons not to like me. My refusal to sing "Onward, Christian Soldiers" was my first political action, my first defiance of conformity and the status quo.

Kids growing up in Wilson Park knew to make friends only with other kids in the neighborhood, not the kids across the tracks. My friends included my neighbor Barbara Myers, the only girl who would communicate with me. She was a slim blonde with buckteeth, glasses, and an unfortunate early case of acne, which never seemed to go away. This made her a fellow outcast, so we had a mutual bond. Mrs. Myers didn't take to the idea of her daughter having a Jew for a friend, but since I was the only one Barbara had, she tolerated me. Barbara eventually became my first sexual relation—well, I'm not sure that's what you'd call it.

Sexuality to my generation arrived in the form of the Sears, Roebuck catalog. That book showcased almost any item that was necessary for the household, including clothing. Every boy waited for the new edition to arrive, and when it did, the first page he turned to was the one with women's lingerie. Let's get this straight: they weren't drag queens in the making searching for an outfit, but normal prepubescent boys looking for their first sexual thrill, and they found it from the various models posing in bras and panties. That didn't really work for me. Actually, the only reaction it stirred in me was to make commentary on color choices. I would think, *Gee, she might look decent if that dress was another color.* What really worked for me was the men's fashion section. My eyes were glued to the men in underwear.

There was no name for it, at least none that I knew, but somehow it seemed wrong that I was looking at the men in the catalog. After all, men were supposed to be eyeing and sizing up women. I decided to try it. And thus, my first foray into hetero-normativity began. Let's call it an experiment.

Somehow, kids in the neighborhood saw Barbara and me as a couple. Puppy love, they thought. We were friends, and for me that friendship might be used to discover this mystery that I couldn't quite solve.

Barbara's parents had one of those above-ground pools in their backyard. It was made of thin aluminum and had a flimsy plastic liner that you hoped didn't get punctured during the first swim. It was about four feet deep and six feet in diameter, and of course it was a calming sea blue. One afternoon while in the pool together, my hand started to feel its way around Barbara. I closed my eyes as my hand traveled down her body. Feeling the top half didn't do a thing for me, so I continued in search of that thrill that had been so well advertised to be at the bottom half. As my hand reached the most important part, it spoke loudly to my brain: *Something is missing here.* With that, I did what any other kid would do: I investigated. I put my head underwater, opened my eyes, and watched as my hand slipped into the bottom of Barbara's two-piece swimsuit. She didn't stop me. When I actually saw my hand there, it scared me so much that my mouth opened in shock and I swallowed so much water I almost drowned—a watery death filled with screams of "Yek!"

To say my experiment was unsuccessful would be an understatement. The thrill that other boys experienced with the scantily clad women in the catalog was, for me, false advertising. Years later, Barbara and I both had a good laugh about our little test. It was her experiment as well and the end result was that she liked boys. Guess we both had the same feelings.

It seems that every time you turn on the news or watch a talk show you hear about someone who was brought up in a public housing project and became a gazillionaire. While I'm not a gazillionaire, I'm well off, and I'm now proud of my roots going back to the Wilson Park housing project, 2333 South Bambrey Terrace.

Almost every politician talks about lifting people out of poverty. As someone who has been there, I can tell you most of them just don't get it. They've never experienced the daily grind of poverty. Their romanticized solution is nothing more than solving a numbers and jobs game. To those of us who have been there, poverty is a culture, one that envelops your entire being, from the constant hunger and degradation, to the fear, despair, and hopelessness that never go away. Even if you get out and get a good job, even if you become a gazillionaire, you still worry, even if irrationally, about being there again. Poverty never leaves you. We poor, those of us who have gotten out, strive every day never to be there again. I for sure never want to go back to Bambrey Terrace.

Our two-story brick row home was constructed as cheaply as the city could get away with. There was no basement. The kitchen was a dark cubbyhole with a slanted ceiling that supported the stairs to the second floor. A bulb swinging on a single cord from the ceiling was the only lighting. There was a closet where washcloths and other sundry items were stored just off the kitchen. When I was growing up, that closet gave me the creeps.

Our dining table and four chairs took up virtually the entire room. It was a typical Formica table with aluminum chairs that had cushioned backs and seats. Next to the dining area was our living room, which consisted of a couch and matching end tables, a chair, and a television atop a faded reddish-brown Oriental-style carpet. On the second floor were two bedrooms, my parents' and the room I shared with my brother. The family all used the same bathroom. Each of the bedrooms had a closet without a door, which my parents covered with curtains. I worried at night about who might be behind those curtains. Every night I prepared myself for Dracula and Abraham Lincoln to come lumbering out. Everyone can appreciate Dracula, the scary Bela Lugosi, but old Honest Abe? As a boy, for some reason the likeness of Abraham Lincoln frightened me.

Children are children even if you're poor. You still ask for the things you want, the things you see that other children have. To this day the moment of my life I feel most guilty about came after I asked my parents to buy me something they couldn't afford. In our house when you wanted something you went to my father. One day, while asking Dad for something, I don't even remember what, he exploded like I'd never seen before. He tried to explain to me why he couldn't get it for me, and then he began to cry. I can't remember what he actually said but I know what it was about. He was crying because he couldn't do better for his kids and felt like a failure. He tried to make me understand the "why" as he talked and cried, but it was way over my head. Finally, he told my mother he was going to take a walk. Ashamed of the pain I caused him, I also ran out of the house.

My mom was Edith Bunker from *All in the Family*—the Jewish version. Fragile, soft spoken, and wouldn't say a word against anyone. She was the most delicate, loving, decent human being I've ever known on this earth, but when it came to Dad she could be strong-minded. She loved that man no matter what. She followed us both out of the house that day and found me sitting on a park bench. "Mark," she leaned over and tried to explain, her words still resonating today, "Dad means well. It's just hard for him to make ends meet. We have to help him. He's a good man." Then she put on her best smile and said, "Let's take a walk and see what we can find."

Getting out of the projects was a treat, especially with Mom holding my hand. Passing Vare Junior High School we headed to Point Breeze Avenue, which in the 1950s was lined with cheap mom-and-pop shops.

After several blocks of walking my mother took me to a variety store, or what was once called a five-and-dime. She looked around and found the engine and caboose of a red plastic train set. They were wrapped in a see-through cellophane bag and were cheap. She asked me if I'd like them, and I screamed with delight. Mom handed the bag to me, and I held on tight. It was my prized possession. We then began our walk back to the projects, taking the same route past the beat-up school, with its overgrown weeds and unkempt ball field. As we entered Wilson Park she asked if I liked my toy. I reached into the bag and my train was gone. I said nothing. Seeing my reaction, she took the bag and found the hole in the bottom through which my toy had fallen out. She just started to cry. Watching my mother cry after all that had occurred that day, I wanted to cry and yell as well, but instead I got sick to my stomach. I just stood there in silence, awash in guilt. I had lost the toy and made my Mom cry. She quickly pulled herself together and we went home. It was never spoken about again, but it still makes me emotional.

The bright light of those dark years was my grandmother, Fannie Weinstein. Grandmom, all four feet seven inches of her, was a smart-dressing former suffragette. In the winter she vacationed in Miami but in the summer she stayed in Atlantic City, and each year I was her guest for two magical weeks. Grandmom was sort of the queen bee of the Jewish ladies' circuit of Atlantic City. And she was proud of her grandson. She made sure that when I was with her I was dressed properly. Each night we'd walk the boardwalk going from one rolling chair to another. She'd delight in bragging about me. How bright, how handsome, and how oh so charming I was. Each year, the two weeks were topped off with a dinner party. Never were the same guests present twice.

Grandmom celebrated diversity before it was fashionable, and the aim of those parties was to introduce me to a variety of people. So avant-garde it all was, it reminded me of one of the first books I had read, *Auntie Mame*, about a boy growing up with his eccentric aunt and her madcap adventures. Her zest for life was captured by her saying, *Live, live, live*, and the famous line, *Life is a banquet, and most poor sons of bitches are starving to death!* It became my motto in life. When Rosalind Russell struts across the screen in the film version, I saw my grandmother, my very own Auntie Mame.

Those parties, as I look back at them, were attended only by women, except for my Uncle Stan, who lived with my grandmother and me. It was not unusual for there to be African American or Latino women among these eclectic folks, but one year I was introduced to Mrs. Goldman and her friend. When I looked at Mrs. Goldman, I thought that something was different about her. She was dressed in a skirt and wore a man's jacket and even walked like a man. Her friend, on the other hand, was dressed in a stylish woman's outfit. I remember that they sat very close together on the sofa. Grandmom asked Mrs. Goldman to tell me about her job. She was a prison warden. How stereotypical that job would be for a lesbian, but back then the only question I had for Grandmom after everyone else left was, "Why were they so strange?" Grandmom smiled and told me that there are all types of people in the world, and one should never judge a person on what they look like on the outside. Mrs. Goldman was a good person, and that was all that counted.

To my delight it wasn't just in the summer that I'd see Grandmom. Sometimes she'd show up out of nowhere and take me to a movie, a speech, the art museum, or, as I remember most fondly, my first civil rights demonstration.

That day when she picked me up, she looked at my mother and said, "I have a very important place to take Mark—we'll be back by dinner." She grabbed my hand and we began to walk. When I asked her where we were going, she said to City Hall.

When we got to City Hall, we saw hundreds of people gathered, mostly black men and women. Grandmom walked up to someone and he handed her a stick with a sign on it. With the picket sign in one hand and me in the other, she marched us around City Hall, alongside everyone else. It all seemed to be some sort of game to me, but Grandmom explained it was about the issue of fairness.

After the march she introduced me to the man who had organized it. His name was Cecil B. Moore, a Philadelphia attorney, president of the local NAACP and a civil rights activist who, along with the Reverend Leon Sullivan and Sam Evans, were the major organizers for the African American community in Philadelphia at that time. He chatted with Grandmom, and it was obvious that they had known each other. At some point he leaned down and looked at me but said to her: "Your grandson certainly is skinny!" Then he laughed and walked away. Some twelve years later, the Democratic Party of Philadelphia honored Cecil B. Moore by nominating and electing him to the city council.

On my return to Philadelphia in the early seventies, one of my first tasks was to lobby for the introduction of nondiscrimination legislation into the city council to protect gay men and lesbian women. It was my job to go to each councilmember and ask if they would cosponsor the legislation or vote for it. At that point Cecil B. Moore was an elder statesman, having led the fight to integrate Girard College and the trade unions; he was always known to be outspoken and confrontational and was clearly unfazed by what people thought of his opinions. He often said whatever he wanted, sometimes just to get a reaction.

When I walked into his office for our designated appointment, he had his feet propped up on his desk and was smoking a cigar. He looked at me and said, "What do you want?" I went into a speech I had put together on why gays and lesbians needed protection from discrimination. About halfway through, he stopped me and said, "Just wait there." And, with what looked like an angry face, he added, "Are you asking me to support a bill for fags and dykes?" I was staring at him in disbelief, wondering if this was the same man my grandmother had asked me to march with, and then he broke into a big laugh and said, "You can count on me."

By the time I was nine years old, I knew that being poor sucked and that I had to get out. That desire to lift myself out of poverty's debilitating grasp led me to me my first newspaper job. There was a company contracted by the *Philadelphia Inquirer* to sell subscriptions to suburbanites. Their plan was simple: take inner-city schoolkids to the suburbs, have them go door to door and read a prepared text. "Hi, ma'am, my name is Mark Segal. I'm in a school contest to win a trip to Cape Canaveral to further my science education. You can help me win by subscribing to the *Philadelphia Inquirer*." Who would not buy from a poor, skinny, yet charming nine-year-old at their door?

Stereotypical as it is for a Jew (though believe me, I didn't care an ounce about stereotypes), I was the best salesman on our team. Those trips to the suburbs gave me my first view of how the other half lived, and put some money in my pocket. The car would pick us up in the projects around six p.m. each weekday.

We'd head to a fast food place for dinner with our team leader (we paid our own way), then spend about an hour or so going from door to door before returning home by eight or nine p.m. Often we'd go to a New Jersey development, mostly single-family homes with a bit of land around them. Those yards! Each house was similar but, to me, large with very nice furniture, and the swimming pools made me realize what my family didn't have. That experience taught me to dream. The money I made allowed me to buy some of the things I wanted; and brought the realization that there must be even better jobs out there for me. The job also taught me about anti-Semitism, from incidents with my coworkers. At that young age I knew life was going to be a fight if I wanted to succeed, but it was one in which I was willing to engage since my parents had promised me it was worth the effort, no matter how hard it might be. My parents never lied.

In my teens, Dad's luck turned a little. He had been driving a cab and made enough so we could move to Mount Airy, a much better neighborhood, well away from the projects. It was a middle-class community, the model of an integrated neighborhood, populated by Jews, Christians, and African Americans. At Germantown High School, I simultaneously got my first taste of organizing and learned an important lesson.

One teacher in my senior year had never taught high school

before, and couldn't handle the students. Most of us were a bit unruly, and even when we weren't misbehaving, we simply found it impossible to understand his teaching. His last resort at keeping control was to tell us that we were all going to fail his class. His class was a requirement to graduate, so I took up a petition. It was the first time I had ever done anything like that. This was the middle of the counterculture era, 1969. The inspiration for my campaign came from the rancor of the antiwar and civil rights movements that I watched nightly on the television news. One of the many items I listed in the petition as a reason for our lobbying was that he was teaching Communism. All the white kids signed, but the black kids refused and were angered by the focus on Communism. Finally, one of the black kids explained it to me. In the South, when the police were pushing around the civil rights workers, they justified it by claiming they were Communists. So I took that item off the petition and even today I still think about what an unfair and cheap shot it was. Once we did it, however, everyone signed. We all passed the class and graduated. It was my first organizing success, and I learned a valuable lesson in compromise and listening.

While other kids were collecting eight-millimeter stag films, my collection was of old J.C. Penney, Montgomery Ward, and Sears, Roebuck catalogs. I didn't think there were any stag films or porn for people like me. One day at a farmers market in Berlin, New Jersey, I stumbled upon an old magazine stall and began flipping through various periodicals. I found a magazine with men modeling in what today would be called Speedos, and in jock straps, some wearing strategically placed loincloths, attempting to emulate the look of a Greek god. Ashamed to take it to the cashier, I put the periodical inside another magazine and purchased that one instead. Telling the clerk that I didn't need a bag and holding it tight like my freedom depended on it, I exited the store posthaste.

I didn't want to kiss the girls. I'd look at the guys in my class and feel far more attracted to them. There was no doubt in my mind about this, but I didn't know the word for who I was or what I was feeling. I knew, however, that I was okay with it. Now, I wasn't going to tell anybody, not in the 1960s.

I did have a few friends in Mount Airy. Randy Miller became my closest friend and my first real crush, which was an obstacle in our friendship, since he wasn't gay. I never told him how I felt about him. This experience taught me that there is more to a relationship than physicality . . . The way I felt about him, the way I desired him, wasn't just for sex because I wouldn't trade the emotional connection of our friendship for that alone. I realized that any real relationship had to include emotional connection.

When I was younger, maybe five or six years old, my cousin Norman was sixteen. His father discovered that he was gay, gave him a major beating, and threw him out of the house. Cousin Norman was the family member whom nobody mentioned. One day, I was in the backseat of my parents' Studebaker while they were discussing him and I somehow picked up on the fact that he was a guy who liked guys—a *fegeleh*. It was rarely brought up in the family and this clued me in to the dynamic that silence was preferred on this topic. Talk or no talk, I knew that whatever it all meant, I too was a *fegeleh*. And I knew never to speak about it.

As a teenager, I read in *TV Guide* one afternoon that on his PBS talk show, David Susskind was going to interview "real live homosexuals." A new word different from *fegeleh*, somehow I knew it also referred to me. I just knew it. In the fifties and sixties, those words were rarely used, but if you were found to be a homosexual, you were a sinner in religious circles; you were a criminal in legal situations; you were insane in the psychiatric community; and you were unemployable by city, state, and federal governments. Pretty much a life of condemnation awaited you. If people found out the word *homosexual* applied to you, chances were you would lose your job, your family, be subjected to electrical shocks, and lose everything else you valued, so most remained inside a closet within a closet. I didn't know all of this as a kid, but I knew it was a dangerous subject to discuss. This would all change later on, but in the early sixties there weren't many places to turn if such a life was yours.

My parents had given me a nine-inch portable black-and-white television set for my bar mitzvah. It was all the rage back then, an itty-bitty set with big round batteries. The David Susskind show came on at late at night and I remember taking my TV up to my room, making my bedcovers into a tent, and watching the show. There was a man from the Mattachine Society in New York talking about gay people. I thought to myself, *There are homosexuals in New York. There are people like me.* Then and there I knew I would move to New York.

It was awhile before I took action, but that night a plan began to form in my head. I was going to be with people like me. For a long while I had no idea how I'd do it, but it eventually came to me. Radio Corporation of America (RCA) had a technical institute that taught high school students how to be television cameramen. That was my ticket. It broke my father's heart since he really wanted me to go to college, and Mom always said I'd make a great lawyer. But the only thing that mattered to me then was to be with my own kind and there were none of us in Philadelphia, at least none that I knew. In New York I would become part of a new breed of gay men who didn't slide easily into the popular and unfortunate stereotypes of the times—and that would work to my advantage.

On May 10, 1969, the day after grades were finalized, I moved to New York on the pretense that I would start technical school in September. My parents drove me up, dropped me off, and I got a room at the YMCA. I dressed up in my best clothes and set off for a gay evening, probably expecting that my gay brothers and sisters would line up to embrace me and welcome me into their community. The problem was, I had no idea where to go. There were certainly no neon signs pointing to the gay area. It seemed the place to start my search was Greenwich Village, which according to the network news was the counter-cultural hub of the 1960s. Getting off the subway in the Village, I had an unhappy, lonely feeling. Leaving the security of home, finding myself in a strange place with no prospects of a job and little money, was a bit daunting. Yet my search was on. It didn't begin very well, though, and that first night I returned to my tiny four-dollar sweatbox room, exhausted and unsuccessful in finding my people.

After a few days of looking around, I came across a Village dance bar, the Stonewall, a mob-owned dive. The search was over. As it turned out, two boys who I'd met at the YMCA from Saint Cloud, Minnesota, were there that night as well.

That first week, remembering the Susskind show with real live homosexuals, I also looked up *Mattachine Society* in the telephone book and went to their office. I had no idea what to expect. All I knew about them from the television show was that they worked on keeping gay people from getting fired. I walked out of the office about fifteen minutes later with a guy named Marty Robinson, who would later become one of the most unsung heroes of the gay movement. Marty was young and evidently frustrated in his dealings with Mattachine. He said, "You don't want to be involved with these old people. They don't understand gay rights as it's happening today. Look what's happening in the black community. Look at the fight for women's rights. Look at the fight against the Vietnam War."

It was 1969 and Mattachine had become old. They were men in suits. We were men in jeans and T-shirts. So he told me that he and others were going to start a new gay rights movement, one more in tune with the times. Marty was creating an organization called the Action Group and I became an inaugural member. We didn't know exactly what we were going to do or what actions we might pursue, but none of that mattered. Others at that time were also creating gay groups to spark public consciousness, similar to the groups feminists were establishing. It deserves to be said right here and right now that the feminist movement was pivotal in helping to shape the new movement for gay rights.

Groups across New York worked independently of each other, but all with the same goal of defining ourselves rather than accepting the labels that society had branded us with. We were on the ground floor of the struggle for equality, and though some might have seen it as a sexual revolution, we saw it as defining ourselves. Years later a friend would remark, "Mark was so involved with the sexual revolution that he didn't have time to participate." The Action Group would hold meetings walking down Christopher Street—our outdoor office, so to speak. We didn't have a headquarters.

Then, just a little over a month after I arrived, on June 28, 1969, Stonewall happened.

Chapter 2

Stonewall

Many in the LGBT community think of the Stonewall vets, as some call us, like heroes. For me it started out as a frightening event.

I was in the back of the bar near the dance floor, where the younger people usually hung out. The lights in the room blinked—a signal that there would be a raid—then turned all the way up. Stonewall was filled that night with the usual clientele: drag queens, hustlers, older men who liked younger guys, and stragglers like me—the boy next door who didn't know what he was searching for and felt he had little to offer. That all changed when the police raided the bar. As they always did, they walked in like they owned the place, cocky, assured that they could do and say whatever they wanted and push people around with impunity. We had no idea why they came in, whether or not they'd been paid, wanted more payoffs, or simply wanted to harass the fags that night. One of the policemen came up to me and asked for my ID. I was eighteen, which was the legal drinking age in New York in those days. I rustled through my wallet, very frightened, and quickly handed him my ID. I was no help in their search for underage drinkers. I was relieved to be among the first to get out of the bar.

As a crowd began to assemble, I ran into Marty Robinson and he asked what was going on.

"It's just another raid," I told him, full of nonchalant so-phistication. We walked up and down Christopher Street, and fifteen minutes later we heard loud banging and screaming. The screams were not of fear, but resistance. That was the beginning of the Stonewall riots. It was not the biggest riot ever—it has been tremendously blown out of proportion—but it was still a riot, although one pretty much contained to across the street on Sheridan Square and Seventh Avenue. There were probably only a couple hundred participants; anyone with a decent job or family ran away from that bar as fast as they could to avoid being arrested. Those who remained were the drag queens, hus-tlers, and runaways.

People had begun to congregate at the door after they left the bar. One of the cops had said something derogatory under his breath and the mood shifted. The crowd began taunting the police. Every time someone came out of the bar, the crowd yelled. A drag queen shouted at the cops: "What's the matter, aren't you getting any at home? I can give you something you'd really love." The cops started to get rough, pushing and shoving. In response the crowd got angry. The cops took refuge inside. The drag queens, loud and boisterous, were throwing every-thing that wasn't fastened down to the street and a few things that were, like parking meters. Whoever assumes that a swishy queen can't fight should have seen them, makeup dripping and gowns askew, fighting for their home and fiercely proving that no one would take it away from them.

More and more police cars arrived. Some rioters began fire-bombing the place while others fanned out, breaking shop win-dows on Christopher Street and looting the displays; somebody put a dress on the statue of General Phil Sheridan. There was an odd, celebratory feel to it, the notion that we were finally fighting back and that it felt good. Bodies ricocheted off one another, but there was no fighting in the street. All the anger was directed at the policemen inside the bar. People were actually laughing and dancing out there. According to some accounts, though I did not actually see this, drag queens formed a Rockettes-style chorus line singing, *"We are the Stonewall girls / We wear our hair in curls / We wear no underwear / To show our pubic hair."* That song and dance later became popular with a gay youth group I was part of, and months after Stonewall, Mark Horn, Jeff Hochhauser, Michael Knowles, Tony Russomanno, and I would dance our way to the Silver Dollar restaurant at the bottom of Christopher Street. We were going to be the first graduating class of gay activists in this country—indeed, most of us are still involved, and we're in touch with each other to this day.

Marty Robinson, after seeing what was happening, disappeared and then reappeared with chalk. Most people don't realize that Stonewall was not simply a one-night occurrence. Marty immediately understood that the Stonewall raid presented a "moment" that could be the catalyst to organize the movement and bring together all the separate groups. He was the one person who saw it then and there as a pivotal point in history. At his direction several of us wrote on walls and on the ground up and down Christopher Street: *Meet at Stonewall tomorrow night.* How did Marty know that this night could create something that would change our community forever?

The nights following the Stonewall raid consisted primarily of loosely organized speeches. Various LGBT factions were coming together publicly for the first time, protesting the oppressive treatment of the community. Up until that moment, LGBT people had simply accepted oppression and inequality as their lot in life. That all changed. There was a spirit of rebellion in the air. More than just merely begging to be treated equally, it was time to stand up, stand out, and demand an end to fearful deference.

Stonewall would become a four-night event and the most visible symbol of a movement. We united for the first time: lesbian separatists, gay men in fairy communes, people who had been part of other civil rights movements but never thought about one of their own, young gay radicals, hustlers, drag queens, and many like me who knew there was something out there for us, but didn't know what it was. It found us. So, to the NYPD, thank you. Thank you for creating a unified LGBT community and thank you for becoming the focal point for years of oppression that many of us had to suffer growing up. You represented all those groups and individuals that wanted to keep us in our place.

The Action Group eventually joined with other organizations to become the Gay Liberation Front, or GLF. In that first year Marty helped create the new gay movement, along with people like Martha Shelley, Allen Young, Karla Jay, Jim Fouratt, Barbara Love, John O'Brien, Lois Hart, Ralph Hall, Jim Owles, Perry Brass, Bob Kohler, Susan Silverman, Jerry Hoose, Steven Dansky, John Lauritsen, Dan Smith, Ron Auerbacher, Nikos Diaman, Suzanne Bevier, Carl Miller, Earl Galvin, Michael Brown, Arthur Evans, and of course Sylvia Rivera.

I'd like to believe that the GLF put us gay youth in a good position to succeed, since many of us have done so in different ways. Mark Horn has had an incredible career in advertising and public relations at top firms; Jeff Hochhauser went on to his dream of becoming a playwright and teaching theater; Michael Knowles is in theater management; and Tony Russomanno, who for a while in those early days was my partner, continued on his path in broadcasting, winning multiple Emmy and Peabody awards as a news reporter and television anchor.

* * *

Over the last few years, LGBT history has become a passion of mine, and sometimes it seems that the younger generation doesn't really care about it. The Gay Liberation Front has mostly been ignored in the history books, even though it helped forge the foundation upon which our community is built.

Stonewall was a fire in the belly of the equality movement. Even so, accounts of it are full of myth and misinformation, and much of that will inevitably remain so, since there are differing accounts from those active in the movement. That's the nature of memory, I suppose. Regardless of the diverging stories, and no matter how intense the fighting was, Stonewall represented, absolutely, the first time that the LGBT community successfully fought back and forged an organized movement and community. All of us at Stonewall had one thing in common: the oppression of growing up in a world which demanded our silence about who we were and insisted that we simply accept the punishment that society levied for our choices. That silence ended with Stonewall, and those who created the Gay Liberation Front organized and launched a sustainable movement.

But Stonewall was not the first uprising. LGBT history is written, like most history, by the victors, those with the means and those with connections or power. Two similar uprisings before Stonewall have almost been written out of our history: San Francisco's Compton Cafeteria riot in 1966 and the Dewey's sit-in in Philadelphia in 1965. Drag queens and street kids who played a huge role in both events never documented those riots, thus they have been widely eliminated by the white upper middle class, many of whom were ashamed of those elements of our community. But Stonewall, Compton, and Dewey's all have one thing in common: drag queens and street kids. For some historians, drag queens are not the ideal representatives of the LGBT community. Oppression within oppression was and is still of concern. Even recently, with the transgender issue finally being taken seriously, there is still a backlash from the community about including them in the general gay movement.

It has been over forty years since the Gay Liberation Front first took trans seriously, but the gay men who wore those shirts with the polo players or alligator emblems didn't want trans people as the representation of their community. Their revisionist history has been accepted into popular culture because they were the ones with connections to publishers, the influence, as well as the money and time to sit back and write about what "really" happened.

The riot of 1966 in San Francisco grew out of police harassment of drag queens at Compton's Cafeteria. It all started with the staff at Compton's telling the drag queens to settle down. It was the drag queens who, night after night, went there and bought drinks, sustaining the business. It was, in a sense, their home. The management's job, according to their deal with the police, was to keep the queens in order. One night, like Stonewall, the queens decided they didn't want to be controlled any longer.

And even before Compton's there were the Dewey's restaurant sit-ins in Philadelphia in April 1965. The restaurant management decided not to serve people who demonstrated "improper behavior." The reality was that they didn't want to serve homosexuals, especially those who didn't wear the acceptable clothing. Meaning drag queens. A spontaneous sit-in occurred and over the next week the Janus Society, an early gay rights organization, had picketers on site handing out flyers. Most were people who had little to lose, the street kids and drag queens once again. Those LGBT people with the little animals on their polo shirts were in short supply.

Both Compton's and Dewey's point to the fact that in the

mid-1960s the fight for black civil rights was beginning to influence the more disenfranchised in the gay community. The major difference with those two early events is that from the Stonewall riots grew a new movement, one that still lives today. Nonetheless, they deserve to be remembered.

The biggest fallacy of Stonewall is when people say, "Of course they were upset, Judy Garland was being buried that day." That trivializes what happened and our years of oppression, and is just culturally wrong. Many of us in Stonewall who stayed on Christopher Street and didn't run from the riot that day were people my age. Judy Garland was from the past generation, an old star. Diana Ross, the Beatles, even Barbra Streisand were the icons of our generation. Garland meant a little something to us, as she did for many groups—"Somewhere Over the Rainbow"—but that was it. And, honestly, that song was wishful thinking, an anthem for the older generation. In that bar, we were going to smash that rainbow. We didn't have to go over anything or travel anywhere to get what we wanted. The riot was about the police doing what they constantly did: indiscriminately harassing us. The police represented every institution of America that night: religion, media, medical, legal, and even our families, most of whom had been keeping us in our place. We were tired of it. And as far as we knew, Judy Garland had nothing to do with it.

While I didn't know it at that moment, I was fighting back against feelings that had been suppressed for so many years. No more J.C. Penney catalogs for me. It was time for the real thing. As the riot was happening all around me, the idea of a circus came to mind, and then it hit me: we can shout who we are and not be ashamed, we can demand respect. It was at that point that Marty Robinson's words hit a chord. We were fighting for our rights just as women, African Americans, and others had done throughout history.

After my Grandmom had taken me to my first civil rights demonstration at thirteen, I'd watch the news every night, waiting to see the latest update on what was happening. My television viewing and newspaper reading included following the Freedom Riders in the South. The sit-ins and marches had a big impact on me. The images of Birmingham, of Bull Connor with his German shepherds snapping, of the fire hoses blasting people marching for desegregation moved me. They led me to ask how one human could possibly treat another in that manner. I realized, too, the brilliance of Martin Luther King Jr., the Atlanta pastor and face of the movement, in his strategic use of Bull Connor and Birmingham to showcase the hatred behind segregation. What's more, Bayard Rustin, MLK's contemporary in the fight for equality and his chief of staff for the March on Washington, was a gay man, vocal on the rights of gay people. The FBI and others tried to use Rustin's "homosexuality" against him, and some of the organizers of the march wanted to drop him, but MLK stood tall in supporting him. It wouldn't be until I interviewed Coretta Scott King in 1986 and she reaffirmed her husband's support of "gay rights" that I got to personally offer my gratitude. It was an unknown fact to many, including those of us in Gay Liberation Front, which would become the only university I ever attended.

Gay Liberation Front, in all likelihood, was the most dysfunctional LGBT organization that ever existed, which shouldn't be very surprising. Born from the ashes of the Stonewall riots, it brought together for the first time the various elements and fractions of the community, to organize, to strategize, and to fight back. Before Stonewall we were polite; after Stonewall we demanded our equality. To that point we had no understanding of who we were as a people, we only had what society told us we were, and at that time a lot of us in New York were attempting to redefine ourselves. There were many individuals who began to set up collectives, lesbian separatist groups, discussion groups, even communes, and everything in between.

In addition to redefining ourselves, we also realized from the beginning that we were focused on building a community, since we couldn't count on any part of society to provide the basic services we needed. We had to create those institutions where they had never existed before. We were trying to establish our goals and figure out what kind of organization we would be. Since we were oppressed by the system, we didn't want to use any of their old tools in our meetings.

Therefore, there was no leadership at GLF, no permanent chair, only the occasional use of *Robert's Rules of Order*. Decisions were made by consensus, and in order to reach that point some meetings went late into the evening. It was total chaos. It worked, but at times it was almost comedic.

At one meeting a woman spoke about how men were trying to control women in the organization. Her example was that the men with beards in the group did not understand how through the ages facial hair had been used to symbolize the dominant male of a community, i.e., the leader. So men with beards at Gay Liberation Front were supporting the oppression of women. The following week several men, in order to show solidarity, came to the meeting with their beards shaved. That upset some of the other men, who saw beards as fashion or a symbol of who they were, accepting their masculinity. That in turn upset the fairies who wanted men to accept their feminine side. And around it went.

We debated everything, with the exception of creating

community—we were all agreed on that goal, and worked to form groups to help us achieve it. There was no debate when I advocated for a gay youth group and little debate when Sylvia Rivera created Street Transvestite Action Revolutionaries (STAR), one of the first-ever trans organizations. There was no debate on health alerts, and the only conflict about opening a community center related to money, not the idea. This is part of why 1969 is often cited as the start of the new gay rights movement. Gay Liberation Front led our struggle from a mere movement trying to change laws into one of harvesting community.

We were so radical that even Harvey Milk, the "Mayor of Castro Street" who lived in New York before he became the first elected openly gay member of San Francisco's Board of Supervisors in 1977 and was assassinated in 1978, stayed clear of us.

Little known fact about Harvey: His former partner and later a friend of mine was Craig Rodwell, founder of the Oscar Wilde Bookshop. He was also the founder of what today is Gay Pride Day, but what Craig then called the Christopher Street Gay Liberation Day. Milk was so closeted in 1970 that he wouldn't involve himself with the event or any other gay movement. He only did so after moving away from his New York family to San Francisco in 1972. It says something about San Francisco circa 1978 that an openly gay man would be assassinated in what was considered the nation's most gay-friendly city. (For those who appreciate LGBT history, the first openly gay or lesbian elected official anywhere in the country was Nancy Wechsler, voted to the city council in Ann Arbor in 1972, then Elaine Noble to the state house in Massachusetts in 1974. It would not be until 1987, when Barney Frank came out, that we would have an out member of Congress, and 2012 when we finally had an out member of the US Senate, Tammy Baldwin.)

Like all caucuses, committees, cells, or communes, each

group within the Gay Liberation Front had its mission. While I didn't form the first youth group, I organized the first one intended to be a foundation on which a community could then be built. We were going to reach out beyond the areas where LGBT youth were thought to be. We took on the serious issues of bullied, battered, homeless, and suicidal gay youth. We created safe spaces and safe activities. And not only were we there to offer our support to one of the most endangered segments of our community, we were there to nurture future activists. We were in some ways the first graduating class of gay liberation. Donn Teal wrote in *The Gay Militants*: "As GLF had given birth to organizations for transvestites and transsexuals and for Third World people, so did it sire Gay Youth." Published in 1971, this was the first LGBT history of those early years.

Our flyers clearly stated that our goals were both political and social. We even surprised our older comrades in the Gay Liberation Front with our media outreach directed at gay youth. We went on radio talk shows and even TV shows. We spoke at high schools. One of my favorite items of that time was a copy of the *Spider Press*, the newspaper of Oceanside High School, and there on the cover is a picture of Gay Youth members Tony Russomanno and Mark Segal with the headline, "Gay Activist Lecture; They Are Not Neurotic." This was October 23, 1970.

At one time or another I was chairman, president, or sometimes just the leader. My steadfast vice president, Mark Horn, whose title never changed, would smirk at my various titles. Tony Russomanno helped us in our goal of becoming the first national gay youth organization by starting our Detroit chapter— and we called ourselves, simply, Gay Youth. We soon had chapters in San Francisco, Chicago, Tampa, Ann Arbor, and even my hometown of Philadelphia. Our Philly chapter started by Tommi Avicolli Mecca, now a housing activist in San Francisco, in-

tended "to act as a basic introduction to Gay Liberation Front."
In Stephan L. Cohen's book *The Gay Liberation Youth Movement
in New York*, our "demands" in various national LGBT organizational meetings, to summarize, were: ending ageism in all
its forms, ending age-of-consent laws, ending abuse by parents,
ending repression by schools and religious institutions, and, most
importantly, an equal voice at the table for LGBT organizations.

I hosted movie nights in my five-story walk-up apartment
on 12th Street and Avenue C, which was a three-room tene-
ment decorated with donations and furnishings from the street;
the bathtub was in the kitchen. It had a nice living room where
we would plug in the borrowed projector and show films on the
wall, before leaving to take a walk across town to Christopher
Street. These movie nights grew too popular for the apartment
so we moved them to Alternate U, where we held our dances.
Gay Youth did all of this with no real funding, with the exception of what came from our pockets or what we received from
the small Gay Liberation Front treasury.

As Marc Stein writes in his book *Rethinking the Gay and Lesbian Movement*, "Interest was so great among young people that
in 1970 GLF-NY established a Gay Youth caucus . . . Led by
Mark Segal, Gay Youth soon was functioning as an autonomous
organization with affiliated groups elsewhere in the United
States and Canada." For me, Gay Youth was a lesson in both
creating lifelong friendships and leadership. It also helped me
prove to myself that my career as an activist was real—as long
as I had no expectations of a salary.

The most contested topic at any Gay Liberation Front
meeting was sexism, but we debated many subjects. At times the
debates became personal and it was not unusual to hear people
being labeled capitalist pigs, fascist, racist, sexist, and for good
measure I'd even toss in the label ageist on occasion.

Somehow even the simple act of a kiss took on political overtones. Perry Brass tells this story: "Someone explained to me that these were 'political kisses,' to show that we were out and proud, especially at a GLF meeting. At my first meeting we broke into discussion groups after the 'business' part of the meeting was over. My discussion group of six people included Pete Wilson, a good-looking young man who also had a program on WBAI radio. Pete had a wonderful voice, and a remarkably sparkling, outgoing personality. I was drawn to him, and I remembered a lot of what he said, talking about how important it was for us to throw off old habits and fears. I certainly had enough of the old habits and fears, growing up in an extremely repressive atmosphere. I noticed, though, there was a distinct coolness to Pete. He was not someone to hug and smooch with other people. But he was very political and could talk an excellent political line.

"Several weeks after this first meeting, I went to Carnegie Hall for an afternoon concert. After it was over, while walking down from the balcony, I spotted Pete in the stairway. He approached me in the midst of a throng of people, and kissed me. He had never kissed me before at a meeting, or any place. I was embarrassed for a second; I was not used to kissing outside. We talked a bit, and I hid any concerns I had about being kissed in the stairway of Carnegie Hall. At the next GLF meeting, on seeing him, I walked up to Pete and kissed him.

"'Why did you do that?' he asked.

"I shrugged. It seemed the right thing to do. 'You kissed me at Carnegie Hall,' I said.

"'Oh, that was a political kiss,' he explained. 'You don't have to do that here.'"

Some topics weren't discussed, such as gays in the military or marriage, but we still had members who went off by themselves and dealt with those issues without the endorsement of the organization. Working with elected officials became a major effort of Marty Robinson and Jim Owles. Gay Liberation Front's support for the Black Panthers, and our numerous demonstrations outside the Women's House of Detention which then was in our neighborhood on Greenwich off Christopher, caused a rift. We'd often join the demonstrations and march and shout, *"Hey hey, ho ho, the house of D has to go!"* And our contingent would then shout, *"Ho ho, hey hey, gay is just as good as straight!"* Ultimately, these types of issues caused Jim and Marty and a few others to break away from Gay Liberation Front and create Gay Activist Alliance. The last straw for them was the support given to the Black Panthers.

Many of us felt religion was a fundamental element in our repression. When Reverend Troy Perry held a meeting in New York at the Summit Hotel on Lexington Avenue to organize a branch of his fledgling LGBT church, Metropolitan Community Church (MCC), we picketed. Yes, one gay organization picketing another. After his meeting, however, Troy came out to speak to us. He took me aside and explained that while we were effective at reaching some members of the community, we had little possibility of reaching those who were religious. His church gave people a place to go where they could be both religious and a member of the LGBT community. His point was pragmatic and started a friendship between us that lasts to this day.

The same holds true for my sisters and brothers in Gay Liberation Front. Being one of the youngest in the group, I was allowed certain liberties, and for that reason I was and am on good terms with most of our surviving members. They were my teachers, and all that I have accomplished has its roots in what I learned in GLF.

* * *

After GLF's incredible first year, many thought we should celebrate Stonewall and our achievements. Chief among them was
Craig Rodwell, so he organized what is now commonly known
as a gay pride parade. As I've already mentioned, its name then
was Christopher Street Gay Liberation Day. I was one of the
many who volunteered to be a marshal those first few years.
One of the original posters from the event hangs in a place of
honor in my den.

It was Sunday, June 28, 1970. No one knew what would
happen since we intended to march up to Central Park without
a permit. We held self-defense/martial arts classes at Alternate
U where we learned how to protect ourselves, since we had
no idea who or what would greet us. After all, we were going
to march through the middle of Manhattan from the Village
to Central Park. That march was one of the great products of
Stonewall.

GLF changed the world in one year. Think that's an over-
statement? Here are the facts: before Stonewall, the movement
for LGBT equality consisted of one large national public demonstration each year on July 4 in front of Independence Hall in
Philadelphia, and of course the Compton's and Dewey's events
and a couple of small regional pickets. But the picket line at
Independence Hall lasted from 1965 till 1969. No more than
fifty to one hundred people attended. That was the preeminent
LGBT demonstration of its day, and the picketers came from
across the nation, though mostly from the East Coast. In a few
major cities there were organizations like One Inc. (Los Angeles), Mattachine (Washington and New York), Daughters of
Bilitis and Janus Society (Philadelphia), and a handful of others.
That was it.

But Gay Liberation Front, along with its brother and sister organizations, wanted to create something more than just

a march for equality. Before Stonewall, these few brave organizations, and the people on those picket lines outside Independence Hall each July 4, all that existed were bars, secret gay hook-up venues, and private parties.

In 1969, the Mattachine Society in New York would not allow anyone under eighteen into their offices, afraid that the police would raid them. So we organized our youth, welcomed them to our meetings, set up a suicide hot line, a speakers' bureau that went to high schools, and, when the *Village Voice* would not publish the word "gay," we marched on them. The laws were wrong; we were not!

That Sunday morning we gathered on Christopher Street. By the time we reached 23rd Street, the crowd still reached all the way back to Christopher Street. Estimates were everywhere from 5,000 to 15,000 people. We had taken the movement from a brave crew of a hundred people willing to march in public at those Independence Hall pickets to what was now a march of many thousands. That first year of Gay Liberation Front was one of the most pivotal years in the struggle for LGBT equality. As my friend Jerry Hoose used to say about that year, "We went from the shadows to sunlight."

And in 1972, when the gay pride march was officially launched, the *New York Times* reported on June 26, "The message of the march, according to Mark Segal, the grand marshal, was simply, 'We're proud to be gay.'" Well, I wasn't the grand marshal, and I wouldn't return to that march again until Stonewall 25—and then again in 2004, when Frank Kameny, Jim Kepner, Jack Nichols, some of my brothers and sisters from Gay Liberation Front, and I, among others, were put on two giant floats and recognized as pioneers of the struggle for LGBT equality.

* * *

New York City was for me the center of everything, especially the East Village, where I lived. At that time, it was not the trendy neighborhood it is today; rather, it was one of the most dangerous in the city and therefore affordable to me. Many of my new friends were connected to the outer fringes of show business: James, a dancer from Ohio, and his sister Kelly, who was dating one of the doormen at Stonewall. Mark "10 1/2" Stevens, who found a career in straight porn films even though he was gay and, as my parents might say, a nice Jewish boy. And then there was my roommate, Rosemary Gimple, and her friend Jeff Hochhauser.

Rosemary and Jeff had written a musical called *Graduation* that was being performed at New York Theater Ensemble. They enlisted me as their stage manager despite knowing that my only previous theatrical experience was in high school where I had one line in our school version of *The Man Who Came to Dinner*. (I was to appear at a pivotal point in the plot and shout, "Stop, I'm the FBI and this is a raid!" When I walked onstage my friends in the audience applauded and I froze.)

Graduation was the story of a teenage boy coming of age and accepting himself. It was, I believe, the first gay-themed musical on the New York stage and it led to my second and last job in the theater, managing a show down the street for Andy Warhol "superstar" Jackie Curtis. All I can remember is a song titled "White Shoulders" and what we would today call a transgender actress, Holly Woodlawn, whom everyone adored. Nearby was La Mama, which seemed to always have a show featuring a drag queen. Sometimes that drag queen was Harvey Fierstein, who went on to win many Tonys on Broadway and be inducted into the American Theater Hall of Fame.

The off-off-Broadway community was flourishing. On nights when you weren't working, you could get yourself invited to see these other offerings. One night for me it was a reading of an unfinished show titled *Small Craft Warnings*, which I knew nothing about. As I watched the first act, I grew increasingly agitated and annoyed. The self-pity of the gay character was precisely what my activism was trying to end. At that point, gays in the media had only three variations: pitiful, villainous, or suicidal, and this was going down that same old path. So with my newfound activism and left-leaning language, I stood up and shouted, "Bullshit! This is oppressive to gay men!" As I continued to go on about gay liberation, a small man made his way down the aisle to my row. He told me he was the playwright and that I should get the hell out of the theater. He was Tennessee Williams, who claimed fame following his blockbusters *The Glass Menagerie* and *A Streetcar Named Desire*. The show, when it officially opened, received poor reviews and closed quickly.

On another night Jackie Curtis invited me to a party at Andy Warhol's Factory right off of Union Square. The Factory was the hip hangout for socialites, drag queens, bohemians, intellectuals, and Hollywood types. I remember walking upstairs and winding up in a large, dimly lit loft with lots of people and not much food or drink. By the time we got there Jackie was already stoned. My fifteen minutes with Warhol were spent watching him walk aimlessly around the loft holding a jar of Hellmann's mayonnaise. Warhol, who lived as an openly gay man even before the gay rights movement, said a few unmemorable, indecipherable words and was off. Later on at the party, someone speculated about what he used the mayonnaise for; I'll spare you the details. There were many solitary people who ambled around without agenda, as well as groups of people who huddled tightly together like pickles.

The off-Broadway theater crowd hung out at Phebe's, which served the best burgers in the city. One night I met a guy who

claimed to be a Broadway producer. Why would a Broadway producer be slumming on East 4th Street with the off-off-Broadway
crowd? He invited me to stand with him in the wings and see his
latest show in previews. The show was called *The Love Suicide
at Schofield Barracks* and it closed after five performances. My
friend Rosemary told me that the guy then tried the movie business. His name was Robert Weinstein. He made the right move.

Another friend, Charlie Briggs, was the assistant stage
manager for the Broadway musical production of *Purlie*, star-
ring Cleavon Little, Melba Moore, and a former Philadelphian
named Sherman Helmsley whose TV audiences would get to
know him as George Jefferson on the TV sitcom *The Jeffersons*.
Little and Moore, who went on to have a major music career,
won Tony Awards for their performances in *Purlie*. On my visits
to the show, Helmsley and I would often compare notes on our
home city. There has been much speculation about his sexuality
since his death in 2012. While he certainly took a keen interest
in our talks and my gay activism, there is nothing more that I
can add to that discussion.

On another occasion Rosemary wanted to go to the theater
to see a revival of an old musical, *No, No, Nanette*. She got us
orchestra tickets in the next-to-last row for the final preview
before its opening night at the 46th Street Theater. While I was
reading the playbill before the show, Rosemary tapped me on
my shoulder. She pointed across the aisle at two of our fellow
theatergoers, Senator Ted Kennedy and his wife.

Rosemary, always a little amused at my dealings in activism,
said with a smirk, "Why don't you ask him about gay rights?"

I smiled, got up from my seat, and made my way to Senator
Kennedy. He was sitting up front in an aisle seat. I tapped him
on the back, which startled him. A life lesson: never sneak up
on a man who has seen two of his brothers assassinated. He

turned in surprise and I introduced myself, after which I asked
him his position on gay rights. He looked a little bewildered—
after all, the gay movement was still relatively new at this point.
I watched each word as it tiptoed off his tongue.

"What?" he said.

I asked again, this time using the h-word instead of *gay*, and
he replied, "I've never been asked that before, but I'm for all
civil rights." I thanked him and made my way back up the aisle
to my seat.

Along with *No, No, Nanette*, I got to see the original productions of *Company* and *Follies*, which resulted in a passion
for the words and music of Stephen Sondheim, one of the only
sophisticated elements of my quite makeshift life.

A few days later Rosemary's friend Keely Stahl somehow
arranged tickets and backstage passes for us to attend a Beach
Boys concert in Central Park. Rosemary suggested that I ask
them to do a gay rights fundraising concert, but I only got blank
stares from them when I explained what I wanted. Keely said
they were too stoned to understand me. We left in utter amusement and wonderment of how they performed in such a state.

There was also a new and unusual kind of performance
space called the Continental Baths in the basement of the An-
sonia Hotel on the Upper West Side, which was actually a men's
bathhouse. I had heard about this crazy lady called Bette Midler
who sang up a storm there, so I decided to check it out. The
bathhouse was a place for gay men to meet discreetly, but this
was the early seventies and gay life was starting to bloom and
smash out of the closets and businesses wanted to cater to this
crowd, so they added entertainment to the mix of faux exercise,
swimming pool, and anonymous sex. When I first saw the divine
Miss M., she was singing by the pool accompanied by her pia-
nist, Barry Manilow. Bette did indeed sing her heart out and she

drew a much larger crowd than the space could hold. Crammed to the gills, people actually fell into the pool trying to watch her perform.

Bette glorified the camp humor in the gay community. In the middle of her performance she'd look down a hallway and call out, "Hey, boys, there's a girl out here working," or, "Come out, come out, wherever you are . . . I know you're in those damn rooms doing who knows what." She was so good that I had to have a recording of her performance, and I did the unspeakable: I took a tape recorder to the baths.

Not everyone walked around in towels, although most did, and it has been reported that even Manilow sometimes did so, though I don't believe that was the case. But Bette certainly brought in people who were there only to see her and who were not necessarily gay at all. Ah well.

After the success of the first two gay pride marches, it was decided that we needed something more than just speeches. We needed a feel-good moment as reprieve from all our internal fights; a moment to identify ourselves beyond turmoil. So Bette Midler's friend Vito Russo approached her and she agreed to sing at our third gay pride event. Susan Silverman, an early Gay Liberation Front member, recently reminded me that someone suggested that Gay Youth be in charge of Bette's security—and I got to be her bodyguard. What the hell did we know about security for a woman who at the time was becoming a national show-biz wonder? I vividly recall how she greeted us on the stairway to the stage that day. She looked up at me, since she was so short, and said: "Yeah, this is my security." She laughed, walked up the steps, and added, "Okay, boys, let's get this show on the road."

* * *

I was still young and poor, with no prospects but hope for the future, and New York was a wonderland; it allowed me to grow. From an emotionally battered kid I morphed quickly into a person with his own identity. The excitement never ended, and there was something new happening almost every day. While worrying about the police or FBI listening in on our phone conversations or planting someone in our meetings (we learned later that J. Edgar Hoover and his FBI actually did this), my group of friends expanded to include porn stars, drag queens, actors, playwrights, musicians, and even the prince of a small country. Then there were the eclectic spiritual beings of various varieties. I helped a friend open a short-lived witchcraft store at 119 Christopher Street. I wanted to explore every aspect of what I didn't have growing up. And thanks to Grandmom I was open to diversity.

My favorite book and movie growing up, as I've said, was *Auntie Mame*. It always reminded me of my grandmother Fannie. Somehow I discovered that *Auntie Mame* was based on a real-life woman named Marion Tanner who lived in New York. It became my mission to find her, and I did. She lived on the West Side and was running a boarding house. When I rang her bell, she invited me in and we sat at her kitchen table. She wasn't at all glamorous. She looked like she had been cleaning the house, which was exactly what I'd interrupted. When I asked her about the book, she delivered a cryptic line: "The book is like a plane: sometimes it's on the ground and other times it's in midair." She gave no details and wouldn't talk about her nephew Patrick Dennis, who wrote the book. I left that house realizing that I already knew Auntie Mame and she wasn't the lady I had just met. Her name was Fannie Weinstein and she was my grandmother.

Most evenings had me picking up my friend Doug Carver at

his place at 11th Street between avenues A and B and walking over to Christopher Street in the West Village to attend meetings, hand out flyers, or just hang out at the Silver Dollar near the pier. We'd walk up and down that street all night meeting our friends and popping into bar after bar like the reopened Stonewall or the 9th Circle to see who was there. The scene was now very sociable, like when Grandmom would take me chair to chair on the Atlantic City boardwalk each summer.

Yet activism was not glamorous. Revolutions are work-intensive and that kept me living on a can of SpaghettiOs and potato salad for dinner most nights. We only bought clothes, usually at thrift stores, when the ones we had were worn thin.

To support myself—barely, since we were creating a revolution and had little time to make money—I had a litany of jobs. The one that kept me going was, like my father, driving a cab. Dover was my garage, and even today I have my hack license hanging on my office wall. My other part-time job was as a waiter at John Britt's Hippodrome, literally a rundown gay dive bar on Avenue A between 10th and 11th Streets. My most vivid memories of working there were from Monday nights when I got to be a bartender, since few people came in and John had no one else who would work just for tips. Only one customer stands out in my memory. Almost every Monday he'd sit at my bar, and often he was the only customer. We'd talk, but not about his business, which I'd learned many weeks into our relationship was dance and ballet. Robert Joffrey, of Joffrey Ballet fame, who was born Abdullah Jaffa Bey Khan to an Afghani father and Italian mother, never talked shop, thank goodness. In all honesty, the only thing about ballet that I actually like are the men in tights. It takes me back to those J.C. Penney catalogs.

As an organizer in the LGBT community, I was willing to drop any and everything just to be involved. This meant that I didn't always show up for my shift at Dover to get my cab. New drivers like me sometimes demanded the better cabs that often went to the longtime drivers, and that didn't sit well with the veterans. This led to a confrontation with three older drivers, all well built and intimidating, who cornered me one day and suggested that the garage didn't need faggots making demands.

Since I couldn't live on the money from the Hippodrome alone, some GLF friends suggested a solution: sign up for welfare. For a guy from a working-class family who had escaped the projects and envisioned never being a part of that world again, this seemed out of the question. But when the rent was due and the landlord threatened eviction, I realized my friends had a convincing case.

According to them, the state was giving us welfare as restitution for the despicable treatment gays suffered. Since it was society that was oppressing us as citizens, why shouldn't we use their tools to fight back? When I researched how to sign up, it surprised me to learn that all one had to do in 1970 was walk in a welfare office and tell them you were "homosexual" and, because of that, you could not keep a job and therefore needed public assistance.

In desperate straits I made the journey and filled out the paperwork. As I waited for my turn to meet with the social worker, I wondered how hard the qualifying questioning would be and expected to be tossed out on my butt. When I finally got my turn, a bland man in a brown suit looked over my paperwork and muttered, "Homosexual." He stamped the paper and said, "You'll have to do counseling," and directed me to another window to finalize my acceptance. That was it, with no further questions. As I got out of my seat, my anger rose. What it all meant was that the state of New York classified homosexuality as a mental illness and we, as a group, were incapable of working.

Was I using the system or was I validating their belief system? Regardless, it angered me. We were both wrong—and this act was somehow further impetus for me to help bring about change.

Back on Christopher Street, welfare somehow gave me cred with my fellow Gay Liberation Front members, which made it a little easier to swallow.

My life now had a purpose: in a very short span of time I had gone from quiet high school student to gay revolutionary with a minor in theater on the side. Meanwhile, my parents still thought I was in school. And I was—at a place called GLF University.

It seemed there was a demonstration almost every week. Leafleting was constant as we grew GLF. There was no Internet, no cell phones—just feet. We handed out papers on the street as people made their way to a club or restaurant or we pasted them onto poles and buildings along Christopher, Greenwich, Seventh Avenue, and other areas of the Village.

Then came a call from my father.

Chapter 3

Mom, Don't Worry,
I'll Be Arrested Today

In 1971, hearing my father's voice on the other end when picking up the phone was unusual. Calls from home always, always started with Mom's greeting. So I knew this was no ordinary call. My father never made demands, he requested, and allowed one's good sense to respond. This meant that he just gave me the facts: Mom had advanced kidney disease and needed a transplant, and an extra hand around the house might be useful at this time. Dad made the point that he wasn't asking me to stop anything I was involved with. Most fathers, after finding out their son was spending his days fighting for LGBT equality, would have taken those words back, but not my father; he rejoiced in them. In many ways my parents soon became activists themselves.

After a visit to the library to research my mom's illness, it struck me hard that what she had was tough to beat. Transplants in 1971 were 50/50 odds at best. The thought of losing Mom frightened me more than anything else that had been tossed my way.

Living, truly living, only began for me in 1969 when New York beckoned. Now I was returning, back to the place where I thought there would be nothing for me. I had a vibrant life in New York; Gay Liberation Front had become my family. We were brothers and sisters, and being one of the youngest in the group, I was often treated like a son. These were the people who brought about my understanding of why I'd felt as I did all my life. Now I had to leave; yet with my GLF University education under my belt, the tools of revolution were in my hands and in my heart.

Then it hit me: I'd been part of the movement and helped to create the Gay Youth organization in New York, so why not do the same in Philadelphia? In retrospect the timing might have been ideal, because soon after my departure from New York, the GLF organization imploded—but not before it gave birth to the next stage in community growing.

After selling his United cab 441, Dad had become a door-to-door salesman. He sold everything from encyclopedias to education courses to Jesus. Literally. His final big job was selling 3-D pictures of Jesus Christ in cheap plastic frames. Watching this short Jewish man hawking this tacky picture to a housewife was amazing. He started off by quoting a passage from the Bible, then he'd talk about Our Lord and the importance of having Him in not only our hearts but also our homes. If the pitch wasn't going well he'd drop to his knee and say, "Let's pray," and begin reciting the Lord's Prayer. That was often a closer.

After Dad decided it was getting too hard to do the door-to-door thing he began a new business buying and selling leather belts. These were slightly defective belts called "seconds" with a nick or some other minor flaw. He started selling them at flea markets for a dollar. He offered to bring me into the business, and though it seemed strange—after all, I was supposedly in an RCA technical repair program—what else could I do? Besides, the belt business was profitable. He was bringing in decent money from working just two days a week.

Times should have been good. But Mom wasn't. Dad never accepted that she was as sick as she was. The only change in their lives now was that there was no more bickering about money that they didn't have. Instead, Dad treated Mom like she was a queen, whereas in the past she had only been treated as a princess. Whatever Mom wanted, she got, but she rarely wanted anything—she would never take advantage of any situation or anyone.

Mom was a trouper, like her own mom. She never complained. When her condition deteriorated and she finally had to go on dialysis, her only complaint was that she'd have to quit her job. She was a floor manager at the E.J. Korvette store in Cedarbrook Mall, an early version of Kmart.

So my new life consisted of working with Dad and taking Mom to dialysis. She was often cheerful on the way to her treatment, but when I'd pick her up she was always exhausted and cold. One day while taking her to the hospital during a snowstorm, the car got stuck on a patch of ice. In a panic, knowing she needed her treatment, I jumped out of the car and flagged the first person who passed by, demanding they assist me in pushing the car out of its rut. For my mom I'd give the world.

In the evenings I began attending the local chapter of Gay Activist Alliance, which proved to be a little tame for me. The one exception was that after the general meeting, run strictly by *Robert's Rules*, with a parliamentarian to boot, there was always a topic for discussion. Many quite interesting. At one of the first meetings I attended, a Dr. Dennis Rubini, who became one of the first in the country to teach LGBT history, at Temple University, was giving a talk on the food supplements he ate to create a more healthy body and save the environment. When a questioner asked him how he could survive with just the supplements, Dennis exploded and yelled about the genocide of cows to feed a capitalist society, and summed it all up with, "Anyone who eats meat, fish, fowl, or processed food is a pig." Thereby trashing nearly the entire audience. Ah, I had now found my people. I was home again.

The Gay Activist Alliance's major objective was to get a nondiscrimination bill introduced into the city council. At the time I joined, they were still unable to find a sponsor for the bill from any of the seventeen members on the council. My entrance from New York's Gay Liberation Front gave me great credibility, and though it was arrogant of me to think that I would create a movement in Philadelphia where there already was one, and one that had been the vanguard for the nation in the past, I would try. What I wanted to do was redefine what that movement should look like and what it should achieve.

Not long after joining I was voted in as the political chair. My platform was built on the promise that, if elected, I'd get the bill introduced. This would be a complete change in my life, going from revolutionary to an elected chairman working with the city council.

I started to meet with city council members, even if they didn't want to meet with me. Standing outside their offices, sitting on the steps of their favorite restaurants, or hanging out at the city Democratic headquarters was par for the course. They'd see me and sigh and I'd say, always with a smile, "You'll break down one day and talk to me." As time went on I'd start to joke with them: "Will this be my lucky day?" "Hey, I'm really a nice guy."

Finally they began to smile and chat with me, first on the street, then having actual meetings in their offices. This was a big deal in those days. Politicians did not meet with "homosexuals." The City Hall press began to notice me as well and started to run news items on my work. Zack Stalberg, the future editor of the *Philadelphia Daily News*, saw something in me that I hadn't noticed as yet—dogged determination—as did show-biz gossip columnists Larry Fields and Stu Bykofsky. Somehow, what I was doing was fodder for good copy at the *Daily News* which, after all, was a tabloid newspaper. In an attempt to be more cutting edge than its sister publications the *Philadelphia Inquirer* and the *Evening Bulletin*, they hyped it up a bit. Those were the days of a big city having at least three daily newspapers.

As more and more people would talk to me, my profile began to grow. Producing a daily column is not an easy job, especially if it's local gossip where you need to keep readers interested. So Larry Fields took almost anything I pitched to him, and as luck would have it, appearing in his celebrity news column miraculously made one a "celebrity." It's basically the same path to fame that Paris Hilton and the Kardashians used, minus the sex. Despite these superficial methods, celebrityhood opened doors. Those media mentions led to a radio talk show appearance to discuss nondiscrimination, which in turn led to a feature article and then to a TV interview. The cycle was then repeated. I soon had my city council sponsors and the bill was about to be introduced.

This first victory plowed the way for me on all other legislative and government successes to come. Our nondiscrimination legislation now had a number, Bill 1275. To become a law in the city it first needed to be read at a city council session. During council, most of the time, the clerk would read the bill number and title, which in our case was "a bill to amend the Philadelphia Fair Practice Ordinance," and just move on. The audience in the chamber would have no idea what each piece of legislation really entailed. On the designated morning I went with my friend Harry Langhorne, president of Gay Activists Alliance, and sat in with the audience to watch the council. They were saluting the Boys Club of America for who knows what good deed this time and the North Philadelphia Catholic High School, which had just won a debate championship. The gallery was full of people from the various local Boys Club chapters and from archdioceses—students, a priest, and some nuns. Harry and I went around telling them that a bill was about to be introduced that supported Cesar Chavez and the California migrant lettuce pickers. We were going to stand and applaud when it was introduced and we would appreciate if they'd join us in the celebration. As we took our seats, Bill 1275 was introduced. Harry stood up and applauded on cue, then I stood and applauded. Like clockwork the remainder of the gallery stood up and applauded, and then everyone on the council joined in on the excitement. The following day, the headline in the *Philadelphia Daily News* was "Gay Rights Bill Introduced, Priest and Nuns Applaud."

All lightheartedness aside, these early successes were meaningful. The bill got introduced, but we couldn't move it out of committee since George X. Schwartz, the city council president, was a major homophobe. This led me to take various actions against the council. One of the most memorable, and one that brought me a lasting friendship, was a simple act of disruption. During a council meeting, we climbed over the railing separating the council chambers from the gallery and began to take over the chambers. Schwartz ran out as I approached. I sat in his chair, which was on a perch above the council, almost like a throne. Trying to do my best George X. Schwartz imitation, I plucked a cigar out of my pocket and stuck it in my mouth as I put my feet up on his desk. I took his gavel and brought order to the room. Just when I was about to do a pretend vote on Bill 1275, the sergeant-at-arms was called in along with the police. The sergeant, a very tall and big man, wrapped his arms around

me in a bear hug and picked me up. While carrying me out of
the chambers he gave me a friendly lecture. Rather than have
me arrested, he deposited me outside the chamber in the middle
of a group of visiting nuns. "*The Wizard of Oz*," he said, and
walked away laughing. That sergeant-at-arms is now Congressman Bob Brady, the ranking member of the US House Committee on Administration and Philadelphia Democratic City Committee chairman. A close friend of Vice President Joe Biden,
he's sometimes called the "Mayor of Capitol Hill." His grace
and good humor at that encounter led to a lasting friendship, a
shopping partner in his wife Debbie, and a gay ally who knows
the political ropes. He was the first politico to try and teach me
"how to get business done."

It was now December and the council was winding down
for the year. If the bill didn't pass by the end of the session we'd
have to start the entire process over again. People were all abuzz
with their gift shopping and holiday planning. In the middle of
City Hall there was a Christmas tree, decorated in ribbon and
ornamentation with a star on top. I decided to chain myself to
it and announced that I'd go on a hunger strike until the city
gave a hearing on the gay rights legislation. The press loved it,
especially when I was asked why I was chained to the Christmas
tree. "I'm the Christmas fairy," I replied.

That headline didn't move George Schwartz, but it did, surprisingly, move one Mayor Frank Rizzo, who sent an aide out
to the courtyard to ask if I'd meet with him in his office. The
reality was that I had no exit strategy on this action, so hell yes.
It was another strange but lucky day in my life, one in which an
invitation came from a mayor who'd once called San Francisco
"the land of fruits and nuts"!

Later I heard from Marty Weinberg, Rizzo's chief adviser,
that when he said he wanted to meet me, his staff had cau-

tioned against it. He overruled them and said, "I like the kid, he has balls." The meeting went well and Rizzo explained that although he couldn't tell the council what to do, he could request that the Human Relations Commission hold the hearings. I left Rizzo's office with a victory and with the knowledge that I would not have to spend the night chained to the city's Christmas tree. Truth is, the reason behind his generosity was that Rizzo was in a feud with Schwartz. They were simply using me as a pawn. Though in reality, we were all using each other. We got two days of hearings out of it that led to two days of media coverage. We also got the final report issued by the Human Relations Commission, which stated, "There is obviously overwhelming discrimination aimed at members of the gay and lesbian community, and we urge council to pass legislation."

This embarrassed Council President George Schwartz (later to be indicted in the infamous Abscam case that cited bribery, extortion, and conspiracy, fictionalized in the film *American Hustle*) so much that he decided to declare where he stood on the issue. He'd hold his own hearing in the council that he would personally chair. We finally got the hearings we wanted, but it was Council President Schwartz's "big top." Schwartz called in all the anti-LGBT troops he could influence to speak out against the legislation, including Philadelphia Cardinal John Krol regaled in all his clerical drag—purple robe, cape, rings, and shoes. All he needed was a tiara.

But Schwartz saved his best for me. As I read my prepared statement, every so often I would look up to gauge the reaction. At the councilman's table, Schwartz looked like a caged lion ready to pounce. The second my statement was completed, when the chair usually asks if any of the other members of the council have any questions, Schwartz said, "I have some questions for you."

In my head I said, *Let the circus begin.* And it did.

In front of a gallery full of spectators and a complete press pool, Schwartz started out by explaining that he didn't understand people like me. *Who are you people? What do we expect from people like him? What is a homosexual?* Then he finally looked directly at me and loudly asked, "Mr. Segal, what do you do it with?" The look on my face and the silence in the chambers made him grow angrier and even more despicable. "I mean," he shouted, "what do you do it with?" I could only stare at him, and in a rage he yelled, "Do you do it with parakeets?"

My reaction was one of shock, downright anger, and a pain that I still cannot explain. I'm not sure what I said in response. Perhaps it was a mere diplomatic brush-off, or more likely I just got up and walked out silently. In the hall, the press crowded around me wanting my reaction. Instead I just nodded and walked out of the building in disgust. Inside the chambers, Schwartz immediately ended the hearings, having what he thought was his pound of flesh.

But a strange thing happened. My friends at the *Philadelphia Daily News* were outraged by Schwartz's behavior, and in the following day's edition they ran an editorial with the headline, "Shut Up, George." They included a picture of Schwartz with that cigar pose that I had imitated. He had never been treated this way by the media before. And his downward political slide began.

That hearing taught me a few lessons. First, being a victim of a bully in front of an entire city and handling it with grace wins a lot of friends; and second, it reinforced my belief that as long as non-LGBT society only thought of our community as a sexual one, we wouldn't get very far in the fight for equality. My silence and unwillingness to talk about sexual practices taught me that sex had nothing to do with nondiscrimination. Most important was that I became a darling of the local press. While it was great for my ego, it was better for the LGBT community since up until then, most people still had no idea who a gay man really was. They'd continued to believe all the longstanding derogatory myths about gay people. Now, with all of this press coverage, they saw one live and could finally identify.

The hope of bringing a new kind of activism back to Philly was at last realized. Not only did I bring a radical movement with me, but I was able to map the next step in LGBT liberation: speak up. To put it simply, Oscar Wilde had been correct that homosexuality was "the love that dare not speak its name," but it was time to change that. And that was the most controversial decision I'd ever make. Since I was using myself as the guinea pig, it would unleash toward me a hatred not only from homophobes but from my own community, which often chews up and spits out its young, then stomps the spit wad into the ground.

The Schwartz fiasco set in motion the path for the next act, the Gay Raiders. I had seen the light. I knew how to get there. Despite the backlash, other people's fear and my ego were not going to stand in my way. Why should they? I had nothing to lose. After all, I had already been there, since my childhood and Wilson Park.

As the vanguard of the new gay rights movement, New York was in turmoil. Gay Liberation Front had died after the birth of Gay Activist Alliance, which would soon make way for the first organization in America that could truly be called Gay Inc., the National Gay Task Force (NGTF), today known as the National LGBTQ Task Force. It was the first organization to have a well-paid executive director, Bruce Voeller, and a full-time staff. They set themselves apart from those of us who were activists. NGTF was also to become the first organization to attempt to market the LGBT community and raised what we thought at that time was big bucks. As far as they were concerned, the day of the sit-in, picket, and other activism was over. It was time for lobbying and legislation. To them we were the radicals, harbingers of shame who needed to be swept under the rug.

In a sense the new guys were taking us back to the days of the Independence Hall demonstration where, to put a good look on "homosexuals," the marchers were told that the men must wear suits and ties and the women must wear dresses. The divide in the community was vicious. People like me from Gay Liberation Front had made a movement for LGBT equality a reality; now the guys with the alligators and polo emblems on their shirts wanted us to leave the stage.

The solution to the problem of invisibility as a people was clear. The general public had no idea who we were since what they were fed about us from the media, with only a few exceptions, was negative. Since, for the most part, we were all in the closet, who was there to refute it? Most non-gays didn't know us. All the public knew were the sins religion gave us, the crimes the law pressed on us, and all the torture the medical and psychiatric profession tried on us to stop us from our "evil ways." There was only one answer: to show people who we really were by using the very media that vilified us, and the time for that was immediately. What you wore was not at all the issue for acceptance. We could conform by wearing a suit and tie forever but still miss the mark on what equality required. People had to—they absolutely had to—get to know you as a person.

So in 1972, Philadelphia became my own test lab. It started with a simple plan. The effort to pass nondiscrimination legislation taught me that using myself as a focal point had resulted in the public seeing and getting to know an actual gay man. It was not about the legislation, since passing legislation would not change minds; it was about using that legislation as a platform to communicate with the public. It had gotten me on a number of television and radio talk shows. At that point many called me a local celebrity. Harvey Milk wouldn't receive that notoriety in San Francisco for several years. That "celebrity" status could help to accomplish our long-term goal, but it also needed to be nurtured and cultivated in the right way. Each piece of news had to be one step up from the last.

A plan was drawn up to use what we called *zaps*. A zap is a disruption. Sort of. They were to be nonviolent protests that put us in a light that was not stereotypical. They were upbeat and of course had a point to communicate. We wanted the public to start talking about us. Talk can eventually lead to education. Education usually leads to less fear and more understanding of the unknown. The word *zap*, and using it as a noun for the action, is attributed to my old friend Marty Robinson. The basic rule in the equality struggle—from its inception back in 1895 with Dr. Magnus Hirschfeld, the German physician and sexologist who stomped for sexual minorities, through the 1960s liberation movement in the US, until this very day—is that progress is based on one word and one word only: education.

Our organizational role, we felt as gay men and women, was exactly that: to educate society. Ask any gay person how easy it was to come out to their parents. Today it's still hard. Those who have come out to their parents usually started with an education process. In some ways, just the act of coming out is a form of gay activism since it is the desire to no longer live a double life but live one's truth. Parents, in turn, often educate their friends and so the process begins.

There's an old saying in the gay community: if every one of us was out of the closet, there'd be no need for a gay rights movement since others would learn that we are their brothers, sisters, uncles, aunts, cousins, and even mothers and fathers.

Back then we were everywhere, but at the same time, we were invisible. The Gay Raiders were about to change that.

Our plan called for a zap or press opportunity every six weeks. A zap followed by the initial press, then the talk show circuit, and by the time that was dying down, another event or zap. The goal was to keep us right up there in the public's face and to create conversation.

When 99 percent of your community is in the closet, and you're one of the few being out, proud, and front and center, you're not a popular person. Up to this point, our gay meeting places like clubs, bars, private residences, and cafés were either secret or not publicized. These were safe places where we could be ourselves, and the feeling from that 99 percent was that I was putting a spotlight on those places and possibly on them. The line that activists like me heard most often was, "You'll ruin it for all of us."

The press knew me from GAA, but I was now striking out on my own with few supporters; it had to be made clear that the Gay Raiders were different and separate and it had to be big enough to get everyone's attention. So, we thought, why not zap the city's icon of independence: the Liberty Bell. The plan was simple. Back then, the bell was on the first floor of Independence Hall and you could easily walk in and even touch it.

We of course leaked what we were about to do to specific press people whom we could count on not giving the plan away. At the prescribed time we appeared. I already had handcuffs on one arm, with the other end waiting to be attached to part of the bell. As I entered Independence Hall there was a cluster of flashes and it dawned on us that the plan had been more widely leaked. Like Keystone Cops, the incompetent fictional characters of silent movies, we were off, with the police trying to catch me before I did the deed and the press in hot pursuit. It truly felt like a Buster Keaton movie: me running from one room to the next, jumping over rope lines and crashing into walls, taking two steps at a time to the second floor and doing a circle around the room, then back down the stairs and another trip around those chairs once occupied by Ben Franklin and John Hancock. Finally, I climbed the stairs to the second floor again and quickly sat down and handcuffed myself to the rail directly above the bell. Then, on cue, as soon as the TV camera lights were on, I began yelling, "Independence for gay people! We want nondiscrimination!"

This went on for about ten minutes until they cut me loose and gave me a ride to jail—a nickel ride. That's when you're cuffed with your hands behind your back, tossed into a police wagon, and the wagon takes off at high speed, hitting every pothole it can and making turns on a dime. The objective is to cause as much bruising as possible without the police laying a hand on you.

Next up was the United Way. Why them? They didn't fund any gay organizations. We found a large bike brace and one morning, when the staff of United Way turned up for work, they discovered it was impossible to enter since I was chained by my neck to their front doors. Any time anyone came near me someone would yell, "Don't touch him, you could break his neck!" It worked better than a bomb, and guess what happened? The next year they funded their first LGBT organization.

Then, according to plan, six weeks later it was time for another zap.

This led to my first interaction with a president, Richard M. Nixon. On November 1, 1972, we disrupted a Republican fundraiser for Nixon's committee to reelect the president, known to some of us as CREP. Clark MacGregor, chairman of the reelection committee, was speaking when I produced a roll of paper that when unraveled read, Gay Power. Again I was wrestled to the floor and took another nickel ride in the police wagon, but this one had a happy ending: the next morning, the White House condemned the disruption.

By that point we had staged a few zaps that had been down-right serious and, for me, dangerous. It was time to lighten things up a little. So why not throw a party? How 'bout free morning coffee and donuts to all City Hall workers? There was only one catch: the guest of honor didn't know he was the guest of honor. Enter District Attorney Arlen Specter, later to become a US senator, and who will forever be linked to the fiasco involving Anita Hill and Supreme Court Justice Clarence Thomas. Prior to that, he was a lawyer for the Warren Commission that inves-tigated the assassination of President John F. Kennedy. He was the one who came up with the single-bullet theory.

Back in those early days of the battle for gay rights, Arlen was district attorney of Philadelphia. He had not taken a stand on the gay rights bill that was before city council. Efforts to set up a meeting went unanswered. So we had to be a little creative. One crisp Monday morning, a caterer delivered two large coffeemakers and dozens of donuts to Arlen's office. His staff thought that he had ordered the special treat, and Arlen thought his staff had arranged it. At the same time, in the City Hall courtyard and in the corridors of the building, members of the Gay Raiders were handing out flyers that read, District At-torney Arlen Specter invites you to a reception in honor of gay rights legislation in city council. Please join him at ten a.m. in his office, room 666. (That really was his office number.)

At ten a.m., we, along with hundreds of city workers and a huge collection of newspeople, arrived at his office. We walked in and there was Arlen's staff trying not to look too surprised at a reception held in their office that their boss was hosting, about legislation he had not endorsed. Arlen remained in his inner office. At first, the media took pictures of me handing out coffee and donuts to City Hall staffers, and we weren't sure if Arlen would even come out of his private office. Finally, the door opened and there he was, all smiles. He walked over, shook my hand, helped me hand out coffee, and we then went back into his private office. His first comment to me was, "Mark Segal, who else would cater a disruption? Did you think I'd allow you to have all the media attention to yourself?" And then he flashed that big smile.

The *Philadelphia Inquirer* the following day (October 10, 1973) had a large picture of the event and reported: *District Attorney Arlen Specter shakes hands with Mark Segal, leader of the Gay Raiders, who parked outside the district attorney's office until he emerged and granted them an interview. The Raiders handed out free donuts and coffee while waiting for Specter.*

Arlen eventually went to the National District Attorneys Association and asked them to get on board and support non-discrimination legislation. Now, here's what most people never knew: in Arlen's Republican years in the US Senate, when it was hard to support LGBT rights, he was always behind the curtain ready to vote yes on gay rights if it was needed to assure passage. Only Human Rights Campaign and I were aware of that. I'll never forget the 1996 vote on the Employment Nondiscrimination Act, when he broke ranks with the GOP and the bill failed by only one vote. He later supported the repeal of "Don't Ask, Don't Tell" and the repeal of the Defense of Marriage Act.

A few years later, while I was waiting in a room with others to officially endorse Arlen, someone asked him about his single-bullet theory. Since I was standing next to him, he used me as the John F. Kennedy stand-in and showed where the bullets entered and exited Kennedy's body. That was an eerie feeling.

* * *

The Gay Raiders' zaps produced the desired effect: Philadelphians were talking about gay issues. We were everywhere, including the cover of the Sunday *Inquirer* magazine. This was not happening in other cities.

The zaps were sometimes downright dangerous. For example, a zap of Dr. David Reuben, author of the book *Everything You Always Wanted to Know about Sex but Were Afraid to Ask*, in which he belittled, embellished, and stereotyped LGBT people, became violent. When we staged a sit-in at one of his lectures in June 1974, the police moved in with their clubs. Although it was a nonviolent protest, Bernie Boyle got his head bashed with one of those clubs.

I had little funds, since my activism kept me from helping Dad with the business, and my parents were supporting me. It took me years to realize the contribution my parents made to the struggle for gay rights. Never did they complain, they only offered words of encouragement.

My partner at the time, Phillip, spent weekends at the house, most of which were filled with making plans for the next zap or demonstration or other issues to be dealt with. One Saturday afternoon we were watching TV and a teenage dance show came on the air. It was Ed Hurst's show in Atlantic City, *Summertime on the Pier*. Watching the dancers made us wonder: *What would happen if a gay couple joined in?* That is how the campaign against the networks began, and once again events swept me up faster than I had planned.

Sage Powell, a friend from Gay Activist Alliance, agreed to go to Atlantic City to be my dance partner on the show. The following Saturday, with very little organizing, a group of us set out. The show was little more than a gimmick to get people to buy tickets to Steel Pier. Teenage dance television shows were born in Philly; *American Bandstand*, the granddaddy of them all, was wildly popular.

We bought our tickets and made our way to the ballroom. The show was already on the air—like *Bandstand*, it was a live show. We watched for a while to get our bearings and then, when a song we knew was being played, Sage and I made our way to the floor. We must have danced for three minutes before we heard Ed Hurst yelling from the stage, over the microphone, "Get them off! Get them off the floor!"

Security was called in and we were royally thrown off the pier. We got in the car and laughed all the way home. Sage, who is African American, said we got kicked off the show because we were an interracial couple, not because we were both men. I'm not sure if we even made it on camera, but it didn't matter, we knew what the next step would be: a demonstration.

Gay Activist Alliance protected our honor by picketing the TV station and demanding an apology. They refused to apologize. And thank God they wouldn't. It led us to the next step: the Gay Raiders decided to disrupt the evening news. It was only logical, right? The ABC affiliate in Philadelphia was, and still is, the local news ratings king. Almost every household tuned in to *Action News* on ABC.

Despite how quickly they seemed to happen, zaps were not usually pulled out of thin air. It was a major process. Once the target was settled on, we went to work on planning. Success depended on planning, execution, and security. A good zap couldn't happen in a few hours. But this time, little planning would be needed since we already knew the station well. Being a "celebrity" means being invited onto the talk shows, and their studios were no exception. I'd been there before.

We knew there was a security guard at the front desk and, once in the building, we knew where the studio was. We even had a hideout where we planned to wait until the show was on the air. All we needed was to create a diversion at the front door. Therefore, we had researched and practiced a trick learned from movie stuntmen. A guy on fire running around would surely do the job. So we employed this to our advantage. As the guard went one way, we went the other, into the building. We waited until the show was on and was reporting the top news story of the night. Their format was the same each evening, and we decided we'd treat the city to a newly written script. As the anchorman said, "But the top story tonight . . ." we became the big story as we burst onto the live set. There were the anchorman, Larry Kane, weatherman Jim O'Brien, and sportscaster Joe Pellegrino.

Larry has written about this in his autobiography, and his version seems to be a little embellished. He writes of blood on the walls. The only fluid that I recall being exchanged was the sportscaster's makeup smearing my jacket as I yelled at him, "Hey, watch it, your makeup is getting on my shirt!" We were pushed to the ground and wrapped in cables until the police arrived and treated us to another nickel ride. This time I had friends to knock against. We got released without bail somehow, and we went to our respective homes to sleep. It was nearing four a.m.

The entire front page of the next day's *Daily News* was devoted to the zap, and the story was picked up by almost every other news media outlet. The phone never stopped ringing. By the end of the day it was obvious that we had perfected the solution to invisibility. *Action News* had its format, now the Gay Raiders had ours. We were a force that could not be controlled. We had a laser beam on the networks. We'd hit them, and we'd hit them hard. No live or even taped show was immune to us, and we started reinventing ways to get into the studios.

First up was a syndicated variety show, *The Mike Douglas Show*, one of those mindless afternoon entertainment programs. I chained myself to the camera while crooner Tony Bennett and the first lady of the American stage, Helen Hayes, were getting their feet read by a professional foot reader. I started to do gay chants like, "*Two, four, six, eight, gay is just as good as straight,*" and almost anything else I could think of until they stopped taping. They brought the police in and before they could cut the handcuff I told them that until we had some form of agreement, I'd keep coming back. They agreed to have a gay spokesperson on the show, but not me. We settled on Reverend Troy Perry of Metropolitan Community Church, the man I had picketed against in my Gay Liberation Front days. His appearance was the first time an afternoon audience in America heard from a gay member of the clergy. Troy is an artful speaker and he made me and many others who saw that nationally syndicated show proud.

Next up was the *Today* show. To familiarize ourselves with the studio we took several tours offered by NBC. They were quite educational. We gained entrance to 30 Rockefeller Center in the early-morning hours and just waited in a closet. While the news was being read live I appeared on camera walking across the studio. I believe the director thought this was somehow part of the show. The news anchor actually got up out of his chair and, as some people described it, looked like he was trying to climb the walls. My first thought was to comfort the guy, but I was there for a reason and had to stay on mission. In mid-sentence I'm tackled and again wrapped in camera cables, then taken out to the hall with a security guard. As we're walking away, me expecting to head off to jail once again, it was a relief to know that Morty Manford of the New York GAA was ready to bail us all out. Before anything else could happen, a woman yelled at the guard and told him to stop. Barbara Walters, the doyen of the morning news network crowd, with pen and pad in hand, walked over and asked me why we were protesting the show. My explanation was that it wasn't just the *Today* show but all of network TV that censors us on their news, stereotypes us on their entertainment shows, and keeps us invisible by not having LGBT people on their programs. In the middle of this exchange a producer came out and told her to get back in the studio since she was about to go on air. She firmly replied that this was a story and she wasn't going back in until she had it.

Years later, in January 2012, the *Today* show celebrated its sixtieth anniversary. To honor the occasion, Running Press published Stephen Battaglio's *From Yesterday to TODAY: Six Decades of America's Favorite Morning Show*. The book goes through the highlights of the sixty years and I'm proud that the zap was included. NBC, to secure my participation in the book, gave me a DVD of my zap, and it was the first time I got to see it in over forty years. But there is another connection with the *Today* show that few know.

I had many friends in the media. Edie Huggins, who had various programs on WCAU through the years, was one of the first African American women to host her own talk show. She called me to explain that the station wanted to do a pilot with a new staff member in order to determine if he had what it took to host a show. Would I do the station a favor and shoot a pilot with him? Then she added, "He is very pleasing to the eye." His name was Matt Lauer. When I met Edie at the station, she explained that the show would be done in two sections. One with me "playing" the angry gay radical, then the second, me being my pragmatic self. They wanted to test Matt Lauer on how he would handle each scenario. He was only given my name and position as a gay activist. I arrived on the set; we were introduced, shook hands, and began the taping.

Matt opened the show then introduced his guest, me, and asked his first question. To my amazement he had done some research and asked me about the slow progress of nondiscrimination legislation. I wanted to get into real dialogue, but with my assignment in mind I replied, "It hasn't moved because the legislative pigs in Harrisburg want to keep gay people in their place." He kept going without a bat of his eyelashes: calm, cool, and polite; it almost made me angry. After ten minutes of this he segued into a fake commercial break. Then we began part two of the pilot. This time he asked a question about AIDS and how the mayor was handling it. While the question surprised me, since I was not used to local reporters doing proper research, my shift in demeanor surprised him. It's a pleasure to meet a reporter who understands the issues and can appreciate all the areas that AIDS encompasses. Again we went on until another fake commercial, and then it was over. As soon as we heard we were done, everyone including Matt broke down in laughter. The pilot was picked up. Matt, you owe me.

Next up in my war against the media was what I thought would be the mother lode, Los Angeles. By this point the campaign against the networks was getting major press coverage as we zapped the networks from coast to coast. Along the way, *Variety*, the show-business bible, had an article on how the Gay Raiders had cost the networks over $750,000 in tape delays and lost revenue, a figure that in today's dollars totals over three million.

Johnny Carson, king of late-night TV, was our next target. We expected this zap would be our largest audience to date and make the networks cave. This time we entered as audience members. During Carson's monologue, which I knew they did in one take and couldn't cut away from, I left my seat and walked to the camera and did my old handcuffs trick. Carson, the true pro, just kept up his monologue as his staff came over trying to cover my mouth. They gagged me and told me if I agreed to be quiet they would meet with us and try to negotiate a settlement. I nodded my head in agreement since I couldn't speak. At commercial they cut me loose and then there were police in the studio. They had no intention of negotiating anything. A producer simply said that to get me out of there.

When the police deposited me and my partner on the Carson zap, Mike Walters (a volunteer for the LA Gay Community Services Center), at the Burbank jail after our zap of the *Tonight Show*, we were fingerprinted, photographed, and put in a holding cell. There were six cells that opened to a communal area where there was a table and chairs. There were only four other prisoners in the cell when we arrived and after all the official paper shuffling was done, we joined them. At first the conversation was basic. Where are you from, how old are you? The other prisoners seemed to be friendly and not dangerous—this was Burbank after all. It was all going well until one of the guys asked two men who looked like brothers why they were in the jail. The taller of the two said, "We killed a faggot. I hate those faggots." They then asked me why we were there. Not giving them a second glance I headed back to my cell and closed the door, and remained there until my old friend Troy Perry of Metropolitan Community Church bailed me out. I sometimes wonder if the Burbank police staged that, and what would have happened if those two men knew the real reason we were in that jail with them. The *Tonight Show* did a good job of editing me out and they refused to meet with us, but *Variety* published an article on March 14, 1973, titled "A Segal Lock or How Taping Can Turn into Gay Time for Carson." As the story reported, "He then ran down the aisle to the rail that separates the audience from the stage and handcuffed himself. Guards followed and, when they told him to unlock the cuffs, were told he didn't have the key. Segal was quoted as saying he had mailed it to Philadelphia."

During this campaign against the networks in Los Angeles, it seemed that every hour was accounted for. Morris Knight and Troy Perry kept me entertained with parties and events almost every night. My living quarters most nights were in the Gay Community Services Center, then on Wilshire Boulevard, or on someone's couch. One evening Troy took me along to a recently opened Jewish temple where they were to dedicate their new Torah. On another Morris visited a campaign cocktail party for a homophobic candidate for city council, telling me en route that the woman had no idea she was about to enter a party of gay men. He then told me he was giving me the honor of confronting the candidate. I'm not quite sure what I said but the next issue of the *Advocate* headlined the event as, "Candidate Flees Gay Party."

On yet another occasion Morris took me to a fundraiser in the Hollywood Hills at the home of Terence O'Brien. Terry was the chairperson of the board of the Gay Community Services Center and had gotten his parents' permission to hold a fundraiser in their home. As I walked around the tastefully decorated place, several items caught my eye. The first was sitting on the fireplace mantle. Slowly approaching the statuette and looking at it closely to see if it was indeed what it seemed, I picked it up. Within an instant Terry appeared out of nowhere, took hold of the statuette, and said, "My father doesn't let anyone touch the Oscar, it belonged to a very close friend of his." As I glanced to the corner of the room I could see Morris smiling. I walked over to him and asked who Terry's father was. Morris looked coyly at me. "Pat, of course." He was talking about the actor Pat

O'Brien, who it seemed always played a priest or mob character. This brought a big smile to my face since it immediately made me remember him from one of my favorite old movies, *Some Like It Hot*.

Feeling a little foolish and not knowing Hollywood protocol, I just sat down to ponder the wonders of Los Angeles. Again Terry scolded me, this time saying, "Nobody is allowed to sit in that chair." Abraham Lincoln, my childhood scare, had used it when he was a statesman in Illinois. I was completely out of my cultural league, but I took it as another lesson and an opportunity to observe a different group of people.

My LA adventures even saw me at one of movie star Rock Hudson's "boy parties" where I felt even more out of place than in a TV studio. There were all these guys in skimpy bathing suits. All seemed to have great chests, short hair, many blond, and all were overly handsome. Hudson, himself exceptionally good looking, had a drink in his hand and seemed to be enjoying the view. Somehow the sight of me wearing old jeans and a T-shirt and my long hair down to my shoulders didn't seem to please him, so we made a fast exit.

The following week I had passes to almost every show at ABC, which became our prime target and would be used as an example. We called Av Westin, the vice president of program development, and requested a meeting before the passes were to be used. Troy and Morris had identified a group of media experts to join us. That was the first meeting between a national network and the LGBT community. While Westin agreed to change entertainment policy, he was honest in explaining that the news divisions of the networks operated separately and he could not assist with our negotiations with them.

NBC and CBS quickly agreed to change programming in their entertainment divisions to be more sensitive to stereotypes and said they would consider adding LGBT characters. The campaign against the networks was almost a success, but we still had to tackle the news departments in New York. It was time to return to the East Coast. Troy Perry had to buy my ticket since I didn't have a dime.

Once home, the brainstorming began. What could we do that would make the news divisions do what the entertainment divisions had done? We decided to follow the same formula and knew what had to happen. And that's the way it was.

Chapter 4

Walter

W alter Cronkite, the most trusted man in America, and his CBS viewership of over sixty million people, would be the target that would fundamentally change the LGBT community's national invisibility, though that never occurred to me at the time. To me it was just another zap, just another visit to jail, and just another long line of interviews about the zap. It was almost like I was going off to work, minus the salary.

It all started thanks to comedian Redd Foxx and his show *Sanford and Son*. Our campaign against the networks had already produced a lot of disruptions. We had gained a national reputation for putting broadcast media on notice. Either meet with us to discuss our grievances or suffer the consequences, the zaps.

Sanford and Son was about to get me on the zap trail again. They broadcast a show in which, for some strange reason, Redd Foxx's son had to pretend to be gay. In order to do this he used every stereotype known to mankind. Swish, limp wrist, high-pitched voice, over-the-top and colorful clothing, the works. We caught wind of this and tried to meet with network executives before the airing, but the network felt they were covered by the agreements we made in Los Angeles. Their explanation was that the script had already been in preparation and it would be the last one.

Once the show aired, several activists from around the country urged me to take action since the media had been my area of expertise. GLAAD, the nation's leading LGBT media advocacy organization, would not be founded until 1985, eleven years later. Until then, as disorganized as we were, there were only the Gay Raiders. There was also a feeling that the agreement the networks had made was not being taken seriously. They were testing our resolve. We needed to show them that the airwaves were in the public trust and not a place to continue to oppress the LGBT community.

Morty Manford, then president of Gay Activist Alliance in New York, called and suggested that I do something in New York again, to get the giants of network television to take notice. He also promised that once I decided on what my zap would be, he'd take care of finding me a lawyer. Both Troy Perry and Morris Knight also chimed in and felt that my kind of action was necessary to make the networks know that we were serious in changing their attitudes toward us. Even Frank Kameny, the first LGBT activist to sue the government in order to keep his government job—not to mention the organizer of those Independence Hall demonstrations back in the mid-1960s—was urging me on and giving advice.

The decision was obvious to me: expose their vulnerability with a zap. I'd go back to that first news zap, only this time it would be on live *national* TV. This would be big, and Morty and his offer for bail and a lawyer were absolutely necessary because we had no funds and no support system and I didn't want to spend the rest of my life behind bars. Harry Langhorne, a close friend from GAA and member of the Gay Raiders, became my rock-steady coconspirator in this endeavor. We were not able to gain access by a tour as we had in NBC—there was no audience, and this was a closed set in a closed building. What could we do?

For some time, my friend Tommi Avicolli Mecca had been president of the gay organization at Temple University, and he was kind enough to allow the Gay Raiders, without the university's knowledge, to use part of their budget to print materials and cover other small expenses. Tommi was a Gay Raider who also sat in on planning meetings. In one gathering at the Temple Gay Student Alliance office, Tommi, Phillip, Harry, and I discussed how to gain entrance to that secure studio. As we were debating, a student dropped by and grabbed a book he had left in the office. "I'm off to RFT," he said. What was RFT?

Tommi responded, "Radio, Film, Television."

"They teach television production here?"

Tommi nodded, and then came my request: "Tommi, I don't care how you do it, but get me a sheet of their stationary."

I had it the next day. We drafted a letter to the producer of the CBS *Evening News* explaining that we were in the RFT program at Temple University and we'd like to view a broadcast from the control room in order to see firsthand how professionals use the equipment that we were just beginning to learn how to operate. It actually worked. We received a letter suggesting a visit two weeks later, on December 11, 1973.

As we entered the control room to the CBS *Evening News* we were introduced to the staff. During that time it was Harry's job to scout the lay of the land, and as I went out to the studio he was to create any diversion necessary to allow me to get on air. Before our arrival at CBS we had timed the show and knew approximately when the commercial breaks would occur. We believed that once the show was being broadcast, everyone would be so involved that they wouldn't notice anything we did until it was too late. We also wanted to time the zap just as Walter was coming back from commercial so that if we were tuned out, CBS would have to explain to the viewers what had happened. No cutting to commercials and denying it.

The usual format for the CBS Evening News was to go live at six p.m. to about 60 percent of the nation. In those days there were no twenty-four-hour news channels. People got their TV news from one of three networks, and the CBS Evening News with Walter Cronkite was the untouchable leader for eighteen years. The audience of millions of people who saw that show and their first openly gay person on national television would not be equaled until April 1997 when Ellen DeGeneres came out on her prime-time show on ABC. Will and Grace, considered the first network show with an out character, finally moved past those earlier milestones in 2000.

Their usual pattern called for CBS to later rebroadcast the six p.m. show to the remainder of the country or, if breaking news warranted, they would broadcast it live again. At about fourteen minutes into the program, as Walter Cronkite was reporting to the American public about security procedures for Henry Kissinger and Richard Nixon, I knew this was the moment, and for the first time while doing a zap my heart started beating very fast. I wasn't scared but somehow I knew that after this event things would change forever. I rushed onto the set, holding up my sign and yelling the message printed on it, "Gays protest CBS prejudice!" The CBS Evening News broke down right in front of Walter. I stepped between him and the camera, thereby shutting him out of the picture to show only that sign. As millions watched, I sat on his desk and held the sign right into the camera lens so that everyone could clearly see the words. Gays Protest CBS Prejudice.

Noted historian Doug Brinkley's best-selling 2012 biography and Washington Post "book of the year," Cronkite, best captures the scene:

The days of lax security at CBS News abruptly ended on December 11, 1973, when twenty-three-year-old Mark Allan Segal, a demonstrator from an organization called the Gay Raiders, with accomplice Harry Langhorne at his side, interrupted a Cronkite broadcast, causing the screen to go black for a few seconds. Cronkite was delivering a story about Henry Kissinger in the Middle East when, about fourteen minutes into the first "feed," Segal leapt in front of the camera carrying a yellow sign that read, "Gays Protest CBS Prejudice." More than thirty million Americans were watching . . . "I sat on Cronkite's desk directly in front of him and held up the sign," Segal recalled. "The network went black while they took me out of the studio."

On the surface, Cronkite was unfazed by the disruption. Technicians tackled Segal, wrapped him in cable wire, and ushered him out of camera view. Once back on live TV, Cronkite matter-of-factly described what had happened without an iota of irritation. "Well," the anchorman said, "a rather interesting development in the studio here—a protest demonstration right in the middle of the CBS News studio." He told viewers, "The young man identified as a member of something called Gay Raiders, an organization protesting alleged defamation of homosexuals on entertainment programs."

Segal had a legitimate complaint. Television—both news and entertainment divisions—treated gay people as pariahs, lepers from Sodom and Gomorrah. It stereotyped them as suicidal nut jobs, flaming fairies, and psychopathic villains. Part of the Gay Raiders' strategy was to bring public attention to the Big Three networks' discrimination policies. What better way to garner publicity for the cause than waving a banner on the CBS Evening News? "So I did it," Segal recalled. "The police were called, and I was taken to a holding tank."

But both Segal and Langhorne were charged with second-degree criminal trespassing as a result of their disruption of the CBS Evening News. It turned out that Segal had previously raided the Tonight Show, the Today show, and the Mike Douglas Show. At Segal's trial on April 23, 1974, Cronkite, who had accepted a subpoena, took his place on the witness stand. CBS lawyers objected each time Segal's attorney asked the anchorman a question. When the court recessed to cue up a tape of Segal's disruption of the Evening News, Segal felt a tap on his back—it was Cronkite, holding a fresh pad of yellow lined paper, ready to take notes with a sharp pencil.

"Why," Cronkite asked the activist with genuine curiosity, "did you do that?"

"Your news program censors," Segal pleaded. "If I can prove it, would you do something to change it?" Segal went on to rattle off three specific examples of CBS Evening News censorship, including a CBS report on the second rejection of a New York city council gay rights bill.

"Yes," Cronkite said. "I wrote that story myself."

"Well, why haven't you reported on the other twenty-three cities that have passed gay rights bills?" Segal asked. "Why do you cover five thousand women walking down Fifth Avenue in New York City when they proclaim International Women's Day on the network news, and you don't cover fifty thousand gays and lesbians walking down that same avenue proclaiming Gay Pride Day? That's censorship."

Segal's argument impressed Cronkite. The logic was difficult to deny. Why hadn't CBS News covered the gay pride parade? Was it indeed being homophobic? Why had the network largely avoided coverage of the Stonewall riots of 1969? At the end of the trial, Segal was fined $450, deeming the penalty "the happiest check I ever wrote." Not only did the activist receive considerable media attention, but Cronkite asked to meet privately with him to better understand how CBS might cover gay pride events. Cronkite, moreover, even went so far as to introduce Segal as a "constructive viewer" to top brass at CBS. It had a telling effect. "Walter Cronkite was my friend and mentor," Segal recalled. "After that incident, CBS News agreed to look into the 'possibility' that they were censoring or had a bias in reporting news. Walter showed a map on the Evening News of the US and pointed out cities that had passed gay rights legislation. Network news was never the same after that."

Before long, Cronkite ran gay rights segments on the CBS News broadcast with almost drumbeat regularity. "Part of the new morality of the '60s and '70s is a new attitude toward homosexuality," he told millions of viewers. "The homosexual men and women have organized to fight for acceptance and respectability. They've succeeded in winning equal rights under the law in many communities. But in the nation's biggest city, the fight goes on."

Not only did Cronkite speak out about gay rights, but he also became a reliable friend to the LGBTQ community. To gays, he was the counterweight to Anita Bryant, a leading gay rights opponent in the 1970s: he was a heterosexual willing to grant homosexuals their liberties.

During the 1980s, Cronkite criticized the Reagan administration for its handling of the HIV/AIDS epidemic and later criticized President Clinton's "Don't Ask, Don't Tell" policy regarding gays' nondisclosure of status while in the military. When Cronkite did an eight-part TV documentary *about his storied CBS career—Cronkite Remembers—he boasted about being a champion of LGBTQ issues. And he ended up hosting a huge AIDS benefit in Philadelphia organized by Segal, with singer Elton John as headliner.*

Here's what's not in Brinkley's book: Within moments a handful of technicians came over and wrestled me harshly to the floor and wrapped me in wires. They were angry and rough. It's my belief they were acting out of loyalty to Cronkite. I was beaten and bruised. For a while I remained outside the studio with two guards while they decided what to do with me. I remember thinking in a daze about the stagehands and technicians. Were any of them gay? How did they feel about what I had just done? Did they hate me?

We were then ushered to an office on the first floor of the building under armed CBS guard, and told that we were not free to go. We were a little confused since at no point did they tell us that we were under arrest. Finally the door opened. In walked the anchor of the local *CBS Evening News* with a camera crew and several guys in suits. They told us that it would help to be interviewed. Who it would help or for what reason they didn't say. Nor would they answer any of our questions. It didn't matter. Our goal was to get the word out to the public and this was one way of doing so. We were proud to assist and would suffer any consequences later.

We were also not aware of how big a deal this all was. Later we discovered that the CBS switchboard was so overloaded that it was brought down, and many of those calls came from other media, so the network knew it had a story and they also had an exclusive story that they could keep for their own broadcast. After the interview, security guards led us down a hall, at the end of which stood a group of New York's finest. A police wagon had been brought to a back door and CBS did all it could to shelter us from being photographed while going from the door to the police wagon. We were their exclusive. When we got to the doors, escorted by the men in suits and the armed guards, all hell broke lose. Every news organization in New York was there. As the CBS guards handed us over to the NYPD, reporters kept yelling questions and flashing pictures.

While we were being transported off to jail, Walter Cronkite was doing his second live news broadcast of the evening. He reported on the disruption of his earlier show "by a group calling itself Gay Raiders and protesting CBS bigotry toward the homosexual community." In commenting on the zap during his own show, Walter was not aware that it was the first time the CBS *Evening News* had ever reported on a gay demonstration.

The next morning the story was on the front page of nearly every newspaper in the country. America wanted to know more about this man who dared hurt their Uncle Walter. It was beyond my comprehension. Requests for interviews started to come in as soon as we were out on bail. A couple of publishers asked me to write a book about my zaps, another wanted a memoir. A memoir? At twenty-three? Others felt they could somehow market me, make me a celebrity du jour, but I had no interest in any of it. My purpose in all of this was gay equality.

As the face of the Gay Raiders, I was invited to more on-air talk shows. News magazines and newspapers called for interviews. At times I felt the country simply could not comprehend a gay man who was not only open, but outrageous, proud, pushy, and also happy and fabulously full of life and humor. Offers came and all I asked for was transportation, a hotel if necessary, and meals. This was not for money; even though I had none; I was still living off the grace of my parents. I became the penniless darling of the media, and the first openly gay person to make the talk show circuit. There were other prominent activists out there like Frank Kameny, Barbara Gittings, and Harry Hay, but none of them had captured national attention as I had by disrupting Walter Cronkite's newscast. My intention was to sell gay liberation like a product, by educating the nation about LGBT people.

The hosts of the shows would introduce me as this radical controversial homosexual, and then I'd do my darndest to be a polite and gracious guest. If it was my plan to show America who gay people were, then I had to play the part, which, luckily, mirrored who I really was. Morty Manford, as promised, had arranged for a lawyer. Not just any lawyer, but Hal Weiner, who had been the attorney to incorporate the GAA. While I zapped people in person, Hal zapped them with the law. In my first meeting with Hal, he looked at me sternly and said with what felt like true annoyance: "Do you know you could get ten years in prison for this?" He waited until it sunk in, then started laughing and added, "You won't get ten minutes."

The morning after the zap, Hal called the CBS lawyers and asked to come in to subpoena Walter Cronkite. The CBS lawyer laughed and told Hal that Walter was too busy and then hung up. Hal did a little research and learned that at that time, New York law allowed a subpoena to be copied and then used as a legal subpoena. So he called the CBS lawyers back and said, "Before you hang up, I'd like to let you know about the subpoena powers here in New York." After he explained the law, the CBS lawyer asked, "What the hell does that have to do with us?" Hal then said: "I've just made one hundred copies of the subpoena and tomorrow at eleven a.m. I'm coming in to CBS, and you will have Walter available for me to subpoena him in person. If not, I'm giving fifty subpoenas to members of the Gay Activists Alliance and fifty to Hell's Angels, and I will offer a thousand-dollar reward to the first to serve Walter." Needless to say, Walter was served the next morning at eleven a.m.

While preparing for the trial, the Gay Raiders even appeared in a *Life* magazine feature called "A Day in the Life of America." Nothing like a couple of gays not making a living.

Most gay people at the time were still not supportive of our efforts. Many believed that we should be quiet, conformist, and stay in the closet. Some were ashamed of me and tried to suppress our work. As the nation's best-known out gay man I was doing national television shows with rips in my socks and holes in my shoes. Harry Langhorne, who stood lookout during the Cronkite zap, had to ask his mother for financial help. A distant relative of Lady Astor finally paid our out-of-pocket legal expenses when Morty, Morris, Troy, and even Frank Kameny, who was having his own problems making a living, were unable to get financial assistance for the defense.

I've kept a few of the notes I received at that time to remind me of where we were. One states: *While we admire your intentions, we do not admire your methods.* Another, from a wealthy friend who loaned me $150, which I thought he understood would be paid back whenever I had the funds, said, *I've never run into such a dishonest person before.* But there were those of support as well: a group of lesbian feminists from Miami sent what they could, and we did receive small donations but not enough to either live on or pay legal bills.

Today, activism is a multimillion-dollar business, with huge budgets and all kinds of wealthy backers. At that time, not one major celebrity or corporation embraced our community, much less the radical Gay Raiders.

At our trial most reporters were surprised to see Cronkite listed as a defense witness. A tape of the zap played, and Walter witnessed his open jaw during the incident. Hal asked him his reaction and Cronkite said, "Not very professional on my part," which gave everyone in the court a laugh.

As for Walter and me, we became friends. As Brinkley wrote in his book and made public for the first time, Cronkite kept his promise, but all the while he never admitted that CBS News was biased on the subject. Not while introducing me to key CBS News staffers—including Marlene Adler, his chief of staff who over the years kept us connected—not after reporting on those cities that had passed gay rights legislation, not when reporting on gay pride. It actually became a running joke between us.

Chapter 5

After Cronkite

Sixty million homes. That's how many people saw the broadcast. There was a burning-bright spotlight on the LGBT community and on me personally. The public just wanted answers. Some wanted me strung up for hurting good old Uncle Walter, and many members of my own community thought I had gone too far. But we had succeeded in our attempt to capture the public interest and we were ready to start a discussion. Percentage-wise, Walter's newscast was a juggernaut; his ratings then were higher than most shows on prime-time television today.

When Harry Langhorne and I had been released on bail and left the police station, only Morty and Hal Weiner, our attorney, were there to greet us. We talked strategy with them, then drove back to Philly. It was my turn to take Mom to dialysis that afternoon. At home she was waiting at the door. She gave me a hug and asked if I was treated okay. It had all become so normal for us. Mom would ask about the police treatment, about the cell, and about next steps. It was like any other mother asking her son, *How was your day at the office?* She was the caring mother to the hilt, no matter how sick she got. I assured her I was all right, then she insisted on cooking breakfast for Phillip, Harry, and me. The phone was ringing off the hook but we ignored it for as long as possible. Once we started to answer, it was call after call of requests for interviews for newspapers, magazines, and radio and television talk shows.

The next two years I was fully engaged with appearances on talk shows, other interviews, and making speeches across the country. I'd fly out to Chicago to do a television show, then to Los Angeles for a speech after the taping, and then do a radio show while waiting in the hotel to leave for my flight to yet another city. We still did the occasional zap, but getting publicity every six weeks via a stunt was no longer necessary; publicity was following me.

At the time, the king of the television talk shows was Phil Donahue. His syndicated show was first taped in Dayton, Ohio, before moving to Chicago and then New York. It's ironic to say that he was the Oprah Winfrey of his day, since many give him credit for inventing the genre and ultimately it was Oprah who dethroned him as talk show champion.

Somewhere along the way, I was invited onto the *Phil Donahue Show*. Before the show he came into the makeup room to explain to me that his audience was conservative. This didn't bother me because I'd known that he had done one other program on the subject of "homosexuals," during which he was sympathetic and respectful. While his other "homosexual" guest had tried to win the audience over with simple facts, my attitude would be very different. Per my Gay Liberation Front training, respect was demanded. This conservative audience was about to be challenged by a gay man, and one who would tell them that all they had learned about the LGBT community was wrong. My reply to Donahue was, "Do you think they're ready for me?" He seemed to enjoy that.

Like most talk shows, after the guests on *Donahue* were introduced, the host would begin with an introductory question or two. The real meat of his show, however, was the audience's questions, where Donahue would run up and down the aisles with his microphone.

For my first question, Donahue wanted to understand why we'd done the various zaps on network television. The answer in this case was simple. "Phil, would I be here today discussing this issue if we hadn't done those zaps?" It was true. "Thanks to those zaps, more televison and radio talk shows are now debating this subject, and so those acts far exceeded any expectations we had."

When that softball question was over he went to a lady in the audience who held up a Bible and wanted to quote from it. Donahue persuaded her not to open the Bible but invited her to say what was on her mind. She looked at me and told me I was going to hell and that God intended for me to die. "Says Leviticus," she bellowed, *"Man who lays with man is an abomination!"* She was just going on and on until Phil interrupted her and asked if she'd like to hear my response.

"Madam, from what you say it seems you don't respect religion," was my reply.

She said, "I'm a true Christian."

I stared her down. "A true Christian respects the rights of other religions. My religion accepts who I am. Are you inferring that Judaism is a false religion? If you'd like to talk religion we can do so, but I'll also quote other parts of the Bible you seem to have forgotten."

She exploded and just started tossing out various biblical verses at me.

"You don't know your Bible well," I said. That sentence would become a trademark comment from me in religious discussions. I continued, "You use your Bible like you were ordering from a restaurant menu. I call that *Bible a la carte.* You choose what parts of the Bible you wish to obey and what others to ignore." Then I looked her over and explained that all she was wearing that day made her an abomination according to that same Leviticus chapter, which condemns wearing clothing of two different fabrics. Polyester-cotton blend, anyone? I followed that up by asking the audience a quick succession of questions about shellfish, metals, pig skin, and all the rest, then asked, "Do all of you obey your husbands? While I know none of you would commit adultery, I'm sure you're aware that in cases of adultery your husband has the right to kill you. So, if I'm going to hell, you're all joining me. As the Good Book says, *He who has not sinned should throw the first stone.* Is there anyone in this audience who has not sinned?"

As total silence fell over the room, I directed my next comment back to the lady with the Bible. "Oh, and one more thing. Remember the Ten Commandments? Gluttony. How many of you are joining me in hell now?" No LGBT person had ever challenged an entire TV audience in that manner before. This kept the Bible-toting crowd focused on issues like discrimination, hate crimes, and entrapment. It was this formula that I'd use whenever I found myself in Bible Belt communities. Take it head on, then move to the real issues at hand.

The end of the show was a chance for Donahue to express his own thoughts and bring about peace in the studio. He started out by saying the obvious: "Don't think there has ever been a discussion like this on television before." And with what seemed to be a smirk on his face he added, "Some of our affiliates might not air this show, but we learned a lot about religious freedom and gay and lesbian people today."

Backstage he gushed and looked at his production team and said, "That's what makes good TV," asking to reschedule me as soon as possible. That would take awhile since I had other media obligations piled up, along with speaking engagements, surveys that we had initiated, my position as GAA political chair, and our work on a nondiscrimination bill. Additionally, I had to attend various legal trials due to the zaps, and I still had my duties at home. But eventually it did happen.

For my second appearance, Phil Donohue asked my parents and my partner Phillip to join me. When I told my parents about this request, Dad jumped at the chance, while Mom felt slightly apprehensive. On the flight over, she remained silent as Dad chatted about our engagement to the stewardesses and fellow passengers; I wondered how things would go.

It was late at night when we landed, and a car picked us up at the airport and drove us to our hotel. Early the next morning we were taken to the studio and led into the green room. About twenty minutes before taping, Phil appeared in the room with his makeup bib on. *Hollywood Squares* was playing on a television in the background, and as Phil noticed us, he looked at me and said, "That's the show I'd love to do." At this point Joan Rivers was on screen making a joke about something and Phil commented, "She's got raw talent." He looked around at my parents and added, referring to *Hollywood Squares*, "I don't think I can do that." In quick order he then told us the run of the show we were about to tape. He treated me like we were old friends and realized that my parents had never done anything like this. He calmed their fears by chatting with them. My mother was almost instantly won over by his charm, while my father decided that this was his opportunity to be comedian Henny Youngman. He asked Donahue about stage setup, timing, and the line of questions. My father, the short, very pudgy cab driver from Philly, whose most exciting event in life to this point had been a full house at the weekly cousin's club card game, was all in. My father had gone Hollywood and showed no sign of nerves. In fact, he was overly excited, which in turn made me nervous.

The first part of the show was just me with Phil and the audience. We discussed the pioneering work I had just begun with Pennsylvania's Governor Milton Shapp in order to find ways to end discrimination, as well as my other exploits as an activist. For the second half of the show Phil brought my parents and Phillip back onstage. No sooner had he introduced them when my father went into his routine: "You know Mark lives at home with us, and on weekends Phillip joins him. We enjoy each other's company, but I know Phillip loves Sunday morning best of all. On Sundays, this nice Catholic boy comes downstairs to breakfast and enjoys lox, bagels, and whitefish." Dad, in the best stage acting of his life, looked at Phillip lovingly and, expecting a drumroll after this statement, had now added religion into the discussion.

Mom sat there totally frightened and silent while Dad was channeling a Johnny Carson monologue. Finally, Phil asked Mom, "How do you feel about all this?" Mom straightened up and said what I think was on the mind of every parent when they learned their child was gay: "I want Mark to be happy, I worry about him when he gets older, but most importantly I want him to find someone who he can love and spend the rest of his life with." She looked at my partner Phillip and smiled and placed her hand on his knee.

Donahue broke for a commercial, and when the sound was off he turned to my mother and said, "That was great, Mom." She was thrilled and Dad, still believing himself to be Henny Youngman, asked, "And what am I, chopped liver?"

After the taping Phil came over to tell us that it was a great show, and kissed Mom on the cheek. She smiled and blushed, and would never in her life miss another Phil Donahue show.

The staff handed us a piece of paper with the airdates and we departed.

Mom and Dad flew home, while Phillip and I headed to Provincetown on Cape Cod where I was the keynote speaker at the first New England Gay Conference. When I got home from the conference there was a bill in the mail from the Donahue people for eighty-six dollars for additional hotel expenses. Of course I couldn't afford it and wrote back promising to pay it sometime in the future. In the same letter I requested a copy of the taping. I'd never asked for tapes before, but this show was with my parents, and I thought it would be a great keepsake. They wrote back explaining that the company that handled those requests charged more than a hundred dollars per copy. They gave me their phone number and mailing address. Since I didn't have the money I didn't respond until a couple of years later.

Flash forward to 2013, at a meeting of Comcast's Joint Diversity Council, on which I serve as the national LGBT representative. The council was formed by company chairman and CEO Brian Roberts and Senior Executive Vice President David L. Cohen, with the mission to transform Comcast NBCUniversal into one of the most diversified companies in the Fortune 100. We were having a discussion about the history of television talk shows, when someone asked me about Phil Donahue and that February 1973 taping, saying that as far as he knew it was one of the first depictions of a gay family on TV. He said it was historic. I explained that he was almost correct, but that we were preceded by An American Family on PBS, which aired a year and a half earlier.

I'm still honored to have been a guest various times on Donahue's show. In the early days of TV talk, there was no other American media person or company who had done as much to make Americans aware of the gay and lesbian community. Ditto for the issues surrounding AIDS. Not only did Donahue broadcast shows on the subject before it became popular, it was, in some cases, dangerous. And he handled them always with respect and care. He got into the AIDS battle early, giving of his time when other celebrities hid the issues from their audiences and themselves.

At the 1993 March on Washington for Lesbian, Gay, and Bi Equal Rights and Liberation, I left the crowd to take a walk to the Washington Monument. As I strolled I passed thousands of people, most of them gay or lesbian. Over the loudspeaker I heard a familiar voice—it was Phil Donahue. On this early Sunday morning, long before the crowd reached capacity, he was once again giving his time to support our community in our fight for equality. He read a speech in which he told a story of discrimination, then paused and commanded America to get over it. Next, he shared a story of antigay violence. Again he said, "America, get over it." This went on and on. It must have taken hours of research to draft the speech. This man, who had brought so many Americans face-to-face with the gay and lesbian community, was rightly an opening act at our march. As I walked back to my group listening to Phil's voice, a chill ran down my back. I was so proud of him and his part in helping our movement progress.

While in the early 1970s the *Phil Donahue Show* was the leader in talk shows, I appeared on most of the others as well. The shows would fly me out to their studio, pay my travel expenses, and pick up the cost of meals and my hotel room. In each city, the night before the show, I'd invite a few members of the LGBT community to the hotel, order food and drinks, put it on the tab of the show, and mostly just listen to their stories. The talk shows were, in a sense, paying for me to witness LGBT America. Sometimes when I got a little downtime, the community would surprise me in some way. Yes, despite my upbeat disposition, I would occasionally get discouraged. In Detroit, for the *Joe Pyne Show*, some members of the community took me to the Cow Palace to see a traveling edition of *Peter Pan*. While I was in Chicago for the *Irv Kupcinet Show*, an incredible dinner party was given in my honor by Chuck Renslow, at his mansion that at one time had belonged to Al Capone. (It had a speakeasy in the basement.)

In between the talk shows I gave speeches, many of which have been long forgotten, or so I thought. In March 2014, the *Gazette*, which bills itself as the Eastern Iowa newspaper of record for over 125 years, published a report on the gay rights movement in Iowa. It chronicled the growth of the community and mentioned that in 1974 I became the first out gay person to speak publicly on the subject in Iowa. When I read the article, those memories washed back to shore.

It had started with Iowa State University sending me an invitation, one that included paying for my expenses and giving me a small honorarium. Honorarium? Progress for sure. At that point, the only thing stopping me from accepting an invitation was if I had dialysis duty. I always asked my parents if they could do without me for a few days before making a decision. They said that they'd be all right for this one.

When I told friends where I was going, their reactions were always the same. *Iowa, they'll kill you out there.* I'd like to believe my speech actually inspired a few in the audience. One guy there that night, Ken Bunch, would move to San Francisco and become one of the founders of the Sisters of Perpetual Indulgence, a beloved group of men dressing in outrageous nun drag while fighting the AIDS epidemic. His name became Sister Vicious Power Hungry Bitch. What a brilliant man.

On the homefront, Mom's kidney condition had deteriorated so much that she was now on the transplant list. Each family member was tested, and when only Uncle Stan was a match, my grandmother, who had been a free spirit her entire life, began to look shell-shocked. The emotional turmoil that she felt over the possibility that her daughter and her son could die on the operating table finally broke her spirit. Uncle Stan soon became her caregiver, and they moved into our house on Fayette Street. At the time it seemed very natural. There were three bedrooms. Mom and Dad had one, I had one, and Grandmom had one; Uncle Stan made good with the couch. Our family life became doctor appointments for Grandmom, dialysis for Mom, and demonstrations and zaps for me. I always told Mom and Grandmom as I left the house that they shouldn't worry; the worst that would happen is that I'd get arrested.

There were no complaints from them. At the time, they never told me about the numerous calls from relatives complaining about my activities. Most were about how I was embarrassing the family. Mom also never told me that she'd stopped going to the cousins club, one of the few outings she looked forward to, because some of her relatives had said derogatory things about my actions. Dad never said anything about the fights he got into until years later. Thanks to his time in the Army Air Force during which he competed as an amateur boxer, which had earned him the nickname Little Atlas, he always won. Years later, he boasted how proud he was of my actions and said, "We love you no matter what." He never lost an opportunity to let me know that I had made him proud. I cried every time.

Dad and Uncle Stan always held down the fort while my "career" without a salary continued. The press in Philly coined me "Supergay" and even the establishment wanted a piece of the action. The Junior Chamber of Commerce announced that I was one of their men of the year. The Jewish Community Relations Council voted me onto their board of directors, a gesture more symbolic than practical since my attendance was rare.

Meanwhile, Grandmom's condition grew steadily worse. My Auntie Mame, my muse, started to drift off into a world of her own. I liked to think that world was the one she loved, strolling on the boardwalk in Atlantic City, chatting with all her friends, and sashaying from one avenue to the next. She did listen to each word that we spoke to her, and always with a smile on her face. We never knew if she understood or not, and her speech slowly disappeared. Each night when I wasn't on the road, I'd go to the living room to sit with her and tell her about my day and future plans. She listened, reacted with that smile, and occasionally uttered a reassuring word. At times she'd perk up at the mention of some new success, but she wasn't that perpetual shining light anymore. I suppose those chats were more for me than her. I needed Grandmom and my family. They kept me grounded while I was becoming a public figure.

At home, my social world consisted of Phillip, my high school friend Randy Miller, and Randy's friends Jan Sergienko and Debbie Dunn. In the evenings we hung out and they'd help me come up with the next great idea. Except for Phillip, they were all non-gays, but today you'd call them LGBT allies. One initiative in particular comes to mind. We were still doing stunts in Philly every few weeks. Someone suggested that we paint a large sign with the words Gay Power and place it on the City Hall tower during rush hour. Soon we discovered what it would take to make a six-story "statement." We bought white sheets and began to do the lettering in Jan's parent's basement. Somehow we all agreed on this crazy project. It would be simple: white material, black lettering. It would be carried into the building in stages and Velcroed together.

We transported it to City Hall and found a friendly office where I stayed overnight. I awoke at seven a.m. and took the banner up to the tower but the doors were locked. I ventured to the top of the north side of the building and found an open window. I tied down the top of the banner and Velcroed the pieces together. Finally, I hung it out the window facing the traffic on Broad Street coming into the city center. It caused a huge traffic problem. The all-news radio stations began reporting on it every ten minutes. For some reason it took the powers-that-be about an hour to hoist the banner back inside. In the meantime I was across the street watching and kicking myself for not taking into consideration the wind, which at times made the words almost unreadable.

There was also Chicago's first gay pride celebration. The Reverend Troy Perry and I were to be the featured speakers in Lincoln Park. We agreed to arrive in Chicago days in advance to promote the event. Troy was fighting the religious establishment and I was off fighting the networks and elected officials, and both of us wondered when our community would begin to help us with building our vision. Troy not only struggled with mainstream religion, but also the antireligious sentiment in the LGBT community. My fight was with those who felt my actions put too much attention on the community and pigeonholed us all as radical.

The schism in the gay rights movement was hitting a fever pitch. Gay Liberation Front had disbanded in New York and the Gay Activist Alliance would see its last day soon thereafter, succeeded by the National Gay Task Force. The 1972 and 1973 Gay Pride Days at times seemed like war zones. In addition to the rivalries of the remainder of the GLF and GAA members, there was still infighting about whether the movement should be a diverse, inclusive civil rights movement or have a gay rights–only policy.

GAA had taken up roots in an old firehouse on Wooster Street in Soho in New York City. At that time, under the leadership of Morty Manford, it became the focal point of the movement. But a rift between Morty and Bruce Voeller resulted in the formation of the National Gay Task Force. The Task Force put several of the pre-Stonewallers on their board since by this point Voeller was in need of credibility. Barbara Gittings and Frank Kameny were brought in, but all that did was reopen the wounds of a past battle in 1970 over whether the community would march in New York to mark the first anniversary of Stonewall or continue the July 4 Philadelphia marches for equality. GLF members at the time unfortunately labeled Barbara and Frank, and all those associated with the Philadelphia marches, as the Uncle Toms of our movement. Most of the younger activists thought of them as dinosaurs. To further complicate matters, Bruce Voeller assumed the role as the first employee of a gay organization with a professional staff. This was the beginning of what we now call Gay Inc., the incorporation and branding of the gay rights movement. Previously, GAA had created what they hoped would be the symbol of our struggle, the Greek lambda icon, yellow on a blue background. But the Task Force took things a few steps too far on policy. No drag queens need apply; no care was given to street kids. Zaps or actions were discouraged; the primary activities were lobbying for issues within government, talking in moderate tones, and always wearing a suit when talking to the media. And then there was the constant stream of fundraising at upper-crust LGBT cocktail parties. To my mind they were complacent and afraid to really fight. They wanted to change laws, but not create community.

Bruce Voeller was as unpopular as a figurehead could get, not only among New York activists but nationally as well. My only relationship with the Task Force was to call and complain when they took credit for my work. Any time a story on the LGBT community would break, NGTF was always there to issue a statement and explain how they were involved.

Out on the West Coast, an investment banker named David Goodstein had purchased the only national LGBT publication, the *Advocate*, which was read by nearly all LGBT activists. It was how we learned what others were doing. We couldn't expect any reports from the mainstream media, and there was no Internet. But Goodstein agreed with Voeller's view on a more formal, professional, and organized gay rights struggle. He created a list of people who should be low priority in their news coverage. Along with longtime activists such as Morris Knight, I was on the list. It felt like censorship. Goldstein's strangest contribution to the movement was when he introduced "The *Advocate* Experience," where people paid to attend a Zen-like weekend getaway, with the emphasis on enlightenment and self-acceptance rather than public opinion and equal rights. At this point, the *Advocate*, a respected publication known for good journalism, slipped into the dark side of history.

Voeller eventually left what resulted in a decimated Task Force. A host of directors followed his departure, each of whom crashed and burned due to various scandals or were ousted for a lack of organizational and communication skills. Eventually the Task Force did find decent leadership and direction. Among those leaders were Virginia Apuzzo, Urvashi Vaid, and Matt Foreman. Under their stewardship, the Task Force became the respectable organization that it is today. And as the group was getting its act together, another organization came along, the Human Rights Campaign Fund. It later dropped the word *Fund*

and become known as just HRC, but due to their early lavish fundraising events, it was coined by one activist "Human
Rights Champagne Fund." As it stands, HRC is now the leading
LGBT civil rights organization in the nation and their fundraising brings in over ten million dollars each year for LGBT causes.

In the mid-'70s, while the New York LGBT community was
busy with their in-fighting, the Gay Raiders were beginning to
blossom into new areas. What we had been doing with media,
we now did with government. Seeing the need for concrete data
that documented the treatment of LGBT people, we conducted
surveys. Individuals donated stamps and stationery, and one
of my new friends on the city council, Thomas Foglietta, who
would become a congressman and then ambassador to Italy under President Clinton, allowed us to use his office and equipment to create the surveys.

One of the leading complaints from our community was police harassment and entrapment. We obtained a list of police
chiefs in every major city and sent them letters asking how their
department treated the gay community. We didn't expect much
of a response and were surprised when over twenty responded.
The answers were sterile, but at least we had opened their eyes
to the issue. At the same time, we forwarded the responses to
the local organizations should they want to follow up and create
a relationship with their local police force.

We also did the first-ever survey of corporate America. We
didn't have the funds to send surveys to the complete Fortune
500 list, but the top hundred would still have an impact. We
asked each of them if they had a nondiscrimination policy in
their human resources departments. It was again an eye-opening
survey, for us and for them. Many wrote back that they had never
even thought about it. A few said they'd look into it. In 1976,

that was the state of corporate America on nondiscrimination.

And then my old friend from New York, Congresswoman Bella Abzug, along with then-congressman Ed Koch, asked me to help with something they had just introduced with little fanfare. The Equality Act (a precursor to the federal Employment Non-Discrimination Act) was first introduced by Abzug in May 1974. She and Koch (whom I always thought had a crush on me but never acted on it) felt that my luster at that time might help it along.

After countless meetings, it seemed to me that something was missing from the legislation: there were no African American Congress members as cosponsors. As the *Advocate* reported in August of that year, I worked to have Congressman Robert Nix, a founding member of the Congressional Black Caucus, become a cosponsor. He insisted that he reintroduce the legisla- tion and later that year it became H.R. 166, with five sponsors.

Congrsswoman Abzug made one other request of me during that time: come up with a PR stunt to promote the legislation. That stunt became the lamest Gay Raiders zap of all time, a White House zap. Translation: we decided to have a public LGBT tour of the White House. In those days all you had to do was line up outside the White House in the morning. We publicized this, but since most of the LGBT community in DC was still deeply closeted, the tour consisted of me, a few members of the Gay Raiders, and a very large group of Secret Service agents. The only coverage it got was in the *Advocate*.

It is so impressive how much Human Rights Campaign has improved upon the effort to pass ENDA and how they've made their surveys so important—many Fortune 500 companies work diligently each year to obtain a 100 percent rating for their support of their LGBT employees. While our simple surveys consisted of one question, each year's Human Rights Campaign

Corporate Equality Index has a booklet of questions that each company's human resources department must fill out. It touches on the full range of LGBT issues that individuals and corporations face. Many of the Fortune 500 corporations now covet a top ranking in the index and advertise and promote the fact.

In the middle of all of this, I wrote a letter requesting a meeting with the governor of Pennsylvania. It seemed simple, but at that time, in 1974, no governor in the nation had ever met publicly with anyone from the gay and lesbian community. So when Governor Milton Shapp agreed, it caught me by surprise. His office called to arrange for a meeting the next day. In all honesty, it never occurred to me that he'd actually agree to such a meeting. Preparation was virtually nonexistent and as was often the case for me, the meeting was off the cuff. We met in Norristown, Pennsylvania, while he was on a statewide tour. When Harry Langhorne and I walked into the room, the governor stood up, walked over to us with a big smile on his face, and gave me a hearty handshake. His smile grew as he said, "I've seen you on TV." When I didn't get it, he added, "Cronkite seemed to be surprised to meet you, but I'm not." It was the first time that I'd ever felt comfortable with an elected official so quickly.

Rather than ask what he could do for us, he asked what he could do to help our cause. This caught us completely off guard. And, as always, I went for the brass ring: "Governor, gay men and lesbians are discriminated against in almost every part of state government."

This was all I got out before he said, "How can we change that?"

I replied with the brass ring again: "Create a commission to explore these problems and find solutions." At that point there had never been an official governmental body to look into

LGBT issues. He knew it, I knew it, and we just looked at each other for a while, knowing that what was requested was, in fact, unprecedented.

Governor Shapp finally said, "Let me consider the options and get back to you." He then did something else unheard of: he asked his press secretary to allow the media in to our meeting, which we had believed was to be off the record. This was another surprise to Harry and me.

The press was out in force. When the door to the room opened, they rushed in. Questions were yelled at the governor, too many to answer, but he gave the usual political statement, "We had a good meeting," then added, "It's a start." To further assure us, he actually posed for pictures with us. At that time most elected officials were running from gay activists; some wouldn't even touch a gay person—but not Governor Milton Shapp. The next day, pictures of the two of us shaking hands were splashed across the state's newspapers. He relished the idea of helping; after all, he was the man who came up with the idea of the Peace Corps (not Sargent Shriver, as most people believe).

Our friendship grew, and it was not unusual for him to call the house in the evening to talk about the LGBT community. He wanted to know all the ways in which we were discriminated against. We started to discuss the organization of the commission. During one of these calls, he said, "It's going to take all the departments of the state." If Milton Shapp was from a different state, such as New York or California, he would be hailed as a national hero of our community rather than a footnote. Shapp, the first Jewish governor of Pennsylvania, also became the first governor in the nation to issue a statewide executive order forbidding discrimination against gay people in all agencies and departments, and the first governmental chief executive in the world to create a commission to look into the concerns of the gay and lesbian community. When he was up for reelection, his Republican opponent, Drew Lewis, was forced to write *Philadelphia Gay News* a letter stating that he opposed discrimination in housing employment and public accommodation, and my favorite part of that letter was where he added, *I do not feel that your preference should result in criminal liability.* If elected, Lewis would continue to support civil rights for gays and lesbians. This marked the first gubernatorial election in America where both Republican and Democrat candidates supported LGBT rights. The credit is due to Shapp, and it also underscored the power we as a community had garnered by 1975.

In April of that year, Shapp established the Pennsylvania Council for Sexual Minorities. He ordered each department to appoint a top official to be a member or liaison. This was real. Yet there was also one disappointment for me, and one that I'd have to become comfortable with if I wanted to continue to plow new ground. I might have provided the seed, but I was not allowed to grow my own child. As the governor told me, "Mark, you're too much of a firebrand, and if I allowed you to chair the commission it would get nowhere, and we both want it to make change, you understand."

I was given two subcommittees: prisons and insurance. Tony Silvestre would lead the commission. The governor appointed Barry Kohn to be his liaison. It seemed to me that both Silvestre and Kohn believed, as had the Task Force, that I projected the wrong image. That old feeling of isolation that I experienced in grammar school returned. Gee, if only I'd worn a suit.

Shapp continued to engage me in new ways. While the commission was toiling, he put me to work with the state police and the legislature. One day he called and asked me to meet him in the governor's residence later that afternoon. "Governor, I'm in Philadelphia, is it so important that I come to Harrisburg?" He insisted, and after a two-hour drive, I was pulling up to the gate and the guard said, "Mr. Segal, the governor is waiting for you."

Entering the governor's ornate residence, I found him standing there, smiling with his arms crossed against his chest. He said, "There seems to be one thing that is lacking in your lobbying efforts, and it's about time someone tells you." With that we went into the state dining room where there was a coatrack with about ten jackets on it. "If you're going to lobby state senators and representatives, you need to look the part. You don't have to wear a complete suit, but a blue jacket will do the trick. Here, try these on." The rack contained blue blazers in various sizes. "Find the one that fits you, and I'll see you in Philadelphia next week." He had me drive all the way to Harrisburg just to give me a jacket!

In quick succession, Shapp issued an executive order banning discrimination in state hiring and services, created the Council for Sexual Minorities (whose title, according to the governor, had to contain the word *minority* since that was something the public would respond to), and, in June of 1975, became first governor in the nation to have his state officially proclaim Gay Pride Month.

Shortly after the governor issued his executive order, I was lying down in my bedroom on Fayette Street one morning when the phone rang at six a.m. I ignored it and just turned over in bed. Then, a knock on the door. Mom said: "Mark, there's a guy on the phone who say's he's Lieutenant Governor Ernie Kline and he wants to talk to you."

Picking up the extension in my room, I greeted, "Governor, what can I do for you?"

He explained that Governor Shapp had had a knock-down

screaming match with the head of the Pennsylvania state troopers over his executive order banning discrimination against sexual minorities in state hiring. It seems that when Colonel James
Barger heard that the executive order included his department,
he marched directly to the governor's office and told Shapp that
there was no way would he have "those people" on his force.

My reaction was, "So what can I do to help?"

"The governor wants you to go to the state police barracks
at Belmont today at nine a.m. and sign up to be a state trooper."
As my mind was trying to grasp this idea, he went on, "Just show
up, fill out the paperwork, and we'll do the rest."

All I could get out before he hung up was, "Ernie . . ."

So on May 14, 1975, I jumped out of bed and began hatch-
ing a plan of action, one taking place in an unfamiliar landscape.
I knew the police, that was for sure, but from a completely different type of experience. I wondered what one wears to sign up
to be a state trooper. Then it dawned on me: How far was this
going to go? Would the governor actually make me go to some
sort of state trooper boot camp? By this time, in the two years
after I had been summoned home to help care for my mom, my
parents had adjusted to almost anything. So as I left the house,
I called out, "Well, at least today you won't have to worry about
me being arrested by the police, seems I'm signing up to become
one of them." Mom gave me a strange look and I added, "You
know, Mom, I'm marching off to war." She smiled; it was our
private joke about that day in grammar school and "Onward,
Christian Soldiers."

As I drove into the Belmont police barracks parking lot, a
swarm of media surrounded my car. Clearly, the governor's office had put out a press release. There was a new reporter for
KYW-TV named Jessica Savitch, who in just two years would
become an anchor on the *NBC Nightly News* and in short order

lose control of her life, then actually lose her life in an automobile accident. But in 1975, she was still a cub reporter. When I got out of the car, she shoved a mic in front of me and said, "Mr. Segal, you're a homosexual."

Like that was something I didn't know. Before she could say anything else I replied, "Isn't that obvious?" After all, I was wearing a button that read, *How dare you presume I'm straight.* Then I added, "I see you got the press release."

She continued, asking why I was applying to become a state trooper. The rest of the media gathered around and I said the first thing that came to mind: "I like men in uniform." Everyone laughed, and then I got down to the serious business at hand. "This is about employment discrimination. If I'm able to do the job, then I should be given the same opportunity as anyone else." Sounded perfectly logical to me, and to the press; they got their three-minute story for the evening news. But no one mentioned that the guy signing up for the state troopers was five-seven, dressed in torn blue jeans, a T-shirt with a peace sign on it, and hair down to his shoulders. This was political theater, and the only way to make it work was with a little humor.

One reporter who saw through the theatrics and went right to the facts when covering one of my political actions was Andrea Mitchell, then with KYW-TV and one whose battles with Mayor Frank Rizzo are now legendary. Our relationship was cordial, but once the camera was on she was as professional and well-researched as any reporter I've ever known.

The activity with the state troopers was written about and broadcast throughout the state. Here's an example of how the media of the day handled this:

Philadelphia AP—Mark Segal, an admitted homosexual, applied Wednesday to join the Pennsylvania State Police, but

admitted later his application was a test of state police policy.
Segal said, and state police confirmed, that he applied at the
state police barracks in the Belmont section of Philadelphia.

But my favorite headline came from the *Times Leader:*
"Shapp Aide Tells Berger to Reconsider Homos Ban."

After one long day of fighting, I asked Shapp why he was
taking this on, and he told me, "Mark, I'm in the closet as well."
When I looked at him strangely, he laughed and followed up
with, "My real name is Shapiro, I had to change it to Shapp to
enter politics. So I understand discrimination."

Almost thirty years later I received a call from a young girl
who explained, "My father suggested that I contact you regarding a report on gay rights I'm doing for a school term paper." My
questions were the usual: What school? What aspects of LGBT
history are you interested in? She replied, "I'm not calling you
about your activism, I'm calling you since I understand that my
grandfather was involved with the gay rights movement and my
father told me you worked with him." Her father was Richard
Shapp, and she was Milton Shapp's granddaughter. She had no
idea about her grandfather's important work in this area, and
unfortunately most Americans still don't. And believe me, he's
one of the most important figures in the early gay rights movement. He was a pioneer in his own way.

Those official Pennsylvania gay pride proclamations started
by Shapp kept coming through various administrations, including Republican governor Richard Thornburgh, who was later
appointed US attorney general by President Ronald Reagan.
When elected governor, Thornburgh wanted to show inclusion
in his administration. He chose an African American Republican doctor who had been elected to the Philadelphia city council to be his secretary of the commonwealth. Her name was Dr.

Ethel Allen, and she was diversity-inclusion all rolled up into one neat package. She was also a personal friend, and a closeted lesbian.

Closeted public officials often look for ways to be a part of the fight for equality. Ethel had been in numerous struggles; as a woman, as an African American seeking a medical degree, and as a black Republican in a Democratic town. She was a fighter.

Soon after Thornburgh chose Ethel, she gave me a call and asked if I'd write the governor's gay pride proclamation. Something felt odd. I asked her, "Does the governor know you're asking me this?"

She responded, "Not to worry," and got off the phone.

A month later she called to ask how it was going. My reply was simple: "It's not going, since if the governor isn't going to issue it, why should I waste the time?" She guaranteed me he would, and then she set up a lunch date for us to write it.

We sat in an empty restaurant called Bramwell's one afternoon, looking over the previous gay pride proclamations and making changes and additions. When we finally completed our task, I grabbed her hand. "I think I know what you're going to do, and you know he might fire you over this."

She smiled and said, "Over this small little thing?"

June rolled around and, lo and behold, one morning I read in the newspaper that Governor Richard Thornburgh had become the first Republican governor ever to proclaim Gay Pride Month. That point had slipped both our minds. It created more of a dustup than we expected. A good deal of the media congratulated the governor on making a brave gesture and an opening to the LGBT community, but they didn't know the real story.

Each week, Ethel had a regularly scheduled meeting with the governor where she'd inform him of the various documents that needed his signature. The last item on the docket was usually proclamations. She read off a list of what they were, she put the pile in front of him, he'd sign, and she'd take them back to her office to issue.

It seems at one of those meetings where she was reading off the list, she didn't mention the Gay Pride Month proclamation that he was about to sign. Now, with the positive media editorials, he didn't know what to do. As with all smart politicians, you wait for the clamor to die down before making a move, and that is exactly what he did. A couple of months later, Ethel was unceremoniously fired. The reason given: she abused her expense account by making too many long-distance calls.

Soon after, she contacted me and suggested that we have a celebratory lunch at Bramwell's. We met and chatted about other things before the subject came up. She told me there was no reason for me to say a word. She was proud of what she had done. It was her contribution to the struggle, and in her eyes it was worth the cost. She never regretted it, and I believe it was one of her proudest moments. While Thornburgh went on to be part of Reagan's presidential cabinet, Ethel took a downward medical spiral. It has always been my belief that she knew her time was limited and she intended to make the most of it. She was a brave and dignified woman.

And one last item: at that lunch she presented me with the signed proclamation from Governor Thornburgh that hangs on my office wall to this day.

It was a busy time. Beyond the media zaps, negotiations with the television networks, the groundbreaking surveys of police chiefs, and workplace nondiscrimination efforts, we issued a survey of all fifty state governors, which actually resulted in replies from half of them, including New Jersey's Brendan T. Byrne, Tennessee's Ray Blanton, and one from Massachusetts by Michael S. Dukakis stating, "If this [nondiscrimination] bill is passed by the General Court, I expect to sign it." Alongside the countless speaking engagements and interviews, and my duties at home, at the end of 1975 I managed to do a press tour of eastern Ohio and western Pennsylvania at the behest of Jim Austin.

Jim, a longtime newspaperman who had the knowledge to make a success of one of America's first local LGBT publications, the *Pittsburgh Gay News*, was now branching out. He had decided to create the *Ohio East Gay News*. To launch his first issue, he thought a speaking tour with the nation's most outrageous gay activist would generate good publicity. We did speaking dates in Cleveland, Youngstown, and Kent State University, and our last stop would be Pittsburgh.

Jim made up posters for the tour, one of which still hangs on my office wall. There's a picture of me in my youthful handsomeness with the line, *Meet Mark Segal, Gay Activist Extraordinaire*. The tour was a hit. A lot of people showed up when I spoke, and there was good press coverage, but it was Jim's show and we always turned the message to the new *Ohio East Gay News*.

On our way back to Pittsburgh, Jim asked why Philadelphia didn't have a gay newspaper. I explained that we had a weekly mimeograph publication, the *Gayzette*. His reply was no, you need a newspaper on newsprint with stories on every issue affecting our community, a professional publication. Then, out of nowhere, he said, "Why don't *you* do it?"

I responded by sharing an account of a recent lobbying experience. I told him that while I never had the pleasure of meeting Princess Grace of Monaco, her brother Jack and I were acquaintances. Jack, a rower and member of the US Olympic Committee, was also a Philadelphia city councilman who at rare ambitious times had higher political dreams. I say rare since Jack was a fun-filled guy who worked to live, not lived to work in a political campaign.

We became acquainted while I was lobbying for a gay-rights bill. On our first meeting he invited me into his inner office to ask some questions. None of them concerned anything to do with the law, rather he asked about what it was like to be gay and about gay relationships. After several visits with Jack we were on a first-name basis and I felt comfortable enough to ask him to be a cosponsor of the gay-rights bill. He replied, "Mark, I'd like to assist, but Mother wouldn't understand."

Our relationship remained that of councilman and lobbyist until an item appeared in the *Philadelphia Daily News*, in a column by a mutual friend of ours. Larry Fields's personality (a.k.a. gossip) column kept tabs on the who's who of Philadelphia society and visiting celebrities. Larry was also a friend to Mayor Frank Rizzo. It was in Larry's column that the Rizzo camp would send up trial balloons or political warnings. Rizzo, nearing the end of his first term in office, didn't want any problem in his reelection bid. There was disgruntlement among Philadelphia Democrats over the manner in which Rizzo had governed both the city and the party political machine; many thought that he was acting more policeman-like than mayoral.

In an unusual mood, Jack had let it be known that he might be interested in challenging Rizzo in the Democratic primary for mayor. It was in this atmosphere that I entered City Hall one morning to do my regular check-in with city council members. At each corner of City Hall there are circular staircases. On various occasions, when feeling that I hadn't gotten my exercise or just wanting to marvel at the magnificent building, I'd take the staircase to Jack's office.

On this day, as I made my way up, I noticed Jack sitting

on the stairs holding his head in his hands. I called up to him, "How's it going?"

He looked distressed and, picking up the *Philadelphia Daily News*, said, "Have you seen this yet?" He told me to check out Larry Fields's column. Then he began to cry.

There we were, the gay activist and Princess Grace's brother, sitting on a staircase in the middle of City Hall as the latter started to sob. I turned to the column and read the tidbit, which began by stating that Jack was thinking about challenging Frank Rizzo for mayor. It then stated that if he did so, several members of Rizzo inner circle would rent a billboard with a picture of Harlow, a well-known transsexual in the city, with the caption, *How would you like her as your next first lady?*

As I read the threat, Jack moaned, "I only went out with her on one date." (Harlow, an incredible beauty, insists to this day that it was more than once.) He continued, "Can you imagine what this will do to my mother?" Jack's mother, though sickly, still controlled his life at this point. As he continued to sob and mumble, I stood him up, put my arm around his waist, and walked him back to his office. He got control of himself and thanked me, saying, "I don't have anyone else to talk to about this." How sad I felt for him.

That evening Jack called me at home, thanking me again and asking me not to talk to anyone about his "breakdown." He said that he was feeling better, and if there was anything he could do for me, I should just ask. To get a laugh out of him I said that he could arrange a date for me with his nephew, Prince Albert. He chuckled, and thanked me once more. I told him that I was always available to talk. Days later it was reported that Jack would not be running against Frank Rizzo. The Rizzo team's dirty work did what it was supposed to.

When I ran into Jack from that point on, I'd always say quietly, "You still owe me that date." He knew that just like everyone else, I really wanted to meet his sister, Princess Grace of Monaco, but I was aware that this was unlikely. One day while sitting at my desk the phone rang and it was Jack on the line. "Mark," he said, "I have someone here in my office I want you to meet. Do you think you can come over immediately?"

My office was only a ten-minute walk from City Hall. When I arrived it was apparent that something was up because there were police everywhere. Since City Hall also served as a courthouse I thought there was trouble with one of the courts or an inmate. As I got to Jack's office, the crowd was overwhelming. I made my way to the door and was stopped. After telling the police officer that I was expected, I was allowed to enter. I was then ushered into Jack's inner office. Several people who I didn't recognize were there, but Jack saw me and said, "Mark, I want to introduce you to my nephew."

There sat Prince Albert of Monaco. He rose and said in a soft voice, "My uncle has told me how helpful you've been to him."

I nodded, speechless, and after a very short while I made my way to the door. Jack noticed me leaving and said with a smile, "I guess I'm off the hook now for that date," then added, "He doesn't bat for your team."

After relating this story to Jim Austin, he looked at me and asked, "What does Princess Grace have to do with you publishing a newspaper?" My response was that I was an activist, what did I know about publishing or business? He remarked, "Mark, someday you'll need to earn a living—this is that way, and it will allow you to remain an activist, just in another form."

We shook hands and became partners on the spot, and my life was about to change yet again. Meet publisher Mark Segal.

Chapter 6

Talking Sex with the *Wall Street Journal*

Philadelphia Gay News was among the first local newspapers for the LGBT community. Like the others, we were building a network where one had never existed before. Until being catapulted into my position as publisher, my knowledge of journalism was limited to school yearbooks, the *Gay Youth Journal*, and a few freelance articles I'd written for *Gay Sunshine* and other small publications. Actually publishing a forty-page newspaper each month was a daunting task.

Jim would do the lion's share of the work in Pittsburgh. Jim now had three newspapers, and this made him the owner of the first-ever chain of publications for the LGBT community. He was smart and knew the networking I had done as an activist would pay off.

Like all that I have done in my life, my newspapering was learned from on-the-job experience and a thirst to give our community the best. I had gotten to know numerous mainstream journalists in my travels and I utilized many of them to help guide us in those early days. Among them were Pulitzer Prize–winning writers such as Richard Aregood, Michael Pakenham, and even Walter Cronkite, who had quietly befriended me after we ran into each other in Miami in 1976 at a debate before the Florida primary he was moderating among Democrat candidates for president, and then later in the year in Philadelphia where he was moderating a CBS-TV bicentennial salute to the 1776 American Revolution.

When he'd spotted me in the wings in Miami, he walked over with a smile and asked, "Mark, what brings you here?" I was really surprised that he recognized me. I explained that I was helping one of the candidates, Pennsylvania Governor Milton Shapp, who had a strong record on gay rights. Walter wrote a note and asked if he could use that in his introduction since all he had about Shapp related to a threatened national independent truckers strike. Governor Shapp had stepped into the negotiations and won praise from the truckers for settling the dispute without a national strike. That night Walter's introduction of the man was, "Governor Shapp of Pennsylvania hopes to bring a coalition of truck drivers and homosexuals together to win the nomination," spoken with that Cronkite air of assurance.

By late 1975, we were laying out the first edition of the paper, which was to be issued in January 1976. Never did I expect the battles that would follow over journalism. Our vending boxes would be bombed, and we would clean them up, repaint them, and put them back. People would run over them with their cars, and we would, again, clean them up, repaint them, and put them back out. People threw bricks into our windows and sprayed graffiti all over our building. The death threats were something we got used to. Me being put on the American Nazi Party's hit list in their magazine was a little more unique.

Another person put on the hit list was the publisher of the *Advocate*; both of us were "Jewish fag publishers." *Philadelphia Gay News* covered myriad gay bashings and murders, crimes that most of the population didn't seem to care about. Many times we were the sole voice yelling out in the darkness of a silent press. We covered the issues of transgender people from day one, while many in LGBT media tried to ignore that part of our community. We were one of the first to publish Alison Bechdel's wonderful and funny cartoon strip *Dykes to Watch Out For*. And she was always thankful that she got paid. (Alison's career blossomed along the way, and she was a recipient of the MacArthur Genius Grant in 2014; her life story was made into a Broadway musical *Fun Home*.) In those early days of LGBT media, many freelancers were never paid. *PGN* got a reputation for not just paying our freelancers but paying them on time.

The news could be emotionally nerve-wracking. One week's story continues to haunt me: the murder of Anthony Milano. His death was covered by our then-editor Tommi Avicolli Mecca. Milano's throat was cut dozens of times, and he died by drowning in his own blood. Then there were other murders that only the *Philadelphia Gay News* seemed to care about. In reporting Nizah Morris's story we hounded the police department and district attorney, and requested assistance from the US attorney general. We even took the city to court to release records. The potential for physical intimidation and harm that Tim Cwiek, the reporter on that story, put himself through was akin to any top-notch crime reporter for any major newspaper.

After twelve years of reporting on a single case—that of transwoman Nizah Morris, who was given a late-night courtesy ride home by the police and later found dead—in June 2014 *Philadelphia Gay News* staff writer Tim Cwiek, editor Jen Colletta, and I found ourselves at the Society of Professional Journalist's awards dinner at the National Press Club in Washington, DC. Our table partners were staffers for the *Wall Street Journal*, who were, like Tim, receiving the award in investigative journalism. As we were preparing to accept the highest journalistic honor that any LGBT media had ever received, we found ourselves in conversation with our tablemates about three things: the murder of a transwoman, the business of pornography, and gay for pay. We explained what we knew about the trans community's relationship with the police and why there might have been physical intimidation. The *Wall Street Journal* people looked like they had entered an alternate universe. We all chatted until it was time for our award to be announced. Everyone in the room heard about the twelve-year struggle *PGN* had waged to answer questions surrounding the death of Nizah Morris. And just like any professional publication, we continue to follow up on the story.

When we started in the mid-1970s, we often covered police raids on gay bars and their wholesale blackmailing of gay men. *Philadelphia Gay News* took on organizations such as the American Red Cross, Blue Cross and Blue Shield, and even the United Way.

I once asked Tommi Avicolli Mecca, an early *PGN* staffer and later editor, what his most memorable story was, and he replied, "The police district that was keeping a list of people with AIDS so that it wouldn't respond to calls from those addresses"—the police chief had to denounce that after the dailies picked it up from us—"and the investigation of the murders of several black transgender women that the police weren't even bothering to investigate."

Al Patrick recalls investigating the AIDS Ride fundraisers that took place in Philadelphia, Los Angeles, and San Francisco, among other cities, and unveiling how lucrative they were for the organizers and how little they did for AIDS organizations who received only a pittance from them. After that report, the group threatened to sue us from their Los Angeles offices and we wrote back explaining we'd be happy to meet them in court in our state. They never took us up on this. Eventually the *New*

York Times did a series about them and in a matter of time they were out of business.

Our community was not always pleased with us. We pushed every envelope; from that very first issue we were defining ourselves as a real paper with hard news. In those first two years we published many features that no other LGBT media would touch. We hit a major nerve nationally with the first-ever feature on lesbian nuns by Victoria Brownworth, which made Victoria the national expert on the subject. We reported on the poor and homeless in our community, the countless "thrown away" gay and lesbian youth; we went to Rikers Island prison in New York City to visit their new experiment with a gay men's wing; we wrote about the perils of Susan Saxe, a lesbian who was accused of robbing a bank; and we led a major investigation into aversion therapy.

Aversion therapy was used in an attempt to change a gay man or lesbian's sexual orientation through the use of drugs or electroconvulsive treatment. The latter was done mostly with electrodes strapped to the genitals. Psychiatrists and other health professionals practiced it nationally, since up until 1973 homosexuality was still considered a mental illness. It was also widely used in prisons—the most notable being Atascadero State Hospital in California, on which writer and activist David Mixner reported extensively.

In Philadelphia, aversion therapy was being conducted at Eastern Pennsylvania Psychiatric Institute, which was part of Temple University and got its funding from the state of Pennsylvania. The paper investigated the institute and was able to have the practice ended, one of our first major victories.

In previous years, doctors had one other treatment to use if the "illness" persisted: lobotomy. And yes, there was a method known as the ice-pick lobotomy popularized by Dr. Walter J.

Freeman. It is estimated that Dr. Freeman submitted over a thousand gay men and lesbians to this torture. When you factor in other doctors who employed the practice as well as the prison systems that used it, this figure increases to the tens of thousands. LGBT media has hardly touched on this dark time in our history.

In 1977, Tim Cwiek conducted one of the first interviews in LGBT media with a presidential assistant inside the West Wing of the White House. Tim wrote a sidebar called "Mr. Cwiek Goes to Washington" where he detailed his experience waiting in the West Wing lobby with Senator Sam Nunn of Georgia, who was there with Miss America to be photographed with the president. Miss America, being polite, asked Tim what he was doing at the White House. Tim told her that he would be interviewing the president's assistant about gay rights. Miss America looked nervously to Senator Nunn, bringing a speedy death to that conversation.

I can't help but get emotional when I think about the beginning of our newspaper. We were in a building with no electricity, no plumbing, and it leaked so badly that we needed a plastic tarp when it rained. Our bathrooms were cans in the basement. At times, the only way we could pay our bills was to use the quarters from our few vending boxes. Don Pignolet, our distribution manager who had many roles at the paper, recalls taking those quarters to the hardware store to buy supplies to shore up the plastic tarp with two-by-fours.

If those issues weren't enough of a headache, our "neighbors" came in one night and removed the small amount of electric wiring we were able to install. To their chagrin and astonishment, we went out and got a generator and were back up and running in just a few hours. When someone trashed a vending box, Don would have another out in twenty-four hours. We continued repairing the boxes until the people gave up. We would not be defeated. I'm proud of this paper and its staff for believing we could make it.

Dr. Walter Lear was the main story of our first issue. With that report he became the highest-ranking public official in the country to come out. He was Pennsylvania's first deputy health commissioner and he came out at a time when some state health boards wouldn't give licenses to openly gay doctors. Any mainstream newspaper of the day would have loved to run that story, but we got it first.

To keep the ball rolling, in our second issue we went even bigger and featured a groundbreaking interview with the governor of Pennsylvania. Others began to notice, especially the dailies that couldn't get an interview with the governor no matter how many times their reporters called. We made it a point that if you were running for office, you'd speak to the LGBT community through its media or be held accountable. But we also went further: it was not only speaking to the LGBT community that mattered but keeping the promises of equality.

In 1975, on that trip to Pittsburgh that had sealed the deal to create *Philadelphia Gay News*, I can honestly say I really didn't understand what I was signing up for. The last forty years as seen through our pages proves that it is our own media that best chronicles our community. You can find reporting on all the debates within our community and recall the struggles that we've long forgotten.

LGBT publications had to battle the mainstream press to be recognized. Moreover, we had to get our community to appreciate that it was not our job to be a mouthpiece for them, but rather to be an independent voice that allowed public discussion in and out of the community. We do share our positions in editorials so the community knows where we stand, but we allow people to voice their differences with us in our letters to the editor and even guest op-ed pieces. That's a key strength of *Philadelphia Gay News*: our willingness to invite people to write in our pages when they disagree. I have received plenty of flack for allowing LGBT Republicans and others whose views do not reflect our own to have space in the paper. But their perspective should be heard, since any good story presents various points of view in order to be balanced and complete.

Our news must contain what all professional stories should have, the simple *who, what, where, when, why*, and *how*. When there's a scandal, run to it, not from it. It might sound strange but if you cover a story objectively, even one that the community doesn't want you to cover, you'll earn respect. And like all communities, someone always thinks they are above the law, or gets a little greedy. In those cases we need to be the first on the scene to report our own misdeeds.

In the early days, one of our advertising representatives was running an escort business on the side. When I discovered this I explained that he had a choice to make. The paper would not be affiliated with a prostitution service. He chose to keep his escort business and start a competing paper, taking one of my editors with him, but it never gained any traction. The sales rep was a pretty indecent guy; he pimped his lover as part of his escort service. To me this became a comedy that could serve a purpose. Why not have competitors who were inept to bolster our own standing. Needless to say, I found ways to help keep them in business.

The earliest American LGBT publication I know of was from 1937. It was a slick magazine that looked like *Life*, but only had articles and pictures about men. It had no masthead or any names in it, or even an address. It was more of a fashion magazine. Then, in 1947, a lesbian magazine appeared called *Vice Versa*, completely written and typed for publication by Lisa Ben. In the 1950s, LGBT organizations such as One Inc., Daughters of Bilitis, and Mattachine were publishing magazines or newsletters of their own, but it wasn't until 1967 that the first professional newspaper for our community appeared. The *Advocate* was launched in response to a police raid on the Black Cat, a gay bar in Los Angeles, and is the only national pre-Stonewall news publication that is still in print today. It is an invaluable resource and reference in researching the community's history.

Local LGBT publications began to flourish in the midseventies. Boston's *Gay Community News* (GCN), the *Washington Blade*, the *Bay Area Reporter* in San Francisco, *Pittsburgh Gay News*, and *Philadelphia Gay News* were soon joined by a host of others in almost every major city. In June 1976 we held our first LGBT media conference, organized by GCN, to discuss our mutual concerns and to find ways to work together. Since few of us had the funds to travel to Boston and pay for hotels, GCN stepped in to arrange housing for us. The second meeting was held in Philadelphia. During this period I was elected president of the first LGBT media organization, the Gay Press Association, which was renamed the National Gay Press Association. We soon changed the name again to the National Gay and Lesbian Press Association.

We were officially incorporated in May of 1981. At our convention in Los Angeles in 1984 we received our first city resolution, and there's one clause that tells volumes about building LGBT media:

> *Whereas, the Gay Press Association has instituted the International Gay Wire service, an intercontinental computer network which provides instant transmission of information*

around the world and provides greater access to news and information to its subscribers, be it resolved . . . that a suitable copy of this resolution be presented to the Gay Press Association, member resolution No. 155, dated this 21st day of May, 1984.

Before I received that resolution onstage at the Sheraton Universal in Burbank, I had lunch with a man I had searched for over many years, my cousin Norman. Norman had read about my coming to LA in *Frontiers* magazine, and called my office. He was living in Long Beach, California, and in order to meet me for lunch I had to send him a check since he had no spare funds. We met in the Sheraton's dining room. I was eager to see him, so I arrived early. When he showed up, he looked like a haggard old man of seventy, but he was only fifty-three at that time. Wearing a white shirt with some print on it and brown jeans that had seen better days, he was escorted to my table and we just stared at each other. I stood up and hugged him and it seemed like he didn't want to stop.

At first he was timid, but after ordering lunch he began to tell me the story of his life. As a youth his dad beat him every time he thought Norman was not acting manly enough. When he saw that a sixteen-year-old sissy was developing, he beat him one last time and told him to get out of the house for good. Penniless, Norman took whatever job he could find and was abused and used in every way imaginable. This led to booze and drugs. He even claimed that in a drunken rage while squatting in an old abandoned building he'd tossed a longtime lover out the third-story window and might have killed him, but he didn't stick around to find out. He finally made his way to California and was now living on public assistance. He was the only person I've ever met who had no joy in life. He had kept in touch with his sister, my aunt, but she couldn't deal with his needs and issues.

As we finished lunch, I invited him to the auditorium where in true Hollywood fashion I was to be sworn in by the actress Lynn Redgrave as president of the National Gay Press Association. Why Lynn Redgrave? To this day I have no idea. Norman said he wasn't dressed well enough to attend, but I insisted. After Lynn Redgrave swore me in, I said a few words about our industry, then, looking at Norman in the back, I added, "I have a special guest here with me today, a member of my family who at the age of sixteen had to leave his home because he was gay. Like other gay youth he learned to survive in a cruel world. Please welcome my cousin Norman."

The audience started to applaud, and then rose to their feet. Norman didn't know how to react. It was, most likely, the first time in his life that a group of LGBT people had given him sympathy for what he had been through. He stood nervously and took a bow, and just started to cry. When the audience sat down Norman rose, blew me a kiss from the back of the auditorium, and left.

He called a few times after that, always in need of funds. Then one day the calls stopped, and there has been no trace of him since.

At the 1984 convention, we were looking for ways to get news and information to our readers faster. This was at a time when there was no Internet, and the wire services, Associated Press and United Press International, didn't carry many LGBT stories. Even if they had, most of us could not afford the monthly fee for their services. Out of necessity we created the first wire news service for the LGBT community; we simply agreed to exchange news stories between us. The reality was that given the limited functionality of the computers of the day, it really didn't work so well.

Like other publishing organizations, we also shared strategies on building circulation and advertising. Our news coalition began to create a list of freelance writers and stringers. Early members included Phil Nash of Denver's *Out Front*, Joe DiSabato, founder of Rivendell Marketing, Morgan Pinney, Pat Burke of *Update* in San Diego, Sally Tyre of *PGN*, Chuck Renslow of Chicago's *GayLife*, Bob Swinden of *Cruise Atlanta*, Richard Rogers of *This Week in Texas*, Mike Rutherford of *Out* magazine, Don Michaels of the *Washington Blade*, Bob Ross of San Francisco's *Bay Area Reporter*, and our vice president Henry McClure from Texas, among others. Like most media and journalism organizations, it was overwhelmingly white and male.

Our first resolution was to request that the National Gay Task Force stop attempting to interfere with the operations of gay media by its "request to editors." A stronger condemnation of the codirectors of NGTF was tabled, but this resolution made it clear to activist organizations that we were independent and that any attempt to control our news coverage would be dealt with, and transparently.

The most serious member of the group in those early days was Don Michaels, publisher of the *Washington Blade*. Don always stressed a good business plan and was often heard lending the advice, "Pay your taxes." Thinking back, it's amazing how important that statement was and still is. Many a publication went out of business because they didn't pay their taxes. Don was echoed by Robert Moore of the *Dallas Voice*, who hosted the next convention, where we shared a hotel with a Bible group and the National Rifle Association. (Our treat on one very hot, humid Texas evening was Robert taking us Eastern city boys to a bar to learn how to line dance.)

Don's early advice was welcomed at the *Philadelphia Gay News*. Understanding the playing field and the absolute necessity of learning good business skills to keep the doors of the paper open were paramount. This began my quest to join every professional journalism organization I could. They knew how to make newspapers work and we needed that information. But like the many LGBT lawyers and doctors who tried to join their industry's associations, *Philadelphia Gay News* was similarly rebuffed for years.

New publications continued to sprout from LGBT organizations, and were operated by volunteers. I was determined that *Philadelphia Gay News* would no longer rely on volunteers; everyone was paid something. In addition to being fair, this was also a form of control. We bought used vending boxes from the daily newspapers and charged fifty cents an issue, which we later raised to seventy-five cents. As I've said, many of those quarters were taken to restaurants for meals, as well as to the lumber store to buy wood to create a ceiling in our office. Some nights I would even buy my dinner with them. We also learned to pay a decent commission to advertising representatives, our bread and butter as we learned the canons of journalism.

After nine months, Jim decided he'd had enough. Running three newspapers was more work than he'd expected and he had been in the business his entire life. Plus, I was moving way too fast for him. He somehow believed that I'd make it all work so we made an agreement, and with nine months of experience under my belt I became the sole publisher of a newspaper chain that included *Philadelphia Gay News*, *Pittsburgh Gay News*, *Ohio East Gay News*, and eventually *Atlanta Gay News*.

My relationship with Phillip had been over for some time now. My friends set me up on blind dates since most of them felt I was not doing anything to improve my own home life; in other words, they thought I needed a partner. One of those men had what I thought was a great sense of humor. We went out once, and while it was fun, I didn't see it as a lasting relationship. He kept calling until I finally went on a second date with him. I still wasn't convinced so he kept calling and calling, which led to a third date. Finally, I asked him what he saw in me and he replied, "Your potential to make money and thereby make me happy." We both laughed, and that was the start of a twenty-year relationship.

One afternoon, in complete disgust over the Catholic Church's history of fighting against our issues, I wrote a column called "Shut Up, Pope," which was prompted by Pope Benedict's speaking out against condoms in Africa where the AIDS epidemic was out of control. For that piece alone, I won several awards. Writing what you're passionate about helps generate discussion. You can't be afraid of debate; just make sure to debate with respect.

There's a question that pops up in almost every interview I give. It goes something like this: "What is the state of the LGBT press?" Or, "Is the LGBT press having the same issues that mainstream media is dealing with?" And some even ask if LGBT media is dying. From my vantage, sitting on the boards of several mainstream media organizations, it became apparent along the way that many news outlets were spending barrels of money on their new web ventures without an understanding of where the Internet was headed. Thus far, most traditional media haven't seen a payday and, worse, have needed to cut back on their print editions to pay for their web expenses. It's not a good move to lose seasoned journalists to pay for your web expansion. Your journalists are bringing you the product that you sell, and the good ones are the reason people buy it. You don't just sell information; you sell accurate and well-told information, which, for the most part, only seasoned journalists can give you.

Local LGBT publications serve themselves and their communities by sticking with the stories of their individual communities, and owning those stories. For us, national marriage-equality stories take a backseat to local news that we own, meaning you won't find it anywhere else. Newspapers have to be alive with opinions and information unique to the community they serve, both geographic and cultural. They cannot just be the same thing you find elsewhere else. Local LGBT publications have to be the first place your community looks for details.

The Internet has something that print doesn't: an instantaneous forum to publish and gather opinion. It satisfies those who need instant gratification and can be extremely inexpensive to run. That last advantage is problematic for the print medium, since it allows for more and more websites and blogs to come online and create competition for those already serving the community. It is also a vehicle for misinformation, and thus needs to be watched carefully.

New media is something that needs to be embraced. In 1997 my friend Andy Cramer was in search of people who would assist in his dream of a gay online site. It was Gay.com and I was one of its first nine investors/founders.

I still believe that print is light years ahead of the web. In almost every major city, there's a local LGBT newspaper with numerous full-time staffers and they are excelling at fusing print and the web. There are few, if any, local blogs or websites with full-time employees. Nationally, it's a different story. *Out* magazine and the *Advocate* have both traditional and new media outlets. They are the top websites as far as hits and clicks go, but their print editions are hurting. *Queerty* and *Towleroad* have also become popular sites and have full-time staff. Aside from those, you might have a few out there with one or two staffers. Here's the big problem for websites and blogs: it takes very little capital to start one, but all the new sites are competing for the same audience and advertising dollars.

Publications like ours have had to count on our local advertising for a long time. Relatively recently we've seen national ads in local LGBT publications because many companies want to be on the right side of history. As President Barack Obama has stated, LGBT rights are the civil rights of this generation. In some sense, the ads from Ford, GM, McDonald's, Taco Bell, and other mainstream corporations make a statement about how far we have come. Or is it how far those corporations have come?

At the 2013 annual National Lesbian and Gay Journalists Association (NLGJA) convention in Boston, it amazed me to hear most print journalists there bemoaning the condition of LGBT media. I was honored to be there to get inducted into the NLGJA Hall of Fame. In my speech, I was originally planning to simply thank the NLGJA and get off the stage, but this feeling of impending doom for LGBT media led me, at the last minute, to change my address.

To offer an air of optimism, I explained that *Philadelphia Gay News*, which is now the nation's most awarded LGBT publication, owns its own building and equipment. All of our bills and taxes are paid to date and we employ a full-time staff of thirteen with full benefits. That is success in print media. Then the most important part—how did we become so strong and how do we stay that way? It's a simple formula, at least to me. One must have a strong business department that embraces the need to hire award-winning journalists. Period. It is imperative to put out not only an LGBT newspaper, but a high-quality mainstream newspaper. The key is hard opinion pieces, unbiased news coverage, and investigative reporting. Here I recalled the Nizah Morris case, which at that time prompted a new report by the Philadelphia Police Advisory Commission and caused rule changes at the Philadelphia Police Department. No other paper that I know of would put the resources into such a story for so long, but it paid dividends in the end.

In the early days of AIDS we began to hear about insurance companies dropping men they discovered to be gay or otherwise refusing to insure gay men. We had a reporter call every major insurance company nationwide. This was at a time when there was no Internet and long-distance calls were expensive. The bill for those calls alone was nine hundred dollars. But it was a story that we owned. Few other publications were producing that kind of in-depth material.

Hard news and features keep you relevant. We were out front on the Boy Scouts issue, reporting on the city of Philadelphia's decade-long battle with its local chapter. We also covered the dangers of pumping parties, attended by poor trans people to get the hormones they can't afford from traditional medical resources. These innovative and relevant stories pushed boundaries and appeared nowhere else . . .

At the *PGN*, we expected controversy, but it managed to find us even when we weren't looking. We conducted a public service campaign that stemmed from a series of features on drug addiction in the LGBT community. We spoke to Nurit Shein, CEO of the Mazzoni Center, the local LGBT heath organization in Philadelphia, which in 2014 had over a hundred employees. The campaign sought to highlight the issue of addiction—how it destroys lives and how to seek help. Many in the LGBT community do not feel comfortable in mainstream drug treatment programs, since they are often judged on their sexual orientation rather than their drug use. We never expected a deluge of letters and calls asking, "Why would *Philadelphia Gay News* show our community in such a bad way?"

Nurit and the *PGN* staff felt the campaign was worth the outrage and continued forth; I suspect that the anger and debate about the campaign might have reached more people than the campaign itself. I explained to the audience at the NLGJA awards ceremony that our paper has partnerships with Philly.com (the *Philadelphia Inquirer*) and the *Philadelphia Business Journal*, the first such partnerships in the nation. We also work with the Philadelphia Multicultural Media Network, which has helped more than twenty newspapers, and allowed us to work with a wide range of publications, making Philly a vibrant, diversified newspaper city. There was much more that I could have added, but my time was limited. My desire was to bring new ideas and optimism, and I believe I succeeded.

The reality is that *Philadelphia Gay News* has been on a winning streak for the last decade; in 2008 something very special happened, which made this really sink in. The paper was informed by the Suburban Newspapers of America that journalistically we were one of the top ten weekly newspapers in the nation. Not one of the top ten LGBT weeklies, but top ten of *all* weeklies. Our then-editor Sarah Blazucki basked in the spotlight, as she should have. Sarah, now working for the Peace Corps in Washington, DC, came to her position at *Philadelphia Gay News* after starting as a reporter.

Our staff has gone on to garner more individual awards than could possibly be listed here, but the overwhelming majority of them are from mainstream journalism organizations. As mentioned, our strength is built on our reporting and our appreciation of our community's needs. You can see this same dynamic in the other successful LGBT publications across the nation.

The *Washington Blade*, due to its proximity to the capital, breaks more national news than any other LGBT publication, and their local coverage of the marriage-equality movement should be studied in journalism schools. Chicago's *Windy City Times* and its publisher Tracy Baim pulled out of their files a questionnaire that a state senator by the name of Barack Obama had signed, stating that he supported marriage equality; they did this while he was president and publicly still evolving on the subject. That is the power of local newspapers. The *Bay Area Reporter* in San Francisco, along with the now-defunct *New York Native*, showed the rest of us how to cover AIDS, and do so professionally, even with the widespread anger surrounding the issue. *Bay Windows* in Boston played an important role in what would result in the first state with marriage equality. In Michigan, *Pride Source* staged what could be called the mother of all wedding expos, made a huge profit, and ended up with an e-mail list that would be the envy of any blog, website, or print publication. Their publishers Susan Horowitz and Jan Stevenson are pillars of our LGBT legacy.

LGBT publishing is awash with new publishers and new ideas. The *Dallas Voice* and *Frontiers* in Los Angeles are pioneering the integration of print and web in what will become the new LGBT media, each with a different viewpoint and style. While they do this, they still foster hard news reporting by writers like Karen Ocamb. The *South Florida Gay News* keeps reinventing itself as all media must do in a time of change, and in Portland, Oregon, Melanie Davis, a second-generation publisher with a long history of involvement with Latino media, has created *Proud Queer* magazine. Along with Chris Cash of Atlanta's *Georgia Voice* and Lynne Brown of the *Washington Blade*, women constitute a major presence in today's LGBT media.

* * *

Like any industry, LGBT journalism has suffered low points. Our brothers and sisters who worked for a chain of LGBT newspapers owned by a company called Windows Media showed up at their offices one Monday and discovered that their publications had closed. At the time, Windows Media was the largest chain of publications for the LGBT community, and included the *Washington Blade*, Atlanta's *Southern Voice*, *David Magazine*, *411 Magazine*, and the *South Florida Blade*. In prior months, the same company also closed down *Genre* magazine and the online-only *Houston Voice*. To say this was the biggest failure in LGBT-media history is an understatement. But what does it say about LGBT media in general? The short answer: nothing.

While the media industry is going through changes, there are some basic publishing lessons that can be learned from this. In some ways, these developments make LGBT media even stronger. Those who were behind Windows Media had little idea how to market to this community and little understanding of the struggle for equality that some of us were covering on a daily basis. From the outside it appeared that journalism took a backseat to advertising. It also seemed like substantive articles played second fiddle to fashion and professional features or just plain fluff pieces. At one point, the *Washington Blade* had an escort featured as a columnist on the front page.

As a local paper your first line of advertisers should be the community itself, which should support its publication of record. Next are the gay-friendly businesses in gay neighborhoods and the non-gay businesses frequented by the LGBT community. Once those bases are covered, this should also cover your bottom line. Any national advertising is just icing. It seemed that Windows Media turned this strategy upside down.

Windows Media's failure affected the employees of their publications and the cities they served, but not local publications elsewhere in the nation. New publications would rise in each of those markets since the communities were strong and loyal. In some of the markets the Windows employees themselves set up the new publications. This all shows growth in LGBT media. The best example is the *Washington Blade*. Lynne Brown and Kevin Naff took it from the trash can that Windows had left it in, and have brought it back even better than it was before. Chris Cash has likewise revived a publication in Atlanta, the *Georgia Voice*.

Media, whether it be newspapers, TV, radio, movies, magazines, or the Internet, continuously evolves. One example pertains to young people. Due to the success of our community's efforts, LGBT youth are coming out at a younger age. Many organizations have popped up to deal with their needs but few publications have given them a voice. Jen Coletta at our paper decided to try amplifying their voices by featuring a quarterly supplement written and edited by LGBT youth. They decide on the content themselves and do almost everything to get their stories ready for publication other than the final edit and layout, which is left to the professionals in our offices. This has served various purposes. In addition to allowing their voices to be heard, it provides an opportunity to work in the publishing business. Worst-case scenario: this experience becomes past employment on their resumes.

The aging gay and lesbian community is a topic that we address as well, via a supplement for seniors. As our community ages and we begin to deal with the first out generation of seniors, there are unique issues of ageism that can be urgent.

PGN also spearheaded an alliance with other multicultural publications in our region to seek advertising that would normally go to mainstream print media. Along with several members of the African American regional media, Asian publications, the *Jewish Exponent*, and *El Día*, the leading Spanish-language publication, we've created a united force. Our value to advertisers is strong in an ever-changing and diverse landscape as together our combined circulation is near that of mainstream print media. Forty years ago, none of these publications would have wanted to be associated with a gay newspaper. Now we're one of the leaders of the coalition.

On of my fondest memories from the early days was learning how to do my first newspaper promotion. A former pro football player by the name of Dave Kopay had recently come out and had published his autobiography, *The David Kopay Story: An Extraordinary Self-Revelation*, cowritten with Perry Deane Young. He was doing a book tour and had arranged with his publisher that *Philadelphia Gay News* would host a cocktail party.

It was the first such event we'd put together so we wanted it to be a success. This meant a packed house and publicity for the paper and Kopay's book. We arranged for a venue called The Steps to let us use their space during an afternoon when it was not usually open. In exchange we gave them some free advertising. We invited LGBT leaders, business and government people, some folks from the pro sports teams in Philly (quietly), the press, of course, and our own friends and families.

The Steps had an upstairs bar with a balcony. With the entire party on the ground floor, I stepped out onto the balcony when the time was right to introduce Kopay. I welcomed all the elected officials in the audience by name, and read the introduction that the publisher had prepared for me. Then I concluded, "Ladies and gentleman, please welcome Dave Kopay!"

He took the microphone and spoke so softly that no one could hear him. He looked nervous. Later, I found out that this was one of the first times he had to address this type of crowd and it was the largest audience of his tour. Unable to hear him, the people began to mingle and we were losing control of the room. At that moment, my four-foot-seven grandmother decided to act. Standing in the middle of the audience, she put her fist in the air and shouted, "Right on, Dave!" And she repeated it, "Right on, Dave!" and then again. She kept going until everyone was shouting along with her. Grandmom, my Auntie Mame, once again saved the day.

It was an exciting, heady period. Things were humming along. We were helping invent a microprofession we termed *advocacy journalism* at a time when little was known about this. Exhausted but elated, every night I'd return home to Mom and Grandmom. I'd spend as many evenings at home as possible and I still cherished every second sitting on the couch with my family.

Chapter 7
Tits and Ass

In early 1978, Mom wasn't getting out much due to dialysis. The drugs she was taking had her staying close to home most of the time; the hospital had given her a beeper in case a donor kidney became available. And she couldn't shake the cold of the winter. Unable to get warm no matter how hot the house was or how many sweaters or blankets she had, she never complained and still attempted to cook dinner each night. Mom loved cooking for my brother and me and she certainly loved our appreciation of her time at the stove. But to be honest, she wasn't a good cook. Her beef was always well done and very dry, her tomato sauce, of which we always requested seconds, was so heavy that antacids were required quickly after the meal. (She never understood why we headed for the bathroom directly after having her spaghetti sauce.) Her meatballs, however, were a bouncy delight. They were more like matzo balls then meatballs. But ever since we were little boys, we were always told by Dad that Mom took pride in her cooking and that we should never say anything that might upset her. So we ate, and we loved it, knowing that this made her happy. What's a little indigestion among family?

The newspaper was beginning to make money at that time. To celebrate and to try to get Mom's spirits up, I decided to take my parents to a restaurant and a show. The restaurant's name

I don't recall, but the show was A *Chorus Line*. I had recently interviewed the show's author, James Kirkwood Jr., who had offered me tickets anytime I wanted, so we went to the theater and Mom was delighted just to be out and about.

During the show I couldn't keep my eyes off her. It was so important that she enjoy herself. Any misgivings I might have had vanished with her first smile, during the second number. After that, she laughed and smiled throughout the evening. Dad and I could feel it and that was magic enough for us. Despite my love of musicals and eagerness to see the show, that night I was focused only on her.

As we left the theater I asked Mom what song she liked best. She looked at me with a sheepish grin on her face, and in the tiniest of whispers she said, "Tits and Ass." She put her hand over her mouth in embarrassment. Dad almost fell over in laughter and he and I just started to howl. Even Mom joined in. For her to say "Tits and Ass" was simply earth-shattering. But as the laughter was dying down, the hospital beeper went off. Then she said it again: "Tits and Ass." This time none of us laughed.

We called her doctor and were told she had to come in right away. We hurried home, she put a few things together, and off to the hospital we went, along with Grandmom and Uncle Stan. We were told that since it was so late, the kidney transplant operation was set for the next afternoon. Mom stayed the night and we all returned the following morning. For the first time in my life I saw my mom nervous. This was the mom who went to battle for me over "Onward, Christian Soldiers," the mom who bought me a shiny red train set when we had no money, the mom who went on the *Phil Donahue Show* and walked in gay pride parades. I wasn't as strong as she was. All I could do was be present and tell her it would all work out. I know I was trying to believe that myself.

This was a dread that I had never felt before. My mother was about to go under the knife for an operation that the doctors explained was very serious, very risky, but necessary. Further complicating things was that at this time in medical history, rejection of transplanted organs was a 50/50 proposition.

Mom tried to look brave. She kept any fears in the back of her mind and remained her gentle self, trying to reassure us, as she was readied for the operating room that afternoon. We hugged her and watched as a nurse pushed her through the double doors and down a long, dark hallway leading to the operating room. Then we were all ushered into the waiting area. We sat there as the quiet hours ticked by slowly, only intermittently interrupted by a nurse or doctor who would come out with prepared statements like, "It's going as planned."

Somewhere during that long night Grandmom became silent. When any of us would ask her something she'd just nod. No one thought anything of it at the time, we were all just worrying about my mother on the operating table. Very late in the evening, or perhaps early the next day, the doctor came out and told us the operation had gone "as well as expected." When pressed, he simply stated: "Now we'll see if her body accepts or rejects the kidney." He sounded more like he was building a car engine than transplanting a kidney. It left me with a sinking feeling. He suggested that we go home since she was in isolation. There was not a word spoken on the entire ride back.

I awoke the following morning to a gloomy winter day and immediately felt something wasn't right. When I got downstairs my father called me over and said, "We think Grandmom is sick." The pressure had gotten to her, and she still wasn't talking. Uncle Stan arranged to take Grandmom to her doctor while my father and I went to the hospital. Mom remained on a ventilator and had numerous transfusions going at the same time. She was very woozy, but we wanted her to know she made it through the operation and we were there with her. She looked as if she desperately wanted to talk with us, and it frustrated her that the tube down her throat prevented her from doing so. The hospital didn't allow much time since they were afraid of germs being brought in from outsiders. So we went home to get a report on our other sick family member.

Grandmom's doctor could find nothing wrong with her and suggested that it was merely nerves and depression due to Mom's hospitalization. When things settled down with my mother, most likely Grandmom's "depression" would pass. He didn't even give her any medication. Just a pat on the back, accompanied by unhelpful reassurances.

As the days wore on and as Mom's condition improved, we were able to visit her more often and for longer hours. Every time she saw me she'd ask how the paper was doing. I appointed myself comedian-in-chief and tried as often as possible to get her to laugh. All I had to say was, "Tits and Ass." She'd put her hand to her mouth so we couldn't see that she was smiling in embarrassment.

Even though my partner and friends Randy and Jan were giving me support by getting me to the hospital, staying with me, or just talking, I continued to drift and feel alone. I'd spend the nights chatting with Grandmom. I'd talk and she'd just smile, but there was always hope that something I said would get her to speak again. I even told her about "Tits and Ass," at which she smiled a little wider, but still made no sound. The two most important women in my life were in trouble and there was nothing I could do.

Dad was a complete wreck, but he wasn't on my radar at all, nor anyone else's. Poor Dad. His whole life was my mother and nobody recognized what this was doing to him. Growing up in our house there was one indisputable fact that you knew: my parents adored each other. In a sense it's a true love story. They saved each other. Mom was from an upper-middle-class family and she had been a sickly child who was not, as we discovered later, expected to live into adulthood. Grandmom took her out of school in the tenth grade so that she could help with the family's grocery store. But this proved to be counterproductive; since she was already not expected to amount to much, being taken out of school only deepened her feelings of failure. When she survived and married she was advised against having children.

Dad grew up in a home where his father had abandoned his mother, which was rare in a Jewish family of those days. My other grandmother couldn't afford to feed her kids so Dad was put into a Jewish home for children, sort of like an orphanage. He stayed there until the Second World War, when he enlisted in the Army and became a tail gunner over the Pacific. When he came home from the war, his dreams of going to college slammed head-on into reality. He needed to help feed his mother and siblings. So he put his own interests aside, only occasionally having a night to himself. During one of those Saturday nights, at a dance, he met Mom. According to both of them, it was love at first sight. Dad made Mom feel like she had a future and could have that family she so wanted, and Dad married up and into a loving, stable family. We might have been poor in my early days, but emotionally we were very rich. My parents set my ideal of a successful marriage. Neither of them began to truly live until they met each other; Mom was Dad's life and vice versa.

Their wedding picture tells it all. Dad looks dapper and Mom is a beautiful bride in a long, flowing gown. The smiles on their faces are incredible. They carried that unconditional love to their children; seeing it between them impacted me in ways I didn't even recognize until many decades later. As it stood, if ever that unconditional love was put to the test, it was by me. Even as a child, my independence was evident. At nine years old I hopped a train to New York to see my first Broadway show and called my mother from Manhattan to express how thrilled I was with myself, unaware that I'd given her the fright of her life. When I did it again at age thirteen, she was no longer surprised. This time she asked what show I saw, and I replied, "*UTBU* with Tony Randall." From her voice I could tell she was happy for me, and somehow I instinctively knew that my happiness more than anything was what she wanted from life. If her son wanted adventure, she'd be happy when he had adventure.

Other kids ran away from home; I went on trips. For me it felt like I had broken away from the projects for the day. Times Square in all its awe was no match for my excitement. Passersby on the streets were in such a rush they hardly paid attention to me, a nine-year-old kid strolling by himself. In that big city, this little boy could be just like anybody else, not the poor Jewish kid from the projects. I can still recall going to the stage door and asking to meet Tony Randall. He actually came to the door in a white bathrobe and asked how I picked his show, and I replied, "It was the only one which had a name I knew." He smiled and patted me on the head. I felt special; I'd met a movie star. If ever I thought I was different, this moment solidified it for me. I was different from my schoolmates and relatives, not because I met a movie star, but because I was there, taking a trip on my own. It was the moment I knew that one day I'd create my own destiny. I had no idea what that would be, but on that day I began thinking about my future.

My parents of course knew that I was a slightly different breed of child. One night, my father decided to punish me for something bad I'd done, and told me to go upstairs and miss my favorite TV show, something about a big-top circus. I hesitated and Dad gave me a wallop on the ass. I screamed and yelled as he again suggested I head upstairs. I kept the crying act up as I climbed the steps in dramatic pain. Dad wasn't going to get the best of seven-year-old me. At the top of the stairs and just out of sight I let out another yell for good measure. Then, as if in a trance, I found myself in my parents' room and saw the makeup on my mother's dresser. Soon I was like a chemist pouring one liquid into another until I found the perfect blend and color. I took off my trousers and my underwear and started to apply the liquid to the underwear. It was a nice deep red, and resembled blood. I quietly went to the stairs and laid them out with the fake blood showing. Then I started to howl. My father came running to scold me, but upon seeing the underwear he thought he had actually hurt me and rushed to my bedside. I just looked at him, and slowly started to smile. At first he didn't know what to say, then finally called out, "Shirley, you won't believe what Mark did." And he was laughing. We were a very forgiving family.

Once, Mom was working to make ends meet in a local department store. She was the manager of the pet department which gave us an excuse for having every kind of pet, from goldfish to piranha, from dog and cat to snake. (Ours got lost in the closet one day and wound up in the coat pocket of the housing project manager. We never figured out if this is why our rent was raised.) We had an alligator named Moishe that Grandmom brought back on a leash from Miami, the fruits of her annual winter pilgrimage. She took to walking the alligator until it died of fright from the bark of our German shepherd.

One day when my brother was working on some chemistry experiments, he let our parrot out of its cage to fly around the room. It had been imprisoned too long, he said. My brother was boiling his specimen and the bird decided to land on his shoulder, but somehow miscalculated and flew directly over the

Bunsen burner. His wings caught fire. My mother, who was pre-paring to go out that evening with my father to a cousins club function, was lavishly dressed, awaiting my father's return from work, when she heard a yell from my brother, something about fire. It seems the parrot with its burning wings landed on the curtains; they caught fire, which then spread to the bed. My mother, seeing the problem the minute she entered the room as only a mother can, shouted, "Everything stay exactly where it is!" I was scared and I know that my brother was scared, maybe even the bird was scared, but that fire didn't give a damn. Mom, thinking fast, opened the window and threw the curtains and bedspread out. Then, once all was quiet, she noticed herself in the mirror. Her dress was full of ash, her hair was fried, her makeup smeared. She was not going to the cousins club that night. Seeing the look on her face, somehow I wished she had tossed *us* out that window. Her only response, with a half-smile on her face, was, "At least I'll get to spend the night with my favorite people in the world." That was Mom. She didn't even scold us, not one word about the fire.

My brother and I never truly bonded. We never had what might be called a brotherly relationship. To me it seemed he resented me from the time my parents brought me home from the hospital. We seldom talked. Once, in anger at something he had done that I've since long forgotten, I stormed over to my parents and said, "I'll never forgive you for giving me him as a brother." Even though he was three years older than me, I always felt more mature. I was the one taking care of things, especially our parents. But I do recall, at the hospital following my mother's kidney operation, him trying to comfort our father.

While she was still in isolation, Mom's numbers began to go south. And then we were told that septicemia had entered her bloodstream. The doctors used lines like, "We're trying to do everything we can." And finally one night while we all sat in the waiting room taking our turns to visit with Mom, one of the younger doctors whom I had become friendly with called me over and told me the truth: "It doesn't look good." It was left to me to tell Dad. I suggested that he and everyone else go home and I'd stay the night.

There was no one but me in the waiting room this time. My partner and my friends Jen and Randy all wanted to stay with me but I asked them not to. For whatever reason, I had to be there alone, and when I think of it now I believe that I didn't want anyone to see me so vulnerable. I spent that night in the tiny waiting room pacing back and forth. Every so often the doctor would come out and say nothing, just stand there. And what could he say? He was just trying to comfort me; it was one of his first cases, and he took it personally. When he'd leave I'd curl myself into a ball on the floor and cry with a sick feeling in the pit of my stomach. I felt as though I was the loneliest person in the world. In an uncharacteristic move, I had a personal chat with God. It was a one-sided conversation.

At about six a.m. the doctor came out and said, "You might want to talk to your mother." By the sound of his voice I knew he meant a final conversation. As I went into her room, all I saw were her arms flailing around in pain. It was the most frightening sight I've ever witnessed. The doctors were holding her down, trying to stop her from hurting herself. There was no conversation possible. It was a scene out of hell.

Going back to that tiny waiting room, I sat on the floor and wondered why there was nothing I could do to solve this. Then the doctor suggested that I call my father. At that point I turned into a machine, no longer human, no longer feeling, just doing whatever had to be done, whatever was asked of me. Dad arrived just in time. Fifteen minutes later Mom passed away, and when she did, Dad screamed and cried in pain and kept saying, "Let me die, please take me." Then he fainted on the spot. They needed a wheelchair for him.

A nurse gave him a Valium. He was so out of it that he just popped it into his mouth without question. Another nurse came over to check his blood pressure and gave him another Valium, and then the doctor who was attending my mom saw him and gave him another. We wheeled Dad to the car and he slept until the following day, which was a blessing. It was February 27, 1978. I was twenty-seven years old.

The next day, with Dad out of it and me still in machine mode, I made the funeral arrangements. My brother just agreed to whatever plans we worked out or were suggested by the undertaker. Word had gotten out that my mom had died and the *Daily News* wanted to run an obituary. It was from that obituary that I learned about what my parents had been through with some of my relatives. In the obituary I'm quoted as saying, "My mom was a gay activist." On the day of the funeral, my Uncle Ralph asked me if I had really said that, and I said of course. He said, "Then maybe it's good she's gone." Can you ever forgive someone for saying something like that? I couldn't.

There is only one part of the funeral itself that I clearly recall. It was the part where they ask the family to review the deceased. All I can remember is Grandmom looking at Mom. She was smiling and I wondered if she understood what was happening. We were ushered into a side room as the lid of the coffin was closed. My mind and body remained on autopilot, doing whatever needed to be done.

My father remained a wreck for some time, so I began to make household decisions to keep things moving as best as possible. My mother and father's best friends were Dot and Gouch who lived up the street. Most nights, Mom and Dad would go up to their house and either play cards or just sit around and talk. Now, every night they came down to sit with my Dad, to sit with their Marty. They were his best medicine. And they were funny. Dot spoke like a truck driver, and I could see why the couples were friends. Like my parents, Dot and Gouch adored each other. It might have taken months, but they nursed Dad back to living.

As for me, it might seem strange but my feelings were mostly guilt. Was there more that could have been done? Why did I not have more knowledge on the subject and should I have asked the doctors more questions? There was no WebMD then, and at that time patients relied, for the most part, on whatever the doctor said. It would take an epidemic less than five years later to explain to me the value of patient involvement and self-advocacy for one's own treatment.

My tears only came when I was alone, and they were slight and silent. I wanted to have a big cry, to break down completely, but somehow it did not happen. To me, this was private. For weeks I was in a zombie state, going through the motions and moving forward but without feelings. A friend finally thought it might be good to get me out of the city and took me to Key West. One night while walking on the beach alone and looking up at the stars, I sunk to the sand and cried. I don't remember how long I cried but I do remember thinking, *Let me get it all out now*. I can tell you that even after more than thirty years, you can never get it all out. What you can hope for is that the pain transitions into the fondness of memories and the good that a person brought into your life. My mother's gift to me, the gift of love and support, was immeasurable.

The pages of *Philadelphia Gay News* did not see my byline again for several months, but the editorial responsibilities were in the good hands of Jack Veasey. Jack was a talented writer with a sharp wit. My favorite line from him was when he was doing a review of a cabaret singer whose voice he just could not tolerate. In describing this Jack wrote, "His voice was so flat that you could land a 747 on it without spilling one cocktail."

In April I finally wrote an editorial. It was titled "Up with Parents":

The old adage that says you don't appreciate something until it's gone is never more true than it is with gays and their relationships with their parents. In most ethnic and minority communities, children who are feeling depressed or somewhat different from other segments of society could always look to their parents for needed support in dealing with their problems. Unfortunately, gays do not, for the most part, go to their parents for support. In fact, many shudder at the thought of outing themselves and asking for help seems insurmountable.

Parents can help ease the suffering of guilt, anxiety, and pressure that many of us go through, but most of all, they can normalize a life torn between different worlds. In a time when we feel so unloved, the attentive love of parents can bring us home to reality and ease the hurts that we all come across on the path of life.

We are not all able to express to our parents the realities of our lives; some might not understand, others might misunderstand. In some cases we are not strong enough to burden them with something that may take them the rest of our lives to digest.

This is a very personal editorial because its meaning brings home the memory of my mother, who recently passed away. She not only knew and accepted me as I am, but became an important part of my work. I have no doubt that were it not for my parents, I could not have achieved what I have thus far.

I remember the first time I tried to tell my mother that I was gay. I called her on the phone, dropped the line very shakily, and listened for her reply. She asked, "What are you going to do when you're old, who do you have to keep you company?" I answered, "I would have my friends and family, and you." I was wrong, but the short period I did have my mother proved to be the most productive and rewarding time in my life. She not only accepted and supported my work but she was proud of that work, so much so that she wanted to be a part of it.

My mother's enthusiasm kept me going when times were difficult, and at times she seemed to be more liberated than I. When her cousin was planning a wedding, my mother was outraged when an invitation was not extended to my lover and balked at attending until my father persuaded her otherwise. She's spoken at gay pride rallies even though illness should have kept her indoors, and when speaking on the Phil Donahue Show, she said in reference to my lover Phillip, "He is also my son." She'd planned to reorganize a local "Parents of Gays" group to aid parents in understanding and accepting their gay children, but illness kept her from completing that goal.

I know that the warmth, love, and encouragement that I received from my mother have resulted in numerous successes, and the existence of this newspaper is one direct result.

I still have my father, who I know will continue to be supportive and loving as he has always been. I am particularly grateful for that when I realize that even only one supportive open parent is more than many gays will ever have.

I'd like to encourage readers, who haven't already, to seriously consider sharing your gayness with your parents. You may be underestimating the power of their love. Closeness with the moral support from parents can be an invaluable source of strength to cope with the day-to-day oppression we all have to face.

Chapter 8

Post-Traumatic Stress Syndrome

There's more to a problem than just finding a solution. There's the creativity used to find that solution. Like most boys of my age in 1969, which happened to be during the height of the Vietnam War, the single biggest personal concern was being drafted into the US military and ending up in that hell. Like all eighteen-year-olds, I was required to register for the draft. Then I awaited the dreaded call to go in, to be questioned, and to be examined, hoping that my birth date was low on the list and I'd escape the draft. Many of us looked for ways out. It would have been simple just to say I was gay and I'd be immediately denied entry and receive what they called a 4-F. The problem would be that a 4-F remained on your record permanently and could affect future employment. So most gay men never used that option. The closet was safer.

I had read somewhere that anything you sent to your draft board was required by law to be kept on file, in a permanent capsule of sorts. Given that, it seemed to me that they would try to figure out what was of interest to an individual, and therefore know whether or not they were a suitable candidate for the draft. Each Sunday, I religiously bought my *New York Times*, and every Monday, after faithfully reading it, I'd package it up and send it to my draft board. I wonder if there is a file somewhere out there with my name on it with over a year and a half worth of the Sunday *New York Times* taking up valuable governmental office space.

The point being that if they called me in, the reviewer would have had to sign a paper saying that he or she had read my complete file. Most likely, unless they had hours and hours to spend sifting through newspapers, they would not have. I'm not sure if that was the actual reason, but I never did get a call from the draft board.

If there ever was a time for creativity in the gay community, it was when we were fighting for our lives in a different deadly war. This war started with one word: AIDS. To put it simply, AIDS in the US affected and defined the LGBT community more than any other issue in our history. Everything from coming out, politics, organizing, to how we dealt with each other changed due to AIDS. To this very day, its impact on the LGBT community has not been fully and honestly dealt with. For many, the anger still seethes of being witness to a government that callously ignored our very existence. For others, the residual effects are pervasive grief, crippling fear, personal, emotional, or physical trauma, and the experience of what is commonly known as survivor's guilt. Even in these days of drug cocktails and preventative care, there are always new controversies that arise around the AIDS crisis. When it first started, every single aspect of the disease was a raging battle. In many ways, it still is.

We seem to still be afraid of saying the obvious: AIDS was a virulent war that an entire generation of gay men got drafted into, whether we wanted to serve or not. It's not enough to say that it was on par with serving in Vietnam, Iraq, or Afghanistan. Vietnam cost 58,000 American lives; AIDS, so far, has cost more than ten times as many. Does the US government owe restitution for ignoring the safety of millions of gay Americans? They provided it to people with hemophilia, who contracted HIV from tainted blood products. They gave it to Japanese Americans who were imprisoned during World War II. We weren't imprisoned; we were just left to die. After all, it was merely the gay disease—the gay cancer, as they first labeled it. What harm could it possibly do to them as non-gays?

Something should become very clear, no matter who you are. Whether a member of the LGBT community, a government bureaucrat, a health professional, or just someone attempting to understand our community, we should still be afraid of AIDS. It seems that most people don't even want to know the statistics of the heavy toll, nor do we want to deal with the trauma of those left behind. We pretend that it's over. It's not.

A couple of years ago at the Walter & Elise Haas Fund's annual LGBT media conference, organized by Bilerico Project's leadership, Bil Browning and Matt Foreman (formerly of the National Gay and Lesbian Task Force), one of the attendees, Mark S. King, asked if the LGBT media had dropped the ball on the coverage of HIV/AIDS. This spurred an incredible e-mail dialogue where many of the journalists pointed out areas where LGBT media might be lacking. As one of the longest-serving members of the LGBT media, my answer to that question was and still is yes, there are areas where we are deficient. I'd suggest that the question might be asked in a different way, but the answer, no matter how it is framed, is still yes.

From 1955 through 1975, the US was involved in a war in Vietnam. During that time 58,220 American service members were killed. If we add the Gulf War, the second "Desert Storm," and our subsequent involvement in Iraq, where 7,000 service members were killed, we find that America lost approximately 65,000 lives to these wars.

In 1982, as reported by the Centers for Disease Control, AIDS became an official disease in the US. Since then, over

600,000 people have died of AIDS here. So you may ask, what's the connection? Survivors. Many of those who went to any one of the aforementioned wars, or endured other US military involvements, have suffered what is called post-traumatic stress syndrome (PTSS). Post-traumatic stress syndrome came from the stress of being in a war and witnessing fellow soldiers get badly injured and die. Would those who witnessed their friends die from AIDS also suffer post-traumatic stress syndrome? I think so. That said, there are many external differences between the two groups of people. While the surviving soldiers of war were considered heroes (with the exception of Vietnam vets who were often mistreated), AIDS patients were treated as trash. Those who died were sometimes refused embalming, funerals, and burial. Some were actually put in the trash heap outside of hospitals. Those of us who fought for dignity in death were forced to take on the government, the health care system, and, in some cases, our very own community. It was a war and it was hell for the victims and survivors. Anybody who lived in that period has their own stories of survival, and they are as terrifying as any of the wars mentioned above. Have we in the LGBT community tried to ignore what we went through? The answer is yes. How often do you hear someone of my generation talking about it?

One treatment for post-traumatic stress syndrome is coming to terms with it by repeated discussion. We in our community shy away from this discussion, and the health care resources that could have helped us deal with it were never given to us. Today, when we try to talk about HIV/AIDS with our youth, they are often uninterested and don't want to hear about a time when sex was dangerous. After all, youth is a time for sexual experimentation, and with the advances of HIV medications and treatments, it can seem like a moot discussion. Conversations around the topic are sometimes labeled old and we are told that we shouldn't deny the young their freedom.

We lost scores of friends. Our people were refused treatment. We had to beg to get our friends buried with any level of dignity. Families of those who died from AIDS were forced to feel ashamed, and many times the funerals were held in secret and the death certificates were fraudulent. Causes of death were listed as cancer, heart failure, pneumonia, or anything else but AIDS. Those of us who survived and were up close and personal with the disease now have what is traditionally called survivor's guilt.

There is not a gay man alive today who went through that time period and, at one time or another, did not think he was going to be infected. Just a bruise would make you believe you had AIDS and were going to die. While taking a shower on a trip to Israel, I noticed two bruises, one on each arm. For three sleepless nights and days I was consumed with fear until I got back home. The reality was that the bruises were from the way I was carrying my hand luggage, yet the anxiety from worrying about my health status was real.

Did people actually want us to die? Was that a solution to societal issues with gay people? During the height of the plague we had just begun to find sexual freedom. Once we knew that the disease was transmitted through sex and through sharing needles, some believed that the government would use AIDS as a way to recriminalize sodomy or any form of gay sex. Joe DiSabato, who represented many of the newspapers in the LGBT community to national advertisers, went to the largest maker of condoms and asked them to advertise in LGBT media. They refused, saying that the content in our publications was too sexual. More sexual than condoms? They didn't want the world to think of their condoms on gay dicks. Perhaps they thought straight dicks wouldn't buy them. We were too dirty, we were trash, and our lives were not to be saved, at least not by condoms. To be fair, they'd sell them to us for a cheap price, but publicly they wanted no connection to gay men.

AIDS to Americans was a gay disease, and to many uneducated people it was a disease carried by *all* gay men. Gay equaled AIDS, AIDS equaled gay. In California, there was a discussion about a referendum on whether to set up containment camps. Proposition 64, a California referendum that would have required mandatory reporting of AIDS to the Department of Health Services, actually made it to the ballot (and was ahead in the polls at one point). Torie Osborn, Bruce Decker, and David Mixner ran the campaign to defeat it. People like Reverend Pat Robertson and Jerry Falwell took to their pulpit and declared that this disease was a punishment from God. It still haunts me that on a television talk show that I did on AIDS, the union stagehands refused to attach the microphone to me. They left it aside and explained how to do it myself. They did not want to touch a gay man.

According to the government, whose primary job is the security of its citizens, we weren't people. During the early years of the Reagan administration, the government spent more funds on protecting livestock, fish, and poultry than they spent on AIDS. Even the surgeon general at the time, C. Everett Koop, later expressed sadness that during his first four years he was not allowed to touch the subject. Finally, when he issued the first detailed report on the study of AIDS, his attempts at spreading the word were seen by some as an effort to victimize gay men and brand us as outcasts.

Sean Strub's book *Body Counts: A Memoir of Politics, Sex, AIDS, and Survival* has a good description of the community's actions during this time. His perspective as a survivor is invaluable to anyone studying the subject. At a speaking engagement with him in 2014, he impressed me with his incredible scope of knowledge, and unlike other survivors he tries to be diplomatic and create needed discussion. Another top-notch depiction of that era can be found in Larry Kramer's play *The Normal Heart*, which shows the utter conflict within the community over this issue. In addition to being one of the founders of Gay Men's Health Crisis (GMHC), he also established the AIDS Coalition to Unleash Power (ACT UP) in 1987. In my view this was his finest achievement. ACT UP went back to the roots of Gay Liberation Front, and even zaps. It used street-theater tactics to get the public's attention, and succeeded far beyond anyone's expectations. ACT UP was Political Theater 101, and Larry is certainly theatrical.

According to David France, the award-winning filmmaker of *How to Survive a Plague*, the New York City government spent a paltry $24,500 on AIDS by 1984, even after the city had created the Office of Gay and Lesbian Health Concerns. A *New York Times* article of August 27, 1989 reported: "Mayor [Koch] says he is meeting the challenge. 'We do more on AIDS than any other city or state in America . . .'"

There are two main speculations about the Koch administration's lack of attention to the AIDS crisis. The first is that he was a closeted gay man and the second is that some communities affected by AIDS rallied hard for it not to be publicized, specifically the black community, where homophobia in some segments of the church was rampant. In the case of the latter, I believe the LGBT community did not work closely enough with the black community, which could have provided greater lobbying and thereby galvanized more support from the city. The effort to combat this public health catastrophe required public, private, and government intervention.

While in New York the funding for AIDS was limited, in other cities the funding grew and information flowed. This is all somewhat amazing when you realize that in the private sector, New York was actually a leader. GMHC was at the forefront of showing the nation how to serve the needs of patients with AIDS, and certainly how to fundraise. American Foundation for AIDS Research (amfAR), the first major organization to fund AIDS research, was also based in New York.

But compare New York's public officials with those in a city like Philadelphia and the differences are striking. Around the same time in the eighties, Philadelphia's first African American mayor, W. Wilson Goode, announced that he was not only creating the AIDS Action Coordinating Office, but he was also doubling the AIDS budget. The city did not have the same resistance from the African American population, possibly because the mayor provided better leadership and faced the issue as a human crisis.

The media in Philadelphia also came out in support of a stronger response to the epidemic. Unlike New York, where such enlightened publications as the *New York Times* downplayed AIDS until much later, Philadelphia stood with the community. While mainstream media might have been light on coverage, it was during this time that LGBT media all across the country stepped up to the plate and found their collective voice. It was to the LGBT media that the community looked to find information about new research and proper organizing. Out of necessity, some of the LGBT publications published only AIDS news and information. Needle exchanges, safer sex practices, condom distribution, and buyers clubs were broadly written about.

On June 26, 1987, Mayor Goode, along with media heads, public health officials, and AIDS activists, held a morning press conference to declare AIDS Awareness Day in Philadelphia. If you lived anywhere near the city it was literally impossible to ignore the messages. The primary purpose of the conference was to give people the information they needed and allow them the opportunity to apply that information to their own lives.

For AIDS Awareness Day, the two daily newspapers, the *Inquirer* and the *Daily News*, along with the *Philadelphia Tribune*, America's oldest African American community newspaper, and *Philadelphia Gay News*, all ran the complete multipage supplement of the surgeon general's report on AIDS. If you read a newspaper in the city, you saw the supplement in print. The community also partnered with local television stations. All three network affiliates and some independents started out every newscast of the day with the story, and they also made it a featured subject on their talk shows. Even Oprah's schedule was changed in Philly that day. We lined up experts from the various AIDS organizations to be guests on radio shows throughout the day. The copy for ads was provided by a committee of the AIDS organizations headed by Jane Shull, cochair of the day. What I am most proud of is that all of this was done without a single dollar changing hands. Not one TV station, radio station, or newspaper asked for a dime. The print publications all donated the space and wrote news copy. The *Inquirer* printed an additional twenty thousand copies of the official AIDS report, which AIDS organizations in the city handed out on the streets.

Thanks to the efforts of the various HIV/AIDS organizations and the political clout of the LGBT community, we were able to keep the issue front and center in Philly up to the 1991 mayoral election. During that election cycle, an HIV/AIDS forum was held in which all the candidates had to present their views on treatment and city services.

One of the candidates running in the Democratic primary was my old friend, former District Attorney Ed Rendell. He and his campaign manager, David L. Cohen, decided that they needed to brush up on the issues before the forum. They came to my office to meet with various AIDS experts. What surprised me most was their ability to quickly memorize the treatments, drugs, and afflictions of HIV.

It was the first time that I got to experience up close the brilliance of David L. Cohen. He was someone who could not only strategize and organize, but he also showed genuine empathy for the people he was dealing with. He and I struck up a friendship almost immediately. David later went on to do great things at Comcast NBCUniversal, specifically around diversity inclusion, and became one of America's top corporate leaders.

When Ed became mayor and David took on the role of chief of staff, David mentioned that Ed was not on good terms with one of the state's leading Democrats, State Senator Vincent Fumo. David knew that I had a decent relationship with Vince and suggested that since I had asked the mayor to come sit at my table for the first ActionAIDS Dining Out for Life fundraising event, I should invite Vince too, in the hopes that they might develop a working relationship.

Vince was chairman of the Senate Appropriations Committee, which of course dealt with the budget of the state, and from that position over the years he literally brought billions of dollars back to Philadelphia. But beyond balancing the budget, I thought the mayor was going to need state dollars to be successful in helping to combat the AIDS epidemic and of course for other programs in Philadelphia in general.

With my somewhat shameless hosting style, I got them both to agree to sit together, explaining that it was the event's head table and all the press would be there. Vince came with his wife and Ed came with one of his assistants who over the years had seemed to take on the role of jester, giving an audience to Ed's adolescent humor. At dinner, all was going well; Ed and Vince seemed to be getting along. When Ed spilled a dessert covered with powdered sugar on his black suit pants, he jokingly leaned over to his assistant and asked him if he wanted some of it. I heard Vince's voice in my ear: "I didn't know he batted for your team." At that point I had to explain to the senator that the mayor was heterosexual but felt liberated enough to make such jokes. The dinner, powdered sugar and all, was a tremendous success, and Ed, Vince, and David developed a solid relationship, allowing for continued funding and support for HIV/AIDS among other issues. The three of them became a force for great change in a growing city, and are proof of how networking and collaboration, even in the face of a crisis, can benefit all parties.

Despite the progress we were making, both medically and politically, all gay men were still suspected by some of being "carriers." If you visited a person with AIDS in the hospital, you had to prepare for something out of a science-fiction novel. The yellow and red tape was everywhere, along with ominous warning signs. You were asked to wear hospital gowns and face masks. Sometimes, hospitals emptied an entire floor for one patient, and nobody would attend to them. Some patients were lucky enough to have friends visit them; some were not. I still hesitate to ask friends about people I've lost contact with from that time, afraid I'll hear the dreaded line, "Oh, they died." Or just get a telling nod of the head.

But from the trauma, the LGBT community learned an invaluable lesson. With little assistance from the government or medical community, friends and loved ones continued to die. When we saw our friends commit suicide rather than go through the daily horrors of being sick and stigmatized, this community learned how to react, fight back, and organize. ACT UP and those who preceded them are the real heroes. In Dallas, the hero wasn't the glamorized heterosexual cowboy in *Dallas Buyers Club*, but Robert Moore, cofounder and former publisher of the *Dallas Voice*, who put a spotlight on the issue. Other heroes were the real-life doctors who put their practices on the line. Those few elected officials who found dollars in their tight budgets to house, feed, and care for people who were tossed aside by society—they are heroes. And yes, clubs allowing members' collective buying power were heroes too, but not the Matthew McConaughey movie versions.

During the height of the epidemic, I was watching TV at home one night and a show on PBS got my attention. It was called, simply, *Plague*. It explored various plagues throughout history. For me, the one takeaway from the show was that most plagues last about twenty-five years. So I began to hope that by 2005 or 2006 we'd be at the end of AIDS.

Soon after watching that show, the AIDS drama hit home in a very personal way. There had to have been some clue to the change in my partner of twenty years, that guy who always joked that he wanted me for my potential to make money, but I hadn't noticed. One night at dinner he said with a tentative smile, "There's something I have to tell you." It wasn't long before he began to cry and told me he "has it." I knew exactly what "it" was. Stunned, sitting there frozen, the seconds seemed like an eternity until it finally sank in. We embraced, and I whispered in his ear, "We'll get through this." Even with this painful disclosure hovering in my mind, I knew we were going to somehow make it through.

That night, the answers to the questions I asked were not reassuring; he said that I was the seventh person he had told. *What?* He explained he hadn't known how I'd react. That was hurtful. After twenty years, he didn't know me!

While I was attempting to stay calm for his sake, inside I was torn apart. Was our twenty-year relationship just a show? I was furious and began to believe that I had somehow let him down. Had I also failed the community? I don't believe I've ever had so much anger inside but I couldn't allow it to explode. There was no sleep for me that lonely night.

This was also the night before I was scheduled to host Mayor John Street on his first venture into a skeptical LGBT community. Though Street hadn't been our ally while serving on the city council, he was making a public statement of his switch to now supporting LGBT rights by having a full-scale tour of the William Way LGBT Community Center, with press in tow. I knew that by leading this tour, I'd be ridiculed by some in the community, but I also knew that Street, as mayor, could make a difference. It was important that I be focused that night. I had twenty-four hours to get my head straight, but the hurt remained palpable. My partner had told six other people of his condition before me, and chose the night before a major press event to share the news.

The tour was somehow going really well, and after taking in several rooms and having a demonstration of the computer-learning center, we came to the ballroom. At that point, acting out of pure impulse, I asked the executive director of the community center to continue the tour without me, saying that I'd catch up later. I pulled the hand of someone who I knew could help, and the two of us stayed behind while the press junket moved on. In an empty ballroom I looked at Jane Shull and blurted out, "He has AIDS, what should I do?"

Jane, president of Philadelphia Fight and cochair of AIDS Awareness Day, was a strong woman, politically smart, and one of the most knowledgeable people on the subject. She shot me a nice smile and said: "Let's finish this up, and we'll get to it."

As the tour continued, questions wound around in my head. Questions I hadn't asked or thought to ask. How did it happen? What was his viral load? How do we tell his parents and my nephew Jeffrey, who was living with us? Should we tell him at all? What should I prepare myself for? What care procedures will I need to learn? The questions never stopped, but somehow no one noticed. I went on talking to people, discussing the evening and how the mayor could help us as a community. I was on autopilot, which was my fallback position when overwhelmed.

After the tour was over Jane took me aside and said, "Have you cried yet?" This sounded so strange, but Jane knew what she was talking about; she had been through this many times before. In a flash I realized that I hadn't, and then the watershed began.

As the city's foremost expert on the subject, Jane knew that there were a number of issues to deal with, both medical and psychological, regarding our relationship. Her next question was one that hadn't even occurred to me: "Do you want to continue the relationship?" How could I not continue the relationship? Me, I'd deal with it like I did with everything else that had been tossed my way.

In short order, my partner and I became clients of Philadelphia Fight. At our first visit, the counselor asked me, "Have you been tested yet?"

That hadn't dawned on me either. I scheduled a test with Karam Mounzer, one of the doctors who dedicated his life to help fight AIDS. Getting tested wasn't a new experience for me, but this was different, as the closest person to me now had the disease. The test was negative.

When it became public knowledge that my partner was HIV positive, things went from bad to worse. While most friends were supportive, a number urged me to leave him, saying things like, "Do you realize he's put your life in jeopardy?" It also spurred on friends to tell me what they knew about him, most of which I had earlier refused to believe, chalking it up to idle gossip. It soon became apparent that he had a secret life I had no knowledge of.

He needed more than what Philadelphia Fight could offer; as the months went on his drinking became worse, and friends told me to wake up and confront my denials. Instead, I did what many people do—blame myself—all the while not realizing what was happening around me. He would openly hurl insults my way, giving venom to a previously humorous line of his—"I always told you the only reason I married you was for your potential to make money." He now told me that it was the *only* reason he had stayed with me. He bragged about his recent infidelities and reminded me of past ones that I had forgiven or tried to forget. He began to confess all facets of his life, a life alien to me, and to viciously ridicule my person. A friend told me I was in an abusive relationship. It broke me, and then rage set in when I discovered that little has been studied about abuse among same-sex couples. Anger, depression, and self-doubt took over my life.

How my nephew Jeffrey made it through this time I'll never understand. As I write this, I'm full of sorrow for putting him through it and realize how much he loves me to have stuck by my side all these years. Some of my friends were not so loyal. To them, I now apologize. I apologize to all my friends whom I didn't believe.

The end came the day I picked him up from yet another stint at rehab. I believe it was his seventh time. We got home and before dinner he already had a glass of wine in his hand. Denial had ended. Calmly I spoke the words, "It's either the wine or me."

He threw the wine at me and was out the door. Later that night, Jane Shull called to tell me that he was at one of her fundraisers, drinking and happily telling people that we were through. She asked if it was true. The answer was yes. It would be great if I could say that life went on, but for me, after a nearly twenty-year relationship, it felt like life was over.

I was about to see bottom, thinking that I'd failed myself and the community too. I could no longer claim that we'd have a normal, long-lasting relationship like some of our straight counterparts, like my mom and dad. In hindsight, I know that every relationship, no matter what kind, is different. But I felt that I had something to prove, from my early days of activism; seeing my parents' and their friends' happy marriages . . . until the end, so happy.

Friends tried to help pull me out, but I built a brick wall around myself. Instead of going to the office, I'd spend days holed up in my house on the Jersey Shore, which I had bought a few years prior. Jim Austin had been correct: I could earn a living as a publisher. It became real to me in 1994, eighteen years after the first issue. We had steadily picked up advertisers and circulation climbed. I had wanted to rent a house at the Jersey Shore for the summer and didn't know if I could afford it, even with others sharing the cost, so I called my accountant and asked if I could do it. I essentially pleaded with him that I needed some time off. He laughed and explained that for the money it would take for a summer rental I could make a down payment on a house and it would serve me well each year with taxes. He also suggested that I give myself a raise, and for the first time in my life I actually felt middle class. Walking into the house for the first time, I felt great pride. Things were beginning to get a little easier, to the point that I was able to purchase a house—rather, a shell of a house—in what was becoming a gentrified neighborhood. Indeed, *I* gentrified it, as the first non–African American on the block. It had one of these bathtubs with the four legs, but one of the legs was missing so when you took a shower it sometimes felt like you were surfing. It actually fell through the ceiling at one point, and we then used it in the kitchen. And when the dining room ceiling plaster started dropping one day, we covered it with egg cartons. The house was falling apart, but it was mine.

But now, after the breakup, I used that house as a place where I could drink in excess and take various prescription drugs for sleeping or depression. I wouldn't even answer the door when my friends Larry Furman and Dennis Cook, who had a house at the Shore a few blocks from mine, came by to check on me. Soon it didn't matter which pill it was or how many. I'd come undone.

It was Pattie Tihey, our editor, and Rick Lombardo, my assistant, who kept *PGN* afloat during that time, as I was useless to the publication. Convinced that my ex-partner's problems were my fault, I had taken an emotional beating and internalized his scathing remarks.

I stayed in that fog for over a year, until one day Pattie stormed into my office and said she'd had enough. "This has gone on too long. You have responsibilities. This publication which you founded supports fourteen people and their families." She then added, in understanding some of what I was feeling, "That is success!"

Get up and get on with it was the message I received.

Patti urged me to get help; she even suggested several psychologists. As always, she was prepared, and her words about supporting fourteen people became my new guiding light.

Seeing a psychologist set me at ease. "Tell me about your last twenty-five years."

Thinking for a minute, I said blankly, "Death, suicides, AIDS, the breakup."

She looked at me for a few moments, remarked at my lack of emotion, and then asked whether anything positive had happened. There was nothing in my mind. Empty. Then she had me tell the full story, sparing no detail.

My last twenty-five years had included my mother's death from kidney disease, Grandmom's Alzheimer's and ultimate death, Uncle Stanley's gambling and death, the suicides of my friends Jan Sergienko (after a gang rape), my friend Carol (after sexual abuse from her husband), my friend Michael (after becoming fed up with medical treatments and watching his own deterioration from AIDS), and my former sales manager and close friend Sally Tyer (who after a bad business deal shot herself in the head). Then there were the AIDS deaths, chief among them my friend Bill Way, and the numerous funerals that were left for me to plan. Then there was my failure as a partner. All relayed in a stream-of-consciousness monotone.

She had one more question: "Did you ever cry?"

I took a long pause before I replied, "We had a demonstration at the city council where we disrupted the session and I took over the president's desk, tossing the papers in the air. The police were called in and it became rough. Several of our members were hurt. The TV reporters rushed me and there were tears coming down my cheeks. In an emotional state, I said on camera that our people are being hurt. Later, a few friends told me sternly that I should never cry during an interview, that it was unmanly."

She didn't judge me, instead asking me to keep relating my life story. Soon I was in tears, hysterical uncontrollable tears; surprisingly, so was she.

Afterward, she stated the obvious: "You need to get in

touch with your emotions and stop covering them up." She also encouraged me to meet with a pharmacologist.

That was the first time I'd ever heard of such a profession. Those two hours with the psychologist were perhaps the best investment in myself I'd ever made. Without her, along with the other key people mentioned above, I'm sure my life would not have had any more chapters. Jane and Dr. Mounzer got me the help I needed, and Pattie and Rick kept the newspaper moving, even hiding the fact that I wasn't at the wheel.

This story isn't unique; it was common to many gay couples when one partner was diagnosed with HIV. Like others, it took me years to accept the situation and move forward, and that is another lesson that those of us affected by HIV/AIDS had to learn. PTSS is real.

By that time in the mid-nineties, the pharmaceutical industry was competing to see who could come up with the best regimen of pills, or "cocktails," to manage the disease. HIV was on the road to being treatable—just like that PBS show had promised—but it couldn't be cured. Those cocktails did indeed work and they have been improved upon. Now there are pills advertised to prevent a person from acquiring HIV. But there's no telling what effect these new pills will have on younger people, if they'll simply forget the lessons we learned and deem themselves invincible. Will we see the return of Fire Island circuit parties—no air of caution and no end to the high? With medical advances in prevention, will those who already have the disease be alienated and forgotten? Even after we've gotten through the worst of it, the work of educating people is not over. Not by a long shot.

Above, the official White House picture of President Obama's first state visit to Philadelphia in 2010, for which I was one of the hosts. Below, the president and I engaging at the event.

The receipt from my first arrest in 1970.

Mark Segal, taxi driver.

Courtesy of the *Philadelphia Inquirer*

The picture that appeared in the *Philadelphia Inquirer* the morning after I held a party in Arlen Specter's office in October 1973.

Courtesy of Mark Segal

My first meeting with Governor Milton Shapp in 1974.

Dedication of a Pennsylvania state historical plaque at Independence Hall, honoring the pioneering LGBT public pickets of 1965–69. (L to R) Lilli Vincenz, William B. Kelley, Randy Wicker, Ada Bello, Barbara Gittings, me, Frank Kameny, and Kay Lahusen in the chair.

Original participants from the first gay pride march in 1970, which was then called Christopher Street Gay Liberation Day. Members of my New York Gay Liberation Front family reunited for this photo on Pride Day 2013 in front of the Stonewall.

Four Chairs in Search of a Table
from left to right
John Chiafalo, GY Chair 1973-4
Mark Horn, GY Chair 1971-73
Tom Approbato, current GLYNY Again Board Chair
Mark Segal, Founding Daddy, GY Chair 1969-71

Gay Youth reunion. Top: John Chiafalo, Mark Horn, Tom Approbato, and me.
Bottom: Michael Knowles, Mark Horn, Jeff Hochhauser, and me.

Messing around at a fundraiser at my home: Congressman Barney Frank dancing with Congressman Bob Brady.

Soon-to-be Mayor Jim Kenney with Jason and me after he paid for our wedding license (yes, he really did).

At home talking policy with California Lieutenant Governor Gavin Newsom.

Scott Drake

Our wedding on July 5, 2014. (L to R) Jason's sisters Jennifer, Ryan, and Lill, Jason's parents Clyde and Rosalina, Jason, myself, Judge Dan Anders, my cousin Ilene, and my nephew Jeffrey.

Courtesy of the White House

Jason meets President Obama and the First Lady for the first time.

Gay History Month, front page of the *Philadelphia Daily News*, October 13, 2011.

Chapter 9

Clout

I n 1993, *Philadelphia* magazine named me the resident with "Most Clout" in their annual Best of Philly issue, crowning me above union leaders, corporate heads, and elected officials. By this time I had been in the public eye for nearly twenty-five years. It wasn't a quick rise, and the clout they attributed to me was garnered out of necessity. Any social justice or civil rights movement needs not only to understand the politics swirling around, but also to have insider clout. Change does not happen without working the system.

One can develop clout from a number of factors, like building coalitions with other communities, organizations, and leaders. Other important facets are the ability to raise funds and deliver votes, and being able to stop a candidate dead in their tracks. And the simple fact is that to get a large program on the boards or to get any sort of legislation passed, you need to be in tune with elected officials, both those who support your issues and those who don't. Knowing how to navigate the latter may indeed be even more important. One last item is getting the attention of media. Today, that means having an understanding of the power of both traditional and social media.

Two organizations that prove this point and deserve recognition for a job well done are Lambda Legal Defense and Education Fund and Freedom to Marry. They get it. They know how to spend funds wisely and use media to their full advantage. Evan Wolfson, founder of Freedom to Marry and formerly of Lambda Legal Defense and Education Fund, is a community treasure: he is bright and articulate, and understands how to create a message that the public can consume. He has been creative with his approach, and no one can doubt that it has worked. Like many activists, he was ahead of his time and kept to his vision, no matter the opposition in the community—and that has a place in my heart.

The LGBT national all-star team also includes the Human Rights Campaign, which exemplifies the slogan that money and media are the mother's milk of politics. It takes funds to elect candidates and launch campaigns that change public perception.

Each time I hear a complaint about the lobbying efforts of Human Rights Campaign, it makes me want to hurl. While one might disagree on the issues, HRC is excellent at raising funds and using those funds to lobby, which is simply playing the game, and playing it correctly. You have to be in the game to win it.

Another member of the all-star team is the Victory Fund. Cofounded by Vic Basile in 1991 to support and groom politicians for LGBT equality, and later infused by the incredible energy of Brian Bond, the Victory Fund raises money and teaches people the fundamentals of campaigns. Their efforts have led to scores of victories around the nation. Both Vic and Brian became important members of the Obama administration and have helped shape the path of LGBT issues, providing a blueprint for future administrations to follow. Human Rights Campaign and Victory Fund can take a bow for the work they have done with Barack Obama to make him the most inclusive president in our country's history.

Along with money and organization, an additional path to clout for our community is to have a mainstream media watchdog, which has largely fallen to the Gay & Lesbian Alliance Against Defamation. GLAAD has had a few bad years but they're getting back on their feet. The low point for them (and Human Rights Campaign to a lesser extent), and our community in general, was the Chick-fil-A disaster. That campaign will also be a blueprint for gay activists—of what not to do.

The quick story: It was discovered that the Chick-fil-A Foundation was giving money to anti–marriage equality organizations. Some LGBT groups and bloggers went off the rails. The Human Rights Campaign and GLAAD, however, were caught off guard; the LGBT community and the marriage equality bloggers were angry, but they were given no direction from our leaders. They grew frustrated, and many began to ask where HRC and GLAAD stood on the issue and what countermeasures should be taken. With no apparent plan, the organizations simply issued press releases about the facts, without offering any leadership of what to do next.

The LGBT community ultimately had to find its own answer, which entailed a national kiss-in at Chick-fil-A restaurants all across the country. Unfortunately, this resulted in perhaps one of the best business days for Chick-fil-A. Our equality was reduced to kissing, we looked weak and silly, and opponents staged a Chick-fil-A appreciation day, which drove more profits to the chain.

People forgot a fundamental aspect of our struggle from the early days of the movement, which was not to allow the opposition to simply reduce our community to sex. Compare the Chick-fil-A story with a similar struggle that occurred much earlier in our climb out of oppression, the Anita Bryant fight against gay rights in Florida. There, the local community had control and leadership. Anita Bryant was a devout Christian and a popular singer of the day who in 1977 went on a crusade

against "homosexuality," attracting national notoriety and support. She used as her slogan "Save Our Children." That played
into the stereotype that gays were child molesters and predators.

Dade County, Florida, where she lived, had passed nondiscrimination legislation, and she used the platform of repeal-
ing that legislation to assault the LGBT community. She was
endorsed and supported by Jerry Falwell and his Moral Majority,
who threw in millions of dollars. In 1977 we had little national
organization, so the locals led the way. Lacking major funds to
combat Bryant, they first fought her and her supporters with
logical, tempered answers. And then they dropped the hammer
on her. Bryant made most of her money as the spokesperson
for Florida Orange Juice, so activist Bob Kunst called a press
conference to announce a boycott on orange juice from Florida.
Today you'd say the campaign went viral, with people around
the nation hearing the call.

In Florida, Bryant did ultimately win the ballot initiative,
but by 1979 she was fired as the spokesperson for Florida Orange Juice. A win and a loss for her, but that win ultimately
faded. She never regained the support and stature she once had.
Anita Bryant, in the eyes of history, looks similar to George Wallace, standing in the doorway to uphold segregation—or in her
case, discrimination.

If I had my way, I'd have taken all the money that went into the
battle against Chick-fil-A and given it to Democratic National
Committee treasurer Andy Tobias, the master of all political
LGBT fundraising for the Democratic Party and its candidates,
through the LGBT Leadership Council. Andy understands
LGBT oppression well. He's best known for his financial writing, but early in his career he also published a book in 1973
about growing up and coming to terms with himself. Using a

pseudonym, the book was titled *The Best Little Boy in the World.*
It's my favorite book of a boy coming of age. He also showed me
how to turn my involvement in the political system into clout
to gain equality.

My first foray into congressional funds, also known as *ear-
marks*, came in 1993. The LGBT Community Center at that
time did not have a permanent location. Their slogan was "A
Community Center without Walls." Fundraising was volatile,
the board of directors mostly transitory, and the vision simply
lacking. Tony Green, chief of staff to my old city council friend
Congressman Thomas Foglietta, met with me for lunch to see
what he and the congressman could do for our community. Formerly married to a woman, Tony was now openly gay. I told him
about the center's predicament and he was receptive to ear-
marking funds. With funding, we'd be able to get a permanent
location. He sent me the paperwork and we began the process.
Along the way, he mentioned that "LGBT" could not appear
anywhere in the paperwork, since that would alert the Republicans, who would vote it down. Our solution was to describe
the building as "a place for the community most impacted by
AIDS." That $300,000 earmark, the largest funding the orga-
nization has ever received, made it possible for what is now the
William Way LGBT Community Center to purchase its building
at 1315 Spruce Street.

Thanks to my early work with media and our efforts to pass
a city nondiscrimination bill, I knew most of the city officials
well. We asked for their support and also got valuable contact
information to build my Rolodex. At my urging, Governor
Shapp created the Governor's Council for Sexual Minorities,
which further cemented my relationships with state leaders.
Invitations to my house parties became coveted, especially by
city officials and those hoping to break into politics. Where else

could you see a Jewish governor singing Christmas carols with the Gay Men's Chorus? Along with regional bank presidents, union heads, a Socialist, and a drag queen all mingling with one another.

In the midst of all of this, District Attorney Ed Rendell, who was thinking about running for mayor, suggested that I form a political action committee (PAC). Almost as quickly as the ink was drying on our PAC filing, there was a fight in the city council regarding a gay pride resolution. It was a perfect reason to launch the Pride of Philadelphia Election Committee. Within weeks a cocktail party was held with leaders of the community, and Ed gave a speech about the importance of raising money in a campaign and the clout that the community could gain. There was also a hint that Ed might run for office again and could use a supportive PAC behind him.

That first fundraiser was memorable, to say the least. Pride of Philadelphia Election Committee at that time saw itself as a local version of the national Human Rights Campaign, and set as its first goal to gain passage of the pride resolution the following June in the city council. But in order to do that, we needed funds. Enter Barney Frank.

Barney Frank was the new gay hero to many of us, an openly gay man in Congress representing both his district and the greater LGBT community. Using the gifts of wit, intelligence, knowledge of history, and his famous Massachusetts drawl, Barney commands attention when he speaks. In 1989, when I first met him, you could say "Barney Frank" was synonymous with "pride." A PAC board member who was involved with one of Philadelphia's namesake organizations, the Franklin Institute, arranged for us to use space in the institute for our kickoff fundraiser. The plan called for cocktails in the observatory, then down to the planetarium for speeches and a private show. We had the venue, but we still needed a headliner. Congressman Tom Foglietta wrote a letter to Barney in July of 1989 asking him if he'd assist an old friend in starting a local gay and lesbian PAC. Tom's letter was accompanied by another letter from me telling Barney about my work.

Barney soon called and told me that he had followed my escapades over the years and would be glad to help. I then called Congressman Bill Gray and Mayor Goode to ask them to serve as honorary hosts. Both accepted.

Next came the arrangements of caterers, printers, mailing lists, advertising, and ticket sales. The date for the event was set as September 15, and by the fourth week in August ticket sales far exceeded our expectations. Then, with less than two weeks to go, Barney was figuratively caught with his pants down. The scandal involved a callboy who was living with him and the rumors that the guy was running a service out of Barney's house. Barney told the nation that he knew about his roommate's background, but was trying to help him change his life.

As with all Washington scandals, it dragged on and on, and the roommate even started to do talk shows and tell about his sexual antics with Barney, true or not. As the scandal broke I tried to talk with Barney about the September 15 fundraiser. He did not respond personally, but several staff members kept telling me that they didn't know his plans. Some of my political friends offered to pinch hit, but none had the same level of name recognition. Others suggested that I drop Barney, but I felt that was a bad signal to send out with our first major fundraiser, not to mention downright disloyal. To me the issue was clear. Loyalty mattered, along with the notion that all are innocent until proven guilty. What's more, Barney was still a national treasure; the public was just coming to terms with the fact that he was human, like the rest of us.

At the same time, board members were calling me every day to ask about Barney and the fundraiser. We continued to run advertisements, but Barney had walled himself in, and nobody was getting any answers. Finally, I wrote to him and explained that the test of a friend's loyalty is when you are down, and in this instance we still wanted him since he was a hero, and heroes are heroes, even after falling from their pedestals. A week before the event, I returned home from a meeting to discover a message on my answering machine: "Ah, hello, Mark, this is Barney Frank, sorry that I've kept you in the dark this long. It's not fair and I'm sorry. I promised you I'd be at your function, and I'll keep that promise. Call my office tomorrow to make the arrangements."

This, it turned out, was the easy part. His staff was concerned about media. The press was now camped outside both his office and home. They followed him everywhere, and he was not commenting to them on the scandal. It was a typical DC feeding frenzy. Someone suggested that our gala premier of a new PAC should be staged without press. Then Barney's staff told us it would be a mandatory condition for his participation. I had to find a way to get this man, embroiled in the nation's number one sex scandal, into the city to attend a cocktail party, give a speech in a public place, and leave, all without the media catching on.

I faced the situation like it was a Gay Raiders zap. We stopped the sale of tickets. Only friends of board members could buy tickets. Security was set up at every entrance of the Franklin Institute. Drivers were informed that no reporters were to come near Barney no matter what. And no press releases were allowed. Meanwhile, a strange thing occurred: since most politicians run for the hills, away from their scandal-ridden colleagues, I was surprised to find that both Congressman Tom Foglietta and Ed Rendell called to offer support, and while neither had planned to attend, they both now felt compelled to in order to support Barney and the cause.

September 15, 1989 was a damp, drizzly, and windswept day. It matched my spirits. Members of my board were telling me that Barney would cancel at the last minute. After all, he had not made a public appearance since the scandal began other than a few attempts at talking with the press. It was decided that I'd be the one to pick him up and welcome him to the city. With my friend Bill Davol, who I thought would have a calming effect on Barney, we set off in the rainy night.

Barney arrived at the train station alone with one bag. I introduced myself and we shook hands, then made a quick exit before he was noticed. Bill was close by in the car. En route to the institute, I expressed my gratitude to Barney for coming, considering the toll that other matters might be taking on him at this juncture. He was mostly quiet, keeping his head bowed. Finally, worried about his state of mind, I said, "I recently wrote you about heroes and the way they sometimes slip. To me a hero is someone who fights for a cause no matter what might fall around them. The heroism is the cause, not their private life. To me you are still a hero." Barney lowered his head some more and began crying. We said little else for the rest of the ride, but I was worried. At the reception, the first thing I discovered was that we had succeeded in keeping the mainstream press unaware of the event. Since we sent out no press releases or advisories, the only way for reporters to know was to read the gay press. Imagine the firestorm that would have greeted us if they read the gay press regularly. For the first time in my life, I was thrilled that they didn't.

At the venue, some members of the board took Barney around the room and introduced him to the attendees. Several local politicians arrived to assist and lend support. It became apparent almost immediately that Barney was mentally not with us. We quickly arranged for a friend in attendance, a psychologist, to usher Barney from person to person, but he told us that he wanted to mingle on his own. Then he sort of ambled around the room, just nodding his head in acknowledgment whenever someone tried to talk with him. At one point he came up to me as I was going over the rest of the schedule with the board, and asked in a low voice, "Where's the bathroom?" I suggested that we'd have someone show him, but he declined and asked us to point the way.

We watched as he slowly made his way to the bathroom. Once the door had closed behind him, we looked at each other in total fear. We honestly believed that he was going to do some harm to himself. As we waited, I found myself thinking of how I would respond to reporters' questions about the dead congressman in the bathroom. Eventually, we all agreed to send someone inside. I asked Jeff Moran and his partner Richard Bond if they would make sure the congressman was okay. As they reluctantly approached, the door opened and Barney came sailing out. My sigh of relief could be heard all the way in Washington.

Congressman Tom Foglietta showed up, and we moved to the planetarium where the program was to begin. After everyone was seated I took to the podium and thanked the attendees for their support. The first speaker was Ed Rendell, followed by Tom who would introduce his colleague Barney. Tom spoke stronger and more eloquently then I'd ever heard him before. He reaffirmed his support of Barney and said he looked forward to working on a progressive agenda with him for many years to come. He then concluded, "Friends, let me introduce a fine gentlemen and a great congressman, my good friend Barney Frank!" The assembled rose to their feet en masse, and I could see the tears in Barney's eyes. Like magic he woke up from what seemed like a walking sleep, and was full of energy. As he spoke he became stronger, and with each comical story he slowly became the Barney the nation had grown to love and appreciate.

After the speech, we had to get him to the airport to make his flight to Boston, and I hugged and thanked him, offering to help in any way I could. The next time I saw Barney was in the spring of 1994 when he and Congressman Gerry Studds came to my home for another fundraiser, this time for Tom Foglietta. My fondest memory, though, came many years later at a different event at my home. He and Congressman Bob Brady were both there, and Bob talked about how close he and Barney had gotten in Washington. Barney was so comfortable and upbeat that he slow danced with Bob, the same blue-collar guy from the tough neighborhood, the sergeant at arms who had the job of carrying me out of the city council thirty-five years earlier.

That first fundraiser at the Franklin Institute was merely an appetizer for the Pride of Philadelphia Election Committee. Over the next couple of years, the committee continually brought political surprises. One development in particular cemented the strength of the LGBT community; it was a perfect storm that I could exploit, and that storm was Fran Rafferty.

Rafferty was a city councilman with strong religious beliefs. He was a blue-collar Irish Catholic who had imaginative ideas about God and AIDS. He had a temper, which once resulted in a brawl with another councilman on the floor of the city council. When a gay rights issue came up in the council, he'd yell slurs like, "Fairies!" Beyond his antigay views, his other behaviors were, shall we say, not representative of the pride Philadelphians took in their city.

Most people thought of Rafferty as the most homophobic

elected official in the city. It all came to a head when we introduced a resolution recognizing Gay Pride Month. He suggested
that it be called AIDS Pride Month. This led to a series of mis-
haps and ended with a televised debate on a KYW-TV talk show
hosted by Jerry Penacoli, who went on to Hollywood to report
for the entertainment show *Extra*. My plan for the debate was
simply to be as quiet as possible (for once in my life) and let him
talk as much as he wanted. Just allow him to flaunt his hate and
ignorance on the subject, let him be the bully he was. Of course,
I'd encourage him along whenever I could.

Just before we went on the air and were having makeup applied, I looked over to him and saw what appeared to be malice
in his eyes. I smiled and said, "Franny, you look so good in all
that makeup."

At every commercial break, my mind found another line
that just kept him roiling. During one commercial he actually
suggested he might punch me. It was difficult to hold tight, but
people viewing saw a bully in action. All we had to do was let
it sink in. We were about to do something that had never been
done in American politics: try to defeat a candidate in a citywide race simply for being a homophobe.

It was 1991 when we announced our campaign against Rafferty's reelection. The political elite of Philly thought the idea
ridiculous. To be truthful, so did I. After all, he was endorsed
by the Democratic City Committee and running in a city controlled by an entrenched Democratic machine. He had also
been the top vote-getter in the previous election. In our own
style we were attempting to take him from number one to number six, since the top five vote-getters would be elected. People
thought we could lower him to two or three, but certainly not
cause him to lose office.

The campaign organization was formed with two goals in

mind. The first was to help Ed Rendell become mayor and the second was to defeat Fran Rafferty. Ed was almost a sure bet to win, but defeating Rafferty didn't seem realistic—until we realized that we could use Ed's campaign to work the ward leaders. We would need to find an acceptable candidate to replace Rafferty who the public could embrace and we needed to make the community and the city believe this was all possible. Television was what I knew, so we decided to produce a commercial. We had little money and a commercial campaign would wipe out most of our funds. This, we realized, would be a smoke-and-mirrors campaign. But it was worth a try. No pain, no gain.

Richard Bond, a public relations executive on our board, had a friend who sold airtime on KYW-TV. Together, we began to research hot-button issues and put together a storyboard. In the end, the commercial would be a thirty-second spot. It was filmed secretly at NFL Films studios in Cherry Hill, New Jersey, at a deep discount. Yes, NFL Films must be thanked for helping produce the first-ever citywide LGBT political campaign television commercial in the nation. We sent Peter Lien out to photograph Rafferty with the instructions to get as many shots as possible with him looking mean. Mission accomplished. From my days at a radio station called Talk 900, we got Bill Davol to agree to do the voiceover. The spot was a collage of Rafferty photos; in each one he appeared progressively meaner. With the voiceover, we used his quotes and his votes to lay out the issues.

"You may have thought it was funny when Fran Rafferty insulted lesbians and gays. But was it funny when he had to apologize to Philadelphia for saying he would salute the Statue of Liberty by getting drunk? Or when he voted against more money for our children's education? Or when he made the city council a laughingstock by having not one but two fistfights there? The sad thing is, Fran Rafferty could be elected again to the city council. If you're serious

about Philadelphia, don't waste $65,000 a year . . . Say no to Fran Rafferty."

I believe the commercial cost us under a thousand dollars to produce. We then tried to place it. There, we ran into a surprise: most of the stations were afraid to sell us time. No one had ever run an ad against a sitting city council candidate without being a candidate themselves.

We called a press conference and announced that only two TV stations would sell us time for the commercial. This was outrageous. We thanked the two stations, KYW and WPHL, and told the assembled press, which included the stations that wouldn't sell us time, that the commercial would begin running the following morning on the news shows. That night the six p.m. and eleven p.m. news on most stations led with the press conference, with the commercial as part of the story. We ended up getting the commercial on TV free of charge and it ran more times on the news than the airtime we'd actually purchased.

But the true magic of that moment was that we were the first LGBT group to ever fight a standing councilman with a TV campaign. We made bumper stickers with the *Say No to Rafferty* logo next to a snarling Rafferty. We handed them out and they began to appear all over the city. People like activist Mike Marsico and members of ACT UP kept coming back for more stickers for their army of friends and colleagues. People saw them and recalled the commercial, and it appeared as if we had a citywide campaign going.

This led to the most powerful member of the Pennsylvania Senate calling and asking to have lunch with me. Enter Vince Fumo, not only a state senator, but also a ward leader, who was trying to help get his friend Jim Kenney elected to the council. Vince felt that if our campaign took votes from Rafferty, it would help Kenney win. The idea was to take Rafferty off the list of endorsed five and replace him with Kenney, and to do it ward by ward. Finally we had found our candidate! Once agreed, Vince began to call ward leaders and I'd take them to lunch at The Palm.

Ed Rendell was at the top of the ticket, and thus far I had not asked him to do anything for us in this election. But now things were moving fast. So fast that Rafferty began to believe he needed to get a stronger campaign together. I was so focused on our own campaign I didn't have time to pay attention to Rafferty's response. It seemed, like other city council candidates, Rafferty expected that the City Committee and Rendell would carry him on their ticket. I don't think he ever expected any ward leaders to request that his name be removed.

I took ward leaders to lunch almost every day, which became one of the largest expenses of our campaign, since there were sixty-nine of them. I became such a regular that my picture now graces the wall of The Palm. We printed new bumper stickers and announced new commercials that didn't exist. There was not a week without some announcement. A month before the election, ward leaders were now publicly announcing that Rafferty was off their ticket.

We now went shopping for an election-night hotel ballroom. We secured the ballroom next to that of the Ed Rendell campaign in the Warwick Hotel. That night saw an early win for Ed. He, his wife Midge, and his son Jesse came over to our ballroom as soon as he declared victory. Our night was just beginning, and to the surprise of everyone our little smoke-and-mirrors campaign had been widely embraced. The city council election was still close, too close to call. We already knew at that hour that Rafferty was no longer at the top, but had we toppled him? We wouldn't know until the following day.

Ed and Midge gave me hugs as they prepared to leave, and I

witnessed a beautiful family moment in politics: the two of them bent down to their little son Jesse to explain that, with his dad becoming mayor, life would now change, but the two of them would always be there for him.

The following morning, I was awakened by the phone ringing. It was Senator Fumo, who greeted me with an incredible laugh: "Congratulations!" He went on to say a lot more, but all I heard was that one word. When I finally roused and regained some ability to understand the situation, Vince made me realize the importance of what we had done, but also some of the finer points of the game of politics. "Mark, you won, but Fran has a family to feed. We have to give him something. How about if we put him on a commission?" This was a level of politics I had no knowledge of, and all I could say to the man who had first reached out to help was, "If that's what you feel is correct."

In hindsight, I realize Vince was explaining to me that we had just knocked off a giant, and in victory we should offer an olive branch. After all, the giant could rise again, if not placated. The fact that Vince even asked me was a sign that he respected the campaign we had launched, and understood that this made the LGBT vote a powerhouse. In the subsequent election, we continued to make a pro-gay difference in local politics, leading the president of the city council, John Street, who at that time was considered a homophobe, to spend $400,000 to protect his own seat.

As Ed began building his mayoral team, he appointed members of our board to his administration. Some elected officials suggested to me that Ed should offer me a position of deputy mayor. This went to my head, and I let it be known to media friends that out of respect, I *should* be asked. Word got around to Ed's campaign manager, David L. Cohen, who called and made the offer, but also told me that I wouldn't be happy, since taking that position meant that I was no longer independent. I'd be part of the administration and would have to voice their positions. David was right, and I quickly declined the offer.

The first week as mayor, Ed called me to his office. He was leaning back in his chair with his feet up on the desk.

"What commission or board do you want?"

"How about the airport board?"

Ed was surprised, and suggested several boards and commissions that offered compensation, and I responded, "The airport board."

He looked at me sternly. "Why? It doesn't pay anything."

My answer: "Mr. Mayor, I want to be Philadelphia's first official flying fairy."

Ed still likes to tell that story.

James Carville, one of the nation's most renowned political consultants, showed me his tremendous charms during our first conversation. Jim is often credited for the Clinton White House victory, and the man knows how to win debates. He is a lover of the political deal and I got a taste of that early in his career. Robert Casey Sr., the father of future US Senator Bob Casey Jr., was running for Pennsylvania governor in 1978, and Carville was his manager, willing to do whatever it took so that this would not be Casey's fourth failure in getting to the governor's mansion. It was during this campaign that Carville uttered his famous description of Pennsylvania. He said in his Louisiana drawl, "On one side of the state you have Pittsburgh, on the other Philadelphia, and in the middle is Alabama." Some have since remarked that his description is an insult to Alabama.

The polls were running pretty even and Casey needed one more thing to go his way to pull off a victory. The old Democratic coalition was drawing together to support him, but the gay community was suspicious of Casey and his devotion to the church. He had not met with gay leaders or made his position on gay rights known. What's more, my newspaper was not offered an opportunity to interview Casey and find out what he stood for and how he would apply that to the gay community.

It was in this atmosphere that I picked up my phone one day and was greeted by: "Mark, what the hell do I have to do to get you to support Bob? This is Jim Carville." Taken aback, I said hello and asked why he was the one calling. He explained that since Bill Bateoff, a campaign fundraiser and acquaintance of mine, had been unable to make a deal and get me on board, he thought he'd give me a talking-to.

I replied that it was very clear what was required for my support. Unlike others, there was no need of patronage, state funding of any particular organization, or bond issues to any law firms I was associated with. All I needed was for Casey to support the state's gay rights legislation when introduced in the legislature, and to recreate the Pennsylvania Council for Sexual Minorities that Governor Shapp had started and which had died under Shapp's successor.

"That's all?" Jim uttered.

I immediately said, "And one more item: an interview in my newspaper, so he can give his remarks on these issues."

"Done deal," Jim responded.

After the interview was published, Jim called to thank me for handling Bob in a polite and professional manner. At that point I asked what I should do when Bob doesn't keep his promises. After telling me that should not be a concern, since Bob always keeps his word, Jim said, "You have Bill [Bateoff] talk to Bob, and if he can't take care of it, you call me and I'll set him straight."

Governor Robert Casey broke every promise, and I'm still waiting for Mr. Carville's return call.

It was around this time that I got a call from an up-and-coming union leader by the name of John Dougherty from the International Brotherhood of Electrical Workers. We set up a meeting and he asked what he could do to help the LGBT community. Never one to shy away from the big ask, I explained that we had just purchased a building to be used as our community center and it needed some electrical work. Being a generous guy, John replied, "Not a problem, consider it done." He sent over a few apprentices to take a look and unfortunately, the building needed a completely new electrical system, which would require more then a few apprentices. To his credit, John never told me what the price tag on that job would have been. Certainly a price tag the center could not have paid.

Later I'd discover that John was doing this in part as a way of showing his daughter his support of the LGBT community since she had recently come out to him. We've gone on to engage in many battles together, sometimes even opposed to one another, but we remain friends and enjoy a special bond.

Councilman Jim Kenney, our replacement for Fran Rafferty, showed gratitude from the beginning. Soon after being sworn in, he arranged a meeting with Council President John Street and me. Basically, we were quickly shown the door. Leaving the office, Jim laughed and said, "Well, that went well."

We thought that Street, who had been opposed to domestic partnership legislation for religious reasons, might see the writing on the wall. Not a chance. Thus began the fight for domestic partnership and another national first when we connected tax savings to LGBT relationships. Yes, we did beat Vermont to become the first government to recognize that domestic partners mean taxation as well.

By Ed's second term he had created a peaceful, working relationship with Council President Street, who was still opposed to domestic partners legislation. Ed was somewhat boxed in, since Street controlled the council with an iron fist. Without the council, Ed wouldn't have a city budget. Knowing this and having to straddle us and Street, he publicly said that if passed by the council, he'd sign domestic partnership into law (though I believe he expected Street would never allow it to pass).

Street was all about power. He understood how power could be a force for good, and he believed his community hadn't gotten the benefits it deserved. We were like-minded in that respect. Enter my partners in this effort. From our PAC's board, Andy Chirls, who would later become the first openly gay chancellor of the Philadelphia Bar Association, and Andrew Park, executive director of the Center for Lesbian and Gay Civil Rights, both stepped up. As with the Rafferty campaign, we knew we had to define our characters. This meant that we had to paint Street as the homophobe who was blocking the door of equality.

Andy Chirls's job was to stay close to Street's coalition members who we knew would be uncomfortable with being labeled homophobic. That was the behind-the-scenes campaign. In front of the camera, Andrew Park commissioned surveys, brought out people who had lost their homes due to unfair tax laws, and showed people in hospitals unable to see their partners on their deathbed, all with the tag line: *John Street Did This.*

Street felt the heat.

He called a special evening session of the city council. It was rumored that he actually intended to force a vote on the legislation while he still had some control. What he didn't know then was that one of his strongest supporters on the council, Republican Thacher Longstreth, was wavering. This was a vote I really hadn't counted on even though he was someone with whom I had developed a friendship. Thacher, his girlfriend Melanie (who he lived with, and who was employed by the council), and I would sometimes have dinner together. Hearing the life story of one of Philadelphia's most blue-blooded and beloved characters was a joy, and as word got around about our friendship, it bemused the city. The conservative, Republican, blue-blooded socialite being friends with the out, loud, and in-your-face gay activist.

So on that fateful night, Street needed Thacher there, but he didn't show. Street went as far as asking the police to find Thacher, requesting his presence in the council chambers. He didn't give up until almost midnight. Which of course irritated the other council members. Later, when I asked Melanie where they were, she said delightedly, "I took him to the circus so John couldn't find us."

The first call to break Street's coalition was from a councilman whom I expected would feel the guiltiest, Michael Nutter, himself a future mayor and president of the US Conference of Mayors. Nutter asked if we would allow him to reintroduce the legislation that Jim Kenney and Councilman Frank DiCicco had previously submitted. Kenney and DiCicco were gracious and stepped in as cosponsors. The votes were now moving in our direction. It became a race, and for the first time Street knew he was in trouble. His designs on power were in jeopardy.

Andrew Park and his team of lawyers had written companion bills to create a domestic partners registry and give tax benefits similar to those offered to heterosexual married couples. As we came closer to a vote, only Street, the Catholic Church, and evangelicals publicly opposed the bill.

On the morning of the vote, I was shuffling from one council office to another. It was clear how close this vote would be. Street would sometimes be coming out of a councilmember's office just as I was going in. Our union friends had packed the galleries and it was said that a certain councilman was told that if his vote was needed, he would give it to us. I must admit that I didn't believe what I heard, until I entered the council and saw two muscled giants having a chat with that councilman.

Thacher was playing it cool, telling both Street and me that he'd make a final decision when he actually voted. Street had to face the fact that he might actually lose a vote in the council he controlled. As council president, he hadn't yet lost one vote. So at the very last minute, he proposed his own domestic partners legislation. Of course it was a sham.

Andrew Park recently shared with me his memory of the vote on the John Street decoy bill, just before the vote on the real domestic partners bill: "I was standing next to you on the railing of the city council behind all the desks. You were on your cell phone with Vince Fumo. You handed the phone to Janie Blackwell who was going to vote in favor of Street's bill. I don't know what Vince said to her, but it changed her vote. I think he offered her a campaign contribution. She was the deciding factor."

By the end of the day we had passed real domestic partnership legislation with a surprise vote from Thacher Longstreth.

Street, to his credit, quickly began to reach out to me. It might be relevant that he was about to run for mayor. I gave him an education on the subject of domestic partners and we soon became friends. I wouldn't be endorsing him for mayor, since he was still painted as a homophobe, but he and I knew that this didn't mean we couldn't start a dialogue.

In time Street began to question his own position on the matter, and this led to us having long discussions. As mayor, he actually did more for the gay community than Ed Rendell. He fought all the way to the state supreme court to protect Philly's domestic partners law, the one he originally fought against. And he won. He also launched a war on discrimination against gay people in the Boy Scouts and he both funded LGBT organizations and hired LGBT staffers.

The highlight for me was when he personally performed the domestic partners ceremony for his gay staffer Micah Mahjoubian and his partner Ryan Bunch. In a front row seat in an ornate City Hall room, I watched as Mayor John Street talked about marriage and how it should be afforded to all. This was the end result of legislation that he had opposed five years earlier and a testament to the power of education. To conclude the ceremony, Street brought out a broom. He told a story about slaves who were forbidden to marry without the permission of their owner. "They'd call the ceremony 'jumping the broom.' " Since it is outlawed for LGBT to marry in our country, like it was for slaves, it is appropriate for you, Micah and Ryan, to jump the broom." When he laid it down before them, there was not a dry eye in the room.

When people ask me about Street, my reply is that we're friends and that he's really funny and often surprising. After winning reelection as mayor, he invited me to lunch one day. I thought we'd meet at the Capital Grille or maybe The Palm. But he had another idea: we'd dine in his office. When I got there, a table had been set up in a little back chamber where Ed used to keep a soda machine. It had white linen on it with china, crystals, and even lit candles. A server was at the ready. It was elegant, and I do not know if I've ever felt more out of place or uncomfortable. Yet he did it for two reasons: first, to show thanks and appreciation for our unlikely friendship, and second, to prove a point.

During Street's inauguration, I had attempted to stop him from limiting the power of the new city council president, Anna Verna. In a strange twist of circumstance, Verna had a delightful and upbeat assistant named Pat Rafferty who I became friendly with, and it turned out her husband was Fran Rafferty. Street had known the power of that city council presidency and didn't want it to get in his way. My attempt at blocking this power grab had failed.

Street said over lunch, "Mark, without a soldier who is willing to fight, you can't win. Anna will never fight."

I told him he was correct, then said, "We're now even."

My coalition had beaten him on domestic partnership legislation and now he had won the battle for city council supremacy. We both had a good laugh to accompany our lunch.

In 2011, the Philadelphia city council passed the most far-reaching LGBT legislation in the nation. It was a well-needed update of an old piece of legislation. Sponsored by our friend and Rafferty replacement, Councilman Jim Kenney, the legislation now included trans issues; it even gave tax credits to corporations that offered trans benefits.

On August 28, 2008, my partner Jason and I, along with our friend Nia Meeks, were sitting in Invesco Field listening to will.i.am and waiting for Senator Barack Obama to make his speech accepting the Democratic nomination for president when my cell phone rang. I tried to answer, but due to security measures in the stadium it was hard to keep a signal. It took several callbacks for me to get the message. Just before accepting the nomination, the Obama people got a tip that the Republican nominee, Senator John McCain, was about to announce his VP choice in order to mute the publicity Obama would receive from his acceptance speech. One of the prospective candidates was former Pennsylvania governor and secretary of Homeland Security, Tom Ridge. If that happened, the Democrats wanted me to be prepared to speak on the subject.

Political pundits and columnists were falling all over themselves trying to guess who McCain would pick and when. Several weeks earlier I'd made a few guesses and offered a detailed analysis on two leading candidates in my weekly column. At the top on my list was Ridge, who as governor was a zero on LGBT rights. Just before becoming governor, I had met with him in Washington. He was serving out his final days as a congressman. In that meeting, he made it clear to me that he was not a friend to the LGBT community. My question to him at the time was simple—was it political or personal? His answer was both. I thanked him: "Congressman, you've saved me a lot of time."

That night, McCain didn't pick Ridge. It wasn't until the next day that we heard his decision. In hindsight, Ridge might have been a better choice than Sarah Palin. I'm not sure how the Obama team would have used me, but it's a testament to how well structured, organized, and disciplined the Obama campaign was in 2008. They had contingency plans for any issue. Ridge, to his credit, went on to support marriage equality in a brief before the US Supreme Court, and of course Barack Obama was elected president.

Chapter 10

Adventures with a Publisher

We drove up to the gate at Fort Indiantown Gap, Pennsylvania, and noticed that it was well guarded. It was one of the detention centers where the administration of President Jimmy Carter housed Cuban immigrants from the 1980 Mariel boatlift, and they were keeping it a secret. Actually, the center was holding prisoners and captives of various types.

I was in the driver's seat. J.R. Guthrie, our reporter, sat shotgun, with photographer Harry Eberlin in the backseat with an interpreter we'd hired for the day. We were all nervous as we pulled up to a guard.

"Reason for requesting entrance," he said, stone-faced.

Looking him straight in the eye I replied, "I'm Father Segal, sent by Metropolitan Community Church to talk with the refugees." He stared at me skeptically, so I added with equal parts seriousness and calm, "It's my missionary work. We should be on your list of clergy." I tugged at the clerical collar around my neck and cleared my throat. We were granted entrance.

Father Segal and *Philadelphia Gay News* became the first media to get inside one of America's military detention centers in the wake of that 1980 Mariel boatlift. The secret that President Carter had not wanted made public was something we in the LGBT community were well aware of. A great number of gay Cubans—considered "undesirable" by Fidel Castro—were put on those boats to Florida in an attempt to rid the island of homosexuals. Castro thought he'd play a joke on the US, since it was our policy to accept all Cuban refugees.

By June the rumor was spreading in the LGBT community. The State Department ran a quiet campaign to find foster homes for the gays through the Metropolitan Community Church and other church groups. Our military and State Department were not used to dealing with gay men, from Cuba or anywhere else. I smelled a story. J.R. and Harry agreed to come, which surprised me, and I happily put on a black jacket and shirt to look like a priest.

Once we'd gotten inside, instead of checking in, we headed straight to where our source said the gay Cubans would be held. We found two full barracks of gay men, well kept and wearing a hodgepodge of clothing. Our interpreter explained to them that we were from a gay newspaper in Philadelphia, and we began handing out copies of the paper. Few spoke English, and those who did spoke poorly at best, but we got permission to interview and photograph them. I kept watch at the door as J.R. and the interpreter asked questions to as many of them as possible. They talked of their lives back in Cuba; of how the police often raided their homes, imprisoned them, and attacked them with guard dogs. Even when showing us the scars from various abuses and atrocities, they radiated joy at being in the US even if they were in a detention center. Those who'd finished interviewing with us went to another barracks to tell a second group about us. Soon there was almost a party atmosphere as these guys paraded and danced before us with their stories.

The carnival soon drew attention and we suddenly found ourselves surrounded by soldiers. One of the higher-ranking men walked in and asked what we were doing there. By that time J.R. and Harry had hidden the recorder and camera.

"Sir," I said, "I'm just doing my missionary work for Metropolitan Community Church and I'm sorry if we have caused a ruckus. It seems we're giving them too much hope." I extended my hand.

"Father Segal, it's a pleasure to meet you." He shook my hand. "I think you've done enough for today."

The soldiers showed us back to our car and we drove off the base. Going through that gate was a relief. We were quiet for a few miles, and then we all broke into laughter. Awaiting us when we got back was a message from the general in charge of Fort Indiantown Gap, who had finally discovered our true identities and intentions. When we returned his call, the general demanded the recording and pictures we took. Apparently we were in deep trouble.

Thoughts of Watergate kept dancing in my mind, but I wasn't about to give in so easily. "General," I said, "I'm a publisher, and as far as I'm concerned we have a great story. You gave us entrance, we left when you requested. I see no reason not to publish. It's our First Amendment right."

He offered a few choice words, more loudly and a tad more threatening, before hanging up with a flair. We published the story on the cover of our August 8, 1980 edition, under the headline, "Meet the Gay Cubans."

Nine years later I spent a week in Cuba, traveling there without any prior contacts or government approvals. I did not want propaganda from either side; all I wanted was to report on the actual state of the gay community there.

I had learned from friends who'd visited the country that there was an ice-cream stand in the center of Havana where gay people went to meet up. After walking around for an hour, trying, albeit poorly, to cruise some of the guys, one of them came up to me and started speaking in Spanish. Seeing my confusion, he brought a friend over who spoke English. The two of them wound up being my tour guides for the week. I didn't tell them I was a reporter, not at first, since I didn't want to scare them. After a few days I told them the truth, and realized I should have done so from the beginning. They opened their lives to me, just as the men in the barracks had.

On my final night, they took me to a private party on the roof of a four-story walk-up in downtown Havana. We paid a dollar to enter, which I quickly realized guaranteed us all the bathtub rum we could drink. I learned that these parties happened at the same hour several times a week. It was an incredible sea of diversity, both men and women, and like most Cubans they were fairly poor. A few hours into the party, there was a commotion and people began to scream; some bolted for the exits. I made my way down to the ground floor with my friends, and as we left, I saw policemen pull up and begin to storm the building. After the raid, I watched from a distance as those who didn't flee the party were carried out and carted away. We returned to my hotel, where I decided to treat my guardians to a good meal.

Fidel Castro later publicly apologized for his government's discrimination against the LGBT community and treatment of people with HIV/AIDS. His brother Raul is a supporter of LGBT rights, and his niece Mariela has become an international voice on behalf of the cause.

In the eighties, I tried my hand as a radio talk show host on a small AM station in Philadelphia. WDVT (Delaware Valley Talk) is what is known as a daylighter, which simply meant that according to Federal Communications Commission rules, the station could only operate during daylight hours. The limited hours, plus competing against the other talk radio stations in the city, meant that the station had to do something revolutionary to garner an audience. Hence, *GayTalk*—the premier commercial gay and two-way talk radio show with your host, Mark Segal.

GayTalk launched on November 1, 1986. Stu Bykofsky, writing in the *Philadelphia Daily News*, described the show as "sort of a cross between Ralph Nader and Ethel Merman . . . *GayTalk* will twit heterosexuals, but not bash them." My first guest ever was Mayor W. Wilson Goode, who pleased me to no end when he said, "I didn't know what kind of show this was when I agreed to come." This is the same mayor who just four months later, during a heated reelection bid, appeared in front of a packed crowd at the annual *Philadelphia Gay News* Lambda Awards ceremony. In the Grand Ballroom of the Warwick Hotel, Philadelphia's first African American mayor stepped onto the stage to great applause. Wanting the gay audience to appreciate his commitment, he said with excitement, "I'm glad to be here, I've come three times." The audience roared. He meant he had attended the award ceremony three previous times.

Every Saturday afternoon for two hours, *GayTalk* held court. My format was to interview guests for the first hour and host a community roundtable for the second. Our guest list was surprisingly varied considering the subject matter and the station's small size. We had visits from politicians, TV personalities, and community leaders. On one particular Saturday we decided to discuss the pope. The Vatican had issued a statement on homosexuality written by one Cardinal Ratzinger, later to become Pope Benedict XVI. The statement declared that homosexuality was intrinsically evil. To which Stanley Ward, managing editor of *Philadelphia Gay News*, opined: "The pope is just a pimp for those abusive priests." Being a special-interest show, on a small station in the middle of Saturday afternoon, you might imagine (and you'd be right) that we didn't receive many calls. Our lines were always open and anyone could get through to us and on the air at almost any time. Once Stanley made that statement, however, the phone lines lit up like the proverbial Hanukkah bush.

Monday morning I heard from the station. While they did not agree with the statements on my show, they felt that speakers had the right to express their views, but in the future I should make it clear that those views were that of the individual, not the station. Several days later the station received a letter from the Anti-Defamation League of B'nai B'rith, supporting the church and asking for an apology on my show.

After I had fully digested the crux of their letter, I wrote back expressing my surprise at their support for an organization that not only has a historical record of oppression against the LGBT community but also the Jewish community. Then I cited the material on sexual abuse of children by priests. In 1986, most were unaware of this rampant abuse; the issue hadn't yet made it to the mass media. After receiving my reply, B'nai B'rith made no more requests for an apology.

A friend by the name of Wade Alexander began to gather clippings on issues that he thought would make good conversation for my show. I soon noticed that in every packet of clippings there were a number of articles on the papacy, so many that I figured there must be an eleventh commandment just for journalists: *Thou shalt not kill a story about His Holiness.* Considering the large audience response to our first foray, we soon had a regular feature—the weekly Pope Report.

We constantly corrected the misinformation sent out by the church, like comparing homosexuality to pedophilia, or the attempts to hide various issues that were, at that time, very problematic within their organization. Week after week, we covered the issue of abusive priests, and we made sure that any attempts by the church to denigrate the LGBT community were answered with facts.

As much fun as this was, it was bound to end sooner or later. After two years of being on the air, the station, always on the brink, succumbed to a buyout offer from a company that owned religious tape stations. These were radio stations that played religious shows on tape from various fundamentalists who paid the company for air time, then would plead with their listeners to send in a prayer offering to keep them on the air.

My friends Bill Davol and Phyllis Furst were running the day-to-day operations and coordination with on-air personalities. When I'd started at Talk 900 I was green to radio. Bill and Phyllis had taken me under their wings and helped me make my show more professional. They loved my energy and applauded the freshness that the show brought to the station. So for my last show they went all out.

My guest was a conservative TV talk show star named Morton Downey Jr., who paved the way for people like Bill O'Reilly and Glenn Beck. I relished the chance to interview a poster child for the right wing. I'd debated many people with his views before and knew what buttons to press. Downey strolled into the studio with a confident air. He was there to promote a new book. My agenda was to get him to tell his followers that he would not accept violence against gays. If possible, I wanted to set him straight on the issue of AIDS; his remarks about the issue were inflaming the nation. An example, which he repeated on my show, was that AIDS wouldn't be a problem if gays would just learn that God gave us the anus with only one purpose in mind.

As soon as we went on the air the telephone board lit up. Most of the early calls were from Downey's fans, then an abortion question or two, and then I asked him about AIDS. He started out by using the same gay-baiting language, and tried to tug at heartstrings by talking about his brother who had AIDS. He said he loved him, but often told him that if he had a different lifestyle, he would not be in that position now. He was chain-smoking at the time and I asked him if he'd say the same thing to someone dying of emphysema. He continued on, insisting that he'd do anything for his brother, and you could almost hear tears in his voice. Then we went to a commercial. During the break, I tried to tell him about a new drug that was being tested that might be of help to his brother. He just asked to use the phone and didn't seem to hear me. When he returned I tried to tell him again, but this time he interrupted me and changed the subject.

The next topic we tackled was violence. It took me some time but I finally got him to say that violence of any type was wrong. Then another break. He told me that while he wasn't as extreme as he appeared on the air, his act was going strong and if he could stand it for another two years he'd make a couple of million and then blow. He was cancelled in two years, right on target.

The lesson learned was that professional right-wing broadcasters like Downey and Rush Limbaugh, and even the shock jocks like Howard Stern, are more entertainment than enlightenment. They have every advantage by controlling the audio button, that magic ability to just cut someone off. They also have their regular callers and supporters, and they control the commercial break. Those things, no matter how good a speaker you are or how professional, mean that you cannot win a debate on their show unless it is agreed beforehand.

As for Downey, he filed for bankruptcy and would later suc-cumb to lung cancer. These people must be admired for the pro-fessional show-biz personalities that they have become. When Howard Stern's show first aired in Philly, his producers did their homework and tried to get local personalities on the air. At one point I was attacked for several days. This was a time to put my ego behind and realize that Stern controlled his own airtime. I didn't take the bait, and I didn't become another of his chewed-up guests. Within a few days I was never mentioned again on his show. But one fun episode: In August of 1994 my editor learned that Stern had a twenty-something gay intern for the summer. He assigned our intern, also a twenty-something, to interview Stern's charge, who arrived with his own public relations repre-sentative. That showed the level of control that must be exer-cised when you're crafting a media personality.

The one unfortunate fact with television media is that many Americans buy in to the unreality of what they see. Many let the shtick influence how they treat people. Ask any Rush Limbaugh listener about gay issues, and it's likely they will simply spurt out his views rather than try to form their own. This misinformation is something that the LGBT community combats every day, and is why it's so important for us to make human connections, talk about the facts, and, whenever the opportunity arises, speak the truth on any relevant or so-called controversial topic. We must protect ourselves as a community, and that includes being able to spread the real word, which is to say, the truth.

Years later, while sitting at my desk one morning and looking over mountains of paperwork and wondering where to begin, the phone rang and it was the ACLU. They asked if I would be willing to go to jail in order to protect the First Amendment. When I told them I'd gone to jail for less, they perked up and explained COPA.

The Child Online Protection Act was passed by Congress and signed into law by President Bill Clinton in 1998. It was an attempt by Congress to restrict access by minors to online material deemed harmful to them, an attempt to control Internet pornography. They were using pedophiles as a justification for the legislation. Any government official or agency that was offended by something placed on the web could somehow argue that it was harmful to minors and then prosecute.

The ACLU representative wanted to know if *PGN* would be interested in being a plaintiff in the case and help sue the US government. She explained that this had inherent danger, like being found guilty and carted off to prison for example. For me, it was an easy decision. *Salon* and *PGN* were among the plaintiffs. As expected, the case made it all the way to the Supreme Court. The plaintiffs were invited to be present while our attorney argued her points and then took questions from the justices. The night before, all the plaintiffs were in DC for a planning meeting, or rather we were told what was expected of us, which was very little. As plaintiffs this was the end of the trail for us. We were instructed to sit respectfully in the court and listen.

The following morning, just going into the elegant Supreme Court building was intimidating. Truthfully, there was very little to be worried about since by this point we had won all three lower court rulings on the First Amendment rights. Indeed, the US Supreme Court eventually ruled that legislation, which was signed into law by President Clinton, unconstitutional.

On another occasion I had an encounter of a different kind with President Bill Clinton. He was in town to deliver a speech to the party faithful at the Warwick Hotel. Several months before I was unable to accept an invitation to the White House due to a trip to China. I asked Ed Rendell, who had then become chairman of the Democratic National Committee, if he'd arrange a photo of me with the president. Once again Ed and I began to act like children. He said, "You bring the camera and I'll take the picture." This was before cell phone cameras. Somehow I got through security with the camera in my coat breast pocket and made it to the front where there was a red velvet rope separating us from the podium. Standing next to me was the city's district attorney, Lynne Abraham, with a Secret Service agent directly in front.

President Clinton's party entered the room to thunderous applause. They took their places onstage; Ed stood directly behind the president. As Clinton finished his remarks, Ed put his hands to his face like he was taking a picture and mouthed, *Do you have the camera?* I nodded. People began to stare at us. The president's speech ended to more thunderous applause. Enter the Marx Brothers, Ed and Mark. The president tried to leave by the left side of the stage but Ed steered him to the right where I was waiting. Clinton climbed down the stairs and Ed, who was directly behind the president, shouted, "Toss me the camera!" Without thinking I reached in my pocket, pulled out the camera, and tossed it over Clinton's head. Ed caught it, then told the president he wanted to get a few pictures, and we began to pose with him. It is amazing that I didn't get shot. The president started laughing and the crowd was stunned.

In my weekly column of November 10, 1994, titled "Presidential Charmer," I told the story. I sent a copy to the White House with the following note on my three-by-five stationary pad with the *Philadelphia Gay News* logo.

Mr. President,
    If you'd sign and send this back to me it will be the highlight of my life . . . Okay, ONLY ONE of the highlights.

Thanks,
Mark

A few weeks later a brown envelope from the White House arrived at my office. Inside was a large piece of white cardboard and in the middle was that three-by-five stationary. Scrawled over my writing were the words, *To Mark, Warm Appreciation, Bill Clinton.* The picture that Ed took is now on my office wall; it shows Clinton and me with the surprised crowd looking on with open mouths.

Most Communist countries have had trouble dealing with LGBT issues. In 1991, soon after the fall of the Berlin Wall, Patsy Lynch, then a photographer for the Associated Press, was covering what is now known as "Soviet Stonewall," a phrase coined by journalist Rex Wockner. It was the first LGBT conference tour in Russia. The organizers chose a wide range of speakers from around the world to showcase gay activism. Bob Ross of San Francisco's *Bay Area Reporter* and I were representing LGBT media. The tour had two stops, St. Petersburg and Moscow. Thanks to President Mikhail Gorbachev, there was new freedom in the air that spring and people wondered how far they could take things. Our conference was a test. The International Gay and Lesbian Human Rights Commission (IGLHRC) had gotten us invited to Russia on a ruse from a medical institution. We didn't know what to expect.

During a break in the proceedings in St. Petersburg, after taking a photo of me on the throne of Peter the Great, Patsy wanted to go shopping. We found ourselves on Nevsky Prospect, one of the main streets in the city. Walking along we noticed that most shop windows and shelves were bare. The streets on the other hand were filled with peddlers hawking their goods on carpets and cloth. These wares were mostly knickknacks, tattered old clothes, family mementos, and Soviet memorabilia. Everywhere you walked, if they knew you were from the West, people would just take things out of their pockets to sell you. A pack of cigarettes would get you a car ride to any destination in the city. People were poor, and the country was on the edge of political and financial collapse.

Patsy had only one shopping item in mind: a watch from the Soviet navy. While tensions in Russia had eased up a little, there still was some restrictive protocol, and military items were not to be sold. A man came up to Patsy at some point and showed her a Lenin pin and a Stalin pin, but she just brushed him off. She started to move on but then turned around and asked him if he had a watch, and lo and behold, her dream item appeared. She haggled for a moment and as the watch and currency changed hands, a black car screeched to a stop in front of us, just like in the movies. Two men in black trench coats grabbed the guy, threw him in the backseat, and made a quick exit.

I looked at Patsy incredulously. "We could have been arrested as spies by the KGB," I said.

"But at least I have my watch," she replied. She still has it today.

To say that the Russians were not prepared for the freethinking American gay people is an understatement. AIDS was just beginning to rear its ugly head in the former Soviet Union and the organizers of the conference had smuggled in thousands of condoms. We handed them out to people at the conference who rushed to grab them. When we asked one guy why he wanted American condoms, he replied, "Soviet condoms taste like machine in factory." So we all grabbed bags of condoms and went back to the main street to give them out. Amazingly, even the police began to assist. Patsy took a great photo of me handing condoms to a peasant woman, who kept coming back for more. I believe she wanted to sell them on the black market. At least they'd find a user.

Though you couldn't even buy a bottle of soda that wasn't rusty, one evening Robin Tyler, the comedian and activist from Los Angeles, was somehow able to rent a white Cadillac limo, complete with a sunroof. She and I and another couple took off to a casino, which turned out to be a dingy little place without much gambling going on. Disappointed, we returned to our dilapidated hotel, but not before getting a bit drunk. We stood up and out of the sunroof and shouted at the tops of our lungs. Nobody seemed to notice these Americans on the prowl in their city.

Tyler went on to Moscow and performed her out lesbian humor for an audience of eight hundred astonished Russians. Earlier in her career she'd paired with her partner as the first lesbian comedy duo, Harrison and Tyler. Back in 1970 they had joined Jane Fonda's *Free the Army* tour at a time when Fonda was being labeled Hanoi Jane, and after their first appearance Fonda canned them. "I don't remember Jane yelling anything," Robin explained to me. "I do remember that she came over to our apartment in Hollywood and told Patty and me that we could no longer be in the *FTA* show because we had showed that kind of open affection onstage. In the 1980s she apologized. But when I met her almost a decade after that she pretended that she didn't know anything about the incident. Very strange. By then I believed her to be a born-again Christian or something like that."

When it was my turn to speak at the conference, I was awestruck looking out at gay and lesbian Russians. They were just beginning to find their sea legs in activism and it made me think of the humble start of LGBT media in the US, not only in our struggle for equality, but in building community. I tossed my prepared remarks aside and spoke from the heart.

Through an interpreter I explained how oppression leads to activism and how important communication is to any movement. I knew they cared deeply about these issues because they took a major risk by being present. We hoped that they'd use what they learned at the conference to foster an active Russian LGBT community. Never would I have expected that years later the "democratic" government of Vladimir Putin would oppress the LGBT community to the point where people were comparing it to the country's historic subjugation of Jews. The homophobia of the Putin government reached its pinnacle in 2014, as Russia geared up to host the Winter Olympics in Sochi.

Through my involvement with Comcast and NBCUniversal's Joint Diversity Council, I had a front-row seat watching the company mitigate the issue of homophobia at the Sochi Olympic Games. The company was getting flack for broadcasting an event from a country with an egregious civil rights record. But it was difficult to advise what steps could be taken to pressure Russia since our television contract was with the International Olympic Committee, not with the country of Russia. Strategically, the company made a brilliant move when they chose an openly gay man, Thomas Roberts, to host the Miss Universe pageant from Moscow, just weeks before the games. It was Comcast telling Putin and the world that it stood with the LGBT community. Roberts bravely took on the task and spoke openly about being gay and the restrictive laws in Russia, thereby sending a message to Putin: *You better not touch anyone during the Olympics.* To make the message even clearer, NBC sent numerous LGBT staffers to cover the various sports, including one flamingly out gay man, retired figure skater Johnny Weir. If he had been a Russian citizen, I believe he would have been arrested without question. He, like all other non-Russian citizens, was left untouched and the games went off with minimal issues. Brian Roberts, David L. Cohen, and the entire Comcast-NBCUniversal team were brave and brilliant, and made me proud.

The LGBT community applauded NBC for pushing the boundaries, yet noted that after the games, when the cameras were off, the oppressive homophobia inside Russia tightened. Putin and his team were taking Russia back to the days of the Soviet Union, with massive restrictions on the press and the alleged murder and imprisonment of many journalists. The opening we saw as a group in the nineties had long gone. I hope that the LGBT Russian community will someday regain a foothold in their country to advance their civil liberties.

At the 2008 Democratic National Convention in Denver, *Philadelphia Gay News* covered the events for many of the LGBT publications that were unable to send their own reporters. Each day we had a preproduced interview to be posted. Before we even boarded the plane we had interviews with Barney Frank, Tammy Baldwin, Howard Dean, and a host of others. We tweeted from many of the LGBT events and meetings, including the roll call of delegates, where the number of LGBT delegates was proudly shouted out for each state. We took polls on gay marriage from people at the convention, including notables like Spike Lee and Maria Shriver. We knew before all the other media about the "secret" set being built for Obama to accept the nomination at Invesco Field. But there was something else I knew and didn't report.

I wasn't surprised when in 2012 Vice President Biden made a very public gaffe preempting the president in support of marriage equality. Why did he do this then? I'd suspected his position for four years already. The morning after Joe Biden was nominated as Obama's vice president in 2008, his first speaking engagement was with the Pennsylvania delegation. It was fitting since he grew up in Scranton and spent his formative years in Pennsylvania.

After making a triumphant entrance at the 2008 convention, VP nominee Biden made his way to the platform to deliver a few remarks to an excited crowd. Jill Biden was standing on the side near us, and we spoke for a while. She knew I was from *Philadelphia Gay News* and I asked her a few questions, including one about gay marriage. She thought for a moment and then said, "Of course I support it."

Jill Biden is a delightful, personable, and brilliant woman, but I didn't do my job as a journalist and instead dispensed some advice: "Since Joe is the nominee, the two of you might want to mirror Obama's position." It was her first day on the job and I didn't want to taint it. I didn't ask the vice presidential nominee the same question. Was this a missed opportunity? I'm happy to say I have no regrets.

The second conversation I had that morning was with MSNBC pundit Chris Matthews, who was considering a run against Senator Arlen Specter, and that conversation was reported in the LGBT press. Here's the exchange:

Mark Segal: *You're running for Senate in Pennsylvania. As you know, there are some very important issues going on. We have a Republican in that seat, Specter, who voted two ways on the Defense of Marriage Act. So what would you be doing?*

Chris Matthews: *Well, first, I'm not going to answer it that way. I always start with freedom. That's where I start* on every issue, whether it's reproductive rights or it's crime. There's a constitutional right that starts with freedom and inherent rights, exclusive rights to the Constitution. But I really do believe that we always as Americans start with that. Then we work our way through things. Do you understand? It's very important. Individual freedom has always been the way we start. First governments, sequestered governments like in England, always start with state power. This country has always started with individual freedom as the basis to work at what you allow the state to do. But obviously, this is an evolving thing; my thinking now is different from what it was ten years ago. [For] a lot of people it's been evolving, and for a lot of gay people it's been evolving. A lot of gay people didn't think marriage was going to be the issue. A lot of friends of mine didn't think it was going to be an issue, because it was too far out. A lot of people are changing on these issues. I think a lot of people are going to work our way through these things.

MS: Well, where are you on the issue?

CM: I have an open heart. I'll have to live with it.

MS: In other words, you won't answer the question.

CM: I can answer it the way I have, which is any fucking way I want. I can answer in my way even if it isn't your way.

What's interesting here is the irritation Matthews had with the question. I'd like to believe he was in that "evolution" mode. Again, no regrets. Watching Matthews show his support of marriage equality now sometimes amazes me. He completely understands the history of the issue, and could give other pundits lessons in the proper journalistic approach to describing marriage equality. He has become passionate in his support of civil rights.

Chapter 11

Bringing Up Baby

In 1996, my nephew Jeffrey called me after years of my trying to reach him. He's one of three children born to my older brother. He and his two sisters, Jennifer and Stephanie, hadn't lived with their father since early childhood. My brother is not the most nurturing person alive and we've been estranged for many years. But his children are my parents' grandchildren, of course, and that led me to seek them out. At first their mother allowed both Jennifer and Stephanie to visit with my partner and me. That was usually around holidays or during the summer. The first time they arrived at the airport from Florida, I immediately saw how beautiful they were.

When I'd ask about their brother there was always a different story. I couldn't find out much about him. This game kept going for years. Once in a while, when I called their mother and asked, Jeffrey was put on the phone, but he spoke only briefly and with trepidation. When I got the call in 1996, he began with the words, "Uncle Mark, may I come to see you?" This time, his mother allowed him to visit for a weekend, or so I thought.

The minute he got off the plane I could see the family resemblance. We did touristy things around the city, and I treated him to dinner, but it took him awhile to warm up to us. As I'd say later, he came to us broken. By the end of the weekend he was trying to either con us (something which I found charming and amusing) or get us to adopt him. (It turned out that he was a ward of the Florida court.) The last night of that weekend visit, my partner went to sleep early to allow Jeffrey and me to have a heart-to-heart—though we had already decided to take him. After all, how hard could it be to have a teenage son?

That night Jeffrey told me his story. We both cried a lot. I'm sure that some of it was embellished to spur me to action, but regardless of what I thought at the time, I soon learned from the court that much of what Jeffrey said was true and much of it was not his doing. I promised then that we'd get him out of Florida. A promise I had no idea how I'd keep.

I also knew we had to act quickly. I called some political friends involved in the judiciary and requested that they contact their colleagues in the Florida court system to see what they could do to help me. Within two weeks I was on a plane to Florida to be interviewed by the court guardian, during which time Jeffrey was placed in a group home. The guardian, almost on sight of me, opened up about Jeffrey. She adored him and wanted him out of reach of his family. I spent two days in Florida, returned home, and almost overnight I had somehow been approved to be his new guardian. I don't believe his mother had any idea this was happening, and since I was never in any court in Florida, I don't even know how this was legally possible. Regardless, my teenage nephew-turned-adopted-son was about to arrive.

Our first thought of parenthood was to give him everything he had been denied. He went from being a rural, hardworking child laborer and ward of the state to a child of a successful gay publisher in an urban setting. My friends in the media were kind enough to ignore all the hijinks with Jeffrey, since many of them were parents and knew very well that I had taken on a challenge. They preferred to sit back and enjoy the show rather than report on it.

When Jeffrey arrived, we gave him twenty dollars and told him to walk around the city and enjoy himself. A few hours later he called in tears. Seems he felt he needed a more contemporary haircut than his Florida crew cut, and went into a fancier-than-he-realized spa. He thought the massage and shampoo were part of the haircut, but panicked when he was handed the bill for eighty dollars. No problem.

He had heard about my many trips to jail. By this time I thought that this part of my life was over. But along came Chris Bartlett, who had put together a demonstration against the local CBS affiliate after their news broadcast did an exposé of "gay men having sex in public restrooms." The real story was that in almost all cases they were married men. Chris explained something to the effect that it was my duty as an elder to show the younger generation the significance of the issue. In other words, he guilt-tripped me.

His plan was to toilet-paper the entire building. Jeffrey went along and wanted to be a part of the demonstration, but in my first parental protective gesture I told him to stay in the car and watch. The police were called, and he got to witness his uncle and new guardian being arrested, handcuffed, and hauled off to jail. (Perhaps it was a good civics lesson?)

Jeffrey and I had a chat one day about family boundaries. He still quotes to me my words: "Jeffrey, there will be times that you'll try to get something over on me, but believe me, I've pulled every stunt that has ever been pulled, and I'll catch you, so don't even try." That was my first mistake as a parent, since Jeffrey took it as a challenge. His first try came very quickly. He noted that we had numerous parties at the house and that it was a great way to get to know people. He got comfortable chatting with the mayor and other notable individuals. At sixteen he was living the life, but it was his uncle's life—and he would imitate it. One weekend, as we were about to leave for our shore house, Jeffrey asked if he could stay home. My partner and I agreed, since we thought he was doing well, adjusting to city life. We didn't really give it a second thought. Until we arrived home. When we got upstairs, the house was oddly clean. Not clean, immaculate. Something was wrong. While taking a walk, I noticed items that used to be in our house in public trash cans. On my way back into the house a neighbor saw me and said, "Quite a wild party you had last night." According to other neighbors, people were hanging off the balconies. Hey, at least we taught him how to socialize.

It was obviously time to have a sit-down with Jeffery. I must admit that I was almost proud of him, but he lost points since I had caught him. I told him he was grounded, and instead of an allowance, which I never understood anyway, he had to get a job. He found one and kept it, all the while dealing with the unforgiving Northeast winter. He was just happy to be out of Florida and with role models for the first time in his life. He had earned his GED, so we investigated getting him into a community college.

Jeffrey hadn't seen his father since he was a young child. He couldn't even remember him. One thing I suggested was that since his father lived in the same region, it might be good to meet him sometime, so at the very least he'd be able to form his own opinion. I handed him his father's phone number and reminded him that the only things he knew about his father were what he'd heard from his mother and me. It was important that he meet him and make his own judgment, then decide whether to continue the relationship. His attitude toward a father who he felt had abandoned him was quite negative. He snapped at me, saying that he didn't want to see him, but I insisted he take the number and call his father when he felt ready.

Having a child about to enter college was a shock for someone who had never paid for school supplies before. Jeffrey made a list of all the things he needed, and I'd supply the cash or credit card. What I didn't know is that Jeffrey had indeed gotten in touch with his father and was asking him to pay for the same items. He was double-dipping. My brother's girlfriend called me out of the blue for the first time in years and asked a question about Jeffrey's school supplies, and I suddenly put two and two together. When Jeffrey came home, I called out to him in a stern voice. He came over to where I was sitting with a smile on his face. "Guess who I was just on the phone with." He knew I knew. "Jeffrey, I've got to hand it to you, that was a good one, but the gravy train just stopped." This was also the end of his new relationship with his father. Jeffrey does not like to talk about my brother, and neither do I, so we just don't. But I've always believed that it's good to know where you come from.

To my great pleasure, Jeffrey became a first-rate IT headhunter, now living and working in New York. It will not surprise me when he opens his own firm. He's talented, sociable, and smart. His success and our relationship come with an added bonus for me. Whenever we chat on the phone, I get to say to him, in my best Jewish accent: "Jeffrey, when are you going to find a girl, settle down, and give me some grandkids to spoil?"

After Jeffrey moved to New York, I began to appreciate the empty-nest syndrome. I also began to ponder what it felt like to be really single. The emotional damage from my twenty-year relationship had filled me with 100 percent self-loathing and 0 percent self-esteem. As I detailed earlier, this breakup, aside from the deaths in my family, was the lowest point of my life. I survived with the help of prescription drugs, my physician Dr. Mounzer, a psychologist, and a pharmacologist. It took them and a team of friends to get me to the point where I'd even consider seeing someone again. And the first two dips into the water didn't work out so well. The first candidate and I weren't quite hitting it off, and on our third date one evening at Ruth's Chris Steak House, I told him we should stop seeing each other. He stood up and started waving his steak knife at me, yelling, "You're breaking up with me?" It took the staff to get him away and out of the restaurant. Then the second guy kept disappearing on various evenings. I later found out that he was picking up drugs from an unsavory guy. Maybe it was best to remain a bachelor.

But life wasn't *all* down at that time. My friends the Mezzaroba family and their matriarch Rita adopted me. At first, when I wouldn't leave the house, they brought over care packages, which were as delicious as any restaurant. They insisted that I spend the holidays with them. Christmas Eve, feast of the seven fishes, in their Italian home, was my particular favorite. Rita grew up in the heart of Italian South Philadelphia. Her husband owned a construction company and did very well. They still lived in a row home and shopped at the Italian market on a stretch of 9th Street where each grocery has stalls out front; it resembles New York's Lower East Side circa 1900. They had their favorite cheese shop, butcher, and pasta maker. Her husband even made his own wine. I'd joke with Rita about being a Mafia princess, and occasionally she'd almost make me believe it. She was elegant and a damn smart woman. I adored her. The warmth between her, her daughter Charlene, her son-in-law Jack, and their children allowed me to believe that decency, kindness, and love were possible for me.

Rita's favorite restaurant was an elegant wood-paneled downtown joint, stocked with antiques. A photo of Marlon Brando as the Godfather sat discreetly next to a tin slide photograph of Abraham Lincoln. It was reputed to be a mob hangout, but the food was incredible. One wintry night with an icy wind blowing, Rita was waiting for me at the bar when I walked in. She had a glass of wine in her hand, and as I dragged a heavy stool across the black-and-white-tiled floor to sit next to her, she shook her head sadly and said: "Things just don't fall off the truck the way they used to." She was serious. "There were fur coats and designer jeans, and the shoes! Now all we have is going to the shops." She sighed and finished, "I miss that kind of living."

Around this time Dad began a slow drift into loneliness. Mom was his world and he had lost her. My attempts at making him feel important were sometimes totally out of place. For his seventieth birthday I used my brand-new video camera to make a *This Is Your Life, Marty Segal* highlights film. Mayor Wilson Goode: "Marty, I have some news for you, hospital records have been found that prove that we are brothers." A hooker played by *Philadelphia Daily News* columnist Stu Bykofsky's former wife Maria Merlino (yes, of *that* Merlino family) telling Dad he's "one of her best customers." Then Philadelphia District Attorney Ron Castille, who went on to become a Supreme Court justice of the Commonwealth of Pennsylvania, explaining that he had just sworn out a warrant for Dad's arrest for using too many prostitutes. Then we took him to dinner where at the restaurant he was surprised to find the complete family waiting for him and applauding as he walked in.

At that time Dad only wore jeans and short-sleeve shirts. I wanted him to come to one of my political fundraising dinners, explaining that it required a suit and tie. He objected, but finally gave in and allowed me to have someone take him shopping to get the proper outfit. He not only picked out the suit, he sat for it to be tailored. He chose the shirt and tie and was very particular about the matching shoes. When he showed up at the fundraiser, he was in jeans, a short-sleeve buttoned shirt, and his old brown shoes. He saw my smile and shrugged. He never wore that suit and when he died it was not among his possessions. I have no idea what happened to it.

During the last couple of years of his life, until he succumbed to myasthenia gravis at age seventy-three in 1996, Dad lived with Aunt Rose, his sister. Her daughter Ilene remains to this day my favorite cousin. Rose's children grew up seeing their cousin Mark on the news being carted off to jail or interviewed on TV. Ilene knew of the various pressures on my time but she attempted to get me to attend as many family functions as possible. Her children went through puberty during the early years of HIV/AIDS. Through my work with doctors, she learned how to explain safe sex to her children as they came of age. And to the embarrassment of her children, when their friends visited them, Ilene occasionally felt compelled to offer safe-sex lessons. Sometimes the other parents did not appreciate this.

One time at her daughter Stacie's school, when they did show-and-tell, Stacie brought me in and told them about the fight for gay rights. But more than anything else, their home became a refuge for many of their young friends who were coming out of the closet. Ilene and family opened their home, and at times Ilene lectured parents who wouldn't accept their children. In a way she was able to show me how my work was used in real time . . . and she never let me feel left out. She has raised three incredible children. That closeness continues; one night her son Michael and his wife called and asked if they could name their first child after me.

When my twenty-year relationship ended my family was there

for me. So was my friend Rob Metzger. He told me of an e-mail he'd received from a young man, a journalism student at NYU. Rob had found the perfect man for me, or so he thought. The e-mail began with something like: *Your friend Rob Metzger suggested I write you since we have so much in common.*

This started a yearlong e-mail correspondence with Jason. No chat rooms and no phone calls, just e-mails. Somehow, after a while, I lost sight of the fact that he was a student. Our messages were intense, full of discussions on current events. He even began to offer advice on some my projects, and eventually the exchanges became emotional, though never sexual. Twice he invited me to New York, and twice I backed out at the last minute.

Then Mayor John Street won reelection and allowed me to create an official LGBT inaugural gala to benefit our LGBT community center. It was on Saturday, January 3, 2004.

At ten p.m. we did the check ceremony, announcing to the crowd that we had raised $110,000, and Patti LaBelle sang "Over the Rainbow" to me and I swooned. The party was jumping and we still had a couple hours to go. But something hit me: I wanted to go home and send an e-mail to Jason. He had worked with me on this project the entire time. Why hadn't I invited him? He should have been standing next to me in the glory of that evening.

By eleven p.m. we were e-mailing away. This lasted till the very late hours of the morning. It was decided that the following weekend he would come to Philadelphia so that we could finally meet in person. We decided on Philly so that I could not back out.

All week I prepared for that first date. I hadn't been on a real date in decades, so I thought it should be special. There was no way to contain my excitement, and this somehow took on the shape of a city project. After I mentioned the date to a friend in City Hall, word seemed to get around. Friends started calling with suggestions. What I didn't grasp was that everyone was working to get me back to my old self.

Jason arrived by train. At the station, I met him with yellow roses and I sang a Bette Midler song. He should have run then, or I should have, but instead we got in my car. The first stop was showing him the Philly skyline, which he'd never seen before. We drove to the top of the Philadelphia Museum of Art with its famous *Rocky* steps. The police had cleared out all cars and people for me, so we'd have that romantic view of the city all to ourselves. There I gave him a treasure trove of Philadelphia tchotchkes, donated to me by various city tourism organizations. Moving along, we went to RiverRink by the Delaware River to go ice-skating. The Delaware River Waterfront Corporation had a guard at the gate awaiting our arrival at Penn's Landing, and he escorted us to our parking spot next to a tent erected specifically for our use. Inside the warm tent were carpet, chairs, and a sofa. Candles flickered all around a bottle of champagne, fruit, and a chocolate fountain. It was a scene out of the *Arabian Nights*. My favorite part was a framed message on a little wooden table, *Enjoy Your Night, Mark and Jason. —Your friends at Penn's Landing.* We looked at each other, hugged, and yes, we had our first kiss. We chatted for a while, held each other, and finally we tried on the skates that were laid out for us in the tent.

When we emerged there were two escorts waiting to take us to the rink. Someone asked over the speaker system that everyone leave the rink temporarily, and we were brought onto the ice. They changed the music to Bette Midler and Jason and I began to skate. On our second lap around the rink, he took my hand and the crowd, who had been forced off the rink, actually applauded. I knew then that this was something special.

After skating, it was time for dinner. We had a reservation at Buddakan, a Stephen Starr restaurant with an Asian twist. Inside the restaurant, a long string of tables usually sits in front of a two-story golden Buddha statue. But not that night. Stephen had rearranged the tables so we had Buddha practically to ourselves. When dinner was done, a giant dessert arrived at the table. I didn't know it at the time, but Jason loved sweets and was delighted. And on top of all that, there was no bill.

Then and only then did we go home, and he saw the house for the first time. That was over a decade ago, and I thank God (a term I rarely use) for each and every day with him. Aside from my parents, he is the only person in the world who has ever truly understood me; he supports and encourages me, and wants nothing in return but my love. He's my best friend and soul mate.

I've left out some details from that first date, but I suppose I should come clean. When Jason arrived in Philadelphia and came up the train station escalator, I almost ran for the doors. Seeing him for the first time shocked me. I had somehow stopped thinking about how he was a student at NYU, i.e., young. In the previous year, his e-mails had made me feel like I was corresponding with someone of my age and maturity level. His knowledge and calmness were new to me. His youth scared me. To make matters worse, after three laps on the ice rink, I stopped. Translation: I was out of shape. He was the star of the NYU swim team, and earlier in his career had been on the Maryland state team with Michael Phelps. He was tall and slim, I was short and portly. His family was Catholic while mine was Jewish. He came from a conservative military family, and I was a left-wing pinko fag. But somehow we connected. He was and is one of the brightest people I know. I am truly turned on by brainpower.

Jason thinks I changed his life, but the reality is that he changed mine far more dramatically. The past decade has been among the happiest and most productive of my life. Like all couples, we have our problems, a primary one being everything that comes along with being me, that circus I call a life. Instead of complaining, he encourages me. He allows me to think big. When I do fail, he's there to suggest new projects to keep me busy and engaged.

Just a few months after Jason and I met, the organizing began for a big Elton John concert. I had somehow gotten engaged, and Jason accompanied me and several others on a related trip to Vienna and then to London for negotiations with the Elton John AIDS Foundation. This trip showed me what a partner should be and that in some ways our relationship was like a fairy tale. At the Hofburg Palace in Vienna on a private tour, when we arrived in the queen's bedroom, a band in the courtyard below started to play, and without a word he took my hand and we danced.

Being part of Elton's entourage was an experience that would scare even seasoned media veterans. Jason was not fazed at all. Motorcades, shopping trips, dinner with Elton—nothing rattled him. The one thing I noticed on that trip is that he challenged me without making me feel threatened. The numbers showed him to be young, the brain showed him to be Yoda.

Shortly after our return from London I hosted a meeting of the National Gay Newspaper Guild, an organization of LGBT publishers, and invited Jason along. On our first day of meetings I asked the mayor to say a few words to open the conference and he obliged. After welcoming the publishers to the city, Mayor Street got up and went around the table to shake hands. When he came to Jason he said, "I've certainly heard a lot about you."

Then he turned to me and said in a loud whisper that all could hear, "A little young, Mark." He patted me on the back with a warm smile and made his way out.

We've had so many special moments and have been through a lifetime of memories, including deeply challenging situations. We even separated for what now looks like the blink of an eye. I was so saddened that I wrote a column about it, and then equally joyful when I wrote another retracting it.

For a time, Jason lived in Japan as an English teacher, and he also worked for a national network news show in Washington. But we always made a point to keep in constant communication, for which our year of e-mailing had prepared us well. When he was in Washington, we only saw each other on weekends. As I expected, he rose through the ranks of the show remarkably quickly, to the point where he was actually assisting the executive producer with running a nightly newscast. And yet as well as he did there, I was delighted when he was able to return home to Philly to work as a producer for another big media company.

We complemented each other in ways that enhanced both of our lives. We couldn't have been happier. But our families were not so thrilled with this union. My first introduction to Jason's family was to one of his two older sisters. We were all visiting New York and a dinner meeting was arranged. It was early in our relationship and I was still recovering from the end of my long-term relationship. It felt like his sister hated me at first sight. In retrospect, she should have. She probably didn't expect an overweight older man who was from a culture totally different from theirs. I'm also sure that my appearance was not as neat as it could have been and my manners not impeccable. To make matters worse, when I get nervous I chat and chat, and often don't let anyone get a word in. I chatted.

Her true impression, she later told me, was of a man telling her how he would try to change the little brother she loved and had helped to raise. In hindsight, she was correct and I simply was not ready for prime time. The guy who had done thousands of interviews had failed this one.

Jason's parents were about as welcoming as his sister. By this I mean that I didn't meet them until we had been together for seven years. But Jason holds that he is really at fault here, since he gave up on trying to introduce us early on. Somehow I was not worried about meeting them and as I expected, at that first meeting, seven years after Jason and I had been together, we hit it off immediately. Jason was the most nervous person in the room. The other three of us got along famously. And I was able to see the love between Jason and his parents, and instantly realized where he had gotten all the qualities that I cherish about him. I adore Jason's parents and enjoy every visit with them.

As for my side of the family, my cousin, upon first meeting Jason, actually walked out of the restaurant and called me later to ask what I could possibly have in common with him. According to her, our age gap was too wide. My lifelong friend Barbara just didn't get it, but guess who did? On Jason's second trip to Philly I introduced him to Rita and Charlene. After we dropped Jason off at the train station, they just kept repeating, "He's a keeper."

Jason gets the credit for bringing me back. He has also taught me how to distance myself from negativity. It's a political tactic, one that I never embraced before. No longer is my time spent defending myself against false allegations or those trying to use me to raise their personal profile. Like me, Jason is passionate, in particular with his writing. On many nights we are both at home writing or reading or, if too exhausted, sitting in front of the television. We treasure our quiet evenings at home.

We've become an old and boring couple and we love our old and boring things.

One night during bedtime conversation I asked Jason, "Do you think I can raise nineteen or twenty million to build an affordable LGBT senior living facility?"

He looked me in the eye and said, "Of course."

Those two words of support were all I needed to start on my next project, the biggest one yet. But it had to wait until after my stint as a concert producer.

Chapter 12

Elton John and a Bag Full of Diamonds

Like many things in my life, the Elton saga began by accident. In the fall of 2003, in the midst of Mayor John Street's reelection bid, a story broke. The FBI had bugged Street's office as part of a federal investigation of political corruption in Philadelphia. The mayor, who at one time was considered one of the most homophobic elected officials in the city, had done a complete turnaround in his first term and was trying hard to correct his past. Any decent man believes in human rights, after all. Street had come to embrace the LGBT community and I endorsed him for reelection. But his history still gave people pause and my endorsement was not very popular in my community.

There was one thing that most people never understood about John Street: he wasn't about personal wealth. For him, politics was all about the power, specifically the power to bring on a progressive agenda. The FBI, as it turned out, taped our calls and many others. Not to leave any stone unturned, they also got the mayor's e-mails. This was discovered when the *Philadelphia Inquirer* successfully sued the government for access to information and materials related to the investigation. Those correspondences appeared on the front page of the paper. Marcia Gelbart wrote a story about the mayor's attempt to understand the LGBT community and published our e-mail dialogue.

It showed a side of John Street that most people never saw, a caring man from a devout background who was trying to accept that his religion, or those who taught it, might have gotten some things wrong.

As a result of the investigation, the campaign for mayor between Street and Republican rival Sam Katz was now a dead heat. Some polls had Katz ahead, even with a five-to-one advantage in Democratic voter registration. As a Street supporter, I tried to change the odds. About an hour after the FBI story broke, I asked myself, *Could a federal bugging of a mayor's office be used as a positive rather than a negative?* It sure could, if it was tied back to someone very unpopular in the city of Philadelphia, someone who nobody in their right mind would ever support. That would be the president of the United States, George W. Bush. So I ordered five thousand buttons that read: *Bug Bush! Reelect Street.*

I then turned my attention to the LGBT community, which, now a decisive political force in the city, was coveted by both parties and could make the difference in a tight election. Katz thought that given Street's antigay reputation our votes were attainable. But Street knew he had an ace in his pocket—me. Katz was somewhat popular in the community, while Street was still hated for rallying against domestic partnership legislation despite his increased support and actions over the past three years. But I knew how to turn the tide. By putting the focus on Katz, I could deflect the negativity away from Street.

The Katz campaign had an advisor, Brian Tierney, future publisher of the *Philadelphia Inquirer*. Tierney was, as some would say, close to the Catholic archdiocese, and a fierce, even vicious opponent who led attacks on Street for one major pro-gay position he had taken. The mayor had promised to combat discrimination in Philadelphia by evicting the Boy Scouts from a very well-situated city-owned property for which they were paying an annual rent of one dollar. The Boy Scouts, you might remember, had taken a strong antigay position, barring adult gays from serving as scoutmasters and young gays from participating in their programs. It was clearly in violation of Philly's nondiscrimination law, so the city began the legal process of bouncing them from their sweetheart deal. The question for the LGBT community became, simply, *Can we really trust Katz to toss the Boy Scouts out?* Katz, as I expected, wouldn't answer. We editorialized in *PGN* that anyone who would not support our community in the fight against discrimination, or even attempt to speak up on our behalf, did not deserve our votes. Since Katz would not support the gay community in our battle against the Boy Scouts, I wrote, no major gay leader could possibly endorse his candidacy. And indeed that is what happened.

Upon his reelection I could have asked Mayor Street for almost anything. I had tarnished my own reputation in the community by working so hard for a candidate who many still viewed as a homophobe, and whom I myself had fought against during his early unenlightened days. But supporting him was the right thing to do. The mayor called to thank me for my help and I asked for an LGBT inaugural gala at the William Way LGBT Community Center. It would be on the Saturday before his official swearing-in ceremony. He agreed. I was pretty elated until I realized I'd have to organize this inaugural gala in less than seven weeks. It was my first opportunity to become a producer.

First thing first, I needed some kind of entertainment. For years, I'd wanted to recognize Philadelphia's favorite hometown diva, Patti LaBelle. Patti was one of the first show-business personalities to support LGBT rights, including being one of the first to raise funds for HIV/AIDS, even before Elton John. She also was a supporter and friend of John Street. In short order, Patti agreed to be the star of the gala.

The next thing was food and drink. If I throw an event, there must be some good food. My ancestors would never forgive me if people went unfed. So we got ten of the leading restaurants in the city to agree to set up tables and bring their best samples: prime rib, oysters, shrimp, fois gras, champagne, and more. Liquor and soft drinks were donated by the LGBT clubs. At one hundred dollars a ticket, it would be the best party in town. Almost every item was donated, and almost every politician wanted a ticket.

On the big night, men arrived in black ties, women in beautiful gowns. It was standing-room only. The evening was going great. The community center ballroom was elegantly decorated and we made sure that every logistical detail not only made sense but would run smoothly. Or so we thought.

Patti wasn't feeling well on the night of the ball. She wasn't ready to acknowledge how serious her diabetes had become; only a few people knew of her illness. But that lady is a trouper, and she doesn't disappoint. Sitting in her limo, I explained that the ballroom was on the second floor, and that there was no elevator. She was concerned at first, but then we came up with a strategy that would allow her to climb the stairs to her dressing room and to the ballroom gracefully. We pushed through the crowd to the foot of the stairs. People pressed in, wildly applauding. We took deep breaths and went up the first five steps. At the first landing, Patti turned around to pose for pictures and receive even more applause. We continued and the applause got even louder. Every two or three steps she would turn, wave, and be photographed. It took many turns and many photographs, but ultimately Patti got up the steps and the crowd was delighted. This solution offered her fans the opportunity to give her the proper worship that she deserved. When she got to her dressing room, she fell into a chair and said with a big grin, "Mark Segal, I should kill you before you kill me! Get out of here so I can get ready."

The mayor took the stage. He thanked us profusely and told the crowd that he could not have won his reelection without the support of the LGBT community. This brought overwhelming applause from an audience who never thought they would hear that kind of appreciation from a purportedly homophobic man. Naturally, there were awards to thank the people who'd made the evening possible. I then had the pleasure of introducing my diva, Miss Patti LaBelle.

"Enough talk," said Patti, shooing me off the stage, "we need some singing!" She sang a couple of her most well-known songs accompanied by my friend Dennis Cook on the piano. Then I reappeared onstage. "You know, Patti," I said, "you don't have any background singers with you tonight, do you? How about we form a new group, Patti LaBelle and the City Hall Bells?" We coaxed both Mayor Street and Governor Ed Rendell to the stage, draped them in blue feather boas that we'd stashed in the wings, and the City Hall Bells rang out. At the end of the night, Patti invited me back on the stage and asked what song I wanted to hear. I told her and she performed a heartfelt rendition of "Over the Rainbow." I melted. I still shiver when I think of that moment.

The following morning the front page of the *Philadelphia Inquirer* carried a photo of the mayor and governor at the ball— looking good in their boas. On that night, January 3, 2004, we raised $110,000.

The Monday after, I received a call from Gary Yetter, a man I'd never heard of before. Gary helped run Lunch Around the World, an annual celebration of Elton John's birthday that raised funds for the Elton John AIDS Foundation (EJAF). He wanted to meet with me about supporting their event in some way. I'd just come off weeks of intensive labor to organize the gala and was whipped, so I tried to politely brush him off by saying that the only thing I'd consider doing was a concert with Elton. To my surprise, the idea excited Gary. Like me, Gary is very focused when he believes in a project. He was relentless about EJAF and putting him off was impossible. A few weeks later he and a guy named Michael Anzalone, who would later become pivotal to this venture, joined me for dinner at Judy's Restaurant in Queen Village. At the end of the evening I arrogantly repeated that I'd only be interested in doing an Elton John concert. I thought that would be the end of it. But a few days later Gary called again, asking for another dinner to further explore the idea of a concert. He said he had brought it up with EJAF headquarters in London and they didn't say no.

Soon Gary, his beautiful wife Maureen, Jason, and I were jetting off to Vienna to Life Ball, Europe's largest and most luxurious AIDS benefit. Thirty thousand revelers would contribute nearly a million euros to AIDS charities in the third world. Some four thousand VIP guests would pay 130 euros each for their tickets. And Sir Elton, seller of 200 million records, master of outrageous stagecraft and costuming, member of the Songwriters and Rock and Roll Halls of Fame, founder of the Elton John AIDS Foundation, and the most famous gay man on the planet, was to perform. Gary informed me that if we did a concert in Philadelphia, this would be an example of what the EJAF expected of us. The whirlwind tour was enhanced by the fact that Jason and I had just started dating five months before and everything felt dreamlike. After Vienna, we were to fly to London for meetings at EJAF's offices to firm up the plans.

Everything concerning Life Ball in Vienna was lavish. Held

on the grounds of Vienna city hall, the event is equal parts fashion show, casino, disco, banquet, costume party, and den of iniquity. Guests were dressed in outlandish and incredible costumes. The liquor and food flowed while celebrities and Eastern European porn stars strutted around or played up to the wealthy.

The day before the actual event, Robert Key, the executive director of EJAF, took Gary and me on a backstage tour. The dressing rooms for the fashion show were a swarming hive of people stitching garments, ironing dresses, models trying on outfits, rooms filled to capacity, racks and racks of haute couture clothes. We saw the stage area and the sound and light setups. We then went around the building to check out the different spaces. Each room had a corporate sponsor, and as we saw, each spent a lot of time and money to make their room the most extravagant at the event. One created a casino with people in animal costumes, while another presented a seventies pop culture room. It was a spectacle even before the main event. Finally, we visited the most important room, one of the main reasons we'd flown all the way to Vienna: Elton's dressing room. Right off the bat, I saw that it had been decked out with new furniture, a new carpet, and, to my amazement, material stretched around the room to cover the walls. Behind the material was diffuse lighting. In another room was a full bar and lavish food for guests. I was already overwhelmed, thinking about having to replicate everything.

Later that day we toured Vienna. We saw the palaces, took in the baroque architecture and the spectacular gardens all around the city. We had been given a specific time to meet at the hotel to go shopping with Elton, but when we returned, we found out that Mr. John had gone on without us! According to rumor, he was expected at a certain time to get something to wear that night at a jewelry store. Soon, with a very good-looking security guard in tow, he came back with a paper bag with a quarter-million dollars' worth of diamonds nestled inside. Not just your average, run-of-the-mill shopping trip, and certainly not one that could wait.

Next we all headed out to the cars. Four of us trailed the car behind Elton's. Inside our car were two women, one a high-powered agent and the other a member of a female rock band. We were explicitly told that when we pulled in to the portico of Vienna's magnificent palace-like neo-gothic city hall, we should get out before Elton did and assemble behind him en route to his dressing room.

As we rolled under the portico, the paparazzi pushed and elbowed to get in optimum position. Then the door opened of the first car in line. The scene exploded with flashes and even more pushing, shoving, and shouting. We had been prepared for this riotous scene by the expert security team, used to protecting the famous: keep your arms at your side, say nothing, nod, smile, and keep walking in tight formation behind our leader. Inside, it only got stranger and more elaborate. For a kid from South Philly, it was like suddenly finding myself in the middle of a Fellini movie. Models in appropriate regalia were posing and strutting in each of the themed rooms.

In Elton's guest room there was a very interesting mix of people. Pop stars, former pop stars, major contributors, the upper echelon of EJAF, some Eastern European porn stars, and the handsome security men. We enjoyed the comforts of his suite as the fashion show continued below, outside our window. We paid close attention to the stage and crowd. Gary and I had already decided that if we were to do this, it would be at the Philadelphia Museum of Art, a much better place to set a stage and on a much grander scale than Vienna city hall. I knew that if our event were to happen, it would have to be spectacular.

After the fashion show we made our way outside, just as it began to pour. Unlike in the US, where we prefer not to be electrocuted, the show continued on full-speed ahead. There seemed to be no worries about the large LCD screens, wires, and cables running around the stage and runway. Politicians and people from various political organizations gave speeches, which went on for some time. It was all in German, so we had no idea what was being said. Finally, they brought Elton on-stage. After a few words from the organizers (also in German), Elton spoke of how much this benefit meant to his foundation and to him personally. He did it in English while holding a live microphone in the pouring rain. He then—wisely, due to the hazard—lip-synched the song "Are You Ready for Love." Soaking wet, Elton gave a bravura performance. He left the stage to a standing ovation and we all headed to the dining hall.

After the show, four of us were scheduled to have dinner with Elton, but he was running a little late. We were told he wouldn't be around for at least an hour. We decided to use our all-access passes and leave the comfort of Elton's suite. Outside the suite was bedlam. People packed everywhere, many of them in costumes: aliens and all types of animals. But an equal number were quite simply not in costume. I remember one guy who wore nothing but a six-gun holster and a ten-gallon hat. Oh, and cowboy boots. There was no one way to dress—anything from white tie and tails to leather, latex, and fur.

Exhausted from the sensory overload, an hour or so later we returned to the dining hall. When we got there, Elton, now dry, embraced us. As we all posed for a photo, Elton whispered in my ear, "Don't worry, Mark, we'll do this." Then an idea sparked. One that I thought might really fascinate the star, whose song "Philadelphia Freedom" celebrated one of his favorite cities.

I had never done anything close to a megaconcert, but the

idea began building in my mind as we flew to London to close the deal with Elton's foundation. Except for Live Aid, nothing of this magnitude had ever been staged in Philadelphia. This wasn't Mickey and Judy putting on a show in somebody's father's barn. This was a very big deal. For some reason, I wasn't frightened by the job ahead.

Elton had already given me the okay in Vienna, so the meetings in London were working sessions to flesh out some of the details, though we still needed to iron out the contract. Elton arrived at one of the meetings with dogs in tow. As the plane took off from London, I looked at Jason, shook my head, and kept wondering what I'd gotten myself engaged in.

My father used to have a saying when he and Mom treated us to an all-you-can-eat buffet. I'd look at the array of food and begin putting every single thing I wanted onto my plate: mac and cheese, mashed potatoes, fried chicken, biscuits, and whatever else. The mound of food would be sky high. Dad would come over with his reasonably loaded plate, smile, and remark matter-of-factly: "Your eyes are too big for your stomach."

First the mayor explained that I'd have to work through the existing contracts with Welcome America, the city's quasi-government corporation that usually produced the July 4 celebration. Welcome America had contracts in place for events such as this. The most beneficial was with WPVI, the ABC affiliate that broadcast the Philadelphia July 4 concert every year. Another was with Sunoco, the oil company that had the naming rights to the events. Obviously, the concert needed to be dedicated to AIDS awareness, to connect us to the work of Elton's foundation. It also had to give our local organizations a chance to showcase themselves. The mayor had no problem with that, but it seemed this was the last concession that Sunoco, WPVI, or Welcome America would ever give us. They viewed us as competitors rather than partners. And fought us on everything including port-a-potties.

My two partners in this endeavor were my friends Dan Anders and Jeff Guaracino. Dan, a lawyer working at the law firm Pepper Hamilton LLP, provided us with pro-bono legal work, which otherwise would have cost us tens of thousands of dollars. Jeff worked for Greater Philadelphia Tourism and Marketing Corporation (now known as Visit Philadelphia), and was given to us by his boss, Meryl Levitz. Jeff had come up with Philadelphia's historic and award-winning LGBT tourism campaign, "Get your history straight and your nightlife gay." To complete the team, we brought on Nina Zucker to do the day-to-day public relations and Rita Mezzaroba to spearhead contributions and in-kind services. That was our team, along with Jason, who kept me calm no matter what situation reared its head.

The mayor, knowing that he had just handed me the key to the city's biggest day, realized his guidance might be needed. Thus began our weekly eight a.m. meetings in his cabinet room, every Wednesday. His reasons were twofold. Primarily, he would help mitigate the inevitable turf wars that would occur with an event of this magnitude. And secondly, he reveled in the fact that, as the most anti-morning person he knew, I had to drag myself to City Hall at that early hour. My reaction, as Dan tells it, was that I threatened to show up to the weekly meetings in pajamas as protest. To his great credit, Dan talked me out of it.

The first point of order was to have a firm contract with Elton. At this early juncture we still had only a loose agreement. Dan, EJAF, Elton's tour manager, one of his lawyers, and I all jumped on a conference call. I thought, logically, that we could save on costs by having Elton onstage solo with a piano.

"What's the projected audience?" the tour manager asked. Before I could finish my reply, he interrupted, "We're bringing the bloody band!" I tried in my best negotiator's drawl to get him to reconsider, but he knew his craft, and a single piano would not work for a huge crowd (expected to be as many as 500,000 people) out in the open. We relented with little fanfare. The band was in. Due to the various agencies and nonprofits involved, Elton had to be contracted by yours truly—a personal services contract. There was no way out now. I had to deliver.

Working with city agencies for a fifty-person block party can be a headache. Multiply that by tens of thousands and it's a nightmare. The agreement with the mayor was that we'd be given the budget that was usually set aside for stage production. (Even here, Welcome America tried to get a share.) All other expenses we'd have to come up with ourselves. We had thirteen months to put it all together; it was a daunting project no matter which way you looked at it. Fundraising, programs, production staff, concessions, souvenirs, everything down to street closings and traffic patterns.

On February 9, 2005, we held a press conference to announce the event, now titled Philadelphia Freedom Concert & Ball. The concept was to give the city a free concert and use it as a way to promote AIDS awareness. There would be a grand ball in the massive Philadelphia Museum of Art, as I'd envisioned in Vienna, which would pay for it all. We were holding the press conference from the mayor's reception room with the mayor and many other elected officials. The room was at maximum capacity and every official who had any connection to the production wanted to be up front and in camera range. Elton was to join us courtesy of the satellite hookup via WPVI from Las Vegas, where he was doing his regular show at Caesars Palace. We scheduled it for 12:05 p.m. so it could be carried live on all the TV channels' noon news programs. Everything was set.

The plan called for the mayor, EJAF president Robert Key, and Elton to speak, and then I would introduce Geno Vento from the famous South Philly Geno's Steaks who was donating $100,000. As we were about to begin, Key told me he'd never given a speech of this importance before. I looked at him and said that I didn't believe him. But it turns out he was telling the truth. Up to that point, EJAF had never accomplished something on this scale, although Vienna was grand and drew 100,000 people.

The foundation was made up of Elton's friends and exiled employees from the business side. It seemed a place for castoffs; even an ex-lover was on the organization's payroll. Key, aside from his EJAF duties, was, according to him, directing the construction of Elton's new French getaway home. (On a side note, let me state clearly that post-2005, EJAF has become a professionally run organization in which Elton can take much pride.)

At the first meeting with the general manager of WPVI, she had told us we could work together on finding mutual sponsors. I asked her what the financial split would be. She had no answer. I then asked her who they had already lined up. Again she wouldn't answer. When I asked how much money they would give us to produce a show that would be financially beneficial to them, her response was that they were helping *us* by broadcasting it in the first place. I understood that to mean we'd receive zero dollars from them and realized, on the spot, that they could be counted on for nothing. It saddened me, since up to that point, other GMs at WPVI had been supportive of the LGBT community and committed to fighting AIDS. They had been a major partner in the original AIDS awareness campaign in the 1980s, which was revolutionary for its time. This woman might have been good for the station's bottom line, but not its soul. And she made it very difficult for us when she proclaimed that no sponsor of the concert would get any airtime, including forbidding us to put our sponsors' logos on the stage unless they bought time on the broadcast from WPVI.

After this woman's departure from WPVI and promotion at ABC, the new general manager once again became a partner in promoting diversity. The current general manager, Bernie Prazenica, is a champion for diversity at every level at the corporation, and a friend.

Back to the broadcast. So, we were all ready for the press conference. The aforementioned general manager of WPVI came over and told me not to introduce Geno's when we were live, since they were not sponsoring the concert broadcast. After I declined her demand, she countered with a different issue: the satellite transmission seemed to have a problem, so they couldn't broadcast at all. It was now past noon. This went on for a while. I guess the tipping point came when she realized that the station needed the publicity too. We finally got clearance before the end of the noon newscast. I made it a point to have Geno on live. What the general manager hadn't realized was that the sponsors WPVI had lined up for the broadcast were calling me directly, expressing how proud they were to be contributing. They were mistaken on that front, since WPVI would be keeping any dollars made from broadcast advertising. But it was not in anyone's interest to let them know they were not actually helping combat HIV/AIDS. Jonathan Saidel, former city controller, told me years later that he stood at the back of the press conference and looked over the scene, saying to himself, *What is Segal doing up there with all those thieves? They'll eat him alive.*

When the conference was over, Dan, Jeff, and I had a meeting to discuss a budget. I took a napkin and a pen and we began to sew things together, stitch by stitch.

* * *

We began adding new acts to the lineup, which now consisted of Sir Elton John, Patti LaBelle, Rufus Wainwright, and Bryan Adams. Comedian Wayne Brady had come on to emcee the show with Bruce Vilanch. We now had our own orchestra with Peter Nero and the Philly Pops, our legendary ensemble made up of musicians who played orchestral versions of a variety of musical genres. And, of course, the fireworks finale! One treat that I was especially proud to have secured to start off the show was a video dedication to AIDS awareness from my friend Walter Cronkite. On the logistics side, we had redrawn the Parkway concession areas, gotten my old friend John Dougherty from the electrical union to agree to line the Parkway with bigger and better LCD screens than previous years, and we even found a more efficient way to reroute the traffic.

Little more than a month before the concert, I woke up one morning to a startling news headline: "Mayor Announces Live 8, a Mega-Concert Celebrating the Twentieth Anniversary of Live Aid." The date of the concert would be July 2, two days before our own megaconcert.

It's during times of crisis like this that you discover who your true friends really are. Many realized what was happening, and stepped up to the plate to help make it all work. We decided to simply accomplish what we'd set out to do: put on the best July 4 concert in city history, and the largest AIDS awareness event ever. In a way, Live 8 freed us. It finally made me realize we were our own bosses; we didn't have to answer to anyone. I stopped worrying about our competition and I didn't think twice about making decisions that I would have previously run by others first. Though I admit I took my newfound autonomy a step too far on one occasion.

We were advised that President George W. Bush might want

to be present and give a speech during the ceremony at Independence Hall, when Elton was getting his award. Citing Bush's homophobic reelection campaign and his generally unwelcome policies, I categorically and not so politely told his representatives that he was not welcome on our stage. Yes, that was a step too far, and I was admonished by the mayor, who politely explained that you never turn down a visit by the president of the United States. In any case, Bush did not end up coming.

One night over dinner, Dan, Jeff, Jason, and I were laughing about the absurdity of it all and recalling the mayor's gentle warning to me that the show had to be family-friendly. It was this advice that made us realize that there was nothing outwardly gay in the show, and we needed to fix that. Fortunately, Jason and I had a trip to New York planned, to see Bruce Vilanch. After watching him play Edna in *Hairspray*, we went backstage to chat about his hosting duties. He was getting out of his costume as we met. We asked him if he'd consider doing Betsy Ross, the woman credited with making the first American Flag, in drag. As two assistants were helping him out of all the padding he needed in his role, he said as only Bruce can, "Please note, I'm a big man, but even I need padding to pull off Edna. How do you think I can get a costume ready in a month?"

On Monday morning Bruce called to say it would be done. Seems the *Hairspray* dressers, wig makers, and costume designers wanted to contribute to our show, and creating a complete Betsy Ross costume from scratch was their way of giving back. How I love the Broadway community!

To assure that July 4 was as patriotic as possible, Congressman Bob Brady arranged for an Air Force flyover just as the show began; the police would sing "The Star-Spangled Banner"; and a color guard of the military would open the show.

Our Wednesday-morning meetings in the mayor's office

were now somewhat calmer since his staff was busy dealing with Live 8 and had to contend with an even more outlandish set of demands. It was fun to watch knowing that we had absolutely nothing to do with that chaos.

Two weeks before the concert, on Wednesday, June 15, 2005, the headline on the front page of the *Philadelphia Inquirer* read, "Caught on Tape: City Deal-Makers," then the subheading, "Lana Felton-Ghee Wanted More Action on City Contracts. The FBI Heard it All." At this point I believe the mayor understood the ongoing problems we were encountering and began to show compassion. While the *Inquirer* story was about the alleged corruption at the top of Welcome America, our concert was unrelated and above reproach. In fact, we seemed to be the only people connected to city government who were not called in to be interviewed in the investigation by the FBI and the federal prosecutor. When I later met the former federal prosecutor, Patrick Meehan, while he was campaigning for Congress, I asked him why we hadn't been called in and he said, "We knew you were clean and we didn't want to give you any more problems than what you already had." That was a kind remark. He went on to be elected congressman for the Seventh District.

In the days leading up to the event, the mayor had a request for me: "Mark, I want you to speak on the July 4 morning at Independence Hall." My response was that I would be too busy that day ushering Elton around; we'd agreed to give him an award at Independence Hall in the morning, then go to the William Way LGBT Community Center and name a portion of the Street "Elton's Way," then jet over to the Philadelphia Museum of Art for sound check.

The mayor insisted, and after each meeting Dan and I wondered why he was pressing so hard. Then it dawned on me: I would be the first openly gay person in history to make a speech on July 4 at Independence Hall. I called the mayor one morning and agreed to do it.

The morning of July 4, Jason and I dressed in our suits and walked to Independence Hall for the award ceremony. We'd done a walkthrough the day before. Elton's security was demanding that they be allowed to carry their guns onto the premises, to which the National Park Service guards firmly said no. I wasn't sure if that situation had resolved itself or not.

At Independence Hall, looking out over the platform in front of the building, a chill went down my back. Then my friends Robert Metzger and Barbara Lichtman came over to wish me luck. As I watched them return to their seats, I noticed a man next to Barbara in the front row. It was Barney Frank. When I approached and asked him what he was doing here, he said he knew this was an historic event and wanted to support me. I was so very honored. This also made me fully realize the magnitude of what I was about to do.

Elton was supposed to make an appearance for the morning program, which was being broadcast live. Our start time came and went and Elton hadn't arrived. The mayor quickly decided that enough was enough, and said we'd start the program and stall until Elton showed up. He made an introduction, and we all stood for the national anthem. I peered up at Independence Hall, marveling at what was happening, when suddenly we heard sirens. *Oh my god*, I thought, *something's wrong*. For a second, I thought it might be a terrorist incident. I turned around to see a black SUV with a police escort screeching to a halt in front of the stage. Out popped Elton and his armed guards. That's one way to avoid being searched by security. At the command of the mayor, I retrieved Elton and brought him into the building to wait until called to the stage.

The program continued, a band played some patriotic music, and finally the mayor introduced me. The boy from the Wilson Park projects at 25th and Ritner, the boy raised on the other side of the tracks, was about to address Independence Day from the nation's birthplace, Independence Hall. Approaching the podium I took out my speech and began:

"Mr. Mayor, Senator, Congressmen, Fannie Weinstein [she was still with me in spirit], ladies and gentlemen, what a wonderful exciting and historic July 4 this is in Philadelphia, and tonight will witness the brilliant musical talent of a legend and the man who gave our city its anthem, 'Philadelphia Freedom,' Sir Elton John. I'm on the stage for two reasons today. First, as a producer of the Philadelphia Freedom Concert & Ball with Sir Elton John, which will raise awareness for HIV/AIDS. That mission began over twenty years ago when Jane Shull and I created the first AIDS Awareness Day in Philadelphia in the early 1980s. Then, AIDS was a gay man's disease; today, more than half of all new cases in the US are not. In most parts of the world HIV is a heterosexually transmitted virus.

"There is another reason I'm here today. I am representing what up to now has been an almost invisible minority, the gay community. On this very spot in 1965, the first gay civil rights march in America was held. Last Friday we commemorated those brave souls with a historic marker which you could see over there on the northwest corner of 6th and Chestnut streets. Millions of patriotic gay and lesbian Americans have watched speeches in front of this magnificent building on July 4 and we've still remained invisible. But today, for the first time in 229 years, a member of their community, an openly gay American, has the opportunity to stand on this podium and say, God bless America."

When I made my way back to my seat, the mayor reached over and said, with a large smile, "Very well done."

Elton was given an award that we had created for him. He accepted with grace, and posed for a picture with the mayor and Barney, before getting back into his SUV. The ceremony now over, Jason and I got into a car and, before we could catch our breath, the motorcade was on its way to the William Way Community Center, our second stop of the day. Dolph Goldenburg, executive director of the community center, was awaiting Elton to unveil a new sign for a street renamed after the star.

In rapid-fire succession, Elton got out of his vehicle, made a few remarks, cut the ribbon, and posed for a few more photos. We then parted ways, Elton back to his hotel to prepare for the concert and me to the Parkway to see how sound check and other preparations were going.

As I walked down the Parkway, I glimpsed the stage. Mike Barnes and his stagehands from the union had erected what must have been the world's largest red ribbon as a backdrop. I was also delighted as I walked past every one of the ten giant LCD screens lining the Parkway. I had badgered my old friend John Dougherty from the Electrical Union to donate the additional $80,000 that we were short for the rental cost. It was beautiful. The sound system was top notch too.

The first words I heard coming out of the speakers were during Patti LaBelle's sound check. She was going off about Elton with more than a few choice words. I rushed up to the stage. Jerry Blavat, a legendary radio deejay known locally as the "Geator with the Heater," whom I had asked to keep an eye on his friend Patti, was standing off to the side. He shrugged as I got to the stage. Patti had just been informed that Elton, who had previously agreed to perform a duet with her, had changed his mind. When I went over to Elton's road manager to inquire about possibly of putting the duet back into the program, he told me that the star had made up his mind and it was final, no questions.

It was now up to me, the producer, to placate Patti. "How's my favorite yelling diva?" I said as I approached. She didn't laugh. She just kept shouting, letting it all out. I wasn't too up-set because I knew she wasn't mad at me, but at the situation. I explained how sorry I was but that there was nothing I could do. Being the professional that she is, Patti eventually concluded her sound check and then said, "I'm all done here now, what time should I arrive tonight?" I gave her the details and kissed her on the cheek, then she said to me sternly: "You owe me."

With that bullet dodged, I went inside the Philadelphia Museum of Art to check on the rest of the Freedom Ball prepara-tions. Fred Stein, our party organizer, had created an atmosphere that was beyond elegant. Elton's signature was emblazoned in lasers atop the grand staircase. Members of the Philadelphia Boys Choir were lined up on each side of the magnificent stone staircase rehearsing the song "Circle of Life" from The Lion King. Food tables and bars were being erected with special buntings displaying our logo. It looked like something you'd expect from a White House event, and even at a thousand dollars a ticket it was still a bargain. For those who paid more, there would be a photo op with Elton that we had negotiated with his team.

Before the event commenced, Jason and I did one last check in-side the backstage production trailer. Bruce, our emcee, ever my friend but now in need of support, walked up to me and asked for his script. I just stared at him. My brain was overloaded. He shook his head and said, calmly and with a hint of a smile, "There is no script, is there?"

My reply was as timid as they come: "Thought you'd just wing it."

Bruce, the consummate professional and take-charge guy, said, "I'll write it. Ask Wayne Brady to come over to my trailer and we'll get it done. But Mark, did you know there is no mirror in my dressing room? Betsy Ross doesn't happen unless she has a mirror. The first lady of the flag must look proper." Even under stress, Bruce had a great sense of humor.

It was five p.m. and time for the ball to begin. Jason and I left the production area and ran up those famous *Rocky* steps. Midway up I tripped, and for an instant believed I was having a heart attack. Jason grabbed me, and as I lifted myself back up, I could hear the Philly Pops playing the overture to *Star Wars*. Enlivened by the music and happy Peter had honored my request, Jason and I walked hand in hand up the remainder of the steps.

For the first time I got a glimpse of the crowd. It was overwhelming. People were stretched far beyond what my eyes could see. With Jason still holding my hand and Peter's music inspiring the crowd, I knew the evening was going to be a success. Bill Fraser, with a long-range camera, somehow captured that moment on film. It is one of my favorite photographs of all time.

Jason and I quickly headed back into the museum and found an empty gallery in which I could change into a fresh suit. I was standing, if you please, next to a Renoir.

When we entered the party it was going very well. Sponsors and people who donated their time, money, or services to help us make the evening a success were mingling with politicos and corporate CEOs. Trumpeters stood at the top of the stairs that were lined by the Boys Choir in white pants and blazing red jackets. Jerry Blavat in his distinctive radio voice announced each of the dignitaries as they descended the steps. They came down in pairs with the trumpeters blaring away like they were Cinderella making an entrance at the ball. Somehow, in the middle of it all, I lost Jason. I didn't have time to look for him as it was my turn to accompany Robert Key of the EJAF, who was having the time of his life, down the magical steps. As the trumpeters blared, Blavat announced, "Ladies and gentlemen, please welcome the producer of our ball, Robert Key of the Elton John AIDS Foundation, and our own Mark Segal." The crowd went wild as we descended the stairs and the Boys Choir serenaded us with "Circle of Life." At the bottom I made a brief speech and then gathered the people who had paid extra money to have their photo op with Elton. We all made a mad dash down to the painstakingly appointed dressing room in the basement to get ready for the star.

Before we actually entered the dressing room, Robert Key said that Elton wanted to skip the photos. I finally snapped. "You call him right now and tell him that if he does not come here, it will be a violation of the contract and he will be fired." Robert, one of the most dignified and stiff-upper-lipped people I've ever known, looked very nervous. He asked what I'd do if Elton refused to come, and I replied: "I'll march onstage and announce that Sir Elton John did not honor his contract and has been fired."

Fortunately, Robert was able to restore the original plan, but as we walked to the photo area, another member of the EJAF pulled me aside. "Just wanted to let you know that Elton prefers to have good-looking guys in the front row. It helps him perform better." Dumbfounded, I glanced around and saw Bruce Yelk, who worked with Jeff Guaracino at the tourism agency, and who I thought might be able to fulfill the request. He took it all in stride and stepped away to make some phone calls. To this day I wonder if Robert was just attempting a joke.

When I paused for a moment to catch my breath, Jason reappeared and asked what he'd missed. I rolled my eyes, too tired to even laugh. We left the ball and went back down the steps to the production trailer. Bryan Adams and Rufus Wainwright had already performed, and Patti was next. As Jason and I opened the door to the trailer, we saw a man arguing with a group of svelte girls in black dresses. The man, a security guard in charge of keeping people off the stage, was refusing to let the girls up. "We are Patti LaBelle's singers!" one of them shouted. Jason recognized them from the earlier rehearsal, and told me they were fine. I ran up to the guard and demanded that he let them through, then apologized to the singers.

We sat in for Patti and her singers as they performed "Lady Marmalade" and then headed backstage again. The next time I saw Elton was just before my introduction. He was chatting with Bruce and said I reminded him of Nathan Lane. Then I was told that it was time for me to go onstage to thank all our sponsors. Yet in all the confusion, we had forgotten to print out our list of sponsors. Dan and Jason, from inside the trailer, wrote out a list and handed it to me just in time.

Walking onto that stage I was exhausted. But the applause, which seemed to go on forever, was humbling and lifted me up. My job was simple: read the list and introduce Elton. I was also there to pump the crowd up for the final act, the most grand performance that had ever graced the July 4 stage. (Afterward people told me that I sounded like a man at the end of a long and arduous ordeal and was simply glad to be rid of it all. Producing this concert was one of the most thrilling things I've ever done but I was never more relieved than when it was all over.)

It was now time for my introduction: "Ladies and gentlemen, it is my honor to introduce you to the man who gave us our city song and made tonight possible, Sir Elton John!" With that it was over for me, but not before one last interesting moment.

Apparently, Elton's band did not start playing on cue after my introduction, so when I returned to join Jason in the wings of the stage I heard Elton screaming, "Play! Play!" Finally they started, and Jason and I took our seats and watched as Elton mesmerized the crowd. He truly gave, in my estimation, and many of his longtime fans agree, one of his best performances ever. He even dedicated a song to me, which was a surprise. As Jason and I held each other toward the end of the performance, Jason said, "It's over, you did it! I knew you would."

When Elton and his police escort were leaving for the chartered plane, the fireworks began. Standing on the stage with Jason watching the fireworks, I let out a sigh of relief. Heading down the steps, we saw Dan passing by on the back of a police cart, waving goodbye. It dawned on us that we hadn't arranged for a ride home, and since the area was blocked from cars, including cabs, we had a nice long walk ahead of us.

Naturally, we still had one more highlight left in the day. As we were walking away from the Philadelphia Museum of Art, out of nowhere came the SUV limo that had just taken Elton to the airport. When the doors opened, it was full of what looked like a group of female hookers. Huh? We continued on, and as we hit Logan Fountain a man yelled out to us, asking if we wanted to buy an official T-shirt. It wasn't; he was a counterfeiter. I stepped up to him and started to call the police over, but once again Jason held me back. We'd been through enough already. We finally made it to Market Street and near City Hall we found a cab. We slept late the following morning.

Chapter 13
Meeting with Mr. President

I had promised Jason a nice vacation after the concert. We went to Greece. With our friends Barbara Lichtman, Rita Mezzaroba, Dennis Cook, and Larry Furman, we rented a four-cabin catamaran out of Athens with Rob Metzger as our captain and set off to sail the Greek isles. The deal with my friends was that there would be no drama. Somehow, no one had told us about the infamous Etesian winds of the Aegean Sea that can whip up waves of fifteen feet or more and tear the sail off a boat.

We made it to two islands before we hit Mykonos where the harbormaster literally shut down the harbor and forbid any boats to sail. I could think of worse things than being stuck in Mykonos for a couple of days. We had a blast dancing on the rocks at Super Paradise beach and visiting the local discos and restaurants. Enjoying the beauty of the island was an additional treat.

Once we were allowed to leave Mykonos, we set sail to our last stop, a small island called Kythnos. As we were approaching we dropped our anchor and it got stuck on the bottom of the channel leading to the harbor. After numerous attempts to get the attention of the harbormaster, or anyone for that matter, it seemed we'd be stuck all night. To heck with it, we'd figure it out in the morning. Then we heard a blast. It was the horn of a 40,000-ton ferry headed directly toward us. Everyone started running around the boat in a panic. Rob was at the controls, and as I saw the ferry heading for a direct hit I yelled, "Just step on it!" He did, and the ferry passed by so close you could reach out and touch it. Later, after the night had gone and turned into early morning, we cut the anchor loose and headed to port in Athens. Drama seems to follow me.

On my return home, it was back to business. I needed a new passion, which became examining LGBT history. October is LGBT History Month and each year the *Philadelphia Gay News*, along with eighteen other LGBT newspapers and numerous websites, coordinates the National LGBT History Project.

Mark Horn informed me that a Gay Youth reunion was being planned for the fall of 2007 and I wanted to prepare myself. I began by doing some historical research of my own for the first time.

On November 3, 2007, the first-ever Gay Youth reunion was held at New York City's Lesbian, Gay, Bisexual & Transgender Community Center. While the organization had gone through many names and mission changes over the years, its doors were still open, making it the longest-serving LGBT organization in the city. Nearly one hundred of us met up that day. Five of the originals members showed up, including Mark Horn, my vice president.

When I arrived, people came up to chat, many of whom I didn't know. Then the chairperson welcomed everyone and said, "Without this guy, we wouldn't be here—the founder of Gay Youth, our papa, Mark Segal." As people got to their feet one by one and explained what the organization had done for them, it felt like an out-of-body experience.

Following the after-party, there was a special moment for the class of 1969. Mark Horn, Jeff Hochhauser, Michael Knowles, and I left the reunion, locked arms, and walked down Eighth Avenue chanting once again and for the first time since 1971, *"We are the Stonewall girls . . ."*

The bubble burst on the train home to Philly. Recalling everyone who had spoken, I sobbed uncontrollably, tears of pure pride. At fifty-six I was still a Gay Youth. My brain had a hard time taking in all that had happened, and it was also the first time my age truly registered with me. On the train, here's how I wrote about that day:

> *It only took thirty-eight years, but today in New York City, it was graduation day. Presiding over this day were members of Gay Youth, GLYNY, and all its other reincarnations through the years. The organizers were brilliant in hosting first a meeting, which served as our graduation, then an after-party which served as a prom, one that most of us never had.*

And Tom Approbato wrote in New York's *Gay City News:*

> *Gay Youth would over time emerge as the parent of every other gay and lesbian student group throughout the United States. From humble beginnings, with a handful of dedicated teenagers, Gay Youth left a legacy for LGBT youth in America.*
>
> *GLNY was in fact one name for an organization whose mast changed several times over the years—Gay Youth; Bisexual, Gay and Lesbian Youth of New York (BiGLYNY); and Bi, Gay, Lesbian, Transgender Youth of New York (Bi-GLTYNY) at different times were the words on the common banner . . .*
>
> *Eighty-nine alumni spanning the years 1969 through*

1994 traveled from their homes all across the country to answer a common call. Members came from New York, New Jersey, Pennsylvania, Florida, Illinois, Wisconsin, Arizona, California, and even the UK. There were men and women of all ethnicities, backgrounds, and even persuasions with one common bond—the feelings of friendship established during our teenage years.

We shared some of the toughest coming-of-age experiences with each other. In a peer-run support group, there was no place for false sympathy. Our bonds of friendship and support were earnest and heartfelt.

Mark Segal, one of the founders of Gay Youth from 1969, addressed the membership with a stirring speech. Although Mark now lives in Philadelphia, he made the trip into New York to see his contemporaries and his surrogate progeny. He spoke passionately about the lifelong friendships he established as well as the ongoing effect that this teen support group has had on his life.

"It's like the graduation I never had," Mark said. "I never went to my high school prom or my high school reunion. This is my prom. This is my reunion."

Many of us in the audience echoed those sentiments as we sat in a big circle and introduced ourselves.

Back home with a new sense of pride, several projects were moving forward, but one that had never been completed was building an elevator at the community center for those in wheelchairs. Councilman Kenney had lobbied the mayor to give the center a grant for the funds required to finally complete this task. A community center is a place where we should all feel free to gather, no matter what our political positions are, and like Switzerland be politically neutral.

Our community was in full preparation mode as we headed into the presidential primary year of 2008. By the time the Democrat wagon reached Pennsylvania in March of 2008 the field of nominees in the Democratic party had been narrowed down to Senator Hillary Clinton and Senator Barack Obama.

Throughout the primaries, in each state Senator Obama campaigned, his staff would often promise the local LGBT media an interview, then pull out at the last moment. As far as we at *Philadelphia Gay News* were concerned, that was not going to happen on our watch. We requested interviews with both Clinton and Obama. Due to Clinton's relationship with Governor Rendell, she quickly agreed. Obama agreed too, but kept putting it off. Finally, with only two weeks to go before the primary, we decided to wait no longer and to act.

On April 4, 2008, the front page of the *Philadelphia Gay News* was filled, on the right side, with the interview with Senator Hillary Clinton. The entire left half of the front page was a blank space, with the exception of a box in the middle that read, "It's been 1,522 days since Sen. Barack Obama has spoken with local gay press. See editorial, Page 11." The reaction was immediate. Every network took notice and newspapers around the nation wrote it up. It was a united and bold decision made by our entire staff. In her interview, Clinton had urged state legislative Democrats to vote no on the anti–gay marriage legislation, so we decided to continue our campaign to get an answer to this question from Senator Obama. The following day we put out a press release asking, "Day 2: What is Senator Obama's position on the antigay legislation in Pennsylvania?" The day after that: "Day 3: What is Senator Obama's position on . . ." This went on each day until a week before the primary, and almost every reporter in the state now wanted the answer. I finally received the following e-mail from Chris May at the local CBS affiliate:

Subject: Obama finally answers, thanks to our friends at Capitol Wire

Hi Mark,

Not sure if you saw it on Sunday, but we put the question about the gay marriage amendment to Barack Obama. In an interview after his town hall meeting in Reading he told us this:

"I have said before and continue to believe that a constitutional amendment banning gay marriage is unnecessary, it's divisive, and it's something I would oppose. I think that it is important for us to recognize that same-sex couples should be able to engage in civil unions, that their rights to transfer property or visit each other in the hospital—all those things are matters of law. Even those of us who may not believe in gay marriage should still be able to confer those benefits. And the problem with a constitutional amendment is—I'm not in favor of gay marriage but I certainly don't want to see a court suggesting that somehow we can't pass laws to make sure gays and lesbians aren't being discriminated against. So I think this is a distraction from a lot of issues we need to be tackling, and if I were in the state legislature I would oppose it."

Thought you would be interested.

A few days before the primary, the Philadelphia Democratic City Committee held its annual Jefferson Jackson Day dinner, where both Clinton and Obama would address a crowd of over a thousand party workers. My friend Congressman Bob Brady, who also served as the committee's chairman, erected a VIP tent outside the union hall for a few of the elite and somehow he managed to include me. Bob's wife Debbie and I watched the scene unfolding together. We were teasing the Secret Service agents; one looked at me and said, "I'm from San Francisco." We laughed, assuming that the guy had just come out to us. There was an air of excitement when Senator Obama entered the tent. He said a few words then went around the tent shaking hands.

City Council President Anna Verna wanted a picture of herself with the senator and shoved a camera in my hands as Obama made his way toward us. "Take our picture," she said. So I did. Then, in a polite gesture, Senator Obama reached out to shake my hand. I'd feared this introduction.

As my hand met his in that VIP tent while a thousand Democratic Party workers waited to hear his campaign speech, I said, "Senator, I'm Mark Segal."

His eyes opened wide. He stood even more upright and pulled me toward him, a serious look on his face. "So you're Mark Segal," he said. Then, with hurt in his eyes and sincerity in his voice, he added, "I really am good on LGBT issues. We have to talk further on this, but I have to go in the other room and speak." He then made a fist and wanted to fist bump. There is just something in me that must win every debate, or at least have the final word. Somehow, he recognized this and said, with that great broad smile of his, "Come on, Mark, give me a fist bump." I did. The man is charming.

That would have been enough drama for me in one evening, but a half hour before, Hillary Clinton had been in that same VIP room. After she spoke to our small group of elected officials, union leaders, and major contributors, Governor Rendell, a major force in her campaign, spotted me and brought her over to say hello. She gave me a warm hug and said, "You're more tenacious than me!" Coming from her, it was the ultimate compliment.

* * *

The following day, Steve Hildebrand, Obama's deputy national campaign manager, called me to follow up for the senator. During that call, Steve told me he was gay and I quickly realized that this in itself was a story. I asked if we could get an interview with him about being an openly gay deputy campaign manager in a presidential race, and Steve said he had to run it by David Axelrod and Obama first. Luckily, they approved. Then in August, in the middle of the race between Barack Obama and John McCain, I finally got that interview with the future president, and to make it sweeter, it was shared with all my fellow LGBT local publications as part of our National LGBT History Project. Here's an excerpt:

> **Mark Segal:** *You are the most GLBT-friendly candidate in history running for president. Are you concerned John McCain and the Republicans might use this as a divisive issue as they did in 2004?*

> **Barack Obama:** *No. I think they can try but I don't think it will work for a couple of reasons. Number one, I think that the American peoples' attitudes with respect to LGBT issues are continuing to evolve. I think people are becoming more and more aware of the need to treat all people equally regardless of sexual orientation. There are some people who disagree with that, but frankly those folks—many of them— probably have already made their minds up about this election earlier.*

> **MS:** *You've talked about your many gay friends. Would you and Michelle be comfortable attending their commitment ceremony?*

BO: We would. But I'll be honest with you that, these days, I can't go anywhere.

MS: The current President Bush has used signing orders to change military rules and regulations. If White House counsel advised you that you could end "Don't Ask, Don't Tell" by attaching a signing order to a military appropriations bill, would you?

BO: I would not do it that way. The reason is because I want to make sure that when we revert "Don't Ask, Don't Tell," it's gone through a process and we've built a consensus or at least a clarity of that, of what my expectations are, so that it works. My first obligation as the president is to make sure that I keep the American people safe and that our military is functioning effectively. Although I have consistently said I would repeal "Don't Ask, Don't Tell," I believe that the way to do it is make sure that we are working through a process, getting the Joint Chiefs of Staff clear in terms of what our priorities are going to be. That's how we were able to integrate the armed services to get women more actively involved . . . At some point, you've got to make a decision that that's the right thing to do, but you always want to make sure that you are doing it in a way that maintains our core mission in our military.

MS: Many lawyers contend that the Defense of Marriage Act passed by Congress is unconstitutional. It takes away more than 1,100 rights, including IRS joint filings. If a suit is filed in federal court, would you expect or instruct your attorney general to join in that suit with an amicus brief questioning its legality?

BO: *I would want to review carefully any lawsuit that was filed. This is probably my carryover from being a constitutional lawyer. Here's where I can tell you [what] my principle is: DOMA was an unnecessary encroachment by the federal government in an area traditionally reserved for the state. I think that it was primarily sent as a message to score political points instead of work through these difficult issues. I recognize why it was done. I'm sympathetic to the political pressures involved, but I think that we need to bring it to a close and my preference would be to work through a legislative solution. I would also point out that if it's going before this court, I'm not sure what chances it would have to be overturned. I think we're going to have to take a different approach, but I am absolutely committed to the concept it is not necessary.*

MS: *In the wake of the torture and murder of Matthew Shepard in 1998, Senator McCain voted against adding sexual orientation to the definition of hate crimes and says he'll vote against it again. Isn't this inconsistent for a man who knows torture?*

BO: *You'll have to ask Senator McCain that. Here's what I can say: There is no doubt that hate crimes based on sexual orientation are all too prevalent. It is something that we have to hit back hard against and identify these vicious crimes for what they are: hate crimes. This is something that I believe in and will continue to believe in when I am president.*

MS: *President Reagan, President Bush, and President Clinton, when meeting world leaders, have raised human rights* *questions. Amnesty International has documented countries that imprison, torture, and kill gay men, some of which are very close US allies. Would you be willing to raise that question when meeting with those leaders?*

BO: *I think that the treatment of gays, lesbians, and transgender persons is part of this broader human rights discussion. I think it is not acceptable that we would in any way carve out exceptions for our broader human rights advocacy to exclude violations of human rights based on sexual orientation. I think that has to be part and parcel of any conversations we have about human rights.*

At this point I personally had no doubts about how Obama would evolve on the issue of marriage equality. As he promised me, he has indeed been great on LGBT issues. Before he was even sworn in, he had appointed a host of LGBT people to high positions in his administration, including Shin Inouye, who had LGBT media in his portfolio as a deputy press secretary.

Once President Obama took office, he quickly stated that he would work to end "Don't Ask, Don't Tell," and his attorney general filed a brief before the Supreme Court opposing the Defense of Marriage Act. Any time a state introduced anti-LGBT legislation he publicly opposed it. But what he should get special credit for is that when Maryland was about to vote on marriage equality, he got personally involved and urged the citizens of Maryland to vote yes, and he urged the pillar of the African American community—the churches—to do likewise. This one act created a sea of change in the black community, not just in Maryland but across the nation. While African American leaders have supported LGBT rights in the past, this was the first black president asking them to stand with LGBT Americans in the struggle for equality.

And when the Supreme Court ruled in June 2015 that marriage equality was now the law of the land, President Obama made an impromptu emotional statement from the Rose Garden, and that night the White House was lit up in rainbow colors.

After the August 2008 interview, I wouldn't speak to Barack Obama again until 2010, when as president he made his first official trip back to Philadelphia and I was asked by Senator Bob Casey to be one of the official hosts. After the president delivered his speech that day, we were ushered into a small room with no windows. Obviously it was chosen for security. A group of us all gathered, chatting away until the president walked in the room and said, "Hi, everyone."

Silence fell and we all seemed overcome with stage fright, even the seasoned political folks. Since everyone else was standing still, I walked over and said, "Welcome to Philadelphia, Mr. President."

He smiled and said, "How you doing, Mark?"

Now I'm sure he didn't recognize me and someone had whispered my name in his ear, but hey, I have no complaints.

He asked, "What's on your mind?" to which I smiled and said, "Mr. President, I appreciate all the great points you've been making about LGBT equality, but what about LGBT funding?"

He asked if there was something in particular I was referring to, so I told him about our plans to build an affordable-living facility for LGBT seniors.

He said, "Send me the plans."

My reply was: "Yeah, like you have the time to look at them."

A big smile appeared on his face and he said to Reggie Love, his personal aide, "Give Mark your card," and to me he said, "I'll look them over and if they seem possible, I'll pass them on."

Then we did the photo op and others stepped forward for their moment.

That night the plans, everything I had on the project, were e-mailed. The only hint I had about whether the president actually looked at the plans came at the 2012 Democrat National Convention in Charlotte, North Carolina. I was at a Human Rights Campaign/Victory Fund lunch with my friend Klayton Fennell where the first lady was speaking. At the end of the speech I went over to the rope line to shake her hand. Giving her my name and my affiliation with the *Philadelphia Gay News*, she said, "The senior project." Then she leaned over to hug me. When the Secret Service got alarmed, she added with a delightful smile, "I forgot, the first lady is not supposed to hug."

This period of time was a whirlwind of activity. Publishing the paper, pushing full speed ahead with the senior building, the *Philadelphia Gay News* winning awards, and more.

Then, in late 2011, my life and history punched me right in the face. My friend David L. Cohen, now at Comcast, called to ask if I'd serve on something called the Joint Diversity Council. My initial thought was that this would just be a rubber-stamp group or show horse for the company. David assured me otherwise, then added what should have been obvious: "Mark, you of all people in the LGBT community should appreciate this opportunity to create change in the media."

On August 19, 2013, at 30 Rock, the NBC News world headquarters in New York City, presidents and producers from NBC News, MSNBC, CNBC, and the *Today* show were packed into a conference room. I was there in my role as an LGBT advisor and a member of NBC parent company Comcast's Joint Diversity Council. The Latino, Native American, and African American

representatives of the council had spoken. When I was introduced all eyes fell on me. Looking over the assembled crowd of
executives I knew what I had to say and it was unrelated to the
bullet points on the paper in front of me. I smiled at the NBC
news brass and simply uttered: "The last time I was in this building was forty years ago, and you had me arrested and taken out
in handcuffs." Silence swept over the room, but soon they all
began to laugh, and then they actually applauded. Phil Griffin,
president of MSNBC, was laughing the loudest. I had met him
at an earlier Comcast event so he'd had a taste of my humor.

At another Comcast Joint Diversity Council meeting, David asked me to talk about my appearances on the *Phil Donahue
Show* in the 1970s. I explained that the 1973 taping with my
parents was one of the first depictions of a gay family on television. I also said that when I ran across Phil Donahue years ago,
he told me that many of his tapes from that time were lost in a
fire. Since then I had searched television museums and private
collections, but a recording of that particular show remained
elusive. At this point they perked up. Klayton Fennell, who
had become my minder at Comcast, asked Beth Colleton at
NBCUniversal if, through their connections, they could help
track it down. They requested any information that I had on
the taping.

At home, I searched through boxes of memorabilia and
finally found the official letters from *Donahue*, and even the
TV release forms signed by my mother and father. A new hunt
through various television archives began. To see my friends at
Comcast and NBC commit the time and resources to search for
what would be a treasured piece of memorabilia for me was heart-
warming. Ultimately, they confirmed that the fire that Donahue
had mentioned had indeed destroyed all copies of that tape.

* * *

On a cold day in January 2013 I watched President Barack Obama give his second inauguration speech.

"We, the people, declare today that the most evident of truths—that all of us are created equal—is the star that guides us still; just as it guided our forebears through Seneca Falls, and Selma, and Stonewall; just as it guided all those men and women, sung and unsung, who left footprints along this great Mall, to hear a preacher say that we cannot walk alone; to hear a King proclaim that our individual freedom is inextricably bound to the freedom of every soul on earth."

My congressman had graciously invited me to the inauguration, but I'd decided to stay warm and watch it on television at home. As the president spoke those words, my mind tried to fully grasp the magnitude of what he was saying. Something came over me. I'm not sure how long I cried but I know that in the end the tears washed away a lot of the pain and hate that had been stored up in me for years—the pain of growing up and listening in fright as my relatives spoke in hushed tones about cousin Norman, the shame of looking at those men in the catalogs and worrying that I would forever cause anguish to my parents, and the belief that I would have no future due to who I was. It erased all the battles I'd witnessed and the battles I'd fought within the LGBT community as it grew and changed. In a flash, all of that was gone. I was still and at peace.

It was a moment that had to be shared with someone who had been there during the Stonewall period with me. I Skyped Jerry Hoose and we just looked at each other with tears running down our cheeks. While the president had compared our work to that of the founders of the nation, and those who fought for civil and women's rights, only we knew the toll it had taken on us, and the toll that it had taken on everyone involved. We had gone from the lowest class of fighters for human rights to equals.

To me, the kid from the projects, who was always the lower class in every category, it meant the world. I also recalled that first meeting with President Obama where he told me, "I'm good on LGBT issues." Yes, Mr. President, you are.

This inspired "We Are America," the following year's National LGBT History Project. The October series was devoted to LGBT people from the American Revolution through the Civil War who had helped build a nation.

Every year the local LGBT media collaborate in publishing articles pertaining to LGBT history. That year we had thirty publications with a combined print run of 650,000 dedicating numerous feature stories on those LGBT people who had helped create the USA. No longer could the far right wing say, *Our founding fathers did not have LGBT people in mind when they created this country.*

Chief among the features was a piece I offered for the project.

> *If it were not for this man, there would be no USA: Baron Frederick Wilhelm von Steuben . . . Von Steuben had a brilliant military mind . . . but he had one problem. He was on the run from several countries for having sex with men.*

Luckily, the colonies had a representative in Paris who was there to win the French courts' financial support for our revolution and find professionals to boost Washington's failing continental army. His name was Ben Franklin.

Franklin interviewed Von Steuben in his home in Paris. Franklin—the Bill Gates of his day—was impressed with him but also knew of the rumors, and passed on the first interview. Several months went by and now Von Steuben was being hunted down by French clergy. At this point a second meeting took place in Franklin's home. This time Franklin, understanding the situation, arranged for Von Steuben to be whisked out of Paris on a boat full of armaments and with a letter of introduction to General Washington. I therefore bestowed the title on Franklin as the father of "Don't Ask, Don't Tell."

We also featured articles on Abraham Lincoln, a gay African American soldier who led a segregated troop in the American Revolution, President James Buchanan, Katharine Lee Bates (writer of "America the Beautiful"), and yes, our first president, George Washington. All had connections to the community, whether they were allies or gay/lesbian themselves.

To top the project off, I wound up being featured on the front cover of the *Philadelphia Daily News*, dressed in a Continental Army uniform. The project was a smashing success.

Chapter 14

An Army of Pink Hard Hats

That night in 2005 when I asked Jason, "Do you think I can raise nineteen or twenty million dollars to build an affordable LGBT senior living facility?" he looked me in the eye and said, "Of course." He might have believed so, but to me it was a pie-in-the-sky dream, and that's what the project became. Inspiration had begun in 1998, when we received a state grant to look at issues facing LGBT seniors.

We conducted a survey, the results of which surprised us all. The number-one issue facing LGBT seniors was housing. Not only the issue of affordability, which affected them like all communities, but the treatment of these seniors in existing low-income housing. Many people seemed to think that "gay" and "low income" could not be uttered in the same sentence. We were being stereotyped as typically childless, two-income households with lots of disposable funds. This was incorrect.

Significant credit was due to Mike O'Brien, my state representative who identified with the problem and was responsive to my interest in creating LGBT-friendly affordable housing for seniors. His advice was simple and something that nobody had told me in a long time: "Mark, you're not pushy enough." Mike, a proud, heavyset, blue-collar Irish Catholic member of our state legislature, sat me down along with his chief of staff, Mary Isaacson, to tell me the political facts of life as he saw them.

"Mark, you've supported the Democratic Party for forty years and you finally want something back. It may not be for yourself, but you want something and they owe it to you. It's about time you start demanding. Be pushy again."

Mike was correct, and that chat is what really put this project on the road to becoming a reality. Once again I was not knocking politely on doors—I was busting them down. But it started a little before those words of wisdom from Mike.

"Senator!" Every time I made a pilgrimage to State Senator Vince Fumo's office in South Philly, he knew the bite was coming. "If we're going to get this senior building off the ground, we'll need some seed funds."

"How much do you think you'll need?"

There's a personal rule in politics that has served me well. It's called the 50 percent rule: you ask for 50 percent more than you hope to get. "A million would work," I replied.

Now, if memory serves me well, his response was somewhere along the lines of, "What the fuck?" Then he continued: "We're talking about a first-of-its-kind, historic project—with a long road we'll have to maneuver." He just stared at me, half in disbelief and half in amusement. "No one would ever—"

"But Vince, you know this is needed and you know there's no other way."

As I left he said, "I'll see what I can do."

The project trudged along after that conversation, but a couple of years later I got a letter in the mail from the Department of Community and Economic Development saying that my organization had been awarded a grant for $500,000.

The funding gave us the ability to do what had become a pattern with each of my successful initiatives: find a partner who can look after the details. After all, I may have a strong vision but I sometimes lack skills in the small-details department.

From Mark Horn and Gay Youth, to Harry Langhorne with the Gay Raiders, Jane Shull with AIDS Awareness Day, Andrew Park and Andy Chirls with the domestic partnership crusade, Dan Anders and Jeff Guaracino and the Elton John concert, the incredible staff at *Philadelphia Gay News* who allow their publisher the time for other endeavors, and Klayton Fennell at Comcast-NBCUniversal—I always surrounded myself with top-notch and highly skilled professionals. Each one was an equal partner, keeping me on track and sometimes in order. And they all had something in common: they were much smarter and much more diplomatic than I am, and they paid attention to details.

Now I needed a partner for what would become the biggest project of my career—the $19.5 million facility would be the largest LGBT building project in the nation created entirely with government funds and tax credits. Enter Micah Mahjoubian.

As he tells the story: "I joined the project around October 2010. I remember being worried about paying the bills. It was after I had finished the Arlen Specter campaign. My only client was Ceisler Media and it wasn't enough. My dog needed surgery and I had no way of paying for it. I literally ran into you on the street with my dog after we got the news from the vet and I said that I didn't know how I was going to pay for it. I said I needed work, and I was interested in helping on the project. You immediately said that was a good idea. I've been thankful ever since."

Micah is a brilliant political operative; he had been an openly gay member of Mayor John Street's administration, as well as a cochair of the local LGBT Democratic Club. He's also very tech savvy. He entered the project as we were finalizing the concept of building the apartments on top of the existing LGBT Community Center, which was actually the second location that we explored. The original location, proposed by Senator Fumo, was an old army armory on South Broad Street that was then being used for once-a-week bingo games. The games were somehow sponsored by the archdiocese and run by a South Philly doctor. The building was in major disrepair, which made it a perfect candidate. We had to talk the archdiocese and the doctor into the deal. Things had been going well, but then the federal prosecutor raided Vince's offices and began to crack down on his staff and friends. While everything we had done was above board, I didn't want to get embroiled in the publicity circus. So I sent the money—that $500,000 grant—back to the state. Two months later, at my annual holiday party, Governor Ed Rendell walked in the door with an angry face. He grabbed me, took me into a corner, and snapped, "Mark, you *never* give money back to the state. Do you know how many nonprofits would kill for those funds?" As I explained that we didn't want to get caught in the middle of whatever investigation was going on, he began to calm down, and I recognized the look that now crossed his face. He had a solution to the problem. "I'll reissue the money from the governor's office." And he gave me one final piece of advice: "Use it correctly." We did. It was the seed money that kept us moving.

A couple of years later I was in the governor's office asking for more. So began an endless procession of meetings with public officials and department heads to find the right formula for the funding. "Equality" was now a key word, and we ran with it, arguing that we were pursuing this project in the same way that Catholic charities and Jewish federations do their senior homes. All we wanted was equality, to be able to build our project in the same way. The first group to understand this was the team at the US Department of Housing and Urban Development. With the assistance of HUD Secretary Shaun Donovan, and his able deputies Dr. Raphael Bostic and my longtime friend Estelle Richman, we became the first federally designated project with the acceptable designation "LGBT-friendly." That in turn allowed us to apply for funding.

Sometimes when you're so involved with numerous meetings to secure funding, gain community support, and round up corporations to partner with, you lose sight of why you're even doing the project.

I remember Veronica, a women in her late sixties, who told me that as she and her partner of thirty years neared retirement age, they faced the real possibility of homelessness. Both women had worked their entire lives, but never earned enough to save for retirement. Both volunteered their time caring for those in shelters and hospices, and now they were in need of the very care that they provided—but where would they turn?

Donald, sixty-two, was a former teacher and longtime activist in the LGBT community. Surviving on Social Security disability for the past twenty years, his arthritis and neuropathy made living alone in a third-floor walk-up—his only affordable option—more difficult with each passing day. Why shouldn't he be able to live with dignity in his golden years among the LGBT community to which he belonged?

Then there were my Gay Liberation Front brothers and sisters. Due to age and illness, some were left isolated, far from the community that they had helped create. There were also those who lived in religious-based low-income homes and were being mistreated by the staff and shunned by the other residents.

This is the first out generation. The way we treat the needs of our pioneers will define our community, just as the call to help our gay youth and trans communities did in the early days of the movement.

And we as a community were failing. Gay rights pioneer

Frank Kameny, for many years and up to his death in 2011, had to constantly call friends to request money. In 1957, Kameny was the first US government employee to fight being fired because of his "homosexuality," thereby launching his activism. He lived long enough to get an apology from the president of the United States, Barack Obama.

Shame on us! Near his death, Frank still lived in his mother's home (he actually owned it), but to generate the funds to live and be an activist, it was mortgaged to the hilt. Frank's friends, including Bob Witeck, Charles Francis, Rick Rosendall, and Marvin Carter, took over his finances and attempted to put him on a budget, but somehow Frank, who for years begged, couldn't or wouldn't conform.

The year before Frank died, my friend Jeff Guaracino, who at that time was working to generate tourism in Philadelphia, asked me to help arrange the honoring of some of our early pioneers. So in a parade on July 4, 2010, Frank Kameny rode past Independence Hall in a convertible car with a banner in front stating, *Early Gay Rights Pioneers.* Forty-six years before to the day, he had been picketing at that same historic building. As always, Frank wore a suit and tie on that hot, humid July 4, but the suit was old and worn. Frank wasn't begging for funds any longer, but he couldn't get used to the changes that came late in life. At lunch after the parade, he asked if he was allowed to order anything on the menu.

No senior, much less a pioneer, should find him or herself at an advanced age with little resources from our community. For a long time, seniors were, literally and figuratively, the last issue to be considered.

Frank is a good example of our pioneers who live in poverty. We need systems and assurances in place similar to what we now have for gay youth.

So what does the future hold for our elder community? To answer this question, we should first ask: how much do we know about them? We know much about youth and bullying issues, much about our LGBT citizens in military uniforms, much about those couples who wish to marry and have children. Even those interested in playing professional sports. But what about the elders? We know very little, and that is a sign that our community's agenda has, for the most part, left them behind.

Financing for the $19.5 million project would have to come from federal, state, and city funds. It would give seniors a safe, accepting place to call home. Los Angeles was one of the few places helping elders in this way, and a facility in Chicago would open about a year after our ribbon-cutting—but there remained an entire country full of LGBT seniors facing serious housing issues. Success in Philly would be a step in the right direction.

There were zero LGBT senior advocacy programs in our region when we began. We started by funding the Delaware Valley Legacy Fund, which resulted in the creation of the LGBT Elder Initiative spearheaded by a man named Heshie Zinman. We met with every mainstream senior service organization in the region and requested their help and lobbied for their inclusion of LGBT seniors. We asked for seats on governmental senior boards and commissions. And we helped fund another study on the concerns of LGBT seniors, this time by the Philadelphia Health Management Corporation, and once again found that housing was a major issue.

The next step in the process was to decide where to build. I was out looking at buildings on Spruce Street one day and bumped into Dolph Goldenburg, then the executive director of the community center. He asked what I was doing. When I told him in confidence, he said why not build it on top of the center?

Dolph is a man courageous enough to think big, and it was a good idea. We could build our space while doing much-needed repairs to the community center. Dolph's timing could not have been better. The week before, I had met with Richard Barnhart from Pennrose, who would become a codeveloper of the building. The community center gave us a site but not the magic words *site control*. Without that you cannot apply for low-income tax credits. Up to this point, only a few people knew of the dream, namely our board, consultants, the elected officials who had agreed to fund us, and our development partner, Pennrose. But in order for Pennrose to draw up plans, they needed to know the full and true condition of the community center and we needed the center's board to give us a document that included those two words. We enlisted the support of the center's cochairs and asked them not to tell anyone what we were planning, including their own board. They nervously and bravely shepherded the project, up until it was time to get the paper with the words *site control*. In order for us to receive the tax credits needed for the project we had to present that document to the Pennsylvania Housing Finance Agency, which was headed by Brian Hudson. We staged an all-out lobbying campaign to get those tax credits and he, poor guy, was on the receiving end. But instead of asking us to stop, he actually encouraged us, realizing that we might be needed later for public support. It must also be stated here that the staff at PHFA, a state agency then controlled by a Republican governor, gave us every bit of support requested. They treated us as equals. Which is all that we asked.

When we went to the full community center board for approval, it was the first time they had heard of the project; we had successfully kept it quiet. Yet there was one additional hurdle: Dolph was about to leave the center to move to Atlanta. Enter the new executive director with no knowledge of the project,

Chris Bartlett, one of the most affable members of the community. He too was a bit shocked by our news. He knew it would be controversial, but he also understood the difficulties faced by low-income seniors. It was a gutsy move for him to take on the job.

As expected, once we made it public, the project irked some in the gay community. The community center called a public meeting to discuss the proposal. While we were ultimately given a yellow light to proceed with caution, my takeaway from that meeting was the image of a young man standing up and screaming at the top of his lungs, "If you build this old person's home on top of the community center, no young people will ever come here again!" After forty long years of fighting, I couldn't resist yelling, "Ageist!" back at him.

That young man soon left the city to go to school out of state. But there were others in the community who felt the clientele for an LGBT-friendly low-income building would be, in their words, "drug addicts, drag queens, and prostitutes." My response was that people selling drugs would be in violation of their lease and tossed out. Who would be calling a sixty-two-year-old prostitute? As for the drag queens, bring them on, we want them!

Another element of resistance came from my personal detractors, who met with our major supporters, Governor Rendell and Senator Casey, requesting that they drop their support of the project. We also had some contentious negotiations with the board of the community center over the repairs that would need to occur if we were to build on top of it.

We were simultaneously negotiating with the community center, designing the building with the architects, working with Jacob Fisher of Pennrose to finalize the paperwork that would be submitted to the Pennsylvania Housing Finance Agency

(PHFA) for funding, and explaining to city and state officials that the federal government would accept the term "LGBT-friendly" and that it was not discriminatory in any way. Micah and I were trying to organize an advisory board from the community to ease any problems with the neighborhood associations, and all along keep our eyes out for any new objections that surfaced. We were in heavy negotiations over our contract with Pennrose regarding ownership, property management, and the responsibilities of each party. We also had to work out agreements with unions, since we wanted to have LGBT contractors involved with the construction. It was an incredible juggling act.

Our negotiations with the community center fell through along the way due to differing expectations related to repairs and operating expenses. We parted on good terms, though, and Chris Bartlett managed to keep the line of communication open, so the center could help out as needed.

When we entered discussions with the city for a parcel of land on 13th Street, Mayor Michael Nutter pushed his administration along with record speed. It was a choice parcel, and some people really didn't want to give it up. The mayor deserves tremendous credit, along with the Redevelopment Authority's board chair James Cuorato, for making it happen. With the new location secure, Jacob Fisher pulled all the strings together and completed a new plan. From the time we parted ways with the community center, came up with that property on 13th Street, and drew up the new plans, a mere ninety days had passed—we were rushing to make the filing deadline with PHFA.

Meanwhile, Republican Tom Corbett was elected governor—and we discovered that Ed Rendell hadn't been able to complete the state's part of the project. So I had to go begging a new Republican governor to finalize the state funding. Pennrose had a good relationship with the Corbett administration, but to ensure our success, I began to make myself known within the governor's circle. Soon I was told that if it was a good project, they'd fund it. They not only did this, but when various issues stymied us, as they usually do on a project of this magnitude, the administration was always fair and helpful. They helped calm the waters. Then, in April of 2012, we were approved for tax credits. This is how I wrote about it that week:

On Monday we announced that the pie-in-the-sky project, which was made public about two years ago, is now a reality. For many of us, it's the most ambitious project we've ever undertaken. To find a home, a safe place to give our LGBT seniors to live; to bring them a home to thrive in their very own community—that's the goal. I have no illusions that the proposal has many more milestones to meet. It is not a done deal yet. And it will take the support and input of the entire community and our elected officials who have committed to follow through on this dream.

Last Thursday, the Pennsylvania Housing Finance Agency met to decide which projects would be awarded tax credits this year. I'm happy to report that the pie-in-the-sky project was awarded credit in that very competitive field.

The project is now fully funded at $19 million. It is, as the mayor said during the announcement, the largest LGBT-friendly capital building project in the United States. The White House and HUD spotlighted the project as "pioneering innovation in US housing solutions for low-income LGBT seniors."

Good things kept coming our way. When our board decided to name the building after John C. Anderson, a former city council member who was both African American and gay, and who had died from AIDS, we had no idea of the impact it would have. At the groundbreaking for the building, State Senator Tony Williams spoke with great emotion: "You may have bridged the gap between the African American and LGBT community with this building, since it is to my knowledge the first building in America purposefully named after an LGBT African American public official."

When Mayor Nutter cut the ribbon, he was joined by former governor Ed Rendell, US Senator Bob Casey, the entire Philadelphia congressional delegation led by my old friend Bob Brady, Brian Hudson, who was president of the National Council of State Housing Agencies, various other state representatives and senators, and members of the city council—headed by Council President Darrell Clarke—along with District Councilman Mark Squilla. The council had suspended rules in order to pass our zoning changes, unanimously.

By the time we started to build, the vision had grown. We understood that we had to nurture a broader LGBT senior advocacy movement. We knew we couldn't do it alone and we wanted this project embraced by the community and dearly wanted them to have a feeling of ownership. So we went back to the community center and suggested that once we opened, they could take charge of the activities and social services. We asked the Mazzoni Center to create courses on law and safe sex. ActionAIDS was chosen as the HIV/AIDS services agency in the building. We even built an office on the first floor for outside organizations to work from.

Joe Salerno became our architect; he was a gay man who wound up, in a way, coming out during the process. My instructions to him were simple. We were building in an upscale area, and the concept must give our residents dignity. I wanted them to feel that "wow" factor when they walked through the front door. Joe and I came to a quick agreement, though Pennrose didn't like how much our vision would cost them. I had learned that a good partnership always involves compromise, so with every change they'd explain how much it would cost, and we'd attempt to find savings in another area.

The vision: Enter the building into a spacious open area with staff offices and resident mailboxes. Walk a little farther and you'll discover the lobby and library, complete with etched glass and fireplace. Sitting by the fireplace, you can peer out through glass windows that reveal a five-thousand-square-foot private courtyard with paths, benches, and even a fountain. There's a community room with an eighty-inch flat screen and seating for sixty. Farther down the hall is a computer lab station for the residents with five computers hooked up to the Internet. On the fifth floor there's a sundeck with sweeping views of the city's skyline.

Negotiating all of those areas, especially my request for glass walls, was a constant battle with Pennrose, with Jacob Fisher in the middle. But they were eventually completed and, in my opinion, completely worth the cost. The one item that most surprises people actually happened by mistake.

At our first meeting with the full construction team, many of whom were men employed by our general contractor, Domus, we all gathered around a table in one of Pennrose's conference rooms. Joe, who was reviewing the architectural drawings, noted that due to the shape of the building and the configuration of our courtyard, four apartments would have larger closets and a smaller bedroom than the others. I explained, "That's not a problem for our proposed clientele. We'll call them 'drag queen closets.' In fact, can we do the same in all the apartments?" The look on their faces was priceless as they all began to smile. Those closets are one of the most popular features of the building.

Residents must be sixty-two and above and earn no less than $8,000 a year and no more than $33,000. Surprisingly or not, there are lots of LGBT people with low incomes, especially those seniors about whom we know so little. Consider, as just one example, a trans person in 1969. What kind of job could they keep, and what savings, Social Security, or pension do you think they would accrue thirty or forty years later? Think of those stereotyped and shunned individuals in the 1960s who had to receive welfare in order to survive.

During the construction, we'd offer tours of the site to those who had taken part or those we wanted to get involved in the project. My friend Klayton Fennell from Comcast sent me a box of pink hard hats to give out on tours, and soon it became fashionable for a public figure to be photographed wearing one while touring the site. Those hard hats with our logo have become collectors' items.

The project was going in so many directions at once and often kept us guessing where we were actually headed. But behind the scenes was my board of directors, each with her or his own specialty. Irene Benedetti, the longest-serving member of the board, worked with the women's community, while Tyrone Smith, a pioneer in black gay rights, did the same with the African American community. Jane Shull coordinated with the HIV/AIDS community, while my good friend Rob Metzger handled small LGBT contractor firms. Larry Felzer was our liaison to the regional senior organizations. Jeff Guaracino dealt with government affairs and public relations and Judith Applebaum connected to the neighborhood organizations. Rick Lombardo worked on security issues while Judge Dan Anders was the guy I'd call and say, "What would *you* do?" No project of this size gets done without the support of its board. I have never been so honored to work with a board in my life. And, of course, there was Micah, who was by my side seven days a week, keeping me on track.

The Department of Housing and Urban Development asked us to showcase the project at their first conference on LGBT senior housing. Webcast live from their headquarters in Washington, DC, they and the White House hailed the project. From that meeting with President Obama in 2012 to the day we took in our first resident, only three years and nine months had passed. Yes, that was record timing for a project like this. Since opening, we have been deluged with requests to both tour the building and assist those wishing to replicate our success.

As I was driving myself to the state capital one day, my phone rang and I had to pull over to the side of the road. The call was from Openhouse, a group planning a similar senior project in San Francisco. They had finally gotten their seed money, found a developer, had site control, and were planning a forty-unit rehab facility. They asked, "How did you do the marketing to get the desired population?" San Francisco was asking *us* how to get members of the LGBT community into their building—the enormity of that question spelled out for me a job well done.

At the ribbon cutting on February 24, 2014, I took the microphone to welcome the large crowd. I pulled out a letter I had recently received and began to read it:

> *I send my warm regards on the opening of the John C. Anderson Apartments. For generations, courageous lesbian, gay, bisexual, and transgender Americans spoke up, came out, and fought injustice, blazing trails for others and pushing us closer to our founding ideals of equality for all. In the*

face of impossible odds, these leaders and committed allies demonstrated that change is possible and helped our nation become not only more accepting, but also more loving. And across America today communities are tackling challenges that remain and writing bold new chapters in this story of progress.

By working together as advocates, business leaders, and officials throughout government, we can address the problems of LGBT discrimination in housing. Offering security and affordability for Philadelphia's LGBT seniors, this apartment community is an example of how we can create a more hopeful world when we better care for one another. My administration stands with all those in the fight to ensure every American has equal access to housing—no matter who they are or whom they love. May this effort inspire us to continue striving for equality for all people in our time.

As the John C. Anderson Apartments opens its doors, I hope it provides warmth and comfort to all who call it home. I wish you all the best for years ahead.
—Barack Obama

The audience stood and applauded, and for an instant in the emotion of that moment I saw an image of my cousin Norman—who had never gotten the chance to live among people who treated him with decency and respect.

Chapter 15

And Then We Danced

I n June 2014, I drove for an hour and a half in the rain to Harrisburg on the boring Pennsylvania Turnpike for a meeting at the Pennsylvania NewsMedia Association, one of the nation's oldest journalistic organizations, of which I now serve on the board of directors. It was the same organization that had refused me membership for fifteen years. The meeting would be held at a grand Georgian mansion overlooking the Susquehanna River, the organization's headquarters.

Pennsylvania NewsMedia Association is just a few blocks from the governor's official residence, where six months before I had met with our Republican governor, Tom Corbett, after he'd made a very public gaffe that caught national media fire. When asked about same sex-marriage in an October 2013 TV interview he'd compared it to incest. Shortly after that show, I received a call from one of the governor's staff members, asking if I'd come to Harrisburg and meet with the governor privately at his residence. The meeting would include Ted Martin, executive director of Equality Pennsylvania, Chris Labonte of consultant firm Sellers Dorsey, gay lawyer Tom Paese who was a codirector of Corbett's transition team, and Betty Hill, executive director of the Persad Center in Pittsburgh. The governor's chief of staff would also be present. This was a high-level meeting with people who meant business on LGBT issues. In a premeeting we had decided to focus on the nondiscrimination legislation currently sitting before the legislature. Martin would bring a slew of data and polling information. Hill would provide the personal stories of her clients and the negative effects caused by the absence of such legislation. Labonte knew how to stage a campaign, and Paese already worked closely with the governor.

In order to move the meeting forward quickly, the governor started out with an apology, which we all accepted. But when we got down to the basics, the governor was concerned that if he did anything now it would just look like a political move since he was about to enter a reelection campaign. That was my cue.

"Governor, as a member of the media, with all due respect, we see a man with a loose tongue. Someone will, in the near future, try to get you to make another statement on marriage. If I can humbly suggest that next time that happens—and it will— turn it around on that reporter. Turn directly to that reporter and say, *Why haven't you asked me about nondiscrimination?*"

And that is exactly what happened. This time the governor kept to the script. On December 18, 2013, the progressive blog *Think Progress* reported:

> *Pennsylvania Gov. Tom Corbett (R) announced Tuesday that he was "coming out in support" of a bill that would create nondiscrimination protections based on sexual orientation and gender identity. In his statement, Corbett claimed that he did not previously realize that the LGBT community was not protected by federal laws.*

The Human Rights Campaign in DC quickly put out a national press release that included the following passage:

In a surprise move today, Pennsylvania governor Tom Corbett announced his support for a bill banning discrimination based on sexual orientation. The governor joins other Republicans in the state who are in support of such legislation, including State Senator Pat Browne. Congressman Dent and Senator Pat Toomey are supportive of the federal Employment Non-Discrimination Act which passed the Senate in early November and now heads to the House for consideration. Their position on the state legislation is unknown.

The governor not only followed the script, he improved on it. At that meeting, all of us present had suggested that we would be more than willing to stand by his side and help field any negativity, particularly from our own communities.

The governor had one more pleasant surprise in store, as well as at least one disappointment along the way. In February 2014, when we had been finally ready to cut the ribbon on the John C. Anderson Apartments, we were hoping that Vice President Biden would do the honors. Mayor Nutter and Senator Bob Casey, along with our congressional delegation, wrote a letter of invitation. When we discovered the VP could not join us, we quickly set another date, which unfortunately came at the same time as the National Governors Association Winter Meeting. Governor Corbett would be unable to attend.

But he made up for it when the marriage-equality issue found its way to Pennsylvania. I began a very private lobbying campaign with my friends in the governor's office. After all, they had now worked with me for three years on the John C. Anderson senior housing project. We expected that Judge John E. Jones III, a Republican appointed by George W. Bush who was handling the case, would rule in our favor, but we never expected how strong his ruling would be.

My campaign was only known by my most trusted friends and of course the governor's office. This was a highly controversial issue for a man who many thought was a Tea Party Republican, and my friends thought it was crazy that I believed Corbett would allow the state to accept the judge's ruling, should he strike down anti-gay marriage laws in Pennsylvania. The judge stated that he would not hear debate, choosing instead to rule from the briefs each side provided to him. During my conversations with Corbett's staff, I became aware of the timing of Judge Jones's expected ruling, which led me to suggest various options to the governor's legal team.

Option 1: explain that the judge had overruled a law that the legislature had passed and toss it back to them to start anew, but don't request a stay.

Option 2: explain that your hands are tied, since the attorney general should appeal this. AG Kathleen Kane had previously stated that based on the Constitution as well as her personal beliefs, she would not defend anti-gay marriage laws.

Option 3: pass it over to the state treasurer, who would have to handle the effect of the new marriage law on taxes. State Treasurer Rob McCord had also stated that he personally believed in marriage equality.

Option 4, the hardest and bravest option: do what Governor Chris Christie of New Jersey did. State that while you have personal objections, you won't get in the way of the judge's ruling, and allow marriage equality in Pennsylvania.

While attending the New York Tech Expo to help my nephew Jeffrey launch his new company, my cell phone rang. It was the governor's chief legal counsel, Jim Schultz.

"Mark, I promised to give this to you first. We're doing the Christie."

After everything I'd been through in politics, Jim was giving me a political surprise I hadn't seen in years. All I could think to do was offer my assistance if the governor needed some cover. Jim declined; they were good. I also knew that it was Jim who'd fought the hardest for this.

Soon after that call, the governor issued a statement: "Given the high legal threshold set forth by Judge Jones in this case, the case is extremely unlikely to succeed on appeal." Corbett went on to say that he still believed that marriage should be between one man and one woman, and that his faith had not wavered. That line was somewhat understandable, as he was running for reelection and needed to preserve his electoral base.

And as would be expected, *PGN* was the first to have the governor's decision up online.

Philadelphia County began issuing marriage licenses to couples on May 20, 2014. Ron Donatucci, the man in charge of this process, deputized me that day and allowed me to work with the applicants and issue licenses myself. It was the ultimate joy to sit down in a cubicle and have two happy people ushered toward me.

As Jason was helping me deal with all of this, our friend City Councilman Jim Kenney appeared and said he just wanted to be present to observe this historic time. Then he asked, "What about you two?" Jason and I looked at each other and said, after ten years together, why not?

We had just agreed to get married. That fact alone was overwhelming enough. But a problem arose as Jason and I walked up to the register. "That'll be eighty dollars in cash, please."

We stared at each other, dumbfounded. Neither of us had any cash on us. We turned to Jim, who, along with Ron, was chuckling. The two of them fished out their wallets and split the fee, forty dollars each—an engagement gift. We posed for some celebratory pictures and then joined the massive celebration outside City Hall.

When we got home that evening, Jason noticed a line in small print at the bottom of the marriage license. "Do you realize we have sixty days before the license expires?" We had two months, basically amounting to zero time, to make wedding plans. My head was spinning.

A few weeks later, back in Harrisburg for the meeting with the Pennsylvania NewsMedia Association, it dawned on me to take a close look at my calendar for the immediate future. Each day was filled with appointments, fundraisers, events, or meetings with developers. The John C. Anderson project was so successful that developers were lining themselves up at my door, pitching similar projects in New York, Washington, DC, and other cities.

Looking at that full calendar and the numerous opportunities ahead, a wave of memories came rolling back, and suddenly I'm standing outside Stonewall again, a boy who didn't know who he was or where he was going, living at the YMCA with no money and no prospects. The reality is that I had feared becoming one of those homeless kids that Gay Youth helped.

I noticed that I had two upcoming visits to Washington scheduled. The following Friday, I'd go with *Philadelphia Gay News* staff to the annual banquet of the Society of Professional Journalists at the National Press Club to accept the 2014 Investigative Journalist Award along with the *Wall Street Journal*. Then, on the last Friday of June, it was back to the White House for the president's reception in honor of Gay Pride Month.

The John C. Anderson project had taken me to the White House and Executive Office Building a number of times in the last few years, but there are two visits that stand out. The first was at the White House after a long day of meetings on Capitol Hill and the Department of Housing and Urban Development. I was joined by Richard Barnhart, one of the owners of Pennrose Management Company. Richard is a very successful man; he's the Ted Turner style of executive, impeccably dressed and often escaping to his retreat out West. At times, he presents a bit of a waspy, holier-than-thou attitude. He was doing that routine as we entered the White House, so I turned and asked him if he'd ever been there before on business. He looked around in amazement and said he hadn't. I replied, "You mean it took a pushy Jew faggot to get you in the White House?" He simply smiled.

The other visit that stands out was when I had the opportunity to introduce Jason to the president and Mrs. Obama. We were at one of the president's holiday parties. As is tradition, the president and first lady pose for pictures with their guests. When it was our turn, the immaculately uniformed Marine introduced us: "Mr. President, may I present Mark Segal and his guest, Jason Villemez."

The protocol is for the invited guest to stand next to the president and their spouse or guest to stand next to the first lady. Me being Mark Segal, I said, "Mr. President, I have enough pictures of us together, but I have none with the beautiful first lady, so I hope you don't mind if I stand next to her."

Laughter came from behind the camera. It was Reggie Love, the president's personal aide who had helped usher the plans for the Anderson project. He gave a thumbs-up.

That was the only time I've ever witnessed Jason in total awe. Nothing, and I mean nothing—with the exception of my driving skills—had ever fazed him before. To see that side of him was a joy.

With all my memorable trips to the White House, I was almost dreading another visit to Washington. But surprises—

delightful ones at that—seem to always pop up if I simply keep my eye on the target.

At the gay pride reception at the White House in June 2014, Jason and I stood near the back of the East Room with the photographers and journalists, giving others a chance to be close to the president. Midway through the president's speech, I thought I heard him say, "We must do more with affordable housing for our LGBT seniors." I did a double take, thinking I might be imagining things. But after the speech, one of the president's assistants, Gautam Raghavan, came over and said with a big grin, "Did you notice we got your line in?"

Later, Jason and I headed to the portico entrance, where the Marine band was playing, and we danced in the White House. The following Saturday, July 5, we got married in a private ceremony with Jason's sisters as best women and my nephew Jeffrey as best man, and my friend Judge Dan Anders presiding over the ceremony. Jason's parents were there too; in our pockets we each had a piece of his mother's wedding veil which she had given us for the ceremony.

Mom, I'm now sixty-four years old, and I finally have a response to that concern you expressed when I first told you I was gay. Rest assured, I'm not lonely. When people ask me, "Mr. Segal, what was the happiest day of your life?" I get to say, "The day Jason and I married."

It has been a long road from 2333 South Bambrey Terrace, from that lonely guy who escaped to New York with seemingly no future. While I haven't accomplished my father's dream of getting a degree, there is no doubt that he would feel very good about what I've done in lieu of that.

At the ribbon cutting of the John C. Anderson Apartments,

each and every public official spoke about how I was a pain in the ass to deal with. What's nice is that they all said it with pride. That's a compliment I welcome.